A CULTURAL HISTORY OF PEACE

VOLUME 6

A Cultural History of Peace
General Editor: Ronald Edsforth

Volume 1
A Cultural History of Peace in Antiquity
Edited by Sheila L. Ager

Volume 2
A Cultural History of Peace in the Medieval Age
Edited by Walter Simons

Volume 3
A Cultural History of Peace in the Renaissance
Edited by Isabella Lazzarini

Volume 4
A Cultural History of Peace in the Age of Enlightenment
Edited by Stella Ghervas and David Armitage

Volume 5
A Cultural History of Peace in the Age of Empire
Edited by Ingrid Sharp

Volume 6
A Cultural History of Peace in the Modern Age
Edited by Ronald Edsforth

A CULTURAL HISTORY OF PEACE
IN THE MODERN AGE

Edited by Ronald Edsforth

BLOOMSBURY ACADEMIC
LONDON • NEW YORK • OXFORD • NEW DELHI • SYDNEY

BLOOMSBURY ACADEMIC
Bloomsbury Publishing Plc
50 Bedford Square, London, WC1B 3DP, UK
1385 Broadway, New York, NY 10018, USA
29 Earlsfort Terrace, Dublin 2, Ireland

BLOOMSBURY, BLOOMSBURY ACADEMIC and the Diana logo are trademarks of
Bloomsbury Publishing Plc

First published in Great Britain 2020
This edition published in Great Britain, 2024

Copyright © Bloomsbury Publishing, 2020

Ronald Edsforth has asserted his right under the Copyright, Designs and Patents Act, 1988,
to be identified as Editor of this work.

Cover image © JOHN THYS / Stringer / Getty Images

All rights reserved. No part of this publication may be reproduced or transmitted
in any form or by any means, electronic or mechanical, including photocopying,
recording, or any information storage or retrieval system, without prior permission
in writing from the publishers.

Bloomsbury Publishing Plc does not have any control over, or responsibility for, any
third-party websites referred to or in this book. All internet addresses given in this
book were correct at the time of going to press. The author and publisher regret
any inconvenience caused if addresses have changed or sites have ceased to exist,
but can accept no responsibility for any such changes.

A catalogue record for this book is available from the British Library.

A catalog record for this book is available from the Library of Congress.

ISBN: HB: 978-1-4742-3839-7
PB: 978-1-3503-8592-4
Set: 978-1-3503-8603-7

Series: The Cultural Histories Series

Typeset by RefineCatch Limited, Bungay, Suffolk
Printed and bound in Great Britain

To find out more about our authors and books visit www.bloomsbury.com
and sign up for our newsletters.

CONTENTS

LIST OF ILLUSTRATIONS		vi
GENERAL EDITOR'S PREFACE		ix
	Introduction *Ronald Edsforth*	1
1	Definitions of Peace *Charles Webel and Marcel Kaba*	21
2	Human Nature, Peace, and War *Douglas P. Fry and Geneviève Souillac*	41
3	Peace, War, and Gender *Donna Pankhurst*	61
4	Peace, Pacifism, and Religion: *Just War Traditions, Nonviolence, Peace Building, Social Justice, Human Rights, Sustainable Development, and Interfaith Dialogue* *Toh Swee-Hin*	83
5	Representations of Peace *Rune Ottosen and Ronald Edsforth*	105
6	Peace Movements *Cecelia Lynch*	127
7	Peace, Security, and Deterrence *John Mueller*	145
8	Peace as Integration *Geneviève Souillac*	163
NOTES		181
BIBLIOGRAPHY		185
CONTRIBUTORS		225
INDEX		227

ILLUSTRATIONS

INTRODUCTION

0.1	Woman weeps over her husband's body, 1965.	2
0.2	Bertrand and Edith Russell lead sit-down demonstration in Whitehall, London protesting deployment of nuclear weapons, February 1961.	6
0.3	Earth Day Poster, *The Whole Earth is Watching*.	18

CHAPTER 1

1.1	Activist Wangari Maathai.	28
1.2	Gandhi leading the Salt March, March 1930.	29
1.3	The Dalai Lama speaking in Tokyo, October 31, 2009.	30
1.4	Dr. Martin Luther King, Jr. being arrested for "loitering" in Montgomery, Alabama 1958.	34

CHAPTER 2

2.1	A temple stands as a remnant of ancient Greek civilization on the southern coast of Sicily.	43
2.2	Anasazi ruins from Chaco Canyon, New Mexico. The prehistoric Anasazi made the transition from nomadic foraging to settled, village farming, and co-existed peacefully in their farming villages with their neighbors for hundreds of years.	47
2.3	Nomadic forager societies are windows to the human past.	48
2.4	The Iroquois Confederacy was a peace system known as Haudenosaunee, which means people of the long house.	51
2.5	The Hiroshima Dome Memorial, Hiroshima Peace Memorial Park, Japan.	53
2.6	Bonobos relax and groom each other.	55
2.7	Grand' Place market square, Brussels.	58

CHAPTER 3

3.1	War workers modeling an assortment of protective goggles, visors, respirator masks, and helmets.	65
3.2	Eritrean People's Liberation Front female guerilla soldiers training.	67

ILLUSTRATIONS vii

3.3 A new female voter preparing to cast her vote 1920. 70
3.4 Women at the head of an anti-Vietnam War peace march, San Francisco 1971. 72
3.5 Women protestors sitting at gateway to Greenham Common Airbase, England. 73

CHAPTER 4

4.1 Mohandas Ghandi. 88
4.2 Palestinians remove a roadblock while a member of the Christian Peacemaker Team stands behind them. 90
4.3 Thich Nhat Hanh in Paris, 2006. 91
4.4 Rabbi Arik Ascherman of Rabbis for Human Rights who campaign to stop house demolitions on the West Bank, October 2012. 92
4.5 Environmental activist Vandana Shiva, 2013. 95
4.6 Asia-Pacific Interfaith Symposium: Women, Faith, and a Culture of Peace; Multi-Faith Centre, Griffith University, Brisbane, Australia February 2008. 98
4.7 Imman Muhammed Ashafa and Pastor James Wuye of Nigeria at the eighth annual gala of the We Are Family Foundation, New York City, October 2010. 103

CHAPTER 5

5.1 Peace sign designed by Gerald Holtom for Ban the Bomb March London to Aldermaston, April 1958. 106
5.2 Philippines President Corazon Acquino salutes the crowd celebrating the victorious People Power Revolution, March 2, 1986. 107
5.3 Children fleeing their homes, Phan Thi Kim Phuc on right, after napalm bombing of Trang Bang, South Vietnam, June 8, 1972. 108
5.4 Zulu Chief and President of the African National Congress Albert Lutuli accepts the 1960 Nobel Peace Prize. 114
5.5 Neville Chamberlain at Heston Airport after Signing the Munich agreement. 117
5.6 Johan Galtung in 1989 when he was a Professor of Peace Studies at the University of Hawaii. 120

CHAPTER 6

6.1 Margaret Bondfield addresses Women's International League for Peace and Freedom rally at the World Disarmament Conference 1932. 130
6.2 King Felipe VI of Spain and Barack Obama view *Guernica* in the Reina Sofia Museum in Madrid, July 2018. 131

6.3	Bayard Rustin 1964.	133
6.4	Hiroshima's first Peace Festival, 1948.	136
6.5	Dutch artists protest in Amsterdam against the Vietnam War, December 1966.	137
6.6	Liberian women demand peace in front of ECOMIL headquarters in Monrovia, August 28, 2003.	140
6.7	Prisoner liberated by crowd in Kasserine during People Power revolution in Libya 2010.	142

CHAPTER 7

7.1	*I Didn't Raise My Boy to be a Soldier*, Sheet Music USA 1915.	146
7.2	American delegates arrive in the Netherlands for Women's Peace Congress, April 1915.	147
7.3	Children of farm workers in Kent, England have their gas masks checked, August 29, 1939.	149
7.4	Adolf Hitler addressing a meeting in Berlin, January 1, 1937.	151
7.5	Memorial for Fallen Soldiers World War I, in Ohlsdorf, Germany overlooks graves of 3,400 Germans, 230 Russians, 6 Serbs, 6 Poles, 2 Romanians, and 1 French soldier.	160

CHAPTER 8

8.1	Memorials honoring soldiers who were killed in World War I, like this one in Saint Cyprien, Dordogne are located in every village and town in France.	166
8.2	Poster by Alain Carrier in 1991 by the United Nations to celebrate the Universal Declaration of Human Rights.	169
8.3	Reading Jean Monnet, the author's book collection.	171
8.4	The expansion of the UN as a forum for cooperation on matters of common interest is evidence of a new institutional global order.	172
8.5	Medieval city hall Frankfurt am Main, displaying the flags of Frankfurt, Germany, and the EU.	177
8.6	Kristof Wodiczko's Arc de Triomphe, Institut mondial pour l'abolition de la guerre, Abolition of War Exhibition, Kuntsi Musen of Modern Art, Vaasa, Finland, 2014.	179

GENERAL EDITOR'S PREFACE

RONALD EDSFORTH

When people learn that I study and teach peace history, they often look puzzled and ask me, "Does peace have a history?" *A Cultural History of Peace* is an emphatically positive response to that question. Yes, peace has a history. The original scholarly essays collected in these six volumes clearly show that peace has always been an important human concern. More precisely, these essays demonstrate that what we recognize today as peace thinking and peace imagining, peace seeking and peacemaking, peacekeeping, and peacebuilding have long recorded histories that stretch from antiquity to the twenty-first century. All of us who have contributed to *A Cultural History of Peace* believe that present and future generations should have the opportunity to recognize and understand the importance of this peace history.

Very few universities and colleges had faculty who taught and researched peace history before the end of the Cold War. Even today, most professors who do peace history moved into it from other specializations in History or other academic disciplines. Most contributors to *A Cultural History of Peace* are professional historians, but Anthropology, Sociology, Political Science, Journalism, Art History, Religion, and Classical Studies are also represented. These fifty-six contributors work on four continents in thirteen different countries. Their participation in this project tells us that peace history has earned a global recognition in academia that not so long ago was unimaginable. Their essays build upon prior scholarship, but they also introduce new research and new interpretations. As a whole *A Cultural History of Peace* highlights our humanity, something that has been for too long overshadowed in history by the inhumanity of war and other forms of violent conflict. Pursuing answers to new and seldom-asked questions, these collected essays expand our knowledge of when, how, and why people in the past pursued peace within their own societies and peaceable relations with people from other societies.

The South African novelist Nadine Gordimer wisely observes, "The past is valid only in relation to whether the present recognises it" (2007: 7). In other words, what happened in the past is not necessarily history. History is made when scholars produce meaningful answers to the questions they ask about the past. The past cannot change, but history can and does change when scholars ask new questions, and when they use previously undiscovered or ignored evidence to develop new interpretations of the past. Evidence of what people said or did, or said they did, are basic materials out of which scholars shape answers to questions like "Does peace have a history?" Of course, to answer this particular question about the past, we must have in mind some definition of peace. Like most people we probably immediately think of peace as *not war*, a classic definition that describes peace in negative terms, as an absence of the type of violent conflicts that still loom so large in popular histories and stories about the past. The American psychologist and peace activist William James succinctly summed up this common way of framing of the past, simply stating, "History is a bath of blood" (1910: 1).

James' description of history still plays well in a world that during the last century experienced the massive casualties and devastation of two world wars, genocides, and numerous civil wars, as well the fears created by transnational terrorism and still-threatening nuclear arsenals. And significantly, a bath of blood framing continues to shape the priorities of most mainstream reporting of the news from around the world—"if it bleeds it leads"—when, in fact, most people today live in zones of peace where their lives are not threatened by violent political conflict. A human being's chances of dying in war have been historically low in this century, and in striking contrast to the peaks of worldwide violence reached during the global conflicts of the twentieth century (https://ourworldindata.org/war-and-peace). Yet so accustomed are we to framing history *and* the present as a bath of blood, most of us have difficulty comprehending these facts. Steven Pinker recently noted this problem in the preface to *The Better Angels of Our Nature: Why Violence Has Declined*, saying "Believe it or not—and I know that most people do not—violence has declined over long stretches of time, and today we might be living in the most peaceable era in our species' existence" (2011: xvi). It is not just a coincidence that the rapid growth and globalization of peace studies has happened since the end of the Cold War. Undoubtedly, some of the questions raised in *A Cultural History of Peace* have been influenced by the extraordinary recent decline of interstate warfare and resolution of many longstanding civil wars.

A Cultural History of Peace demonstrates that for several thousand years peace has been regarded as a highly desirable social condition, perhaps most especially when the violence and cruelty of war have been in the ascendency. Describing this collection of peace history essays as a cultural history—rather than social, political, diplomatic, or international history—is appropriate because throughout history peace has emerged from the cultures of groups, societies, and nations that developed practical ways to peaceably settle serious conflicts. Here I employ the broad environmental definition of culture that psychiatrist and classics scholar Jonathan Shay uses in his brilliant book, *Achilles in Vietnam*: "Our animal nature, our biological nature, is to live in relation to other people. The natural environment of humans is primarily culture, not the 'natural world' narrowly defined as other species, climate, etc" (1995: 207). Surely, no human culture is ever truly homogeneous or free from conflicts that arise from serious differences between individuals and groups. Murder and warfare are the bloodiest ways that humans have dealt with those with whom they have serious differences. Bath of blood history foregrounds these activities when we peer into the past. Peace history does something very different. It reveals the long, unfinished task of making human cultures peaceable environments that encourage the expression of our most humane instincts: respect for all others who are human like us, and sympathy for those humans who are fearful and/or suffering.

In a remarkable book, *Humanity: A Moral History of the Twentieth Century*, philosopher Jonathan Glover describes respect and sympathy as "human responses" that although they are "widespread and deep-rooted" are often blocked. Frequently aggressive and cruel instincts find expression in warfare and encouragement in cultures that reserve the highest honors for warriors and their blood sacrifices. Yet clearly respect and sympathy have been absolutely necessary for the survival of our social species. Respect and sympathy are, in Glover's words, "the core of our humanity which contrasts with inhumanity." However, as Glover recognizes "humanity is only partly an empirical claim. It remains also partly an aspiration" (1999: 24–25). *A Cultural History of Peace* presents strong evidence for the empirical claim, as well as the aspiration. It focuses on the many people in the past who worked to establish peace within their own societies and peace with other societies by institutionalizing respect and sympathy; people who are unlikely to be highlighted as heroes in bath of blood histories.

GENERAL EDITOR'S PREFACE

As General Editor of this title in Bloomsbury Publishing's cultural history series, I have had to follow two major guidelines. The first required six volumes of essays that follow the same chronological order as other titles in the series. Accordingly, *A Cultural History of Peace* is presented in volumes focused on Antiquity, the Medieval Age, the Renaissance, the Enlightenment, Age of Empire, and the Modern Era since 1920. This chronological order is Western-oriented and something of a barrier to producing a truly global history of peace. Nonetheless, some of the essays in the first five volumes of *A Cultural History of Peace*, and all the essays in Volume 6 present peace history in a global perspective. Indeed those essays show that envisioning a more peaceful interconnected world and finding ways of realizing that vision are crucial components of the complex of historical processes we today call "globalization."

Bloomsbury's other major guideline required the eight topical essays in each volume of *A Cultural History of Peace* to concentrate on identical themes in peace history. My first task as General Editor was developing the eight major themes for these collected essays. Developing the major themes was difficult, particularly because I recognized that a kind of "translation" problem arises when applying modern ideas about peace to the study of peace history in earlier eras when those ideas, or at least modern formulations of them, were absent. I only started doing peace history in 1998 after two decades of teaching and writing concentrated almost exclusively on American history. Not surprisingly, I remained focused on the modern era when preparing my first peace history courses and new research projects. That focus on the modern era was reinforced by what I learned in a peace research seminar at the University of Oslo in the summer of 2007. Thus, I knew that my initial selection of themes for this collection could be criticized as present-oriented. Many hours of discussion with my colleagues in Dartmouth's History Department convinced me that this "translation" problem was not insuperable, and that after significant revision my original ideas would be viable focal points for *A Cultural History of Peace*.

These six volumes validate this conviction. Each one contains an introductory overview of the historical era written by its editor and eight thematic essays written by specialists. They develop the following themes: Definitions of Peace; Human Nature, Peace, and War; Peace, War, and Gender; Peace, Pacifism, and Religion; Representations of Peace; Peace Movements; Peace, Security, and Deterrence; and Peace as Integration. This structure facilitates long views of key subjects in peace history. Anyone interested, for instance, in putting together a chronologically ordered history of how peace has been defined from antiquity to the modern era can achieve this goal by reading in order each of the first chapters in the six volumes of *A Cultural History of Peace*. When they do so, they will discover the distinction between "negative" and "positive" definitions of peace that are commonly used in peace research today is useful when formulating questions about pre-modern definitions of peace. But they will also see that the modern distinction between negative peace and positive peace is a simple model that may hinder understanding the variety and richness of what people since antiquity actually meant when they spoke and wrote about peace.

How people in different times and places have understood what we usually call "human nature" has deeply influenced what they said and did about making peace and war. Human nature is, of course, a tricky term. Does it even exist? If it does, is it an endowment of fixed characteristics, or malleable and evolving? And if by human nature, we mean "instinctual," does this mean "inevitable," or are instincts better understood as potential behaviors that have been repressed or expressed depending on environmental influences produced by particular cultures at particular times in the past? The essays in this collection that develop the theme "Human Nature, Peace, and War" make clear that prevailing beliefs about human nature, whether faith-based or secular, have always played an essential role in how people understand what kinds of peace are possible in their imperfect material world.

Peace and war are among the most clearly gendered historical categories, as Chapters Three in *A Cultural History of Peace* make abundantly clear. It has been common all over the world for women to be regarded as "life-givers" and men as "life takers." Of course there are deviations from this global historical pattern. The Truong sisters of Vietnam and Joan of Arc are among the most famous transgressors of the male monopoly of military power. However, women like them have been exceptional. More commonly, women have provided material and psychological support to male warriors. And perhaps most significantly, some of them have been peace thinkers and peacemakers. Indeed, the widespread idea that peace is feminine has been a source of political legitimacy for women, not just a barrier to achieving political power.

Although pacifism in Western democracies is now usually understood as a principled and often religiously inspired refusal to engage in violence, in other historical settings people who could justify certain violent actions and some wars were still considered "pacifists" whenever they opposed militarism or an ongoing war. On such occasions the deeply subversive cultural implications of nonviolence—its resistance to the idea that history must be written in blood—have been manifest. The essays herein that develop the theme "Peace, Pacifism, and Religion" enable readers to better understand the ambiguous role of religious faith in peace history. They describe religious traditions that link faith and peace, but also ancient and enduring traditions that link religion to the promotion of war.

Since antiquity countless artists, sculptors, composers, poets, playwrights, and writers have produced representations that reflected, but also shaped, understandings of peace in their cultures. Ancient symbols of peace like the olive branch and the dove that were incorporated into religious iconography have never lost their currency, even when used by secular peace activists. Many other representations of peace created during the last two millennia have also survived. Chapters Five in this collection present a long history of these representations of peace. These representations have often been of peace imagined because their creators could not find real peace in contemporary political cultures. The accumulated representations of peace now form a vast and priceless cultural reservoir, much of it easily accessed via the Internet. Currently, new representations of peace are being deposited in this cultural reservoir every day, while old ones are revived and reconfigured by peace activists around the world.

Peace and anti-war movements have always produced and deployed representations of peace, but they have not been a constant presence in the past. Chapters Six of *A Cultural History of Peace* describe collective efforts to prevent wars, or to stop them from continuing, as well as organized opposition to militarism. Throughout history, peace movements have been condemned as subversive, especially when they resisted ongoing wars authorized by political authorities. And even when they have failed to achieve peace, as they have frequently done in the past, peace movements extended the contemporary cultural bases for challenging militarism and the glorification of warfare. Peace movements have over the long run produced traditions of anti-militarist thinking that in this century are mobilized by peace activists whenever interstate warfare threatens global peace.

Today most global peace activists regard the achievement of security via the threat of force as itself a problem, partly because this kind of negative peace has so frequently broken down in the past. The six essays in this collection that explore the theme "Peace, Security, and Deterrence" nonetheless demonstrate the strong and enduring appeal of this approach to peace. Although the perception problem modern political scientists call "the security dilemma" has been recognized since antiquity, the political practicality and immediately recognizable results of deterrence have almost always prevailed in the face of building threats made by military rivals. Enshrined in the modern era as a form of political realism, deterrence policy shaped the nuclear arms that saw rival superpowers each deploy tens of thousands of nuclear weapons that if used would have certainly destroyed civilization. Yet today, most national governments still equate peace with security and produce deterrence policies that create military alliances and threaten adversaries with war.

The last chapters of each volume of *A Cultural History of Peace* address a theme that many people mistakenly identify as a modern phenomenon: peace through integration, as if it must be something resembling the European Union. These chapters show that the social order imposed by expanding empires, kingdoms, and nation-states has long been proclaimed as a form of peace, even when peace was not the reason for the warfare that preceded it. Moreover, its principal beneficiaries have often identified their empires as an expanding civilization, most famously Pax Romana and more recently Pax Americana. Yet since the medieval age another kind of peace achieved by nonviolent agreements built upon shared characteristics of identity has been imagined, and occasionally implemented.

Christianity's claim to be a universal church that could bring all people together in a brotherhood of Christ opened the door for identifying "humanity," a word first used during the Renaissance. Then science, especially eighteenth-century taxonomy, provided a secular path to a similar end: the recognition that all humans are in very important ways, a single unique species of life. In the modern era, threats to the continued existence of this humanity in the form of global catastrophes such as nuclear warfare and climate change have contributed to an unprecedented "species consciousness" and the claim that all humans have rights that must be respected. Unprecedented communications technologies that today allow us to see and hear people from all over the world in real time have facilitated the expansion of global peace and human rights networks. Although during the five years that *A Cultural History of Peace* has been in the making, politics that divide people into hostile groups have gathered strength in many countries, the long history presented in this collection suggests the cultural foundations for peace, so long in the making, will weather the present storm, and humanity will continue to make itself a global reality.

Introduction

RONALD EDSFORTH

This volume of *A Cultural History of Peace* offers readers fascinating ways to consider, or perhaps reconsider, modern global history. Thus far, the modern era, as it is defined here, spans the century since the global catastrophe that its contemporaries called "the Great War," and we know as World War I. Unlike the historical epochs that are the subjects of the first five volumes of *A Cultural History of Peace*, the modern era is *unfinished* and thus impossible to characterize as a whole with confidence. Will it be remembered more for the frequency and intensity of the armed conflicts that produced the extremely widespread bloodshed and destruction of its early decades? And that perhaps will mark its denouement? Or will recent trends like the steep decline of interstate warfare and the global diffusion of democratic values, nonviolent civil resistance, campaigns for human rights, and programs for sustainable development continue to shape peaceable politics among diverse groups within societies as well as peace between nations? We cannot know for sure. However we do know that a new and truly unprecedented global cultural environment for making relations between nations, as well as politics within nations, less violent has emerged in recent decades. These developments reflect the work of a multitude of peace thinkers, peace activists, and peace-seeking political leaders who have been creating intergovernmental organizations (IGOS) and nongovernmental organizations (NGOs) that form the institutional foundations of an unprecedented global peace culture. This modern peace culture today challenges longstanding beliefs that warfare and threatening violence are legitimate forms of politics. The many millions of people who turned out in over six hundred cities and countless smaller towns in at least sixty different countries in early 2003 to protest against the imminent invasion of Iraq by the United States and the United Kingdom, and to support of the United Nations' refusal to authorize it, dramatically revealed the geographic scope and political significance of this truly new global peace culture (Walgrave and Rucht 2010, xiii; and Cortright 2007).

I. A LONG VIEW OF WAR AND PEACE IN THE MODERN ERA

During the modern era, profoundly important changes in the character of warfare have undermined its cultural standing and moral legitimacy all across the world. Modern peace activists, building upon a foundation of ideas and institutions inherited from earlier generations, have shaped this disillusionment, creating during the last one hundred years a global culture in which aggressive violence is almost always regarded as shameful and illegal. During the early twenty-first century, despite what looks like contrary daily evidence appearing in global news media that still generally adheres to the maxim, "if it bleeds, it leads," most human beings have lived in zones of peace free from the fear of imminent political violence. In these most recent decades, the chances that a person will

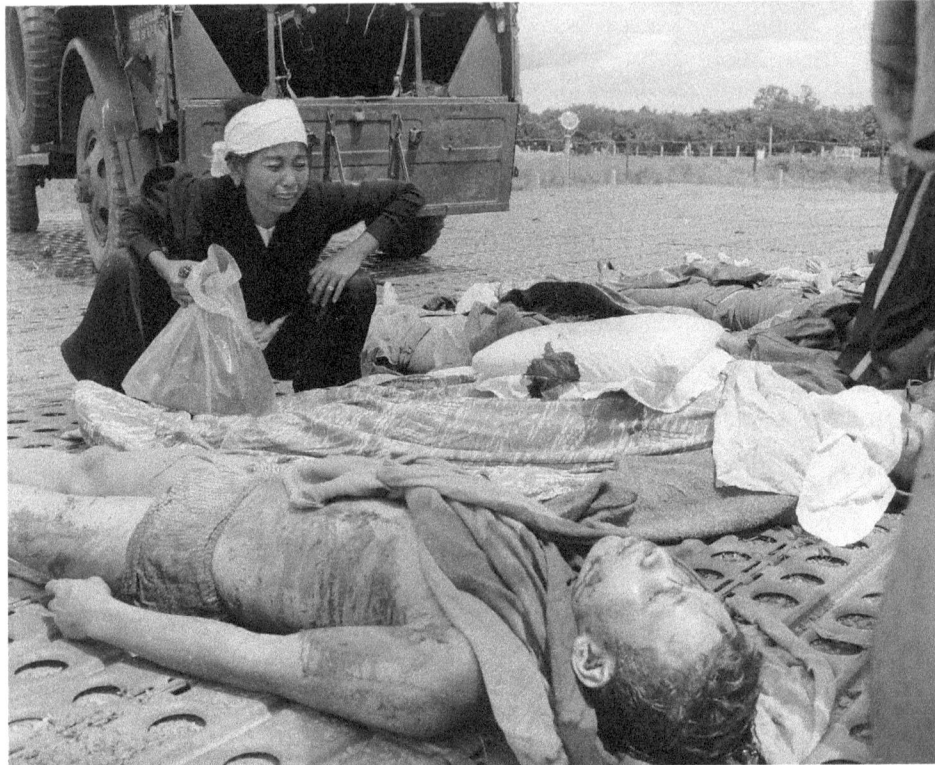

FIGURE 0.1: Woman weeps over her husband's body 1965. More than 200,000 South Vietnamese soldiers were killed fighting as allies of the United States. Wikimedia Commons (Public Domain).

be killed in warfare have been miniscule, a striking contrast to the historic peaks this measure of worldwide political violence reached during the two World Wars and during the Cold War when military interventions of the rival "superpowers" turned decolonization and many subsequent civil wars into boodbaths.

While world population has been growing rapidly (from three billion in 1960 to 7.4 billion in 2015), the total numbers of people killed in warfare has declined steeply.[1] Globally, battle deaths in wars involving at least one national government averaged about 215,000 per year in the period 1970–89. In the late 1990s, after the collapse of the Soviet Union and the Cold War, and as the conflicts in the Balkans and central Africa were contained, the number of battle deaths dropped to fewer than 100,000 per year. In this century, the annual average has been close to 50,000 per year (Goldstein 2011: 13–16). The US-UK invasion of Iraq in March 2003 stands out as the sole example of a major international war in the twenty-first century.[2] Estimates of the numbers of casualties in the Iraq War vary greatly, but it seems likely that at least 250,000 people were killed in its first decade, and that more than half of them were civilians (Crawford 2013). In 2016, only four conflicts produced more than 10,000 violent deaths a year: the long internationalized civil wars in Afghanistan, Iraq, and Syria; and Mexico's "drug war" (IISS 2017: 5). Many of the world's remaining violent conflicts, while producing appalling bloodshed, are nonetheless rightly described by John Mueller, as "remnants of war" that "are more nearly opportunistic predation waged by packs, often remarkably small ones, of criminals, bandits, and thugs" (2004: 1).

Of course, every death in each of these ongoing wars and in all of the world's other smaller armed conflicts is someone's loss and worthy of notice. Even 1,000 battle deaths a year (the social science standard for naming an armed conflict a "war") is an abomination. But when presenting a modern history of peace, we need to apply the sense of proportion that emerges from historical comparisons in order to assess the efficacy of the multitude and variety of peace policies, peace organizations, and peace movements that are uniquely modern. For instance, consider how our understanding of the historical significance of the numbers of total combatant and noncombatant deaths in these current wars changes once we realize that their *annual* death tolls are dwarfed by many of the atrocities of World War II, such as the deliberate indiscriminate killing of tens of thousands of unarmed civilians in Allied bombing raids against European and Asian cities. For example, Operation Gomorah, the British air raid on Hamburg in July 1943, killed more than 45,000 people (almost all noncombatants), wounded over 37,000 others, and destroyed 250,000 homes, thus creating a million internally displaced people (Ferguson 2006: 562). And it took just fifty minutes! Three hundred and thirty-four of America's new B-29 aircraft dropped over 1,667 tons of napalm bombs on Tokyo in a single raid in March 1945 killing over 100,000 people, leaving nineteen square miles of that wooden city a smoldering blackened desert (Reichhardt 2015). Five months later, two B-29s dropped just two new atomic bombs, destroying two cities, Hiroshima and Nagasaki, killing tens of thousands people instantly, and tens of thousands more from radiation sickness and related illnesses over many years afterwards.

In the aftermath of World War II none of the major combatant nations could genuinely claim the moral high ground, although the victorious Allied nations did so. The indiscriminate mass killing of noncombatants had long been regarded as shameful among warrior elites, and had been made a violation of the international laws of war by the Hague Conventions of 1899 and 1907. Nonetheless, mass killing of civilians was a deliberate strategy used by both the Axis and Allied nations. The Japanese Army in China moved under general orders known as the Three Alls: "Steal All, Burn All, Kill All" that left millions of civilians dead and tens of millions more homeless. The Nazi regime implemented Hitler's goal of establishing a new racially "pure" Reich by organizing the mass murder of more than six million Jews and more than a million other noncombatants deemed undesirable including Romani, the handicapped and mentally ill, homosexuals, and political opponents. Soviet soldiers raped hundreds of thousands of German women, leaving many of them dead, as they marched on Berlin during the last year of the war (Beevor 2002).

In what many Americans still call "the Good War," Allied bombing raids like those described above were justified as part of a "total war" strategy that would hasten victory and defeat truly evil enemies. But British Prime Minister Winston Churchill revealed another Allied motive—revenge—when he promised in a radio address in 1941 that the Royal Air Force would produce in German cities "the measure and more than measure" of death and destruction that the Luftwaffe inflicted on Britain during the Blitz (Bridcut 1998). Of course, with these words, Churchill aligned himself with countless other war leaders who since antiquity responded to the blood shed by their people with even greater bloodshed among their enemies. As a proud member of Britain's military elite, he knew that for those who end wars as victors, violent revenge confirmed not just their superior military might, but also their honor because they did not allow their dead to have sacrificed their lives in vain. Throughout history, the victors have felt they have earned the respect of others, and from that feeling they gained an increased sense of their own worthiness. On the other hand, among the defeated, the survivors of a war who failed to make good the blood sacrifices of their fellow citizens, shame and anger have been common responses that all too often compelled them (or their descendants) to again take up arms against a hated enemy. And thus, cycles of violence and warfare are created and sustained. This explanation of World War II is implied every time the punitive peace the Allies forced Germany to accept at Versailles in 1919 is cited as its primary cause.[3]

In the late 1940s, after having witnessed six years of incredible inhumanity including the first instances of nuclear bombardment, people all over the world reconsidered the ancient ethics of martial honor and other very old moral questions. Most importantly, does the end (always) justify the means? They understood that in order to preserve the future for the human race, a new way of organizing political life had to be found quickly, lest the next turn of the cycle of Great Power violence become apocalyptic. "We can distinguish those who accept the consequences of being murderers or the accomplices of murderers, and those who refuse to do so with all their force and being," the great French writer Albert Camus explained in "Neither Victims nor Executioners." He continued, predicting correctly that

> Over the expanse of five continents throughout the coming years an endless struggle is going to be pursued between violence and friendly persuasion . . . And henceforth, the only honorable course will be to stake everything on a formidable gamble: that words are more powerful than munitions.
>
> —1946 in Barash ed. 2000: 183

The scholars who have contributed to this volume of *A Cultural History of Peace* are continuing the struggle that Camus recognized as beginning in 1946. Their work highlights developments of great importance that are often missing or marginalized in popular histories and textbooks that typically focus readers' attention on the great inhumanities of the modern era. Their chapters bring to light some of the many unprecedented efforts to make the diverse societies of the modern world, and relations among them, more peaceable. Of course, as the first five volumes of this collection demonstrate, peace has always occupied an important place in human culture. But before our own modern era, and more precisely prior to 1945, nothing like our contemporary global peace culture had been created. Some of the most important intellectual, institutional, and political foundations of this modern peace culture had been established during the Enlightenment, and more added a century later when a transatlantic peace movement and the first world conferences of peace activists were organized. Nevertheless, before the modern era, institutions and individual leaders who promoted militarism, honored war heroes, and celebrated colonial empires flourished in the most highly developed nations. Early twentieth-century international relations were dominated by tensions between the older European empires and new empires, especially Germany, Japan, and the United States. Competition for colonies and arms races fueled by the marriage of modern industry and their military establishments generated widespread fear of Great Power warfare, especially in Europe and North America. The devastating consequences of the new Great Power military-industrial complexes were made apparent in Europe during World War I that began in August 1914, and then much more widely during World War II that was finally brought to an end by the atomic bombing of two Japanese cities in August 1945.

II. NUCLEAR FEAR

World War II was the greatest demonstration ever of our species' inhumanity, even as it also produced countless stories of self-sacrifice, rescue, and caregiving that are strong evidence of our humane capacities for respect, empathy, and sympathy. The mobilization of whole societies for what their leaders called "total war" spread technologically enhanced warfare across most of Europe, Asia, North Africa, and the Pacific. Whole regions of the earth were turned into immense war zones where the slaughter of soldiers and noncombatants and the mass executions of innocent prisoners, killed merely for being different from their captors, occurred every day for six years. By the end of 1945, scores of cities that for centuries had been monuments to their civilizations lay in ruins. And in Hiroshima and Nagasaki, where the death toll caused by the world's first nuclear bombardments continued to rise long after the mushroom clouds had dissipated, World War II had produced something else for which there was literally no historical precedent: *nuclear fear*, a reasonable and terrifying presentiment of a third world war in which thousands of nuclear explosions might literally end human history.

This dread-filled apprehension of massive, apocalyptic destruction unleashed from afar by a handful of political leaders became in the mid-twentieth century a quintessential emotional component of modern culture. Nuclear fear has been expressed, and stoked by the policies of the few nations that have actually built nuclear arsenals while always claiming deterrence as their aim. The UN has recognized the United States, the United Kingdom, France, Russia, and China as nuclear powers since the 1960s. This so-called "Nuclear Club" had deployed and stored more than 60,000 nuclear weapons (the vast majority of them American and Russian) by the mid-1980s. Israel, India, Pakistan, and North Korea—nations that have hostile relations with neighboring states—have also developed and stockpiled nuclear weapons. Thus in our lifetime, the human condition has always included knowing at some level that our deaths along with the deaths of hundreds of millions and perhaps billions of our fellow human beings could happen in a nuclear conflict. Nuclear warfare, unimaginably more devastating than the two 1945 bombings in Japan, remains a real threat. Nuclear fear is a unique and globalized characteristic of modern culture that has for three generations inspired the organization of global resistance to nuclear weapons development and deployment, while also contributing to broader opposition to war and to uniquely modern forms of peace politics.

Public expression of nuclear fear peaked twice during the Cold War. Each time the superpowers escalated the nuclear arms race, new and enduring peace organizations formed to counter the threat. The atmospheric testing of massively destructive hydrogen (fusion) bombs prompted a group of world-famous scientists including Bertrand Russell, Albert Einstein, Linus Pauling, and Joseph Rothblat to meet in London in July 1955 and issue a manifesto calling on all people to set aside political differences and consider themselves "only as members of a biological species which has had a remarkable history, and whose disappearance none of us can desire." The Russell-Einstein Manifesto argued that as long as nuclear arsenals existed, political issues "whether Communist or anti-Communist, whether Asian or European or American, whether White or Black . . . must not be settled by war." It concluded famously, "We appeal as human beings, to human beings: Remember your humanity, and forget the rest" (http://umich.edu/~pugwash/Manifesto.html).

FIGURE 0.2: Bertrand and Edith Russell lead sit-down demonstration in Whitehall, London protesting deployment of nuclear weapons, February 1961. Sally and Richard Greenhill/Alamy Stock Photo.

The science-based *species consciousness* expressed in the Russell-Einstein Manifesto is a hallmark of modern-era secular peace activism. It led Rothblat and Russell to establish the Pugwash Conference on Science and World Affairs that held the first of its annual meetings in Nova Scotia in 1957. The next year, the Campaign for Nuclear Disarmament began demonstrations against developing and deploying weapons of mass destruction in Britain. Yet, atmospheric testing of ever-more powerful weapons continued, their threat increasing at the same time with the development of accurate long-range rockets and submarine launch platforms. In 1961, the Soviet Union tested in the Arctic "Tsar Bomba," a hydrogen bomb 3,000 times more powerful than the atomic bomb that destroyed Hiroshima. Although relatively "clean" by the standards of the time, Tsar Bomba contributed to radioactive fallout that turned up around the world in milk, meat, and other foods. In 1961, tens of thousands of women marched in anti-nuclear protests in US cities that were organized by the newly founded Women's Strike for Peace. In the wake of the Cuban Missile Crisis in October 1962, a moment when superpower nuclear warfare seemed imminent, the anti-nuclear weapons movement achieved its first significant victory. After more than 500 air-burst nuclear explosions, the United States and Soviet Union ratified in 1963 a treaty banning atmospheric nuclear testing.

In the 1980s, a wave of global protests against renewal of the nuclear arms race led to the negotiations that have during the last three decades produced massive reductions in the arsenals of the United States and Russia. Jonathan Schell's chilling description of a nuclear winter that would be triggered by warfare between the United States and USSR, *The Fate of the Earth* (1982), inspired the nuclear freeze movement, and the first real reversal of the nuclear arms race. But today, despite massive reductions in American and Russian stockpiles required by the Intermediate Range Nuclear Forces Treaty (1987) and the Strategic Arms Reduction Treaty (1991), the nine nuclear nations still possess close to 15,000 nuclear warheads (www.armscontrol.org/factsheets/Nuclearweaponswhohaswhat). And recently announced plans to upgrade US, Russian, and Chinese nuclear forces are again ratcheting up nuclear fear. But the now permanent and well-organized networks of anti-nuclear organizations are already resisting these new nuclear policies.

Two other major developments since 1980: (a) the abandonment of nuclear weapons programs by at least eleven nations; and (b) the incorporation by treaties of 115 countries (including all of Latin America, Southeast Asia, the Pacific, and most of Africa) into nuclear-free zones, never made headline news in the nations maintaining nuclear arsenals (www.un.org/disarmament/wmd/nuclear/nwfz/). Nonetheless, they suggest a radically different historical trajectory than the one projected by the experts and political leaders in nations that continue devoting enormous material and intellectual resources to nuclear weapons in order to ensure what is sometimes called "nuclear peace." The actual arms reductions resulting from the INF and START treaties and the establishment of vast nuclear weapons free zones have been important steps towards the complete nuclear disarmament to which the United States, Russia, and 189 other nations are committed by the Treaty on the Non-Proliferation of Nuclear Weapons (NPT). A world free from the threat of nuclear war remains a possible end to the modern era.

III. WAR AVERSION

Nuclear fear is one strong form of a broader, more complex cultural response to the actual warfare that has produced massive bloodshed, destruction, physical suffering, and psychological trauma across much of the world during the modern era. Although many other wars in history were extremely bloody and destructive, warfare between coalitions of industrialized nations during the first half of the twentieth century was, as Niall Ferguson has observed, "much more intense (in terms of battle deaths per nation per year) than warfare in previous centuries" (2006: 649). Previously, Ferguson explains, "Occasional massacres occurred, it is true, but massacre did not become a routine military method" in conflicts between "developed Western societies" until the modern era (Ibid: 653–4). However, mass killing had frequently occurred during wars of conquest and while repressing revolts in the less developed regions of the world where the Great Power nations exercised colonial rule. New military technologies certainly contributed to the extreme lethality of World Wars I and II, but the deliberate breaking down of longstanding social and institutional restraints on the killing of noncombatants and wanton destruction in warfare in Europe itself was equally significant. The major wars of the twentieth century taught the peoples living in Great Power nations, who had learned to think of themselves and their cultures as "civilized," something that most inhabitants of their colonies had always known: self-proclaimed "civilized" human beings could, in the midst of the environment we call war, become the bloodthirsty savages of their own nightmares.

During the modern era's Great Power wars, what still seem even in retrospect almost unimaginable atrocities were, in fact, first imagined, and then deliberately planned and committed by many of the world's richest and best-educated people. In those wars, self-proclaimed "advanced" nations combined scientific and organizational techniques, as well as a vast and ever-growing array of technically sophisticated weapons, to produce hundreds of millions of dead, wounded, and displaced people and turn into rubble many of the great cities of the world. Casualty figures for the World Wars are still being revised, but general patterns are clear. In the modern era, Great Power warfare became more deadly for civilians as well as uniformed military personnel. As Niall Ferguson has noted, "significantly larger percentages of the world's population were killed in the two world wars ... than had been killed in any previous conflict of comparable geopolitical magnitude" (2006: xxxiv). The Centre Européen Robert Schuman has calculated that World War I produced 20 million deaths (including from war-related famine and disease) and 21 million wounded; with the dead about equally divided between soldiers and civilians. At least 60 million people or nearly 3 percent of the world's 1940 population died as a result World War II, about half that total on battlefields. The deadliest war zones were Eastern Europe and China (where at least twenty million died). Fully one-quarter of the population of Belarus died in the war. Over 15 percent of the populations of Poland, Ukraine, and the rest of the Soviet Union died. There are no reliable counts of the exact numbers wounded, but for some of the most developed countries including Germany, the Soviet Union, and the United States the numbers of soldiers who survived their wounds exceeded those killed in battle.

In the immediate aftermath of World War II, political violence continued all over Europe and East Asia including score-settling murders, the execution of prisoners of war, and the combination of massacres and the forced removal of civilians that we now call "ethnic cleansing" (Buruma 2013: 75–127; and Lowe 2012). Since 1950, most of the warfare in the world, including the great majority of terrorist attacks, has occurred far from Western capitals during civil conflicts in less developed countries. The deadliest of these many conflicts have been the internationalized civil wars in Korea (1950–53) and Vietnam (1955–75) between Communist and anti-Communist armies; and the ethnic/cultural civil wars in Nigeria (1967–70), Bangladesh (1971), Sudan (1983–2005), the Congo (1996–2003). During the four decades of the Cold War, interstate warfare pitting countries that fielded well-equipped armed forces was infrequent and usually brief, like the Arab-Israeli wars of 1967 and 1973 and the war between the United Kingdom and Argentina over the Falkland Islands in 1984. The biggest exception to this pattern was the Iran-Iraq War (1980–88) that killed nearly a million soldiers as it settled into a long stalemate eerily similar to Western Front of World War I.

The history of modern wars reflects what Jonathan Glover calls "the erosion of moral identity" and "festival of cruelty" that have always emerged when military victory, or avoiding humiliating defeat, become so important that they justify any and all means used to achieve them (Glover 1999: 26–39). It also shows how much modern military technologies have increased the killing capacities of national armed forces, rebels armies, and guerillas. The geographic scope of modern warfare has resulted in widespread acknowledgment of massive atrocities and the frightening experiences of modern warfare's victims felt directly, or even more commonly, witnessed via modern media including in news stories, newsreels, and television news, as well as photographs, documentary and feature films, and most recently in real time on global news and social media.

Direct and mediated experiences of modern warfare have led to profound reconsideration of the beliefs, ideologies, and archetypal stories that have since antiquity legitimized war and honored warriors. The global results have been a widely diffused and deeply felt *war aversion*. Modern war aversion has inspired new definitions of peace, a myriad of new forms of resistance to war, and new ways to make societies more peaceful. In other words, the cultural history of peace during the last century seems dominated by an ever-growing global recognition that modern war is inherently inhumane and therefore hard to justify. This change has been reflected since 1945 in international law that stipulates that only defensive warfare or war authorized by the United Nations is legitimate. The UN, the world's biggest peace organization, expresses in all its varied agencies and projects, this modern rejection of war by asserting for all of the diverse peoples of this world a common moral identity, *humanity*.

John Mueller, author of Chapter Seven below, has long argued that the global growth of war aversion and the disappearance of major wars between Great Powers since 1945 are related phenomena that together form a momentous break in the history of war and peace (1989). Mueller defines *war aversion* as "the notion that war is a bad idea and ought to be abolished" (2004: 32). War aversion is a radical revision of ideas about war that have, since antiquity, strongly influenced the frequency and cultural significance of warfare. War aversion is a protean cultural change that first emerged in Europe during and after World War I in response to the unique characteristics and consequences of that modern war. Since then, war aversion has been expressed in many forms. Some of them like the 1928 Kellogg-Briand Pact and the UN Charter embedded a prohibition on aggressive warfare in international law. Attempts to regulate modern warfare are stipulated in the UN-organized Geneva Conventions of 1949 and 1977 and other international treaties banning particular classes of weapons like land mines (1997). The modern elaboration of international law and organizations have been built upon intellectual and political foundations, now identified as Kantian or liberal internationalist, inherited from earlier generations of peace thinkers and peace movements. Other uniquely modern expressions of war aversion like peace research, post-conflict peacebuilding, and the multiplication of strategies and tactics used in nonviolent revolutions have emerged from the thinking and actions of dedicated peace activists. War aversion is emotionally grounded in the reasonable fears created by the violent political conflicts of the twentieth century that are still found in the framing of daily news stories, and are still conjured up in the war stories presented in fiction, drama, and films. The intensity of the fears of industrialized warfare, of nuclear war, and of genocide and its close cousin "ethnic cleansing" have waxed and waned during the modern era. Nevertheless, war aversion has been ever present in the collective memories of nations and the cultural minorities who live within nations all over the world.

In the modern era, war aversion has fed dissatisfaction with longstanding "negative" definitions of peace as "not war," that have underpinned all government policies that define peace in terms of military preparedness. Negative definitions of peace assume correctly that conflict is a normal part of human interactions and politics. Warfare and threatening war have been widely recognized for millennia as legitimate forms of political communication. Therefore, negative peace is presumed to be unstable, and lasting peace an almost impossible dream. When the United States and USSR inaugurated a new form of this political communication in the 1950s, atmospheric testing of hydrogen bombs, the longstanding political axiom "if you want peace, prepare for war" appeared absurd and immoral to a critical mass of concerned physicists and other atomic scientists, as well as many philosophers and social scientists, peace activists, religious and political leaders. A new scholarly discipline, peace research, and a new academic field, peace studies, were born in response to these concerns. Since then, hundreds of independent peace research and conflict resolution centers and university-based peace studies programs have been created all across the world. Peacemaking, peacekeeping, peace enforcement, and peacebuilding policies that are now in the twenty-first century routinely deployed by IGOs and NGOs to stop warfare and prevent violent conflict are the most widely known product of this modern intellectual development.

Peace research has been just one source of the many modern definitions of peace described by Charles Webel and Marcel Kaba in Chapter One. But as they explain, the most politically significant revision of the definition of peace presents it as a positive condition characterized by peaceable relations within society, as well as among nations. During the last half-century, attempts to create "positive peace" have produced new political priorities and policies in many countries. Since the 1960s, Johan Galtung, the Norwegian founder of the Peace Research Institute Oslo (PRIO), the world's first peace research center, and the many scholars and activists inspired by his work have been identifying what he calls "structural violence," deeply rooted ideologies (like patriarchy and white supremacy), social conditions (such as economic inequality and illiteracy), and political practices (including disenfranchisement and censorship) as the causes of civil war and other forms of politically organized violence inside societies, and war between nations. Viewed from this modern perspective, the achievement of (positive) peace requires democratic governments that protect all persons' human rights while promoting economic and social justice and sustainable development. In recent decades, positive peace and the policies developed to achieve it have been frequently honored, and thus promoted, by the Norwegian committee that annually awards the Nobel Peace Prize. It is very difficult to show a direct causal relationship that runs from the growth of war aversion since World War I, through the development and global diffusion of positive peace theories and policies via new networks of peace-oriented institutions after World War II, to what appears to be a truly unprecedented decline of warfare in recent decades. Yet the evidence for this interpretation, much of which is examined in the chapters of this book, has been growing even as what appears to be contrary evidence in the form of resurgent nationalism, ethnic conflicts, militant Islamist groups, and the global "war on terror" proclaimed by the United States and many other nations appears almost daily in the news.

IV. THE CULTURAL CONSEQUENCES OF MODERN WARFARE

In the twentieth century, actual warfare changed much faster than prevailing ideas about war. The changes appeared first in the ways that military establishments of the highly developed Great Power nations planned and fought battles. Mass killing and maiming of soldiers were often the result of attrition strategies that relied on the development and continual improvement of new military technologies that increased the range, lethality, and destructive power of modern weapons. As early as World War I, the results of the enormous investments of capital, labor, and brainpower necessary to achieve and maintain

Great Power status appeared in battles on the Western Front like the Somme and Verdun that continued for months, each of them producing over a million total casualties—dead, wounded, and missing (Baggett and Winter 1996). The deliberate targeting of civilians with modern weapons greatly expanded the total casualties and refugee flows of World War II, as in the above descriptions of some of that war's worst atrocities.

In one sense the dramatic escalation of bloodshed and destruction in both World Wars revealed what Carl von Clausewitz famously described in the aftermath of the Napoleonic wars: that although violent, war results from reasoned decisions designed to force a political opponent to accept what is demanded of them. However, emotional reactions increase during protracted conflicts when the stakes are great. In long bloody wars like the modern era's world wars, victory itself becomes the most important goal of warfare. Franklin Roosevelt surprised his alliance partners, Churchill and Stalin, when he declared at their Casablanca Conference in 1943, that their war aim was the "unconditional surrender" of their Axis enemies.[4] Achieving this kind of victory, forcing the Axis nations to accept whatever terms the Allies offered, justified whatever means could be created to achieve it, including the bombing of often undefended cities. During World War II, no moral or legal barriers slowed the moral slide into a massacre strategy, a strategy made more effective in 1945 by the development of terrifying weapons of mass destruction.

The coalitions of powerful imperialist states that made both world wars developed and employed new military technologies that greatly expanded the scale and scope of death and destruction produced by their armed forces. This change was qualitative, not simply quantitative. In the modern era, the nations that had claimed to be the epitome of human civilization created "total war." This kind of warfare required mass conscription of men to ensure a sufficient and continuous supply of replacements for the soldier-citizens who fell on the battlefield. The major powers also mobilized most of their civilian-citizens, women as well as older men and in some cases older children, on the home front where the war effort began. Thus, there was a certain brutal military logic to the destruction of industrial centers without which the warfare at the front could not be sustained. But such an inhumane form of warfare, especially after it culminated in the nuclear disintegration of two cities, could not be explained or justified by age-old ideas about war.

Archetypal war stories, first told in antiquity and retold ever since in every media devised for telling stories, have framed warfare as an extraordinary experience in which men can obtain honor and glory by displaying physical and psychological strength, courage, and initiative in the face of enemies who could be seen, and for a very long time, only killed at close range. During modern wars these types of archetypal stories have still been reproduced in descriptions of genuinely heroic soldiers, and especially in the propaganda produced by governments and patriotic journalists. Moreover, they remain a staple of very popular "action and adventure" feature films. But these archetypal narratives make little sense of the battles most soldiers have experienced in the modern era. The use of machine guns, long-range artillery, high explosive shells, poison gas, tanks, and aerial bombardment during World War I produced slaughters of soldiers that challenged ancient ways of understanding war. "War, which used to be cruel and magnificent, has now become cruel and squalid. In fact it has been completely spoilt," Winston Churchill wrote as early as 1930. Still proud of his service during the late nineteenth century as a British cavalry officer on India's frontier and in the Sudan, but deeply troubled by what he had witnessed during World War I as a Cabinet minister and also as a battalion commander on the Western Front in 1916, Churchill explained his meaning by evoking contrasting mental images of war that we have probably all seen many times on a variety of pages and screens, as well as in our mind's eye:

> Instead of a small number of well-trained professionals championing their country's cause with ancient weapons and a beautiful intricacy of maneuver, sustained at every moment by the applause of their nation, we now have entire populations pitted against one another in brutish mutual extermination, and only a set of blear-eyed clerks left to add up the butcher's bill.
>
> —*My Early Life*: 65

Total war as it was waged by the Great Powers during the twentieth century looked to Churchill and many of his contemporaries an abomination: death dealt from a distance, often indiscriminately, by death dealers most of whom never saw the bloody and dead flesh their work produced.

The enormous psychological, cultural, and political implications of modern total war were felt most strongly for the first time in Europe during World War I, but by now have been experienced, or at least witnessed in some mediated form, by most people on earth. Clearly opportunities to achieve the kind of glory and immortality that heroes have won on the battlefield fighting enemy soldiers for millennia have not disappeared in the modern era. Indeed they have reappeared during every modern war, and as Rune Ottosen and I argue in Chapter Five, they remain an important feature of the news media's reports about recent wars, as well as in recruiting advertisements for militaries across the world. But that kind of opportunity to demonstrate heroism and establish a place in a war's story was far less available in the World Wars and many other modern wars in which slaughter on the battlefield and the deliberate killing of noncombatants, an action that proud soldiers have traditionally viewed as shameful, has been incorporated into strategy and tactics.

Brave strong skilled soldiers, the most manly of men, are still the central characters of history's most popular war stories. But as Donna Pankhurst shows in Chapter Three, modern warfare itself has challenged the ancient idea that men are warriors and women are pacific, partly because so many women have been warriors in the modern era, but even more so because the stereotype of the masculine warrior hero has been undermined by men's actual experiences in battle. In modern war stories, the citizens who become soldiers often appear themselves as *victims* who suffer psychological as well as physiological damage; victims whose *survival* is often celebrated as kind of victory. This reconfiguration of the soldiers' experience is one of the most significant cultural changes that emerged during and after the major wars of the twentieth century. In his study of autobiographies written by soldiers who served on the Western Front during World War I, Samuel Hynes found that they had redefined courage as "simply going back into the trenches and standing there, enduring the shells, the misery, and privation, and *not trembling* . . . a stoic endurance where there is nothing to be done" (1997: 58). In other words, these soldiers, like noncombatants, saw themselves as victims of modern warfare who displayed what they recognized as bravery whenever they did not mentally break down as death and destruction arrived from afar, and who felt victorious if they merely survived the bombardment.

Steven Speilberg's feature film, *Saving Private Ryan* (1998) illustrates the difficulty of integrating a truthful depiction of modern technologically enhanced warfare and an ancient archetypal war story of a brave and intrepid group of soldiers. As the film begins, the audience finds itself among the American soldiers invading German occupied France on D-Day 1944. There are no panoramic shots of the landing or scenes of generals sending out orders, just soldiers in their landing craft, in the water, and on the sand simply trying to survive the storm of exploding metal that rains down upon them. In this portrayal of the establishment of the first beachhead in Normandy, no heroes appear on the screen. Many men are killed, many others wounded, their screams and moans drowned out for the most part by the terrifying noise of the battle. These opening scenes of the assault last just twenty-one minutes, but they seem much longer. Viewers feel relief when Speilberg, perhaps because he realizes most people would not be able to stand much more, shifts from realism into an archetypal narrative as a handful of soldiers form the band of brothers that during the next two hours and twenty-nine minutes will sacrifice a few of their own, but in the end complete a seemingly impossible mission. The two very different war stories Speilberg presents sequentially in *Saving Private Ryan* are never integrated because they cannot be integrated. The film's first story, the battle for the Normandy beach that the Americans will claim as a victory, is appalling and frightening because it realistically presents modern battle as a slaughter in which the individual qualities of the soldiers have little to do with their fate. Those soldiers who survive this battle without being killed or wounded are just lucky. The second story that follows the landing presents war as an adventure featuring just a few soldiers, each of whom is presented as a unique character. Their adventure is fraught with danger, but for that reason, it creates opportunities for individual ingenuity, heroism, sacrifice, and the achievement of the kind of memorable victory that has prompted young boys to play war games throughout history.

Honoring as heroic the mere survival of those who have experienced—that means directly seen, felt, heard, and smelled—warfare is a profoundly important break in the cultural history of war that occurs in the modern era. So too are modern-era changes in the treatment of the bodies of soldiers who have been killed in battle. In the mid-nineteenth century, the first modern military cemeteries that honor all the victors' dead soldiers by name were created by an act of Congress during the US Civil War, but this democratic form of memorializing the fallen did not become widespread in Western Europe until the twentieth century (Capdevila and Voldman 2006: 43–6). Before then the bodies of fallen officers, typically from the higher classes of society, were usually carried away from where they fell for burial later in marked graves, either nearby or back home. Meanwhile the vastly greater numbers of bodies, those of common soldiers, were left on the ground until their burial in mass graves or mass cremations could be organized. During the interval, these dead were robbed, often systematically, of everything of value including sometimes body parts.

The aftermath of the decisive and very bloody battle of Waterloo in 1815 is instructive on this point. The bodies of tens of thousands of dead soldiers from both armies were looted and stripped on the battlefield by victorious soldiers, camp followers, and local people. Teeth, removed by looters wielding pliers, were sold to dentists who made from them such great quantities of high-quality dentures that for several decades they were commonly known in Britain as "Waterloo teeth" (Pain 2001). A few years later, under the direction of entrepreneurs from England, Waterloo's mass graves were dug up by local workers so that the bones of the dead soldiers could be shipped to Yorkshire where they were pulverized and sold in popular fertilizers. In November 1822, a British newspaper reported that more than a million bushels of bones had arrived during the previous year via the port at Hull, and that

> It is now ascertained beyond a doubt, by actual experiment upon an extensive scale, that a dead soldier is a most valuable article of commerce; and, for ought known to the contrary, the good farmers of Yorkshire are, in a great measure, indebted to the bones of their children for their daily bread.
> —*New Annual Register for 1822*: 132

These early nineteenth-century examples of the commodification of the bodies of soldiers killed in the Battle of Waterloo seem an outrage to us today because we are so familiar with modern practices of honoring as sacrifices (in other words, as sacred acts that reaffirm the solidarity of the community) the deaths of all soldiers who fall in battle. These practices include, whenever possible, individually marked graves or monuments listing the names of the dead. Modern war, it must be remembered, helped usher in democracy for the dead as well as the living. In the many forms of individualized commemoration of the deaths of common soldiers, we see a direct reflection of the spread of democratic values and the belief in individual dignity and human rights within many national cultures. But we also see reflected the unprecedented human requirements of total war on both the battlefield and the home front. The global result, now seen and felt in every place touched by modern warfare, has been "a move away from the cult of national heroes to a recognition of the sacrifice made by ordinary individuals . . . and the inclusion within the collective memory of all members of society, women as well as soldiers, minorities as well as majorities" (Capdevila and Voldman: 173).

The now globalized practice of erecting monuments to commemorate unknown soldiers, tombs that represent the thousands of killed whose bodies were disassembled and disappeared in the extreme destruction of modern battles, began in the United States and Western Europe after World War I. In the twenty-first century, these memorials to the unknown and unnamed are among the world's most visited war memorials. But arguably the most significant and most visited sites that remember those killed in violent political conflicts during the modern era, commemorate not fallen soldiers, but the millions of noncombatant victims of wartime massacres. Commemorative sites such as Vad Yashem in Jerusalem, Auschwitz-Birkenau in Poland, Tuol Sleng in Cambodia, the Hiroshima Peace Park, the September 11th Memorial in New York City, and the Kigali Memorial Centre in Rwanda (that itself houses the remains of over 250,000 victims of that small country's recent genocidal conflict) acknowledge the greatest inhumanities of the modern era. They are grim reminders that modern war always produces slaughter, and sometimes genocide. Thus we find war aversion in the modern world's built environment, especially in these uniquely modern forms of remembering wars and honoring the memory of the multitudes of noncombatants who died in them. Indeed, together they express what has become, since World War II, the formation of a globalized "collective memory of wars that is of individuals and the tragedies which befell them" (Ibid: 174).

Of course, traditional forms of representing warfare as a peak masculine experience and of honoring warrior heroes still flourish in the twenty-first century. Yet the once hegemonic cultural power of longstanding masculine/martial ideas, images, and stories has been seriously challenged in our collective historical memories of modern warfare, and by the foregrounding of the experience of the victims of warfare in so much contemporary news of ongoing conflicts. In the twenty-first century graphic mediated images of big and small massacres of defenseless civilians appear daily on our screens while survivors and fleeing people bear witness using words, facial expressions, and body language that effectively convey fear, grief, anger, and other powerful human emotions that cannot be simply ignored. As Stanley Cohen argues in a brilliant examination of how we moderns cope with so often finding ourselves a bystander, witnessing from a distance the suffering of others, deliberate ignorance and denial are normal responses, not aberrant behavior (2001: 249). But acknowledgment of the suffering of others that leads to action, even an action as simple as just telling another person, has in recent decades become a new norm. "Everything is coming closer and faster, the faces of people in agony, the space and time it takes to reach them, the life-saving work of doctors," Cohen observes. And significantly, "Contrary to the rational self-interest model, people *continually* respond—not just to mass disasters, but by supporting traditional charities, development/aid agencies, and other causes" (Ibid: 290–1).

In our globalized world, the acknowledgment of atrocities and the actions people take to publicize the resulting suffering and deaths often create a snowball effect, especially when twenty-first century networks of international and nongovernmental humanitarian and human rights organizations that can influence policy responses are activated. Today's global audiences recognize that industrial enhanced modern warfare has typically produced the slaughter and suffering of noncombatant civilians, and that it will continue to do so.[5] As a consequence, in the twenty-first century, the morality, and not just the political rationale, of every decision to prepare for, to threaten, and/or use modern warfare has been immediately questioned by millions of people living all over our networked world who find in traditional philosophical and moral justifications for war no justification for slaughter.

V. GLOBAL PEACE CULTURE

A global peace culture has been created during the modern era. Global peace culture is an umbrella term under which the work of an amazing variety of individuals, secular and religious groups, local and national and international nongovernmental organizations, and the intergovernmental institutions of the UN system can be effectively gathered and understood. At the turn of this century, in a study of international organizations titled *Global Community*, Akira Iriye described a new global formation separate from the international system of sovereign states and the business world that had been created in the twentieth century. Iriye prophetically concluded that if its development continued "there would truly emerge a human community that would consist of various complementing organizations sharing the same concerns and seeking to solve them through cooperative endeavors" (2002: 209). Today, what I am calling a global peace culture, defined by its commitments to positive peace, is that human community. Of course, it is anti-war. Indeed, global peace culture expresses in a multitude of forms the deeply felt war aversion produced by the total warfare of the twentieth century and by the unceasing flows of news about contemporary wars and political violence and terrorism. But global peace culture embodies much more than opposition to war. It includes all the diverse and growing intellectual and political efforts to create human communities that are just, humane, and ecologically sound. In other words, all efforts to achieve positive peace by eliminating the causes of violence within and between societies, whether or not they succeed, are part of contemporary global peace culture. Its development has generated, and continues to foster new experiments in reducing political violence and the deeper structural violence in societies that have so often produced violent political conflicts.

Global peace culture includes all the new ideas, methods, and organized efforts directed towards eliminating the many different forms of structural violence in all parts of the world, now connecting them in real time via the global communications networks that are unique to our century. The making of global peace culture since World War II has been facilitated by a convergence and interaction of several major historical developments in addition to nuclear fear and war aversion, each hugely important in themselves, that are uniquely modern. Unfortunately, there is no way to fully describe these developments in this already long Introduction. But they must be briefly noted here if we are to better understand the historical timing of the creation of global peace culture in the modern era.

First, the world political order that had for many centuries been shaped by imperial expansion and competing empires has been destroyed by a combination of the world wars, violent revolutions in the colonies, and perhaps most significantly from a peace history perspective, by nonviolent revolutionaries inspired by the strategic ideas and tactics of the Indian independence movement led by Mohandas Gandhi. The decision to employ nonviolent revolutionary strategies instead of violence, and the numerous successes of nonviolent revolutions have undoubtedly made the modern era more peaceable. The long process of decolonization, including the extraordinary wave of nonviolent revolutions that brought down the Soviet Union's Eurasian empire from East Germany to Mongolia, undermined the legitimacy of all the ideologies of European imperialism including white supremacy, civilizing mission, and Soviet Communism.

Secondly, during the twentieth century, as Amartya Sen has argued, democracy was embraced across the world as a "universal commitment" that "cannot be disposed of by imagined cultural taboos or assumed civilizational predispositions imposed by our various pasts" (1999: 3, 16). Struggles to create and/or maintain democracy have shaped global politics since World War II. Although human rights are often treated separately from democratic forms of governance, the development of this universal commitment to democracy has been infused with the belief that real democracies must include protections for the human rights of all people, women and men, minorities as well as majorities (Goodhart 2005). Moreover, the rapid global diffusion of democratic ideas and governance during the late twentieth century resulted most often from nonviolent revolutions, not revolutionary violence. Beginning with the toppling of dictatorships in Greece, Portugal, and Spain in the mid-1970s, nonviolent revolutions subsequently swept away authoritarian and military governments throughout South America as well as in the Philippines, South Africa, and South Korea during the 1980s before destroying the USSR and its empire as that decade ended (Sharp 2005, and Schock 2005). When able to mobilize great numbers in "People Power" movements, increasingly sophisticated nonviolent revolutionaries who share strategies and tactics in global networks have shown their methods of engaging in political conflict to be far more likely to succeed, and far more likely to lead to the establishment of democracies than violent revolution (Chenoweth & Stephan 2011). And, of course, as the inspirational history of the Civil Rights movement in the United States demonstrated, nonviolent civil resistance has since World War II perhaps been the most effective strategy for attacking the structural violence within societies that denies ethnic, racial, religious minorities and women equal rights (Ackerman and Duvall 2000: 305–33; and Roberts & Ash 2009: 58–74).

Thirdly, the development of a truly global peace culture during the last three decades has been made possible by the acceleration of what we call "globalization." The rapid multiplication of integrative technological, economic, political, and cultural networks has provided for truly unprecedented coordination and sharing of all kinds of ideas and work, including that done by all of the people around the world who promote peaceable politics, champion and protect human rights, provide humanitarian relief to victims of war and natural disasters, and promote sustainable economic practices. Of course, modern-era technologies like jet airliners, digital computing, satellite communications, fiber optic cables, and the now almost ubiquitous cell and smart phones that have dramatically compressed time and space are tools that have no inherent political trajectories. Militant nationalists, fascists, radical Islamists, racists, misogynists, and others who promote political violence are just as skilled at using them as groups that promote nonviolence, peace, social justice, and equal rights. So too are governments intent on suppressing dissent and eliminating political opponents (Morisov 2011).

Nonetheless, it is important to recognize how these new technological capabilities have contributed to the making of a genuinely global peace culture at this particular point in history. Using them, millions of people around the world have formed networks, including those described by Toh Swee-Hin in Chapter Four and Cecelia Lynch in Chapter Six. These unprecedented global networks have resisted nuclear proliferation, opposed particular wars, supported nonviolent revolutions and human rights campaigns, and assisted the IGOs and NGOs that promote peaceful resolution of violent conflicts. They have also contributed new methods for building peaceable politics inside the many mostly former colonial countries that have been ravaged by episodes of civil warfare since 1945.

Finally, although it is easy to miss its profound historical significance because it so quickly became embedded in what is literally our contemporary view of the world, humans have been exploring outer space since the mid-twentieth century. As Neil Armstrong recognized when he walked on the moon in July 1969, space travel was truly "one giant leap for mankind." Photographs of earth taken by the first humans in space, and especially the now famous "Blue Marble" image of earth sent from a distance of 29,000 kilometers by the crew of Apollo 17, did far more than confirm Columbus' insight about the shape of earth. Framing earth against a black background of what appears to be endless emptiness, those unprecedented images confirmed the beauty and fragility of our planet at precisely the moment when the nuclear arms race between the United States and USSR was peaking, and movements expressing fears about the degradation of the natural environment of our earthly habitat were emerging around the world. Since then, recognizing homo sapiens as a single species sharing an increasingly vulnerable habitat has become part of our uniquely modern universal understanding of humanity.

Recent international efforts to reverse global climate change that have been organized by the United Nations are perhaps the clearest example of how this species consciousness has been incorporated into global politics. Responding to warnings issued by climate scientists, the World Meteorological Organization and the UN Environmental Organization founded the International Panel on Climate Change (IPCC) in 1988. Using scientific reports produced by IPCC experts that warned of catastrophic global warming, the UN-organized Kyoto Conference produced the first drafts of an international convention on climate change that was presented for ratification at the 1992 Rio Earth Summit. The Kyoto agreement to reduce greenhouse gases took effect in 1997. Every year since, the IPCC has met to update its climate change analysis and issue new recommendations. Since then, its work has led to the 2015 Paris Agreement on sustainable development and ongoing efforts to get all of the world's countries to accept their responsibility to implement stronger programs that will significantly reduce greenhouse gases by 2040.

FIGURE 0.3: Earth Day Poster, *The Whole Earth is Watching*. Wikimedia Commons, Yanker Poster Collection, Library of Congress (Public Domain).

In 2007, the IPCC was awarded a Nobel Peace Prize.[6] This award and its history illustrate how modern positive definitions of peace have been mainstreamed in what is now a global politics that aims to make a more peaceable world by bringing all peoples together in a common recognition of their shared humanity. Before the four major global developments described above, this political project was most often rejected as naïve, idealist, and/or utopian, partly because dominant ideas about human nature rooted in ancient religions and poor scientific understanding of "primitive" peoples encountered by Europeans in their colonies emphasized male predation, violence, and cruelty. In recent decades, as Douglas Fry clearly explains in Chapter Two, this profoundly pessimistic view of human nature that still underpins most "realist" foreign policy making, has been successfully challenged by a new anthropology that shows the powerful effects of social instincts like respect and sympathy in human evolution. Most importantly from our own twenty-first century peace history perspective, this new science shows that our species has survived especially because we thrive in communities that build cooperation.

The unique characteristics of our contemporary world, which include the widely recognized possibility that we humans may from our own activities make our species extinct and the unprecedented technical infrastructure that every day facilitates global cooperation in peace culture projects (including this collection of essays) does not guarantee the success of the new politics of humanity. But the history presented in Geneviève Souillac's Chapter Eight does show that there have been in the modern era unprecedented cooperative achievements among groups within countries and between nations that have histories of violent political conflict. Our world in which democracy and human rights have the greatest political legitimacy; ideas, goods, the arts, and people circulate more widely, freely, and quickly than ever before; and an ever-growing number of interconnected IGOs and global NGOs promote positive peace is now more integrated than ever before. Of course, it would be naïve to think that this historical trajectory must continue. But it is neither naïve, nor utopian to think that it might.

To paraphrase the famous essay by Albert Camus quoted above, people like myself who identify as contributors to our new global peace culture, do not expect a world in which there are no extremely contentious political conflicts, only a world in which violence and the threat of violence are no longer accepted as legitimate ways to resolve political conflicts. In this century, nations and people build positive reputations and standing in the world by their contributions to science and the arts, by producing improvements in health and the welfare of children and the elderly, in athletic competitions like the Olympics and the World Cup, and in a multitude of other peaceable activities. The chapters in this book explore this still-growing recognition of our common humanity that is very much the result of being able to share and celebrate with people across the world actions that demonstrate our respect and sympathy, like the billions of dollars in assistance sent by millions of people around the world to help the millions of strangers who were victims of the Indian Ocean tsunami in 2004 (www.theguardian.com/world/2009/dec/23/2004-tsunami-five-years-on). This humane consciousness is now deeply entrenched in the institutions of global peace culture, and more broadly in the minds of multitudes of people across the world.

Of course, there are many good reasons to temper the optimism that rises when we focus our historical attention on the development of global peace culture. During the last few years, while this collection has been in the making, we have witnessed political revolts against globalization, a surge of militant nationalism in many countries, and the terrors that a militant form of that global revolt, radical Islam, can spread across the world. In many countries, campaigns to dismantle patriarchy and ensure the human rights of ethnic and religious minorities are currently producing reactionary political violence. Moreover, the United States is trying to maintain an unstable global military hegemony it claimed after the collapse of the Soviet Union against what its leaders have already framed as growing military threats from Russia and the new global economic powerhouse, China. At the same time the United States has been conducting overt and covert wars including long-distance drone strikes against radical Islamists in South Asia, the Middle East, and Africa.[7] The American Congress has also recently set in motion programs to modernize the country's nuclear arsenal, a policy change that is raising fears of a new nuclear arms race. But this year is not 1913 or 1938. The networked global peace culture and a global politics that honors those who make peace and shames those who make war had not yet been made then, nor had the potential for a nuclear war far more catastrophic than World Wars I and II yet been created. Although we cannot say with any certainty that the unprecedented developments that have made the world more peaceable since 1945 will continue, the cultural history of peace presented in this volume gives us reasons to believe they will.

CHAPTER ONE

Definitions of Peace

CHARLES WEBEL AND MARCEL KABA

INTRODUCTION

Most of us think we know what *peace* is, but people often have very different definitions of this apparently simple word. And although almost everyone would agree that some form of peace—however it is defined—is desirable, there are often forceful, even violent, disagreements over how to obtain it. Frequently, there is an unstated assumption in peace discourses that peace is universal and unifying. This premise underlies much peace talk, both Western and non-Western. But few if any peace scholars and activists provide reasons and arguments to justify this belief. And most of the conversations about peace prior to the past century have been among Western and East Asian men of privilege. This is gradually changing, however, as female, non-Western, and previously ignored peace advocates and peacemakers have made their voices heard.

Occidental peace theories, especially prior to the twentieth century, defined peace as "the absence of war," almost always referring to interstate political violence. In other words, they defined peace "negatively." This binary opposition between peace and war entails the further belief that peace and war are mutually exclusive—e.g. nations are either "at peace" or "at war"—and that there is no continuum between war and peace. It also implies that nations (at least from the seventeenth century onward) and empires (through the end of World War I) have been the major peacemakers and belligerents.

However, since roughly the mid-twentieth century and the end of World War II, other actors, including multinational corporations, non-governmental organizations, peace and related social justice movements, spiritual and religious leaders, and groups labeled "terrorist" by states, have become important players on the global stage. Since 1945, intrastate conflicts and proxy wars, especially in the decolonized "developing" world, have been more frequent than wars between great powers. Additionally, significant violent conflicts have developed within nations formally "at peace" and without declared civil wars. For example, perhaps the three most powerful nation-states—the United States, Russia, and China—while officially "at peace" among themselves, are riven by internal conflicts and "terrorist" attacks. Systemic racism still lingers in the United States, there is widespread lack of freedoms for Uighurs and Christians in China and for Muslims in Russia, and all three countries have endemic and increasing inequities of income and power. These and other factors catalyze violent social conflicts, including violence between "alt-right" and "anti-fascist" fringes, as occurred in Charlottesville, Virginia, in

2017, and atrocities against civilians and officials committed by disaffected jihadists, violent xenophobes, ultra-nationalists, and non-Muslim zealots, in all three countries, labeled "terrorists" by government officials and the mass media.

During their Cold War (1945–91), the United States and the Soviet Union provided military assistance to belligerents in many countries in Central America, Africa, and East Asia, and more recently in proxy wars, most noticeably in Syria. These wars resulted in the loss of millions of lives, mostly people of color. And China, whose current political posture extends its long history of internal consolidation rather than overseas military adventurism, has recently expanded its global economic presence in less developed nations and, while reluctant to do so, may become directly involved in international conflicts, especially those involving the United States and the Koreas. Even in such failing states as Iraq, there are regions like its Kurdistan that are largely free from the civil warfare raging in the rest of the country. Hence, there is a *peace–war continuum* between great powers and within many nations.

Moreover, most Western peace discourse still typically signifies "outer," i.e. political and social peace, rather than the "inner" peace denoting the "peace of mind," or "mental harmony," of a peaceful person. This contrasts with many non-Western spiritual and religious traditions, particularly Buddhism, which prioritize inner peace and often claim it to be a pre-condition for outer peace in the public realm. The relative paucity of influential Occidental political discourse about inner peace and about the links between inner and outer peace has since the 1970s become somewhat less egregious, largely due to the attention given in some Western circles to such influential East Asian peace thinkers/activists as Vietnam's Thich Nhat Hanh and Tibet's Dalai Lama.

THE MEANINGS OF PEACE

Peace, like many abstract terms, is difficult to define. Like happiness, harmony, justice, freedom, and other theoretical concepts, peace is something we often recognize *by its absence*. Johan Galtung, a founder of modern peace studies and peace research, has, among others, insisted that the negative definition of peace is insufficient and propagated the important distinction between "positive" and "negative" peace.[1]

Positive and Negative Peace

Negative peace denotes the absence of war. It is a condition in which no active, organized political violence is taking place. Until roughly the mid-twentieth century, negative peace was assumed to be virtually synonymous with peace per se, at least for most "political realists." When the noted twentieth-century French intellectual Raymond Aron (1966: 151) defined peace as a condition of "more or less lasting suspension of rivalry between political units," he was thinking of negative peace. Aron's is the most common understanding of peace in the context of conventional political science and international relations, and it epitomizes the so-called *realist* view that peace is found whenever war or other direct forms of organized state violence are absent.

An alternative view to this realist (or *Realpolitik*) perspective is one that emphasizes the importance of defining peace in positive terms. Positive peace refers to a social condition in which exploitation is minimized or eliminated and in which there is neither overt violence, nor the seldom-articulated phenomenon of underlying structural violence. It is characterized by the continuing presence of an equitable and just social order as well as ecological harmony. In the West, positive peace denotes the simultaneous presence of many desirable states of society, such as harmony, justice, equity, and a sustainable economy. The elimination of all political violence and of the kinds of institutionalized exploitation that Galtung and others call "structural violence" would describe the ultimate achievement of positive peace. Positive peace thus stands for the creation of equitable and just social orders as well as ecological harmony. The many peace research and conflict resolution centers and university programs established since Galtung founded PRIO (Peace Research Institute Oslo) in 1959 have elaborated positive peace theory and practices.

The semantics of peace gets us remarkably far in defining peace as the word has been most commonly used, at least in standard English. In many philosophical, religious, and cultural traditions, peace in its positive sense comprises both "inner" and "outer" dimensions. In Chinese, for example, the word *heping* denotes world peace, or peace among nations, while the words *an* and *mingsi* denote an "inner peace," a tranquil and harmonious state of mind and being, akin to a meditative mental state. Many other languages also frame peace in its "inner" and "outer" dimensions. Two additional denotations of the term are "interpersonal or intersubjective" peace, and "divine" peace. The former refers to the peace, degree of harmony, or lack of concord, between people and within groups or organizations; the latter recognizes the belief held by billions of people that God is the ultimate "peacemaker" (although God, as in Hebrew scripture, may also be a notable war-bringer).

However, in some circumstances, the word "peace" may have an undesirable connotation. The Roman writer Tacitus spoke of making a desert and calling it "peace," an unwanted place of sterility and emptiness. Similarly, although nearly everyone seeks "peace of mind," or "inner peace," the undesired "peace" of a coma or death may not seem desirable. Even the most peace-loving among us recognize the merits of certain aggressive attitudes, acts, and metaphors, especially when they refer to something other than direct military engagement, including President Lyndon Johnson's "war on poverty," and the medical profession's "war on cancer" and "battle against AIDS." The use of militant language to describe efforts to improve society and health is not mere wordplay. Fighting, striving, and engaging in various forms of conflict and combat (especially when they are successful) are widely associated with vigor, energy, courage, and other positive virtues. Nonetheless, peace may be (along with happiness) the most longed-for human condition.

Nuclear Peace

The term "nuclear peace" refers to the assumption that the existence of nuclear arsenals contributes to international peace and stability. While Steven Pinker (2011) presents much evidence suggesting a historic decline of interstate wars and other forms of collective violence, which contribute to a surprising contemporary state of "global peace," there are other analysts who claim that the peace Earth has enjoyed since the end of World War II (the absence and/or decline of officially declared interstate wars between great powers) can be attributed primarily to the deterrent effects of nuclear weapons. Nuclear peace, it is claimed, results from the costs of war being too high in a confrontation between nuclear powers. The costs of nuclear warfare (national, regional, and/or global annihilation of life) are unacceptable, and thus serve as a deterrent. Following this line of thought leads to the desirable outcome of controlling the proliferation of nuclear weapons. An analysis by Victor Asal and Kyle Beardsley (2007: 139–55) indicates that the presence of states with nuclear capabilities reduces likely levels of violence. But is the alleged 37 percent reduction in the probability of war between nuclear powers worth the numerous risks associated with proliferation of nuclear weapons? What happens, for example, when a nuclear arsenal is controlled by a lunatic president or an aggressive dictator? Robert Rauchhaus' research reveals that the probability of war declines in the presence of so-called nuclear symmetry (2009). However, Rauchhaus also concludes that the probability of military conflict is actually higher in cases of nuclear *asymmetry*. Nuclear peace proponents often struggle to explain the fiscal burdens, the tradeoffs, and long-term costs to human health and ecosystems associated with developing, testing, maintaining, and disposing of nuclear weapons and materials.

According to *The Bulletin of the Atomic Scientists*, mismanagement and security threats at nuclear sites in the United States continue to occur despite the country's advanced technologies and capacities. The United States spends almost $6 billion annually to restore the environment and manage the waste related to its nuclear weapons. Costs for compensating affected workers are also extremely high. The total cost of nuclear cleanup is estimated to far exceed the actual cost of producing the weapons (Sagan and Valentino, 2017). In addition to the diversion of resources to nuclear weapons from peace and other socially desirable policies, and the environmental and health damage they create, Richard Falk has also warned of the "moral depravity of relying on genocidal capabilities and threats to uphold vital strategic interests of a West-centric world" (2012). Furthermore, as David Barash and Charles Webel have argued, there are numerous other "skeletons in the closet of deterrence," which, taken together, cast doubt on the claim that nuclear deterrence has "worked" to prevent wars between great powers. Finally, should nuclear deterrence "fail," no one may be left to assess why (Barash and Webel 2018: 132–8).

On July 7, 2017, 122 nations voted at the United Nations to approve a global treaty to ban nuclear weapons. While a landmark achievement, none of the nine states with nuclear weapons voted for the treaty; they boycotted the meetings. Therein lies another major problem with nuclear peace. While most countries voted to ban nuclear weapons, the nuclear powers remained committed to their nuclear programs, and instead of backing a global ban and nuclear disarmament, continue to support nuclear non-proliferation. Deterrence, therefore, does not actually apply globally, and the legitimacy of decisions already made about who can own nuclear weapons continues mostly unchallenged. These factors are threats to peace rather than contributors to stability. In his 1964 Nobel Peace Prize acceptance speech, Martin Luther King Jr. declared: "Somehow we must transform the dynamics of the world power struggle from the negative nuclear arms race which no one can win to a positive contest to harness man's creative genius for the purpose of making peace and prosperity a reality for all of the nations of the world. In short, we must shift the arms race into a *'peace race'* . . ." (King 1964). Since King spoke these words, at least eleven nations (South Africa, Brazil, Argentina, Taiwan, South Korea, Iraq, Sweden, Libya, Ukraine, Kazakstan, and Belarus) have abandoned their nuclear weapons programs.

PEACE AND RECONCILIATION

Two starting points for a "peace race," especially after violent conflict, are addressing past injustices and building a transparent and trustworthy system for administering justice. As Jeremy Farrall noted: "The most difficult reconstruction . . . lies in rebuilding the trust and confidence of people in their own society . . . from public officials in the local post office right up to the head of state." (2009: 138–9)

If parties in conflict are to productively interact in the future, some kind of reconciliation that satisfies demands for justice needs to occur. Since the end of the Cold War, one way countries have dealt with the problem of transitional justice has built on precedents set in the 1945–46 Nuremburg trials: criminal prosecution for war crimes in such special courts as the International Criminal Tribunal for Yugoslavia (1991–2017) and International Criminal Court. These courts dispense so-called *retributive* justice in long costly trials of alleged major perpetrators. People in post-conflict Rwanda and South Africa chose to complement retribution with *restorative* justice. The national South African Truth and Reconciliation Commission and local *gacaca* ("grass-roots justice") courts in Rwanda have provided victims (or their family members) with an opportunity to confront and ideally forgive the perpetrators for their crimes. But many difficulties arise when the emotions of war are revived in postwar courts and truth commissions. As East Timor's first president, Kay Rala Xanana Gusmao, suggests, true reconciliation is a *proactive long-term process* that must address structural injustices in all the social, economic, political, and judicial dimensions of national life. (Gusmao 2003).

PEACE AND DEVELOPMENT

Without peace, there can be little development, and without development there can be little peace. During times of violent crises, development is generally delayed or postponed; while without education, justice, healthcare, protection of human rights and the environment, peace, if achieved at all, would be, as former president of Egypt Anwar al-Sadat (1978) recognized, "a structure of sand which would crumble under the first blow." Accordingly, the more equitable, free, and transparent a society, the more likely it is to have meaningful peace. Societies with basic freedoms, universal education, and the provision of adequate medical care, food, water, and other necessities of life are more likely to be at peace with surrounding nations.[2]

International peace has been linked to democracy since the Enlightenment. In a classic quantitative analysis of democratic peace theory, Dean V. Babst examined the relationships between the occurrence of wars and types of governments, especially democracies. Babst referred to Quincy Wright's study of 116 major wars from 1789 and 1941, according to which no wars have been fought between nations with elected governments. In 1964, Babst claimed that "a general review of the main wars since 1941 appears to be consistent with the findings here reported . . . the existence of independent nations with elective governments greatly increases the chances for the maintenance of peace" (1964: 9–14); and thus efforts at promoting elective governments should be one of the main tasks of war prevention. Democratic peace theory was revived after the Cold War (Russett, 1993; and Russett and Oneal, 2001). It remains controversial partly because it was one of the official justifications for the US/UK invasion of Iraq in 2003.

STRUCTURAL AND CULTURAL VIOLENCE

In stark contrast with peace, however it may be defined, is violence. Violence is commonly regarded as physical and readily apparent through observable bodily injury and/or pain. There are also other forms of violence, more indirect and insidious. *Structural and cultural violence* are typically inherent in social, cultural, and economic institutions. For example, both ancient Egypt and imperial Rome practiced slavery and were highly despotic, although they were technically in states of negative peace for long periods of time. Structural violence is widespread yet often unacknowledged. It denies people, among other things, important civil rights; economic well-being; social, political, and sexual equality; a sense of personal fulfillment and self-worth; and a healthy environment. When people starve to death or go hungry, a kind of violence takes place. Similarly, when people suffer from preventable diseases or when they are denied a decent education, affordable housing, freedom of expression and peaceful assembly, or opportunities to work, play, or raise a family, a kind of violence occurs, even if no bullets are fired and no clubs are wielded. A society commits violence against its members when it forcibly stunts their development and undermines their well-being whether because of their religion, ethnicity, gender, age, sexual preference, or some other reason. Structural violence is a form of social oppression, and maltreatment of the natural environment is a kind of structural violence.

Many contemporary peace activists affiliated with democracy, human rights, and environmental justice movements have embraced Johan Galtung's ideas about structural violence. Under conditions of structural violence, according to Galtung, many people who behave as good citizens and who think of themselves as peace-loving people may participate in "settings within which individuals may do enormous amounts of harm to other human beings without ever intending to do so, just performing their regular duties as a job defined in the structure" (Galtung 1969: 167–91 and 1990: 291–305). The philosopher Hannah Arendt famously advanced the concept of "the banality of evil" in her appraisal of the role of such "normal" people as Adolf Eichmann, who helped organize the Holocaust. Arendt emphasized that routine, workaday behavior by otherwise normal and decent people can sometimes contribute to mass murder, social oppression, and structural violence (Arendt 1966).

Structural violence typically permeates social and economic institutions, even in societies that are experiencing external and internal negative peace. The violence of such *de jure and de facto* social structures as apartheid, caste systems, segregation, and patriarchy denies people important political rights, economic well-being, a sense of self-worth, and social and gender equality. The structural violence involved in homelessness, hunger, political repression, and psychological alienation often goes unrecognized. Normalized, it works slowly to erode humanistic values and impoverish people's lives. By contrast, direct violence is quicker, with more visible and dramatic effects. In cases of overt violence, even those people not directly involved in the conflict may want to take sides. Most reporters and mass media believe that "If it bleeds it leads." News coverage of bloody events is often intense, so modern consumers of the news are likely to pay attention to highly visible violent acts without considering the underlying structural factors that may have led to them.

The concept of *cultural violence* extends structural violence. Cultural violence occurs when any aspect of a culture, including its art, language, symbols, ideology, dress, diet, (pseudo-) science, and religious practices, may be used to legitimize violence, either in its direct or structural forms. Cultural violence does not kill or maim like direct violence or the violence built into the social structure. However, it legitimizes either or both, as for instance in the theory of a *Herrenvolk*, or a superior or "master" race, that informed Nazi mass murders. At present, however, structural and cultural violence remain contested concepts. Clearly, structural and/or cultural violence take place wherever there is slavery or gross political, cultural, and/or economic oppression. However, it remains debatable whether social inequality is structural violence and whether differing cultural norms and practices constitute violence.

A WORLD OF PEACES

From our twenty-first century viewpoint, when considered historically and cross-culturally, peace does not appear as a universal and unitary phenomenon. Rather, it might be more accurate to speak of *peaces*, not of peace. Thus, definitions of peaces—and such presumed opposites as war, violence, conflict, and other "lacks of peace"—reveal more about the definers and their historical and cultural perspectives and contexts rather than disclosing the "universal" components or "essence" of peace.

Until the mid-twentieth century, the dominant discourse of peace was a virtual monopoly of two groups: Western male policy makers and their strategic advisors, mostly political *realists* who in the Hobbesian tradition defined peace negatively as the absence of war for them and their compatriots; and Western philosophers, legal theorists, and diplomats, following the lead of Immanuel Kant and Woodrow Wilson, who continued to articulate *idealist and liberal* visions of peace as the bearer and result of democracy, human rights, the rule of law, and free trade. Since then, however, positive peace discourse has been truly globalized in large part by recognizing the theories and practices of nonviolence stemming from Mohandas Gandhi and Martin Luther King Jr., whose influences have been notable in peace talk and peace work in South Asia, Africa, and Latin America. At the same time, realist or negative peace definitions have also been strongly voiced outside the West, most notably in Russia and China.

The recent globalization of peace talk and peace work is unprecedented. In what follows below, the voices of some notable recent peace-definers, mostly from outside the dominant Western tradition of talking and making peace are heard. Although they voice a range of views found among their Western counterparts, non-Western definitions and theories of peace augment the now conventional Western and once hegemonic peace talk in important ways. They often do this *by situating peace within such broad social and political concerns as anti-imperialism and national liberation, economic equity, women's and children's rights, social justice, and environmental protection—in other words, what in the West has in the past half-century has been called positive peace—which may, at times, take priority over negative peace*. Recent peace-definers also tend, especially in Asia, to *focus as much on inner peace as on outer peace*, and on the interaction between the two at both personal and political levels. Finally, while what follows is by no means a comprehensive or even a truly representative sample of influential peace-definers, it should provide readers with a more globalized view of the definition of peace and its vicissitudes than is usually presented in Occidental sources.

SOME AFRICAN DEFINITIONS OF PEACE

Muḥammad Anwar al-Sādāt, a Muslim, was the third President of Egypt, serving from 1970 until his assassination by fundamentalist Muslim army officers in 1981. As President, Sadat led Egypt into the Yom Kippur War of 1973 to regain Egypt's Sinai Peninsula, which Israel had occupied since the Six-Day War of 1967, making him a hero in Egypt and, for a time, the wider Arab world. Sadat then engaged in negotiations with Israel, culminating in the Egypt–Israel Peace Treaty of 1979, following the Camp David Accords, which were facilitated by former US President Jimmy Carter. This won him and Israeli Prime Minister Menachem Begin the Nobel Peace Prize, making Sadat the first Muslim Nobel Peace Prize laureate.

Like many non-Western political leaders, Sadat *linked peace inextricably with justice*:

Let me share with you our conception of peace: First, the true essence of peace, which ensures its stability and durability, is justice . . . Second, peace is indivisible. To endure, it should be comprehensive and involve all the parties in the conflict. Third, peace and prosperity in our area are closely linked and interrelated . . . And last . . . peace is a dynamic construction to which all should contribute . . . It goes far beyond a formal agreement or treaty, it transcends a word here or there.

—Sadat 1978

Bishop Desmond Tutu, a black Christian, was born in 1931 in South Africa. Tutu became active in non-violent struggles against apartheid, and maintained his nonviolent resistance. Although an ally, Tutu challenged Nelson Mandela and his supporters whenever they advocated and used violent resistance. Tutu's integrity and positive influence across Africa led to his selection for the Nobel Peace Prize award in 1984. In his Nobel lecture, Tutu stressed *the vital relationship between peace and justice*: "There is no peace in Southern Africa. There is no peace because there is no justice. There can be no real peace and security until there be first justice enjoyed by all . . . . peace without justice . . . would be crying 'peace, peace, where there is no peace'" (Tutu 1984).

In 2004, for the first time in history, the Nobel Peace Prize was awarded to an African woman, *Wangari Maathai* who connected peace with sustainable development. In 1977, Maathai founded the Green Belt Movement in Kenya with the intention of combating the deforestation that was threatening the livelihood of rural populations. She gained renown through her environmental activism and the role she played in the struggle for democracy in Kenya. Her environmental conservation initiatives were made famous by her tree-planting activism, which she envisioned as a practical way of supporting poor women, but

FIGURE 1.1: Activist Wangari Maathai. Wendy Stone / Contributor / Getty Images.

also as a symbol for women's rights, democracy, and peace. In her Nobel Peace Prize acceptance speech, Maathai stressed the *connections between peace and sustainable development:*

> Using trees as a symbol of peace is in keeping with a widespread African tradition . . . *There can be no peace without equitable development; and there can be no development without sustainable management of the environment in a democratic and peaceful space.*
>
> —Maathai 2004

SOME ASIAN DEFINITIONS OF PEACE

Mohandas K. Gandhi is revered by many Indians as the founder of their nation and is also venerated by millions of others around the world as the leading exponent and practitioner of nonviolence. Gandhi pioneered the modern use of nonviolent resistance as both a spiritual and ethical approach to life and also as a practical technique for achieving political and social change. Gandhi discussed and practiced *non-violence*, a term he usually preferred to "peace."

Gandhi often explicated his idea of non-violence in terms of *satyagraha*, literally translated as "soul-force," or "holding firm to the truth." *Satyagraha* requires adherence to love and mutual respect, and demands a willingness to suffer, if need be, to achieve these goals.

FIGURE 1.2: Gandhi leading the Salt March, March 1930. New York Daily News Archive / Contributor / Getty Images.

For Gandhi, *satyagraha* required strength in practicing nonviolent methods. In his words:

> Truth (*satya*) implies love, and firmness (*agraha*) engenders and therefore serves as a synonym for force. I thus began to call the Indian movement Satyagraha, that is to say, the Force which is born of Truth and Love or non-violence . . .
>
> —Gandhi 1968: 109–10

Gandhi's teachings emphasized not just love, compassion, and nonviolence ("doing no harm," or *ahimsa*), but also courage, directness, civility, and honesty. It is difficult to overstate Gandhi's impact on nonviolent theories and practices during the past century.

In contrast, *Mao Tse Tung*, also known as Chairman Mao, a Chinese revolutionary and the founding father of the People's Republic of China, did not flinch from advocating and using violence as a method of political change, and is often held responsible for the deaths of millions of Chinese. In his 1956 address to the Communist Party, Mao stated:

> Our country and all the other socialist countries want peace; so do the peoples of all the countries in the world. The only ones who crave war and do not want peace are certain monopoly capitalist groups in a handful of imperialist countries which depend on aggression for their profits . . . To achieve a lasting world peace, we must further develop our friendship and cooperation . . . and strengthen our solidarity with all peace-loving countries.
>
> —Mao, 1956

FIGURE 1.3: The Dalai Lama speaking in Tokyo, October 31, 2009. Jeremy Sutton-Hibbert / Alamy Stock Photo.

During the Cold War, this rhetorical emphasis on "world peace" and "solidarity" was shared by Mao's "socialist comrades" in the Soviet Union, Cuba, and in the "anti-imperialist" bloc more generally.

Tenzin Gyatso, born Lhamo Dondrub in 1935, the fourteenth and current *Dalai Lama*, is the leader of Tibetan Buddhism. During the 1959 Tibetan uprising, the Dalai Lama fled to India. He advocates nonviolent resistance to Chinese rule over Tibet. He has proposed *"A Human Approach to World Peace,"* which stresses the importance of compassion as the source of *inner peace*. According to the Dalai Lama, during the twentieth century, tens of millions of people lost their lives due to violence, and the economies of many countries were ruined because of violent conflicts. He has stated:

> Peace, in the sense of the absence of war, is of little value to someone who is dying of hunger or cold ... *Peace can only last where human rights are respected,* where the people are fed, and where individuals and nations are free. *True peace with oneself and with the world around us can only be achieved through the development of mental peace* ... Without ... inner peace, no matter how comfortable your life is materially, you may still be worried, disturbed or unhappy ... Peace ... starts with each one of us. When we have inner peace, we can be at peace with those around us. When our community is in a state of peace, it can share that peace with neighboring communities ...
>
> —Dalai Lama 1989

A LATIN AMERICAN DEFINITION OF PEACE

Oscar Arias Sánchez started his political career in 1970 as an assistant to José Figueres, the Costa Rican president who had abolished the country's military in 1948. By spending money that would have been in a military budget on education and healthcare, Costa Rica has sustained not only steady economic growth and domestic peace internally, but this demilitarized country has also contributed to peacemaking internationally. Sánchez was elected Costa Rica's president in 1986. He dedicated himself to reducing violence and ending civil wars in Central America. While critical of the political systems in neighboring countries, Sánchez engaged them in peacemaking processes. He also lobbied against US interventions in Nicaragua and rejected the US government's request to use Costa Rican territory as a sanctuary for the Contra rebels.

In his 1987 Nobel Peace Prize acceptance speech, Sánchez emphasized the links among peace, justice, and democracy. He declared:

> *Peace is a never-ending process* ... It is an attitude, a way of life, a way of solving problems and resolving conflicts. It cannot be forced on the smallest nation or enforced by the largest. It cannot ignore our differences or overlook our common interests. It requires us to work and live together ... We seek ... not peace alone, not peace to be followed some day by political progress, *but peace and democracy, together.* ... an end to the shedding of human blood, which is inseparable from an end to the suppression of human rights ... We believe that justice and peace can only thrive together ... peace can only be achieved through ... dialogue and understanding; tolerance and forgiveness; freedom and democracy.
>
> —Arias Sanchez 1987

SOME RUSSIAN DEFINITIONS OF PEACE

Vladimir Ilyich Ulyanov, aka *Lenin*, a Russian revolutionary and Marxist theorist, was the first leader of the Soviet Union. He was partially incapacitated by strokes in 1922 and died in 1924. During World War I and its immediate aftermath, when the Western Allies sent troops into Russia to support counterrevolutionaries, Lenin stressed the "hypocrisy" of the "imperialist phrasemongers" who preached "democracy" and "peace," but practiced exploitation and war:

> Most people are definitely in favor of peace in general ... *each* of them wants an end to the war. The trouble is that every one of them advances peace terms that are imperialist (i.e., predatory and oppressive, towards other peoples), and to the advantage of his "own" nation ... socialists must explain to the masses the impossibility of anything resembling a democratic peace, unless there are a series of revolutions and unless a revolutionary struggle is waged in every country against the *respective* government.
>
> —1921

In 1962, during the height of the Cuban Missile Crisis, when it appeared that nuclear war between the United States and the Soviet Union was imminent, then Soviet Premier *Nikita Khrushchev* proposed to President John F. Kennedy a nonviolent way to settle the crisis. Khrushchev suggested that if the United States dismantled and removed its nuclear missiles from Turkey, the USSR would do the same with its installations in Cuba (Kaba 2009: 34). This "off-the-record" arrangement settled the crisis. In his letters to Kennedy, Khrushchev declared:

> measures indicated in your [US during the Cuban Missile Crisis] statement constitute a serious threat to peace and to the security of nations ... Everyone needs peace: both capitalists, if they have not lost their reason, and ... Communists ... *We, Communists, are against all wars between states in general and have been defending the cause of peace since we came into the world.* We have always regarded war as a calamity, and not as a game nor as a means for the attainment of definite goals, nor ... as a goal in itself ... *War is our enemy* and a calamity for all the peoples ...
>
> —1962

Mikhail Gorbachev was the last leader of the Soviet Union. When he came to power in 1985, he pursued many internal reforms, including *glasnost* (openness) and *perestroika* (restructuring), which contributed to ending the Cold War, the collapse of Communism in Central and Eastern Europe, and the disintegration of the Soviet Union. In his 1990 Nobel Peace Prize acceptance speech, Gorbachev asked:

> What is peace? ... I found ... a definition of "peace" as a "commune"—the traditional cell of Russian peasant life ... people's profound understanding of *peace as harmony, concord, mutual help, and cooperation* ... Peace "propagates wealth and justice;" a peace which is just a respite from wars ... is not worthy of the name; peace implies general counsel ... And, *ideally, peace means the absence of violence.*
>
> —Gorbachev 1991

Vladimir Putin has been the leader of the Russian Federation since 2000. Before entering Russian politics, Putin worked for the former KGB. During most of his rule, he has enjoyed high domestic approval ratings. However, Putin is also widely criticized for both his domestic and foreign policies, and especially for Russia's military support of the Assad government in Syria, its annexation of Crimea, and its alleged instigation of violent separatism in eastern Ukraine. Putin views peace and use of force in international relations from a *realpolitik* perspective. He has stated:

> Peace, as a state of world politics, has never been stable ... *Periods of peace in ... history were always based on securing and maintaining the existing balance of forces* ... we must be realistic: military power is ... and will remain for a long time ... an instrument of international politics ... this is a fact of life. The question is, will it be used only when all other means have been exhausted? When we have to resist common threats, like, for instance, terrorism, and will it be used in compliance with the known rules laid down in international law? Or will we use force on any pretext, even just to remind the world who is boss here, without giving a thought about the legitimacy of the use of force and its consequences, without solving problems, but only multiplying them.
>
> —Putin 2015

The above voices from non-Western nations are, like their Western counterparts, far from uniform in their framing of peace. Nonetheless, they pose important alternatives to an Occidental hegemonic peace-discourse focused primarily on "negative, democratic, and outer" peace, often at the expense of sincere and effective forms of participatory and emancipatory peacemaking.

SOME NORTH AMERICAN AND WESTERN EUROPEAN DEFINITIONS OF PEACE

Albert Einstein is best known for his revolutionary contributions to physics. But he was also a politically engaged pacifist who spoke out frequently on the subjects of civil rights, nationalism, capitalism, and war and peace. In 1932, along with Sigmund Freud, Einstein was invited by representatives of the League of Nations to contribute to a public debate on the causes of war. Einstein posed the following question to Freud:

> This is the problem: Is there any way of delivering mankind from the menace of war? ... The quest of international security involves the unconditional surrender by every nation, in a certain measure, of its liberty of action—its sovereignty ... The craving for power which characterizes the governing class in every nation is hostile to any limitation of the national sovereignty ... I have especially in mind that small but determined group, active in every nation, composed of individuals who ... regard warfare, the manufacture and sale of arms, simply as an occasion to advance their personal interests and enlarge their personal authority ... Is it possible to control human mental evolution so that people can resist the psychoses of hate and destructiveness?
>
> —Einstein 1932

Sigmund Freud, the founder of psychoanalysis and a fellow pacifist, responded to Einstein:

> There is *but one sure way of ending war and that is the establishment, by common consent, of a central control* which shall have the last word in every conflict of interests ... *How long have we to wait before the rest of men turn pacifist?* ... Meanwhile ... whatever makes for cultural development is working also against war.
>
> —Freud 1932

After his emigration from Germany, following Hitler's rise to power, Einstein lived in the United States, where he wrote: "The economic anarchy of capitalist society as it exists today is, in my opinion, the real source of evil" (Einstein 1949).

Martin Luther King Jr. is one of the most famous civil rights activists in history. A black American, born in 1929 in Georgia, King became a Baptist preacher and a leader in the struggle against racial discrimination by American whites against blacks, and later against economic discrimination by the rich against everyone else.

King was best known for his leadership of nonviolent struggles for equal civil rights for African Americans and desegregation in America's southern states and northern cities. Reflecting on the successful Montgomery Bus Boycott of 1955, he stated:

> The "turn the other cheek" philosophy and the "love your enemies" philosophy were only valid, I felt, when individuals were in conflict with other individuals; when racial groups and nations were in conflict a more realistic approach seemed necessary. But after reading Gandhi . . . I came to feel that this was the only morally and practically sound method open to oppressed people in their struggle for freedom . . . *True pacifism is not unrealistic submission to evil power . . . It is rather a courageous confrontation of evil by the power of love*, in the faith that it is better to be the recipient of violence than the inflicter of it . . . *nonviolence became more than a method to which I gave intellectual assent; it became a commitment to a way of life.*
>
> —King 1958: 478–81

FIGURE 1.4: Dr. Martin Luther King, Jr. being arrested for "loitering" in Montgomery, Alabama 1958. Archive PL / Alamy Stock Photo.

King's leadership of mass protests and sustained nonviolent civil disobedience actions were widely regarded as key to achieving landmark Federal civil rights legislation in the mid-1960s. Accepting a Nobel Peace Prize in 1967, King declared:

> In spite of temporary victories, *violence never brings permanent peace*. It solves no social problem: it merely creates new and more complicated ones . . . We adopt the means of nonviolence because our end is a community at peace with itself . . . We will not build a peaceful world by following a negative path. It is not enough to say "We must not wage war." It is necessary to love peace and sacrifice for it. We must concentrate not merely on the negative expulsion of war, but on the positive affirmation of peace . . .
>
> —King 1964

For his dedication to social justice and economic equity, King suffered discrimination, imprisonment, FBI surveillance, death threats, and attacks on his home. In 1968, he was murdered in Memphis, Tennessee, while supporting a strike by local sanitation workers.

It may come as a surprise to some that former US President *Richard Nixon* discussed the meaning of peace in a way that shows he understood the limitations of a simple negative definition of the word:

> I have often reflected on the meaning of "peace" . . . Peace must be far more than the absence of war. *Peace must provide a durable structure of international relationships which inhibits or removes the causes of war*. Building a lasting peace requires a foreign policy guided by three basic principles: [1] Peace requires partnership . . . [2] Peace requires strength . . . America's strength. Peace . . . cannot be gained by good will alone . . . [3] Peace requires a willingness to negotiate . . . But the most fundamental interest of all nations lies in building the structure of peace . . .
>
> —Nixon 1970

Barack H. Obama, another former President of the United States, was awarded the Nobel Peace Prize in 2009 for his vision of a world free from nuclear weapons and his strong verbal support for international human rights and democracy. While claiming inspiration and influence from Martin Luther King Jr., and endorsing a broad definition of peace, Obama used his Nobel Prize acceptance speech to stress *the importance of war as an instrument for peace*, saying:

> Still, we are at war, and I'm responsible for the deployment of thousands of young Americans to battle in a distant land. Some will kill, and some will be killed . . . In today's wars, many more civilians are killed than soldiers; the seeds of future conflict are sown, economies are wrecked, civil societies torn asunder, refugees amassed, children scarred . . . *So yes, the instruments of war do have a role to play in preserving the peace* . . . Three ways that we can build a just and lasting peace. First . . . we must develop alternatives to violence that are tough enough to actually change behavior . . . [Second], only a just peace based on the inherent rights and dignity of every individual can truly be lasting . . . Third, a *just peace includes not only civil and political rights—it must encompass economic security and opportunity. For true peace is not just freedom from fear, but freedom from want* . . . The non-violence practiced by men like Gandhi and King may *not* have been practical or possible in every circumstance.
>
> —Obama 2009

In contrast with the aforementioned politicians, the Norwegian peace scholar and conflict transformer, *Johan Galtung*, has written scores of books and worked for peace in more than 100 countries. Galtung has stated:

> Building Peace Through Harmonious Diversity is a marvelous title, combining three words of honor; peace, harmony, diversity. *Peace . . . is another word for equality, equity, equal rights/dignity, symmetry, reciprocity, diversity/symbiosis etc.*; harmony is creative cooperation, beyond absence of violence; diversity celebrates our manifold, within peace and harmony.
>
> —Galtung 2004

Finally, when speaking in Poland in 2016, a day after a Catholic priest was murdered in France, the Argentinian *Pope Francis*, stressed the pacifistic nature of religion, declaring:

> . . . the world is at war because it has lost peace. When I speak of war I speak of wars over interests, money, resources, not religion. *All religions want peace, it's the others who want war.*
>
> —Pope Francis 2016

PEACE TALK, PEACE MAKING, AND PEACE MOVEMENTS

As evidenced by the global voices quoted above, there are probably at least as many recent and contemporary definitions of peace as at any point in recorded history. The diversity of peace-speak is both a tribute to, and an implicit critique of, *the popularity of peace talk and the lack of consensus regarding peacemaking.*

Since virtually every war bloodies the human record, the work of peacemaking is not only essential but remains unfinished. During the modern era, there have been numerous efforts at building peace, some long-standing and others quite recent. There have also been more than a few successes, including the demilitarization of Japan and the integration of Europe after World War II; the banning of nuclear weapons programs in 115 countries in South America, Asia, and Africa (www.un.org/disarmament/wmd/nuclear/nwfz); the waves of nonviolent revolutions that have forced out dictators from Portugal to Manila and brought down Communist regimes from East Germany to Mongolia (Chenoweth, 2011), and the negotiated settlement of at least sixteen civil wars since 1990 (Sigdel, 2014). Moreover, whereas the toll of war can be tallied, it is impossible to assess exactly how many wars, and how much associated death and destruction, have been *prevented* by the efforts of people seeking peace—that is, by the various "peace movements" of the modern era.

Peace movements worldwide have accomplished a great deal. In the twentieth century, for example, conscientious objection became widely recognized in most Western countries as a basic legal right, although exercising that right was sometimes perilous. The Vietnam War was terminated in large part because of American discontent with the war, fueled by immense pressure from the domestic peace movement, as well as, of course, by the fierce resistance by millions of Southeast Asians to what they perceived as American imperialism. Similarly, in the 1980s and 1990s, nuclear weapons underwent a rapid process of delegitimation, much to the dismay of militarists and cold warriors.

It remains to be seen whether contemporary peace movements can sustain their momentum when and if immediate, readily perceived threats to international peace no longer exist and when militarily powerful governments modulate their militaristic rhetoric but not their strategies, perhaps co-opting peace movements by making headlines with relatively trivial policy concessions. More specifically, it is uncertain whether antiwar sentiment in the United States will outlast current crises in Africa, Northeast Asia, and the Middle East, and also whether the antinuclear movement will regain its momentum or be quieted and "pacified" by political rhetoric that equates nuclear weaponry with patriotism and security. Contemporary peace movements may profit by developing alternative foreign policy concepts, alternative defense strategies, a pragmatic view of social goals, broader motivations beyond single-issue rallying points, a workable model of a disarmed (or, at least, substantially demilitarized) economy, and staying power. In addition, successful peace movements could be more realistic in confronting the power of the state while also, when possible, breaking out of a strictly state-centered model of politics.

WHAT IS, AND WHAT MIGHT BE, PEACE?

So what then is peace, and what might it become? Perhaps peace is like such other human ideals as happiness, justice, the rule of law, and health—something almost every person and culture claims to desire and venerate, but which few if any achieve, at least on an enduring basis. But perhaps peace is also somewhat different from happiness, since it seems to require social harmony and political enfranchisement, whereas happiness appears, at least in Western culture, to be largely an individual matter. Alternatively, perhaps peace does indeed resemble individual happiness—always there, implicit in our psychological make-up and intermittently explicit in our social behavior and cultural norms. Peace is a pre-condition for our emotional well-being, but a peaceful state of mind is subject to cognitive disruptions and aggressive eruptions.

Peace is a linchpin of social harmony, economic equity, and political justice, but over the long run peace seems also to be constantly ruptured by wars and other violent conflicts. And as is evident from some of the aforementioned citations, spiritual and religious leaders have been especially inclined to *equate peace and love*, both in their inner dimensions and in the manner in which people who are spiritually developed interact with others, most acutely with those who may hate and envy them.

For many contemporary peace advocates, especially Johan Galtung, it has been mandatory not only to "manage" and "resolve," but also to *transform* the conflicts rampant in our interpersonal and political realms of interaction and division. *If peace*, like happiness, *is both a normative ideal in the Kantian sense*—a regulative principle and ethical virtue indicating how we *should* think and act, even if we often fail to do so—*as well as a psychological need*—something of which we are normally unaware but sporadically conscious—then why are violence and war (the apparent opposites of social, or outer, peace), as well as unhappiness and misery (the expressions of a lack of inner peace), so prevalent, not just in our time but for virtually all of recorded human history—a topic, as previously noted, addressed by Einstein and Freud? Given the facts of history and the ever-progressing understanding of our genetic and hormonal nature, *is a unitary conception of peace even conceivable, and is global peace possible?* These are issues that have been addressed from time immemorial, in oral form since the dawn of civilization and in written form since the periods of the great Greek and Indian epochs. But to many influential observers they seem no closer to, and perhaps even further from, resolution than they were at the times of the *Iliad* and the *Mahabharata* several millennia ago.

THE "EVOLUTION" OF PEACE

Are the pessimists mistaken about the possibility of global peace? Has there been an "evolution," or "linear progress," in the development of peacemaking in the modern era? Over a century ago, Bertha von Suttner, presaging Freud, articulated the fundamental dilemma in her Nobel Peace Prize lecture:

> ... two philosophies, two eras of civilization, are wrestling with one another ... there is taking place in the world a process of internationalization and unification ... The instinct of self-preservation ... acting almost subconsciously ... is rebelling against the constantly refined methods of annihilation and against the destruction of humanity. Complementing this subconscious striving toward an era free of war are people who are working deliberately toward this goal ... powerful vested interests are involved, interests trying to maintain the old order and to prevent the goal's being reached ... Thus pacifism faces no easy struggle. *This question of whether violence or law shall prevail between states is the most vital of the problems of our eventful era* ... The beneficial results of a secure world peace are almost inconceivable, but even more inconceivable are the consequences of ... world war which many misguided people are prepared to precipitate ... The advocates of pacifism ... will, however, defend their objectives and ... their goal ... which ... affirms the duty of all governments "to bring nearer the time when the sword shall not be the arbiter among nations."
>
> —1905

More recently, according to Steven Pinker (2011) and Joshua Goldstein (2011), the answer to the question has there been an "evolution of peace?" is, perhaps surprisingly, a qualified "yes." According to them, long-term historical trends indicate:

1. Wars today are measurably fewer and smaller than thirty-five years ago.
2. The number of people killed directly by war violence has decreased by 75 percent in that period.
3. Interstate wars have become very infrequent and relatively small.
4. Wars between "great powers" have not occurred for more than fifty years.
5. The number of civil wars is also shrinking, though less dramatically, as old ones end faster than new ones begin.

Based on recent trends, Goldstein claims that we are "winning the war on war." Why? Because of the efforts of international peacekeepers, diplomats, peace movements, and other international organizations (such as the UN, EU, NATO, African Union, and other nongovernmental actors) in war-torn and postwar countries. Goldstein concludes that world peace is not preordained and inevitable, but neither is a return to large-scale war (Goldstein 2011).

Steven Pinker further argues that *today we may be living in the most peaceable era in our species' existence*. Pinker's evidence for this possibly striking and counterintuitive claim includes the recent trends described above, and these facts:

1. Homicide rates in Europe have declined thirty-fold since the Middle Ages.
2. Human sacrifice, slavery, punitive torture, and mutilation have been abolished around the world.

3. Wars between developed countries have vanished, and even in the developing world (civil) wars kill a fraction of the numbers they did decades ago.
4. Rape, battering, hate crimes, deadly riots, child abuse, cruelty to animals—every category of violence—from deaths in war to the spanking of children to the number of motion pictures in which animals were harmed—has declined.
5. And Pinker predicts that forms of institutionalized violence that can be eliminated by the stroke of a pen—such as capital punishment, the criminalization of homosexuality, and the corporal punishment of children in schools—will continue to decline. (Pinker 2011)

Regardless of whether one accepts all or any of the recent arguments for seeing the emergence of unprecedented peace in the most recent decades of the modern era, it should be clear that *peace and war exist on a continuum of violent/nonviolent interstate and intrastate political behaviors, and that their incidence varies over time*. Neither peace nor war should be taken for granted, and neither is humanity's "natural state."

A DIALECTICAL DEFINITION OF PEACE

Accordingly, while there may be some reasons for optimism, an "increase" in, or an "evolution of," peace is neither a linear development nor assured. But some recent empirical measures provide support for the claim that *negative* peace may be on the increase in the modern era. Like other abstractions, peace denotes something intangible, but which virtually all rational people prize. *Peace refers to a historical ideal and is simultaneously a term whose meaning is in flux*, sometimes seemingly constant (as in "inner peace of mind") but also noteworthy for its relative global absence, at least until very recently. Notably, peace has most often been defined or determined negatively; peace is the *absence* of war. Peace is also synonymous with *non*violence and security *from* threats. Paradoxically, *we become most aware of peace if it is missing*.

Peace remains a conflicted and contested term and activity. Peace is thus a *dialectical* concept. Peace is neither a timeless essence—an unchanging ideal substance—nor a mere name without a reference, a form without content. Peace should neither be reified by essentialist metaphysics, nor rendered otiose by postmodernist and skeptical deconstruction. Peace is, moreover, not the mere absence of war in a Hobbesian world of unending violent conflict. *Peace is, normatively speaking, both a means of personal and collective ethical transformation and an aspiration to cleanse the planet of human-inflicted destruction*. The means and the goal are in continual, dialectical evolution, sometimes declining during periods of acute violent conflict like the World Wars and sometimes advancing nonviolently and less violently to actualize political justice and social equity. Accordingly, *peace in this dialectical sense denotes active individual and collective self-determination and emancipatory empowerment*. Peace entails continuous peacekeeping and peacemaking. And peacemaking requires active and continual personal and collective transformation. Therefore, the words and deeds of those who both think and practice peace, and of those who actively seek to attain it by peaceful (nonviolent) means, demonstrate that true pacifism is not *passiv*ism. *Genuine pacifism is transformative and activist, employing nonviolent means of social and personal change to resist oppression, war, and injustice and to promote personal and social moral integrity and radical, peaceful means of transforming conflicts and actors.*

IS PEACE POSSIBLE?

Given the bloody character of much human history and the current parlous state of our world, one might understandably be skeptical about the prospects for enduring peace on Earth. Our modern era is after all the first to be living with the capacity for instantaneous and massive destructive global war. In these circumstances, it is worth recalling that other political ideals once thought unachievable also came to pass. It took millennia to outlaw slavery and legitimize human rights. It might take at least as long to delegitimize political violence, both from above (by the state) and from below (by non-state actors). Although irreversible "peace on Earth" might be unachievable, this thought does not invalidate the struggle to achieve a world with greater justice and equity and without violence, or at least with significantly less violence, injustice, and inequity. On the contrary, the nonviolent struggle to liberate humanity from its means of self-destruction and self-enslavement is its own end. The absence of a guarantee of "success" in the effort to bring peace to humanity, and the real possibility of the failure of the human experiment, do not undermine efforts to pacify human societies, but instead bestow on them existential nobility and moral virtue.

There is no essential, unchanging definition of peace. That is as it should be. Peace, like humanity itself, is both a work, and a word, in progress.

CHAPTER TWO

Human Nature, Peace, and War

DOUGLAS P. FRY AND GENEVIÈVE SOUILLAC

Our modern era inherits a longstanding legacy of beliefs about human nature in relation to war and peace. A classic view of human nature, at least as old as Greek civilization, portrays war as intrinsic to humanity. Although of dubious validity, this classic view today still holds considerable sway in science and society, art and religion, and politics and policy-making. However, in recent decades the view of human nature as warlike has been increasingly challenged as an alternative more balanced and peace-focused understanding has gained a foothold in modern thinking. This chapter explores how over the last hundred years, and especially in recent decades, a growing corpus of evidence derived from multiple disciplines presents a viable, evidence-based alternative to the classic war-steeped view of human nature.

Over the last century, there have been many developments contributing to peace, and at the same time warfare has become more devastating (Gittings 2016; Pinker 2011; Wodiczko 2012). Shifferd (2011) argues that the twentieth century constitutes a turning point for peace as the roles of international law and global institutions have increased markedly, and Gandhi, followed by Martin Luther King, Jr. and many other activists worldwide, successfully applied nonviolent resistance in place of violent rebellion (Chenoweth & Stephan 2011; Popovic & Miller 2016). Additionally, the human rights movement developed, and in the academic sphere, the discipline of peace studies was born (Shifferd 2011; Gittings 2016). These peace developments notwithstanding, the last hundred years have also seen millions of war deaths. Wodiczko provides a five-page listing of US military interventions since Wounded Knee (2012: 101–5). And the twentieth century witnessed the release of the nuclear genie from its bottle, a lethal event unparalleled in world history.

This chapter argues that the classic narrative of a warlike human nature is simply wrong and considers many lines of evidence, mostly amassed during the modern era, that instead support a new more peace-centric view. It is time to retire the classic view and replace it with a new conceptualization of humanity, not just because the old view is inaccurate, but also because the classic view continues to bolster militarism and foments fear, hostility, and violence among nations, religions, and ethnic groups. As Sahlins writes, "Western civilization has been constructed on a perverse and mistaken idea of human nature ... [that] endangers our existence" (2008:112). A strong alternative to the Western classic view of human nature has emerged in the modern era. Whereas the classic narrative rests on longstanding beliefs and historical traditions, the new narrative is based on scientific knowledge that reveals the deficiencies of the classic view.

THE HUMAN NATURE CONCEPT

Human nature is a slippery concept. To what degree does the concept of human nature imply fixed, immutable characteristics? Are some features that are assumed to be embedded in human nature, merely idiosyncratic cultural characteristics? Can there be more than one human nature, or does this possibility distort the concept beyond recognition?

Kluckhom & Strodbeck (1961) suggest that societies view human nature as good, bad, or neutral, and also vary regarding how mutable or immutable human nature is seen to be. Do cultures consistently have a mental map that humans everywhere—across cultural circumstances and geography—share? Are there certain pan-human characteristics? This assumption seems to be invalidated by Gregor's (1994) report that the Brazilian tribes of the Upper Xingu River basin in Brazil recognize three categories of humans: themselves as peaceful, their warlike neighbors, and the most brutal whites. However, does this understanding that two other categories of people, the warlike indigenous groups and white Brazilians, are more violent than themselves really mean that the Upper Xingu tribes see three kinds of human nature? Or, alternatively, are they simply aware that people in different societies sometimes behave differently from them?

In Western thinking, the concept of human nature centrally entails characteristics that are common to all humans. Merriam-Webster (2017) defines the concept as "the fundamental dispositions and traits of humans." A parallel construct from biology is species-typical behavior, which reflects how most members of a species behave in a natural setting (Verbeek 2013). The key idea is that during a species' evolutionary past, natural selection has operated to narrow the range of behaviors in any given species because some behavioral patterns have conveyed higher reproductive success than others. Human nature, or human species-typical behavior, should encompass those characteristics and dispositions that occur species-wide across a variety of ecological and cultural environments. The ability to learn language and to use language to communicate, to walk upright, to enjoy rough-and-tumble play in childhood, and to make extensive use of tools in daily life are examples of characteristics of human beings found all over the world. Such behaviors can be viewed as part and parcel of human nature or as species-typical behavior.

In the preface to his book *Human Universals*, anthropologist Donald Brown (1991) recounts how his friend and colleague Donald Symons, an evolutionary anthropologist, made a bet about whether Brown could find exceptions to Symons' observations about cross-cultural patterns of human sexual behavior. He explains, "I thought it highly unlikely that sex differences in temperament or behavior would show any complex similarities in all societies ... But I did not win the bet—and I began to think more carefully about human universals ..." (Ibid.: vii). In his book, Brown chronicles many elements of human nature, from cooking food to weaning children at roughly the same age, and from following the universal etiquette of greeting other people to applying social pressure on those individuals who break the social rules. He discovered that such species-typical behaviors as these occur across human cultures.

THE CLASSIC WESTERN VIEW OF HUMAN NATURE: NASTY AND BRUTISH

On human nature, the second US President, John Adams, wrote, "from the Fall of Adam to this time, Mankind in general, has been given up, to strong Delusions, Vile Affections, sordid Lusts and brutal Appetites" (Quoted in Sahlins 2008: 5). Anthropologist Marshall Sahlins traces this view of a selfish, violent human nature back to the ancient Greeks two millennia ago in the writings of Hesiod and Thucydides, then onward in time through Saint Augustine's trumpeting of *Original Sin*, Machiavelli's perception of men as "ungrateful, fickle, liars and deceivers, fearful of danger and greedy for gain" (Quoted in Sahlins 2008: 64–5), and onward still to Alexander Hamilton's summation in *Federalist Paper 34* that "fiery and destructive passions of war reign in the human breast with much more powerful sway than the mild and beneficent sentiments of peace" (1788).

It is clear that the classic view of a selfish and violent human nature long predated the thinking of philosopher Thomas Hobbes (1588–1679), and that numerous writings of the modern era continue to reflect this historically entrenched view of human nature. For example, in *Civilization and Its Discontents*, originally published a decade after World War I, Freud concludes in Hobbesian style that humans are savage beasts, lacking

FIGURE 2.1: A temple stands as a remnant of ancient Greek civilization on the southern coast of Sicily. D. P. Fry photo collection.

consideration for others of the same species, and draws upon a litany of historical barbarities to bolster his conclusion:

> The atrocities committed during the racial migrations or the invasions of the Huns, or by the people known as Mongols under Jenghiz Khan and Tamerlane, or at the capture of Jerusalem by the pious Crusaders, or even, indeed, the horrors of the recent World War—anyone who calls these things to mind will have to bow humbly before the truth of this view.
>
> —1961: 59

Freud's approach here is reductionist since it presumes that the causes of war and violence are inherent in human biology. Furthermore, Freud's historical cases of slaughter from which he deduces that all humanity is violent, are, in fact, limited, first because he ignores acts of nonviolent kindness, cooperation, and altruism within the same cultural contexts, and second because his historical examples do not represent the diversity of human societies including the non-warring and nonviolent ones that exist around the world.

The conceptions of a greedy, warlike human nature akin to those of Thucydides, Machiavelli, Hobbes, Hamilton, and Freud have appeared frequently over the last hundred years in popular writings, the media, and academic fields such as biology, psychology, and archaeology (Fry 2006a; Sponsel 2016; Sussman 2013). In the 1950s, anatomist Raymond Dart drew upon Australopithecine fossils to argue that humankind is not really so kind. In Dart's dramatic prose, we are supposedly descendants of killer apes, who were "confirmed killers: carnivorous creatures, that seized living quarries by violence, battered them to death, tore apart their broken bodies, dismembered them limb for limb" (Dart 1953: 209). In the 1960s, playwright Robert Ardrey and filmmaker Stanley Kubrick popularized Dart's views; Ardrey in best-selling books such as *African Genesis* (1961) and *The Territorial Imperative* (1966), and Kubrick in a dramatic scene of ancestral apes smashing adversaries with bone clubs in the blockbuster film, *2001: A Space Odyssey* (1968). Making reference to eighteenth-century philosopher Jean-Jacques Rousseau's writings on the "noble savage," Kubrick (1972) remarked,

> The question must be considered whether Rousseau's view of man as a fallen angel is not really the most pessimistic and hopeless of philosophies. It leaves man a monster who has gone steadily away from his nobility. It is, I am convinced, more optimistic to accept Ardrey's view that, ". . . we were born of risen apes, not fallen angels, and the apes were armed killers besides. And so what shall we wonder at? Our murders and massacres and missiles and our irreconcilable regiments?"

Renowned Harvard biologist, Edward O. Wilson (1978: 99), echoed Freud's reference to history as supposed proof of humanity's warlike nature when he addressed the question whether humans are innately aggressive: "Throughout history, warfare, representing only the most organized technique of aggression, has been endemic to every form of society, from hunter-gatherer bands to industrial states" (1978:99). And Wilson did not change his mind. Thirty-four years later he wrote, "Wars and genocide have been universal and eternal, respecting no particular time or culture" (Wilson 2012: 65). This classic Hobbesian view of a bellicose human nature is also reflected in a host of popularized science writings from *The Dark Side of Man* (Ghiglieri, 1999) and *Demonic Males* (Wrangham & Peterson, 1996) to *The Murderer Next Door* (Buss, 2005) and *Noble Savages* (Chagnon, 2013). "If one traces these theories into the history of modern biology, we can see that the Hobbesian view has predominated," concludes Sussman (2013: 99).

A MODERN SCIENTIFIC UNDERSTANDING OF HUMAN NATURE

Jean-Jacques Rousseau is routinely placed in opposition to Hobbes as an early spokesperson for a gentler view of human nature. In the Freud–Einstein letters of 1932, we see a Hobbesian–Rousseauan tension reflected between Freud's assessments of a bellicose humanity as contrasted with Einstein's more pacific view (Gittings 2016). In recent decades the longstanding Hobbesian orientation, while arguably still the dominant paradigm, has received an increasing number of serious challenges. In the midst of World War II, legendary anthropologist Bronislaw Malinowski (1941: 540) concluded that war "made a very late appearance in human evolution. It could not occur before such high differentiation in types of culture . . . War cannot be regarded as a fiat of human destiny, in that it could be related to biological needs or immutable psychological drives." Paleontologist Louis B. Leakey, famous for discoveries made with his wife Mary Leakey at Oldovai Gorge in Tanzania, debated with Robert Ardrey about the killer ape view of humanity. In *The Nature of Human Aggression*, Ashley Montagu (1976: 59) argued that "There is nothing either in the nature of war or in the nature of humanity that makes war inevitable" (1976: 59). Even archaeologist Lawrence Keeley (1996: 31, 32), who often has been cited in support of bellicose views, acknowledges in *War Before Civilization* that "Pacifistic societies also occur (if uncommonly) at every level of social and economic complexity . . . The idea that violent conflict between groups is an inevitable consequence of being human or of social life itself is simply wrong" (1996:31–32). To summarize, in the modern era, the classic view of an inherently violent human nature continues as a dominant narrative, while at the same time a growing number of voices challenge this portrayal of human nature.

EVALUATING THE EVIDENCE: HUMAN NATURE IS NOT SO NASTY AFTER ALL

Over the course of the last several decades, evidence has accumulated that portrays a brighter narrative of human evolution (Fry 2006a; Lee 2014; Sponsel 2016; Sussman 2013). Unlike the classic perspective that recounts prehistoric, historic, and ethnographic examples of warfare as supposed evidence that war stems from human nature, the new perspective is more holistic in the types of evidence it considers, more scientific in its research design and methodology, more data-centric in its orientation, and more self-reflective of how historical, cultural, and philosophical traditions affect human nature narratives. As Hart and Sussman (2009: 283–4) observe, "Discrepancies among the theories and the evidence must be evaluated. Once these discrepancies are seen to be overwhelming, the new paradigm will be accepted in favor of the old" (2009: 283–4). In this section, we review developments across a variety of fields—from archeology to zoology—that, when viewed additively, present overwhelming evidence in favor of a more peaceful narrative of human nature, peace, and war.

Archaeological Data

Mark Allen and Terry Jones (2014), sticking with the classic view in a recent book that they co-edited, assert that war goes way back in prehistory to the earliest hominins about five million years ago. However, they turn a blind eye to the fact that time and again archaeology shows war to originate along with population growth, sedentism, storage, intensified use of localized resources, and other elements of social complexity, notwithstanding the fact that their book presents some illustrative examples of war's link to social complexification processes (Darwent & Darwent 2014; Des Lauriers 2014). Allen and Jones' assertion that the chapters of their book "support a long chronology for war and violence" (2014: 354) fails to be substantiated by worldwide archaeological evidence in two significant ways. First, with one possible slightly older exception, the earliest evidence for war anywhere on the planet is within the last 10,000 years (Haas 1996; Ferguson 2013a, 2013b; Keeley 1996; Nakao, Tamura, Arimatsu, Nakagawa, Matsumoto, & Matsugi 2016)—not millions of years as Allen and Jones assert. Second, while much more remains to be learned about what drives warfare, the actual origins of war in diverse locations around the world have been documented as arising in conjunction with rising social complexity time and again. In other words, the social changes and conditions associated with the origins of war are not shrouded in mist and mystery. The origins of war are visible archaeologically, and occur very recently in the archaeological record.

Worldwide archaeology clearly indicates that homicide has been around for a very long time, and that war appeared much later. Archaeologist Marilyn Roper (1969: 448) reviews the skeletal finds for early humans—or hominins—over the last three million years, and she reaches the conclusion that sporadic homicides occurred in the deep past, but that warfare did not.[1] In the absence of any corroborating evidence of war such as defensive sites, fortifications, specialized weapons, or mass graves showing trauma, the discovery of a single victim of lethal aggression does not justify a claim that war existed at the time of the victim's death (Ferguson, 2013a). In the absence of other war indicators, skeletal trauma likely represents a murder, a group-sanctioned execution, or even a hunting accident rather than war (Ferguson 2013a, b; Fry 2006a).

Hisashi Nakao and his colleagues (2016) looked at all cases of skeletal violence in Japan across the mostly forager period beginning 13,000 years ago and extending into historical times less than 1,000 years ago. The percentage of violent death was 2 percent, averaged over the entire period, which is a much lower figure than the 14 percent advanced by Pinker (2011) for prehistoric nomadic foragers (see Ferguson 2013a, Fry 2013a). Absolutely no cases of lethal violence were discovered among the skeletons for the earliest 5,000-year period. Nakao and his colleagues point out that some if not all the lethal trauma would have resulted from homicides and accidents rather than war, and they conclude that their findings are "inconsistent with arguments that warfare is inherent in human nature" (Nakao et al. 2016).

Various archaeological examples show the birth of war in association with hierarchical systems. For instance, in the Near East, between 12,000 and 10,000 years ago, nomadic foraging gave way to plant and animal domestication. In this region, there is no evidence of war or hierarchical social organization in this archaeological record at 12,000 years before the present, sparse evidence for war by about 9,500 years ago, and then clear evidence of spreading and intensifying warfare after that (Roper 1975). Multiple kinds of data validate the fact that war in the Near East emerged from a condition of prior warlessness. The evidence shows growing defensibility of settlement sites, increase of violence apparent in human skeletal remains, and rapid introduction of new artistic styles. This last kind of data suggests the arrival and imposition of a conquering group's cultural tradition. All this factual evidence contradicts the view that war is millions of years old and thus species-typical behavior.

FIGURE 2.2: Anasazi ruins from Chaco Canyon, New Mexico. The prehistoric Anasazi made the transition from nomadic foraging to settled, village farming, and co-existed peacefully in their farming villages with their neighbors for hundreds of years. (D. P. Fry photo collection).

Another archaeological case illustrates a similar sequence. Archaeologist Herbert Maschner (1997) chronicles changes in type and severity of violence and the rise of social complexity in an area of the northwest coast of North America. Beginning at about 5,500 years ago and persisting over at least a couple millennia, skeletal trauma almost exclusively involved nonlethal injuries—and not many of these. This was a period of nomadic foraging. The rarity and non-lethality of the injuries in conjunction with absolutely no other indicators of warfare strongly imply the presence of only interpersonal aggression. Later in this prehistoric sequence, evidence of war appears along with social hierarchy and inequality. Maschner summarizes: "The first large villages appear, status differences become apparent, a heavy emphasis on marine subsistence develops, and warfare becomes visible in the archaeological record" (270).

Warfare originated at various times in different locations as some, but not all societies underwent shifts toward intensification of resource extraction and greater social complexity. There is no evidence that war existed anywhere before such changes began just prior to the Agricultural Revolution.

Nomadic Forager Studies

In the modern era, anthropology has continued to amass much data relevant to questions of human nature, peace, and war. One pool of data pertains to nomadic forager societies. Taking mobile forager data into account when considering human nature is important because for most of our evolutionary past humans lived and evolved in this form of social organization. Nomadic foraging is not merely a subsistence mode. It also represents a pattern of sociality based on equality and cooperation. A careful examination of nomadic forager ethnography is centrally relevant to understanding the psychology of our species-typical behavior (Bicchieri 1972; Bjorklund & Pellegrini 2002; Marlowe 2010). The cross-cultural mobile forager data calls into question the familiar narrative about humanity as sinfully self-centered, brutal, and corrupt. Instead, the mobile forager data suggest a human predilection for keeping the peace. Typically, mobile foragers reflect pro-social behavior, a preference for nonviolent conflict management over violence (although violence sometimes occurs), and, importantly, a paucity of warfare at this level of social organization. On the basis of the extant nomadic forager data, it seems likely that humans have evolved predilections for using restraint against lethal aggression; developed species-typical inclinations to empathize, care, share, and cooperate in communal childcare and the quest for food; engaged in reciprocal exchanges of goods and services; favored nonviolent conflict resolution and avoidance over violence; employed social control mechanisms to maintain peaceful social life; and respected the personal autonomy of the individual (Fry, 2006a, 2012; Fry & Szala, 2013; Hrdy, 2009).

Until about 12,500 years ago, all humans and their ancestors lived as nomadic foragers. Consequently, when seeking to gain insights about human nature, it is absolutely necessary to consider the salient characteristics of nomadic forager societies.

In band social life, the reciprocating of good deeds prevails. There are many examples of cooperation in the quest for food. The sharing of resources such as water holes or

FIGURE 2.3: Nomadic forager societies are windows to the human past. D. P. Fry photo collection.

periodic food bounties across group lines parallels the ubiquitous within-group sharing that is regularly described for nomadic foragers. Uniformly, mobile foragers share meat (e.g. Apicella et al., 2012; Birdsell, 1971; Boehm, 1999; Clastres, 1972; Dyble et al., 2015; Fry, 2006a and references therein; Gusinde, 2003; Knauft, 1991; Leacock, 1954; Lee, 1993).

The typical mobile forager response to conflict is simply to walk away (Fry & Söderberg, 2013b). Lacking authoritative leadership, egalitarian nomadic band societies manage to deal with much conflict through avoidance, discussion, group meetings, contests, and in other nonviolent or aggression-limiting ways (Boehm, 1999; Fry, 2006a, 2011; Söderberg & Fry, 2017). Disputes tend to be personal, such as between two men over a woman or an insult (Fry, 2006a; Service, 1966). The most common reasons for homicide are sexual jealousy or to avenge the death of a close family member (Fry, 2011). Another reason for killing is when overly violent persons or serious deviants, if not ostracized, are executed (Balikci, 1970; Boehm, 1999; Fry, 2011; Lee, 1993). All in all, most conflicts in nomadic forager societies are handled without the loss of life.

Mobile foragers offer insights about human nature; the data about them suggest that war is neither an intrinsic part of human heredity, nor destiny. A paucity of warfare at the nomadic forager level of social organization is not surprising for a number of reasons (Fry, 2006a; Fry & Söderberg 2013a, b; Gardner, 2004; Kelly, 1995; Knauft, 1991; Meggitt, 1965; Tonkinson, 2004). In mobile forager societies, there is nothing of value to plunder; groups are interconnected by cross-cutting ties of kinship, exchange, and friendship; population density is very low; and military leaders are lacking (Fry & Söderberg 2013a, b, 2014). Additionally, the motivations for keeping the peace also can be seen as important since foragers depend on each other for assistance, marriage partners, and access to critical resources.

Souillac and Fry (2016, 2017) point out that the classic Western view of human nature as demonically violent is chronically non-self-reflective, biased, and based on simple narratives that depart dramatically from the complexity of the anthropological data on mobile foragers. For example, the narrative of a shockingly violent past and an indigenous world staffed by "savage primitive peoples" ignores the facts that a wealth of conflict resolution mechanisms exist that mobile foragers and other indigenous peoples successfully apply; resources are shared more often than defended in the nomadic forager world; core values reinforce prosocial behaviors such as cooperation and generosity rather than greed; and instead of living in bounded, competitive groups, nomadic forager social organization actually links individuals across human networks encompassing malleable, temporary groups (e.g. Fry 2006a; Fry & Souillac 2013; Lee 2014; Myers 1986; Souillac & Fry 2013, 2017; Tonkinson 1978, 2004).

Internally Peaceful Societies

Another body of anthropological knowledge collected and compiled in large part within the last hundred years is on peaceful societies (Bonta 2013; Fry 2006a; Sponsel 2016). If the Hobbesian views proposed by Freud (1961), Niebuhr (2013), Dart (1953), Pinker (2011) and various others were correct, peaceful societies simply should not exist (Bonta 2013; Fry 2004). The mere presence of peaceful societies contradicts the classic view that human beings are basically violent by nature. Dozens of internally peaceful societies have been described and documented (Bonta 2013; Fry 2006a; Howell & Willis 1989; Kemp & Fry 2004; Montagu 1978; Sponsel 2016; Sponsel & Gregor 1994).

Bonta (2013) concludes that the paucity of violence in internally peaceful societies follows from belief systems that promote and cherish peacefulness. "Peacefulness has its own validity—it has become an end in itself ... People are horrified at the thought of violence—they have no words for it, they get nervous at the mention of it, they can't conceive of it. They identify themselves as peaceful" (Bonta 2013: 125).

Nonwarring Societies and Peace Systems

A solid body of ethnographic evidence showing that some societies shun warfare has also emerged during the modern era. Ethnographically, it is now clear that most societies engage in warfare—from small-scale to large-scale—but some do not (Fry 2006a; Otterbein 1970; Wright 1942). Nonwarring societies can be found in various locations around the planet. For example, among the Hanunóo of Southeast Asia, "warfare, either actual or traditional, is absent" (Conklin 1954: 49). The Saulteaux of North America "have never engaged in war with the whites or with other Indian tribes" (Hallowell 1974: 278). The Veddahs of Asia "live so peacefully together that one seldom hears of quarrels among them and never of war" (Davie 1929: 50). Thus, in contradiction to the classic view of human nature, anthropology has documented that war is not always and everywhere present.

Additionally, peace systems—groups of neighboring societies that do not make war on each other and sometimes not with outsiders as well—have been documented within Malaysia, Australia, India, Brazil, Canada, and elsewhere (Fry, Bonta, & Baszarkiewicz 2008; Fry 2009, 2012, 2013b; Souillac & Fry 2014). The Chewong, for instance, are one member of the nonwarring peace system of Malaysia that also includes the Semai, Jahai, Btsisi, and Batek (Endicott & Endicott 2008; Howell 1988, 1989; van der Sluys 2000). In terms of values and behavior, these Malaysian societies emphasize nonviolence and conflict avoidance. The Malaysian peace system is not a new development as evidenced by early accounts of these societies shunning violent resistance, even to defend against slave raiders, and descriptions of their "extraordinarily peaceful nature" (Endicott 1983: 238; Skeat & Blagden 1906).

An examination of peace systems provides insights into successful strategies for preventing intergroup violence. Features hypothesized to be important in the creation and maintenance of inter-societal peace include: (a) an overarching social identity; (b) interconnections among subgroups; (c) interdependence (ecological, economic, and/or defensive); (d) nonwarring values; (e) symbolism and ceremonies that reinforce peace; (f) superordinate institutions; (g) mechanisms for conflict management; and (h) leaders who promote peace (Fry 2009, 2012, 2013b). The existence of peace systems demonstrates that it is possible to create social systems that are free from war.

Under conditions of pluralist modernity, the construction of peace systems among nations and ultimately on a global scale may involve, first, the critical examination of social identities, values, structural violence, and conditions of inequality with the intention of promoting peace, and second, the forging of higher level ethical standards, applicable across peace systems, to promote human well-being, justice, equality, human rights, and peace, not only within parochial social groups, but across the broader field of humanity (Souillac 2012; Souillac & Fry 2015, 2017). In the modern era, the total interdependence of global humanity in the ecological, economic, political, and social realms necessitates an expanded transborder set of norms based on nonviolence and cooperation, shared humane value orientations, and political institutions that outlaw war and promote peace.

FIGURE 2.4: The Iroquois Confederacy was a peace system known as Haudenosaunee, which means people of the long house. D. P. Fry photo collection.

Existing peace systems have accomplished such goals and provide a model for transforming war-based systems into peace systems (Fry 2012, 2013b).

Empathy, Cooperation, Caring and Sharing

Primatologist Frans de Waal (2013) proposes that a massive theoretical and conceptual revision is currently underway regarding not only human nature, but also animal nature more generally. "Developments in psychology, neuroscience, economics, and animal behavior have begun to question the view, dominant until a decade ago, that animal life, and by extension human nature, turns around unmitigated competition" (de Wall 2013: xii). Caring can be linked evolutionarily back to the basic mammalian pattern of nurturing dependent young, a tendency that is clearly evident in the Order Primates and particularly in the human species with its lengthy period of child dependency. Caring for offspring and other relatives is ubiquitous in human societies, but humans also regularly extend kindness and assistance to nonrelatives. De Waal (2008) points out, for example, the tremendous empathic potential, not merely in humans, but also more generally in other species. "Qualitative descriptions of spontaneous assistance among primates are abundant, ranging from bringing a mouthful of water to an incapacitated individual to slowing down travel for injured companions . . . The help provided can be quite costly. For example, a female chimpanzee may react to the screams of her closest associate by defending her against an aggressive male, thus taking great risk on her behalf" (de Waal 2013: xiii).

The origin of human caring has long and strong evolutionary roots. It should, therefore, come as no surprise that caring is well represented among nomadic foragers. Hrdy (2009) documents how childcare extends well beyond parents in nomadic forager society: "The fact that children depend so much on food acquired by others is one reason why those seeking human universals would do well to begin with sharing" (18). A prominent feature of the nomadic forager group is "an ethic of sharing that selectively extends to the entire group the cooperation and altruism found within the family" (Boehm, 1999: 67).

Souillac and Fry (2013) have proposed that it may be particularly easy and rewarding for children to learn empathy, cooperation, helping, sharing, in a word, prosocial behaviors. Engaging in cooperative activity can activate a neuro-chemical reward, as does punishing someone who breaks the social rules. "The strength of the neural response increases with the persistence of mutual cooperation over successive trials; it is cumulative and self-reinforcing," writes Sussman (2013: 105). Such evolved neuro-physiological responses may make it relatively easy for the developing individual to learn how to become "a good and useful human being," to quote the life philosophy of the nomadic Yahgan foragers of Tierra del Fuego (Gusinde 2003).

Given the longstanding evolutionary legacy of prosociality, empathy, and cooperation, human minds and dispositions may be especially inclined toward the empathic, caring, egalitarian, prosocial, cooperative behaviors. These prosocial behaviors may have been essential to survival for the millions of years that humans and their ancestors foraged for a living.

Military Science

In recent decades, a wealth of knowledge has been accumulating from military science that supports the proposition that humans actually have an aversion to killing members of their own species. This research pounds one more nail into the coffin of the classic warlike view of human nature (Fry, Schober, & Björkqvist 2010; Grossman 1995; Grossman & Siddle 2008; Hughbank & Grossman; Marshall 2000). The resistance of soldiers to killing other human beings has been documented across diverse wars and societies including French officers in the 1860s, Argentine soldiers during the Falkland Islands War, the battle of Gettysburg during the American Civil War, US troops in World War II, and more generally throughout history (Grossman & Siddle 2008: 1802).

A study of weapon firing rates was conducted by US Army historian Brigadier General S.L.A. Marshall on World War II combat soldiers. Marshall concluded that only 15 to 20 percent of the men fired their weapons at a human target (Grossman & Siddle, 2008: 1802; Marshall 2000). Some combatants fired without aiming, or into the air, or did not fire their weapons at all. This phenomenon of avoiding the killing of others, even during times of war, is also reflected in statistics on aerial "dog fights" of World War II. Less than 1 percent of US fighter pilots accounted for 30 to 40 percent of the enemy aircraft shot down, whereas the majority of fighter pilots did not bring down a single enemy plane, and many pilots never even tried to do so (Grossman, 1995). Marshall wrote that "the average and normally healthy individual . . . has such an inner and usually unrealized resistance towards killing a fellow man that he will not of his own volition take life if it is possible to turn away from that responsibility" (2000: 79). Furthermore, Marshall reports that "fear of killing, rather than fear of being killed, was the most common cause of battle failure in the individual" (Ibid.: 78).

This resistance towards killing is also reflected in the greater amount of psychiatric symptoms in the soldiers who were involved in killing in comparison with military

FIGURE 2.5: The Hiroshima Dome Memorial, Hiroshima Peace Memorial Park, Japan. D. P. Fry photo collection.

personnel who were not expected to kill but who still faced high risks of being killed, such as medical personnel or soldiers on reconnaissance missions behind enemy lines (Grossman & Siddle 2008). In light of the military "problem" of getting men to kill, it is not surprising that combat training has been re-designed since World War II to overcome the inhibitions towards killing on the part of typical soldiers that cause them "to posture, submit, or flee, rather than fight" (Grossman 1995: 28).

Another set of evidence that not only supports the proposition that humans possess a natural resistance towards killing other people, but also shows that participation in killing is psychologically very costly and traumatic are the high rates of depression, PTSD, suicide, and domestic violence faced by returning war veterans. Nagler quotes US combat veterans: One says "I no longer like who I am. I lost my soul in Iraq," and another shares, "I am still haunted . . . I would give anything to be able to go back and undo some of the things we did" (2014:2). De Waal points out, "We might not have the problem of PTSD, nor the reluctance of military men to kill, if it weren't for empathy with all life forms, including enemy lives. So, while empathy has trouble reaching beyond the in-group, it resists political indoctrination and does not allow itself to be fully suppressed" (2013: xiv).

Zoological Contexts: The Primacy of Restraint

The modern era has seen the development of modern biology and the collection of a mountain of behavioral data on mammalian and other species from around the world. Never before have detailed behavioral data existed on so many species. A ramification is that with modernity, as never before, comparative studies of animal behavior have become possible. Modern biology shows that agonistic behavior is widespread in the animal kingdom and suggests that it has evolved to fulfill survival and reproductive functions time and again (Fry & Szala 2013).

The agonism concept encapsulates not only physical acts of aggression, but also a variety of competitive behaviors such as dominance and territorial displays, threats, and acts of spatial displacement (Fry & Szala 2013). Intraspecific agonism, including physical aggression, tends to be much less bloody than predatory aggression, and is rarely lethal in mammals (Fry & Szala 2013; Gómez, Verdú, Gonzáles-Megías & Méndez 2016). In a recent landmark study that draws on data from over a thousand mammalian species, Gómez et al. (2016) report that the overall percentage of mammalian deaths attributed to members of the same species averages to a mere one-third of 1 percent. The percentage of conspecific lethal violence is higher in social and territorial species than in solitary or non-territorial ones. The Order Primates, which includes humans, has a higher average percentage of within-species killings, about 2 percent, than the overall mammalian average, which is not surprising given the large number of primate species that are either social, territorial, or both (Gómez et al. 2016).

The researchers drew upon mortality data for more than 600 ancestral, historical, and contemporary human populations to assess how the human species compares with other mammals (Gómez et al. 2016). Two conclusions are noteworthy. First, the overall average percentage of lethal aggression for humans corresponds with what would be predicted on the basis of human phylogenetic position as a primate species. Second, this percentage of conspecific lethal violence varies across time and cultural setting. In both Old World and New World archaeological chronologies, lethal within-species violence was initially low, meaning that it did not differ significantly from the phylogenetic prediction for the human species, then increased recently in the Old World Iron Age and Medieval periods and in the New World with the development of hierarchical chiefdoms and ancient states, only to decrease below phylogenetically predicted levels in the Modern Age.

When Gómez and his colleagues turned their attention to lethal violence in relation to type of social organization, they document that bands and tribes in the prehistoric record were not significantly different from the phylogenetic predictions for the human species, whereas the shift to hierarchical social organizations in the form of prehistoric chiefdoms resulted in an increase in lethality. However, contemporary bands and tribes are more violent than their prehistoric counterparts, and Gómez and colleagues suggest that this reflects increased contact with colonial societies and recent increases in population. Finally, this study found that within-species killing decreases in states. Thus, when Pinker (2011) makes the argument that the human past was shockingly violent and that violence has decreased recently with the rise of state control, he is shown by these scientists to be simultaneously wrong and right, respectively. The past was not shockingly violent until the arrival of social complexity in the most recent millennia, but state-level social organization is correlated with a lower rate of within-species killing than occurs in prehistoric bands, tribes, and especially ranked chiefdoms.

The findings of Gómez et al. (2016) are important for validating that conspecific mammals, including humans, for the most part do not kill one another (Enquist & Leimar 1990; Fry 1980; Hrdy, 1977; Kokko 2013). The study is also important for showing—drawing upon truly impressive amounts of data—that the deep past was not racked with lethal violence and does not statistically deviate from the phylogenetical predictions of

2 percent violent lethality. This finding flatly contradicts an estimate of 14 percent war lethality in the Pleistocene (Bowles 2009; Pinker 2011), an estimate which also has been critiqued previously on various sampling and methodological grounds (Ferguson 2013a, b; Fry 2013a; Fry & Söderberg 2014; Lee 2014).

Fry and Szala (2013) conclude that limited aggression has been favored by natural selection in many different species (Fry, Schober & Björkqvist, 2010; Kokko 2013; Maynard Smith, 1974; Maynard Smith & Price, 1973). They argue that there are more continuities than discontinuities between human agonism and typical mammalian agonistic patterns. In making this evolutionary argument, Fry and Szala (2013) develop a comparative model of agonistic behavior that, instead of focusing merely on mayhem, highlights the typically ignored but important and widespread feature of restraint against aggression. Agonistic behaviors can be classified into categories of increasing severity: avoidant responses, non-contact display-oriented behavior, restrained physical aggression, and unrestrained physical aggression. Consideration of intraspecific competition across species reveals a variety of ways that individuals minimize the risks of injury and other costs of aggression (Fry et al. 2010). Non-contact displays are employed in substitution for physical fighting between conspecific rivals. When physical altercations do occur they usually consist of restrained "ritualized" aggression. Unrestrained aggression is exceedingly rare among mammals, an observation that is corroborated by the findings of Gómez and

FIGURE 2.6: Bonobos relax and groom each other. Unlike chimpanzees, bonobos have never been observed killing one of their own species. D. P. Fry photo collection.

colleagues (2016) that on the average a fraction of 1 percent of mammals are killed by members of their own species.

In sum, in nonhuman and human primates, as well as in mammals generally, natural selection has clearly favored restrained judiciously employed aggression over escalated, severe forms of violence (Fry & Szala 2013). The findings of Gómez and his colleagues (2016) substantiate this interpretation. The classic view of human nature as aggressive and violent takes a major hit when faced with overwhelming data compiled in the zoological sciences over the last hundred years or so. An important implication of this fact is that any claim that humans are by nature "killer apes" or "natural born killers," in other words inclined toward lethal fighting as a species-typical behavior, must be strongly justified, rather than simply assumed a priori, since such claims fly in the face of an extremely well-documented mammalian pattern of restrained agonism. Fry and Szala (2013: 454–5) point out that, "The burden of scientific proof reasonably rests with any claimants that human agonism in this regard constitutes an exception to a widespread mammalian pattern. The logical default proposition would be that human aggression fits within the typical mammalian framework of limited and controlled agonism, rather than constitutes a reversal of selection pressures to favor homicide or war" (2013: 434–5).

Us versus Them: A Part of Human Nature?

Only within the last 12,500 years or so has humanity made a sociopolitical shift toward centralized leadership and authority with the rise of the first chiefdoms (Fry 2006a). The subsequent development of the first ancient civilizations—a mere 5,000 to 6,000 years ago—gave birth to the state as a new form of social organization. Chiefdoms, ancient civilizations, kingdoms, and modern nation-states have social hierarchies with rulers at the top who hold positions of authority. In these stages of social complexity we see also the elaboration and multiplication of social identities.

Despite the fact that a global system consisting of nation-states is largely taken as a fact of life in the twenty-first century, humanity's very first states are only several millennia old, whereas the modern version of the state, the nation-state, is only a few hundred years old. A social lens that captures a broader view of human history and prehistory, including variations in human social structure and behavior, shows that there is nothing inherently natural or normal about nation-states, national identities, or nationalistic "Us versus Them" conceptualizations of the social world. Examinations of social systems across time and place undermine the assumed fixity of "Us versus Them" forces that are commonly believed to reside in human nature. The unification of disparate social units with the concomitant development of a common, overarching social identity—or normative belonging—helps to reduce bias and hostilities as it simultaneously enhances cooperation and positive attitudes across group lines (Dovidio, Gaertner & Kafati 2000; Dovidio, Gaertner & Saguy 2009).

A frequently voiced proposition is that "Us versus Them" identity, as a foundational element of human nature, results from and contributes to intergroup hostility (e.g. Haidt 2012; Konner 2006; Wrangham & Glowacki 2012). However, this is only sometimes the case. We suggest that the "Us versus Them" in-group loyalty and out-group hostility pattern witnessed widely in the twenty-first century has developed recently, archaeologically speaking, accompanied by the emergence of more complex forms of social organization, sedentism, social hierarchy, the adoption of agriculture, and other associated changes in human social evolution, as opposed to having evolved as an immutable human tendency over the course of the Pleistocene. Clearly humans can and do develop strong "Us versus Them" orientations under some social conditions. The key is the "under some social conditions" part, which means that we would be wise to question the common assumption that "Us versus Them" mentalities are solidly fixed in human nature. The nomadic forager data suggest that this is a behavioral capacity of humans in some circumstances, rather than a pan-human tendency.

As Kelly (2000: 2) points out, "In the relatively brief span of 4,500 years, a global condition of warlessness that had persisted for several million years thus gives way to chronic warfare that arises initially in the Near East and subsequently in other regions where a similar sequence of transformative events is reduplicated" (2000: 2). As we have considered, the archaeological evidence for war before 10,000 years ago anywhere on Earth is negligible, whereas the evidence for the multiple origins of war in different regions, always within the last ten millennia, is clear-cut (Ferguson 2013a, b; Fry 2006a; Haas 1996; Haas & Piscitelli 2013; Kelly 2000). Thus, archaeological findings on the recent origins of war are in agreement with the nomadic forager data in contradicting the assumption that "Us versus Them" identifications have played significant roles in intergroup violence—war—over the long expanse of evolutionary time.

Expanding the Us to Include the Them

Anthropology provides information about successfully operating peace systems from different world regions that have various psycho-social mechanisms to counter "Us versus Them" identification by creating inclusive overarching social identities (Fry 2006a, 2009; see also Dovidio et al. 2000; Dovidio et al. 2009). For example, the nomadic foragers of the vast Australia Western Desert region are interconnected by overlapping networks, which transcend local band membership and language dialect (Myers, 1986). The Western Desert peoples view themselves as "one country," for they see the land as boundary-less, as reflected by their inclusion of all inhabitants of this region within an overarching kinship system (Myers 1986; Tonkinson 2004). Thus children of each generation are socialized into this view of an inclusive social world which encompasses peoples from many small groups spread over an extensive area. The Western Desert groups constitute "a vast interlocking network of persons" (Myers 1986: 27). Berndt (1972: 183) observes that the Western Desert peoples do not limit their travels to particular areas, but in fact interact with Aborigines from different language dialects as they crisscross extensive areas of the region. As Myers explains, territories are "flexible, if not insignificant" (1986:93). Creation of a larger, inclusive identity across social subunits prevents "Us versus Them" perceptions from crystallizing into hostile relations. After studying in detail one Western Desert society, the Mardu, Tonkinson (2004) explains that in this arid environment of sporadic and unpredictable rainfall, open borders permit resource sharing among groups as they forage in a non-hostile social atmosphere. The Mardu and their Western Desert neighbors recognize their mutual reliance and employ creative ways of maintaining peaceful relations through kinship, friendship, and spirituality. The friendly relations among bands in the Western Desert area are maintained through intermarriage and joint ceremonies conducted at periodic "big meetings," at which time people from different groups "exchange weapons, ochre, pearl shells, sacred boards and other objects and, importantly, resolve disputes to maintain links of friendship and shared religion among the groups present" (Tonkinson 1974: 97).

FIGURE 2.7: Grand' Place market square, Brussels. Brussels is the seat of a successful peace system, the European Union. D. P. Fry photo collection.

As an example of a similar process in the modern era, a higher-level European identity is in the process of emerging within the European Union, not as a substitute for national identities, but rather as an added level of European identification. Concrete signs of a developing pan-European identity include the issuance of EU passports, expanding use of the Euro currency (now legal tender in most member states), the creation of a European Parliament, an EU flag, and so on (Fry 2009, 2012; Bellier & Wilson 2000). The trend across Europe involves the progressive development of a new regional identity. Such higher levels of identification, in concert with other social features and institutions, can play a role in the creation and maintenance of peaceful relations.

In sum, group identification does not in-and-of-itself lead to war, but in times of conflict, the psychological states that accompany it can feed hostility and facilitate intergroup violence. Once conflict intensifies, a group can come to hold an increasingly negative image of another group, eventually dehumanizing them and excluding them from the realm of moral obligation (Deutsch 2006; Konner 2006; Staub 1989). However, social identity is not always an obstacle to peace but can also be engaged for the advancement of peace, as we have seen with the Australian Aborigines of the Western Desert and currently within the European Union. Socializing children and socially promoting a twenty-first century cosmopolitan view of *expanding the Us to include the Them* can contribute to bringing the peoples of Earth closer to achieving peace (Fry 2012; Souillac 2012).

PARADIGM SHIFT: CHANGING THE HUMAN NATURE NARRATIVE

In conclusion, we suggest that the dominant human nature narrative over the course of the modern era since 1920, especially as it informs the foreign and national security policies of most states, continues to be predominately Hobbesian. This classic view of humanity as inherently violent and warlike like Lord Alfred Tennyson's "nature, red in tooth and claw," goes back two millennia. Since then it has become deeply embedded as a cultural belief in the West, where it long has been expressed in monotheistic theologies that describe human nature as fallen from God's grace. Currently, we can also witness an evidence-based alternative human nature narrative—to have some fun with Tennyson's phrase, "nature, read in truth and law"—that challenges with findings from many fields the classic belief that humans are innately predisposed towards violent mayhem. As Nagler points out, "It is only recently that science has undergone a remarkable shift toward a more balanced vision not only of human nature but also of nature and evolution in general" (2014:4). We have also considered how human identity is malleable and multi-faceted and thus has the contradictory potentials to facilitate hostility and violence among social groups as well as to promote peaceful, cooperative interactions as identity belonging expands to include human rights and peace values and ultimately "expand the Us to include the Them" (Fry 2012, 2013a, 2014; Fry & Souillac 2016; Souillac 2012; Souillac & Fry 2015, 2016).

Souillac (2012) proposes that higher levels of citizenship are emerging in recent democratic thinking as vehicles that contribute to solidarity across multi-layered, complex societies, both within and across national borders. Expanding shared identity to the level of all humanity has important functions in the creation of positive peace (Souillac & Fry 2016). Enhancing a shared normative belonging challenges the exclusionary effects of borders and national sovereignty in a state-based modernity and raises to top priority the common responsibility of reducing direct and structural forms of violence within and among groups (Souillac 2012). The structural violence reflected, for example, in the widespread abject poverty produced by the global economic system is a matter of common responsibility for states and citizens alike. An above-the-nation normative approach to citizenship can expand the framing of civic belonging that is currently tied to cultural and national units in order to foster global allegiance to core peace values and expected standards of ethical behavior. Rather than a single-minded emphasis on national security, policies designed to ensure a future for *Homo sapiens* should focus more on the necessity of global cooperation (as in the climate change crisis) and the augmentation of human security as spelled-out by the UN's Sustainable Development Goals for 2030 that express the pan-human requirements for justice, rights, peace, health, and ecological sustainability.

Just as slavery has been outlawed and shamed, so can institutionalized warfare be. Doing so will free up hundreds of billions of dollars each year for human needs. Abolishing war can be facilitated through the development of a common human identity and a set of transnational ethics backed up by just and enforceable international law and the mobilization of civil society for both social justice and peace (Souillac 2012). However, if a majority of people continue to adhere to the classic view that war and greed are primary characteristics of human nature and prime motives behind human actions, then it seems unlikely that the necessary developments for human well-being and survival will move forward. Lee (2014: 224) draws a key connection:

By constantly asserting the dominance of the side of human nature that emphasizes war over peace and competition over cooperation, the dominant forces in the modern world order can more plausibly maintain a permanent war economy, justify the obscene profits of multinational corporations and their CEOs, and affirm the inevitability of winners and losers in life's sweepstakes.

—2014:224

On the other hand, underpinned by a revised view of human nature that acknowledges a balanced view of human capacities for both positive and negative deeds, warring and making peace, and parochial as well as expansive normative identities, a new path can be opened to a more humane future.

CHAPTER THREE

Peace, War, and Gender

DONNA PANKHURST

INTRODUCTION

The practices and conceptions of peace and war have been highly gendered throughout world history. Indeed, the defining of genders has often itself been rooted in ideas and experiences of war and violence, with men as warriors, and women as the embodiment of peace (Pierson, 1989). It is certainly the case that throughout human history the majority of war combatants have been men. By contrast many women have used their gendered identities, as mothers and guardians of life, in their activism in global peace movements, and in peacemaking at very local levels all over the globe (Cockburn, 2012).

These gendered experiences of women and men have resonance everywhere in the world, but are also stereotypes. As well as being warriors and the bearers of violence, men have also resisted dominant social pressures to fight, and been active in movements to build peace. Women have also cajoled men, and socialized boys, to fight, and shamed those who did not. Famous examples include women in World War I publicly shaming men in England for not joining the army to fight, by presenting them with a white feather, representing cowardice. Women constituted significant minorities in fighting forces, such as in guerrilla wars against colonialism and occupation, and were key players in acts of organized violence, such as the Rwandan genocide. In very exceptional circumstances individual women have become notable warriors and military leaders. In all wars women have also played highly significant roles in supporting warfare and fighters, whether on battlefields or by taking up so-called men's roles in their absence.

Thus, whereas a focus on the stereotypes suggests that the differences between women and men are due to their violent or peaceful *natures*, paying attention to the full range of behavior of women and men makes it self-evident that these differences cannot be explained by biological differences alone because they are so varied. Nonetheless, the roles played by women and men that go beyond the simple stereotypes are persistently regarded as transgressive or insignificant in many cultures, making it difficult to keep the broader picture in mind. However men's and women's actual lived experiences of war throughout this period, and the gendered ideologies and practices which persist today, are far more complex and varied than the simple, binary, stereotypes suggest. That is not to say that gender differences are not significant, however; gender remains one of the most important lenses through which to understand war and peace.

GENDERING PEACE AND DEVELOPMENT: THE CONCEPTS

Today we can see that the idea of equality between women and men gradually became prevalent as a condition of "ideal" or positive peace, based on cooperation rather than conflict, initially made famous by Galtung (1969). But this inclusion of gender equality was not present in popular visions of peace for much of the modern era. As we shall see, they were much more focused on the reduction, if not complete removal, of organized, physical violence and any security threats which might cause a return to outright war. The inequalities that can be seen in societies even with low levels of such violence also prompted Galtung to conceptualize "structural violence" as occurring when a social structure or institution harms people by preventing them from meeting their basic needs. He explicitly referred to sexism as one of those social structures. This term has been in use by peace analysts ever since, because it links the injustices and inequalities of society that can harm those people "at the bottom" even in peacetime.

These concepts of peace remain influential throughout the world today. They have also been linked to ambitions to remove other forms of inequality, and the need for "development" in poor countries. By the end of the century, these ambitions had become common even among powerful international organizations. Feminist scholars and activists developed the use of the term *gender*, and it use became commonplace throughout much of the world. As gender entered policy fora in the Global North, it also became part of the lexicon of international aid and development organizations, and thereby became incorporated into high-level official discourse in many aid-recipient countries, even where English is not the official language. It ostensibly distinguishes the biologically determined from that which is socially created and is, in theory, variable. In this regard gender has proved useful. It is often illustrated with reference to the differences between cultural descriptions of a "real" man or woman, and the relationships between them. However, widespread use in these ways has not always included the feminist political project of identifying how to decrease the disadvantages faced by women.

Gender *analysis* involves more than a binary division of populations based on a mixture of biology and cultural ideology. It focuses on human relationships, and particularly on power. The political power of the term gender lies in the way in which it highlights inequalities between women and men that overwhelmingly work to women's disadvantage, thus emphasizing difference as a problem for society in need of correction. Increasingly gender analysis considers multiple identities which do not fit into simple binary categories, as acknowledged by the World Health Organization (WHO) on the "Gender, Equity and Human Rights" section of its website:

> It varies from society to society and can be changed. While most people are born either male or female, they are taught appropriate norms and behaviours—including how they should interact with others of the same or opposite sex within households, communities and work places. When individuals or groups do not "fit" established gender norms they often face stigma, discriminatory practices or social exclusion—all of which adversely affect health. It is important to be sensitive to different identities that do not necessarily fit into binary male or female sex categories.

This section is followed by a short explanation of what *Gender Analysis* means to the WHO, "Gender analysis identifies, assesses and informs actions to address inequality that come from: 1) different gender norms, roles and relations; 2) unequal power relations between and among groups of men and women, and 3) the interaction of contextual factors with gender such as sexual orientation, ethnicity, education or employment status."

www.who.int/gender-equity-rights/understanding/gender-definition/en/

Nonetheless researchers and policy-makers to date have focused on the ways that most societies have ascribed one of two genders to all individuals. The analytical challenge is to discover how inequality is maintained and consequent opportunities for including a feminist project for change, and the constraints on the ability of women and men respectively to effect change. How older men exert power over younger men, for instance, is an important part of the explanation of how patriarchy works, and it is not revealed by focusing solely on women, or even how men exert power over women. Studying gender relations nowadays requires us to focus on specifics in time and place, to answer questions such as what it is to be a man or a woman here, and what are the different manifestations of these identities? How do they relate to each other? Are poor men expected to behave differently towards women than men from other social classes? Do middle class women have lives less violent than in other classes? What makes it possible for some women—and men—to resist violent behavior, and why are others drawn to it?

All the major international organizations that are concerned with peace, conflict, and development have now incorporated gender analysis into their policy-planning processes. For instance the United Nations Development Programme (UNDP) annually produces, in part to counterbalance the annual data produced on economic development by the World Bank, a Human Development Index (HDI) that presents important measures about gender inequality.[1] Since 2015, all state-members of the United Nations have agreed to a set of seventeen Sustainable Development Goals (with a total of 169 targets). The targets follow the Millennium Development Goals 2000–2015. Gender is mentioned, or mainstreamed, throughout the descriptions of the goals, and one is called, "Gender Equality—Achieve gender equality and empower all women and girls." It seeks "to realize the human rights of all and to achieve gender equality and the empowerment of all women and girls." Number 16 is called "Peace, Justice & Strong Institutions—Promote peaceful and inclusive societies for sustainable development, provide access to justice for all and build effective, accountable and inclusive institutions at all levels" (https://sustainabledevelopment.un.org/sdg16 accessed September 28, 2017). All international aid funding, and all major public expenditure in every member-state (including those in the Global North), is supposed to recognize these goals and make regular progress updates to the UN. These international commitments represent a very great change in the understanding of gender inequalities and how they are maintained, and the problems that such inequality is presumed to cause. Recently, extreme gender inequality has been identified as a problem for peace and prosperity, and even security, by powerful international organizations such as the UN, World Bank, OECD, and the World Economic Forum (World Economic Forum website, section on "Gender parity," www.weforum.org/agenda/archive/gender-parity, for the World Bank).

The process of incorporating gender into policy discourses has not been straightforward. Precisely because the binary divisions between women and men have strong resonance everywhere, highlighting the need for change often rankles those in power who benefit from the status quo. The varieties within and between locally defined genders are complex, and not always well understood or agreed on. Thus, outcomes of interventions sometimes have unintended consequences. "Doing gender" has often become focused solely on improving the lives of women. Indeed, the term *gender* has often in policy practice been used, with some unforeseen consequences, as a codeword for *women*. Recently, the inter-changeability between the term "gender" and concerns about women's lives have become so ubiquitous that we have reached the point of knowing more about women than men in many societies. Policies and research have become so focused on women that our understanding of men's gendered behaviors, vulnerabilities, and potentials for peace is often less complete than that of women.

For instance, while it is not surprising that more men die than women as a direct result of war-violence, men also tend to die younger than women in non-war settings. The reasons are not fully understood, but probably include some socially determined factors, such as riskier behavior, and men seeking fewer medical interventions. Far more men die through homicide than women, although women constitute the vast majority of domestic violence fatalities (UN Office on Drugs and Crime, www.unodc.org/gsh/en/index.html,). Men also commit suicide more often than women, although women tend to make more attempts to do so (World Health Organization, Global Health Observatory, www.who.int/gho/mental_health/suicide_rates_male_female/en). The gendered nature of these issues was not highlighted as a social problem for most of the twentieth century; perhaps because of the powerful ideologies of masculinity, of what it is to be a real man, as being tough, strong and powerful, and that any men that did not conform were often ignored. A broader conception of multiple types of masculinity has intellectually paved the way for inquiry into these issues and open access to data via information technology has made it possible.

The relative benefits of being a man are nonetheless self-evident. The economist Amartya Sen (1990, 1992) suggested that more than two hundred million women, mostly in China and India, might be said to be "missing" in the sense that they have died prematurely due to discrimination. This difference cannot be explained by biology alone, particularly given the data about men's longevity and rates of violent deaths. Rather, this macro-inequality is due to the inferior care given to girls, as compared to boys, including: selective abortion and infanticide, along with inferior nutrition and healthcare from childhood into adulthood. Bias in the care of girls and women is rooted in the higher value placed by many societies on boys and men. Wherever there exists a strong gendered bias in the care of children, it is consistently in favor of boys. Gender therefore affects domestic arrangements, such as who has a greater burden of labor in bringing food to the table, and ensuring the well-being of children. Questions also arise about public lives: who will gain the greater level of education, employment, pay, and legal rights? The arrangement of social roles is not fixed by biology. It changes over time, not always in the same direction, or at the same time everywhere.

The important issues raised by recent gender analysis remained largely hidden and absent from public discourse prior to women's political action in the 1960s. From the beginning of the modern era women had continued actions to improve their practical circumstances all over the world, but these actions did not coalesce in international campaigns until much later in the period. Not until the late twentieth century did the intellectual development of "gender analysis" combine with political action against the oppression of women and their inequality with men, bringing these questions to the fore in many parts of the world.

GENDERED WARS

In the 1920s much of the world was focused on recovery from the terrible experiences of World War I, and in this women and men shared a common purpose. A great deal has been written about the difficulties faced by former allied soldiers in adjusting to civilian life after experiencing the horrors of trench warfare and some of these analyses (Shephard, 2003) still resonate in contemporary discussions about what society expects of its soldiers. It is often said that rather than dwell on the suffering that occurred at home and on the front, most people wanted to "get back to normal" and lead a secure and peaceful life (Ibid., 2003). Much of the fighting in this war took place far from soldiers' homes. They had not witnessed first-hand wartime changes on the home front, and many who returned assumed that social arrangements should remain as they left them.

World War II had many battle zones with different types of fighting and varying impacts on civilians too great to detail here. In urban areas still populated by civilians, there were efforts by governments to protect some women and children by evacuating them. But many others stayed at home. Compared to World War I, far more women and children faced death resulting from strategies of both sides that targeted civilians. In some places most of the adult men were fighting away from home, and so women and children bore the brunt of bombing raids and had to live in dangerously damaged buildings if they survived. Women and children were targeted just as much as men in the Holocaust. The estimates of

FIGURE 3.1: War workers modeling an assortment of protective goggles, visors, respirator masks, and helmets, USA circa 1943. FPG / Staff / Getty Images.

civilian deaths are not precise, but are massive, ranging from fifty to fifty-five million. Total deaths by some estimates reach seventy million, making it the deadliest war in history.

During World War II, women took over conscripted men's work in many countries. Gender norms about work were flexed to enable women to contribute directly to the war-effort just as they had done during World War I. "Rosie the Riveter" became the cultural icon of this strategy in the United States. She is usually portrayed wearing a headscarf and overalls, showing off her muscles in a brightly-colored poster-image, with the slogan, "We can do it!" Rosie represented women who worked in shipyards and factories producing munitions and war supplies. She encouraged people to feel positive about this change in gender roles (Honey, 1985).

Women were also recruited to a wide range of military activities in the Allies' special forces and intelligence, many of which remained secret until long after the war was over. In other parts of the world women faced challenges which have been repeated in subsequent wars as set out below, with an almost complete absence of peace activism.

The Cold War (1946–91) between the United States and the Soviet Union produced a new threat in the form of nuclear arsenals that made human extinction a technical possibility. The nuclear threat triggered many different anti-war campaigns. During the Cold War liberation struggles against colonialism, and civil wars in many liberated countries of the Global South caused a great deal of bloodshed and suffering, but generally these conflicts did not involve the same intensity of mechanized killing as the world wars. Fighting often took place in defence of homes and with heavy artillery and aerial bombardment. There were very bloody exceptions, particularly in Korea, Vietnam, Angola, and Namibia, where for geopolitical reasons, the United States and Communist powers poured in military assistance that added millions to the Cold War casualty lists, but these wars left most of the world unaffected. "Post-Cold War" conflicts prior to 9/11 were predominantly civil wars, often described as "New Wars" because they were characterized by identity-based hostilities, and the widespread use of relatively unsophisticated technologies—largely small arms and land mines.

Retrospective research into women's experiences during all the wars in the twentieth century throughout the world has revealed much about the variety of their roles as fighters, community leaders, social organizers, workers, farmers, traders, and welfare workers.[2] Women in war exercised old forms of influence-as-power; in private they guided men's decisions; in public, they performed as singers or poets; they gave direction as elders or leaders in cultural activities; and acted as informal negotiators while visiting kin or engaging in trade. Women played both "peacemaking" and "war-mongering" roles (El Bushra, 2000: 71-2; Mukta, 2000: 175; 181), including direct involvement in violence (Bennett et al., 1995; Goldblatt, & Meintjes, 1998: 43–5; African Rights, 1995), or motivating men to fight (Vickers, 1993; El Bushra, 2000: 71; Mukta, 2000: 175; 181; Kelly 2000).

Women's war experiences were also mediated by contrasts in age, class and regional or ethnic background, yet they also share commonalities. Where men were absent in battle zones, women tended to bear a much greater burden than men for the care of survivors, and always for children, while keeping social and political activities going. This shift of social responsibilities from men to women was common. Even in wartime, this change was experienced by many women as liberation from the old social order. When the need arose for women to take on men's roles, they had to shake off cultural restrictions and live in new ways. Their "liberation" was nonetheless violently threatened by the risk of injury and death (although not usually as high as for men) and by the particularly brutal war

FIGURE 3.2: Eritrean People's Liberation Front female guerilla soldiers training. Eye Ubiquitous / Alamy Stock Photo.

injury of rape (always with much higher frequency than men). Women's testimonies also often show that they had little choice about the roles they played in wartime.

It has often been asserted that for the first time in history, since the end of the Cold War 90 percent of casualties in war have been civilians (Giles and Hyndman 2004: 3, 4–5). This figure is contested, and sometimes it leads to a highly questionable claim that women are "more victimized" by war than men. Women survivors outnumber men at the immediate end of war because more men than women die directly from violence, including combat (Pearce 2006). Some of the confusion results from inaccurate data for war-related deaths, and from different definitions of casualties of war. Statistical analysis of gender differentials in post-Cold War conflicts indicates that more women than men die or suffer serious disease from long-term consequences of warfare. Plümper and Neumayer conclude that "over the entire conflict period interstate wars, civil wars and internationalized civil wars on average affect women more adversely than men . . . we also find that ethnic wars and wars in 'failed' states are much more damaging to women than other civil wars" (2006). The global focus on women's war suffering has, however, been so great as to lead one commentator to suggest that it plays down the suffering of men (Mack, 2005: 111).

The post-9/11 "war on terrorism" conflicts in Iraq, Afghanistan, Pakistan, Syria, Libya, and Yemen reveal somewhat different patterns from the warfare of the 1990s. They share some aspects of the "New Wars" outlined above, and are certainly gendered in similar ways. But the direct engagement of troops and other military personnel from the United States, the United Kingdom, other NATO forces as well as Russia has controversially introduced violence inflicted by some of the world's most sophisticated weaponry. Since these war zones are places of "extreme patriarchy," it has not been common for women to experience wartime as a liberation or improvement in their circumstances (Enloe,

2010). Even the much-feted US "liberation of women" in Afghanistan from the Taliban's constraints has been widely criticized by Afghan women who still live with some of the world's most restrictive gender norms (Rostami-Povey, 2007).

In this century, international focus on wartime violence committed by men against women, sometimes referred to as gender-based violence (GBV), has increased. GBV exists in all societies, whether at war or not, but in widely varying degrees. During the twentieth century, popular opinion shifted in the Global North and many other parts of the world to regard this violence as transgressive, rather than natural, normal, or inevitable; and calls for those in power to prevent it grew louder. International outcries against GBV during war, particularly with a sexual element, add to the tendency to focus on women as victims of this crime, sometimes marginalizing every other effect of war on them and men's wartime experiences. Sexual violence against women during recent wars has often been claimed to be increasing despite historic incidents such as the Nanking massacre in 1937 and the "rape of Berlin" in 1945.

In these discussions, rape during warfare is assumed to be distinct from "ordinary" rape. Indeed, war itself is often assumed to be a cause of rape. But there is little agreement among writers on conflict resolution and peacebuilding about what distinguishes war-rape from other forms of rape. Rape as a war crime has been linked to genocide (i.e. in Bosnia), but it does not have to be genocidal. From various commentaries, we might deduce that war-rape is less personal, part of a military plan (Enloe, 1993) and must have a different motive from rape at other times. However, explanations for "ordinary" rape at other times are hardly straightforward either, although the complexity of motives is rarely acknowledged by non-feminist writers. Male rape has received more attention recently (Sivakumaran, 2007). It seems also to have been present in many past wars, as part of "normal" behavior of heterosexual male soldiers. Since research on male rape in non-war settings is scanty, making comparisons with male war-rape is very difficult.

For many analysts the sexual element in GBV is more about power and violence than sexual gratification. Pioneered by feminists in the 1970s, this understanding of rape has been maintained for decades by mainstream criminologists, psychologists and sociologists. The perpetrators' sexuality is claimed to be activated as part of the development, or even transformation, of masculinity during war (Enloe, 1988). Much recent research shows that military commanders have commonly regarded the commission of rapes against women witnessed by comrades as a significant bonding experience (Baaz and Stern, 2009). The same argument is not made about male rape, however. By contrast, war-rape is commonly assumed to be a way to undermine the sexuality of the victim/survivor, whether male or female. Both of these types of analysis are often used in examinations of rape in other contexts, and so do not really assist much in clarifying what is distinctive about war-rape. "Rape as a weapon of war," with its intentional humiliation of the enemy, only tells one story. Other "explanations" include: inevitability due to the removal of social constraints; the de-humanization of war; following orders; the bonding of soldiers (by choice or under orders); proof of loyalty. All of these interpretations have been criticized (Wood, 2006; 2009; Cohen 2013).

Furthermore, the rate and prevalence of rape in war are highly variable, but explanations for the variety are poorly developed and rarely investigate what perpetrators themselves say about it. Not all men commit these crimes, but little attention is paid to understanding what makes the difference. Academic disciplines work in silos on this issue. Thus, psychological and psychiatric research with convicted men is rarely considered in policy discussions about reducing GBV. The very high rates of sexual violence against women in conflict in the Democratic Republic of the Congo prompted some outstanding research in exploring the ways the perpetrators described it (Baaz and Stern, 2009; 2013). A similar approach was also undertaken in Sierra Leone (Cohen, 2013). Both cases suggest that there can be multiple motives among perpetrators. The issue becomes even more complicated when we also consider that in some wars civilian men commit the same crimes. Whatever we think about the explanations, it is often the case that relationships between women and men become strained and violent during wartime, with GBV becoming common in many places. Women therefore have some distinct and common experiences in war, particularly of the types of violence to which they are all vulnerable regardless of differences in location and social status.

Men also share common experiences during wars, whether they are fighters or not, but these have seldom been the subject of gender analyses even as the way men's lives are gendered prior to war has increasingly been identified as a cause of war itself. Men's gendered behavior is evident within defense planning organizations (Cohn, 1987) and organized sport (Cockburn, 2012). Many writers have considered hegemonic masculinity in different societies and how it has been manipulated and changed during build-ups to war. Anti-war organizations in different parts of the world often say that gender relations themselves are to *blame* for war (Cockburn, 2010). However, this well-articulated view has not changed orthodox thinking about the causes of war in which gender and masculinity remain absent.

PEACE MOVEMENTS, PEACEBUILDING, AND WOMEN

Many, perhaps most, women during both World Wars, and those living in warzones afterwards, actively supported and encouraged men in their families and communities to fight. After all, women were also nationalists, separatists, and fighters for human rights and against authoritarianism, Nazism and fascism. However, women's impact on movements for peace whether local and small scale, or international and globally influential has been greater than their numbers might suggest. At the same time women have also campaigned to improve their own rights compared to men, and sometimes chosen to protest for peace separately from men. Thus, peace activism and campaigns for women's rights have a long history of being intertwined.

Within the belligerent nations of 1914–18, opposition to war was itself widely seen as feminine, and many male conscientious objectors were ridiculed as being feminine (Bibbings, 2003). The social divisions within countries at peace afterwards were still strongly shaped by persistent gender conventions. Individuals certainly had private visions of postwar peace, and we know (Shephard, 2003) that many soldiers envisioned returning home to a loving wife and mother. Their ideas of peace did not include a profound challenge to gender relations. The common view, held by many women as well as men, was to assume that women ought to maintain socially defined feminine qualities of submission, low professional ambition, and devotion to meeting the domestic needs of men and children while putting their own needs last. This feminine role was sometimes labelled "Angel of the House," a reference to a popular sentimental poem (Moore, 2015). In the United Kingdom and the United States for instance, women also faced major adjustments as they were expected by society to give up to men their many and varied wartime jobs. Adjustment to peacetime in a context where they could be sacked in order to "return" jobs to men was especially difficult for women who wanted to continue to earn their own living.

In 1919, women in the United Kingdom, the United States and Canada resumed the political struggles (now recognized as the First Wave of Feminism) that they had started but suspended to support the war effort. Their campaigns, included women of different classes who undertook dangerous acts of civil disobedience and suffered brutality at the hands of the state in the United Kingdom and United States. In both countries, women gradually achieved greater recognition in law—to vote, to work in the public sector, and not to be arbitrarily sacked. Nonetheless, they were consistently paid much lower wages than men, and continued to face unequal protection from violence and have unequal access to divorce (Bolt, 1993). During the 1930s, the economic depression aggravated tensions between women and men as it became harder for men to get employment due to the rapid decline of old industries. At the same time in many urban areas new opportunities for women to work in offices and new industries emerged, albeit for much lower pay than men. These opportunities were restricted to unmarried women, with the expectation that

FIGURE 3.3: A new female voter preparing to cast her vote 1920. RBM Vintage Images / Alamy Stock Photo.

married women should resign and only consider work like domestic labor that conformed to dominant ideas about femininity. As World War II loomed, the situation for women was slowly changing but there was a long way to go before anything approaching equality would be in sight (Hapke, 1995).

No major movements committed to new feminist reforms emerged during the interwar decades. Social changes occurred because the privileged classes recognized that the antebellum social order could not be restored in its entirety after so many men from poor backgrounds had not only died, but also had shown themselves to be highly effective soldiers; and because former soldiers had witnessed that the elite were not impervious to fear, and often were not effective leaders. But the widely shared vision of peace included the persistence of widespread inequalities and poverty as long as there was no return to international warfare. In other words, prevailing contemporary ideas of peace confirmed Galtung's idea that most societies in a state of negative peace also contained considerable structural violence.

However, despite their reduced roles in society women played prominent roles in anti-war political actions and the hundreds of protests that took place in Britain during the interwar decades. Women marched alone in organizations like the Women's Peace Crusade and Peace Pilgrimage, and they also joined with men in others such as the No More War demonstrations. For instance, the Women's International League for Peace and Freedom (WILPF), which had been founded in 1915 as a rare resistance against the World War, grew in strength after the war, and anti-war campaigning became respectable in the official mood of "never again." The WILPF continued to thrive and expand internationally, and later achieved consultative status with the United Nations. As another example, in 1933 the British Co-operative Women's Guild first promoted the sale of white poppies as an alternative to the red poppy promoted by the British Legion to mark the death of British servicemen on the annual Remembrance Day, and anti-war organizations have continued this tradition.[3]

Lack of space prevents a parallel analysis of the experiences of women in other parts of the world, but it is worth highlighting that in British and French colonies, many returning soldiers who had served under Allied command joined emergent anti-colonial political organizations. Those who engaged in the primarily nonviolent anti-colonial struggles of this era realized achieving genuine enduring peace required nothing short of revolutionary changes in their societies. In some parts of the world, the male dominated anti-colonial movements were not only supported by women activists, but also challenged by them to be more radical. Perhaps the most famous of such women's protests took place in Nigeria in 1929, where tens of thousands of women protested and used an old tactic of removing their clothes to make their point (Matera, 2011).

During World War II, women's activism was not pitched against the war but rather to increase their war efforts in replacing men's labor. As the war ended and once again social pressures to abandon their wartime roles grew, women confronted official and popular cultural emphases on their roles as wives and mothers in the new welfare state. For feminists in the United Kingdom and the United States, the predominant postwar concerns were improvements in welfare and legal rights, rather than fundamental changes in gender relations. In wealthy countries, the 1950s were a decade of strong economic growth and recovery from the war that reinvigorated conservative norms about women's rights. In this sense the 1950s in the United Kingdom is still regarded as a bleak period for feminism (Ward, 2004). Feminist demands for radical change in Western countries did not fuel major movements until the 1960s, as they also did in parts of the decolonizing world.

FIGURE 3.4: Women at the head of an anti-Vietnam War peace march, San Francisco 1971. Harold Adler / Underwood Archives / Contributor / Getty Images.

Until then, demands for equality between women and men were widely rejected by many as being against the natural order of things, or too threatening to the social order.

Beginning in the 1960s feminist activism combined with anti-war activism, particularly in the anti-Vietnam movement in the United States, and anti-nuclear protests there and in many other countries. From then until the end of the Cold War, some women chose to make these women-only campaigns to highlight their responsibility as women in caring for the children of the future, as well as rejecting the dominance of men in political action. Two movements that made international headlines were the Women's Strike for Peace (WSP) in the United States and the Greenham Common protests in the United Kingdom. The WSP was part of the international network of protest against atmospheric nuclear testing (see video at www.youtube.com/watch?v=zcgZ5kPTpRA accessed April 9, 2018). Anti-nuclear protests erupted in different parts of the world, but most dramatically on November 1, 1961 when between 12,000 and 50,000 women demonstrated in sixty US cities. WSP is credited by many with forcing the United States and USSR into a nuclear test-ban treaty (Swerdlow, 1982). WPS remained active for the rest of the period with a focus on demonstrating against US militarism and nuclear weapons.

The Greenham Common Peace Camp remained in place from 1981 to 2000 at the Royal Air Force base in Berkshire, England, which had been loaned to the United States to house Tomahawk Cruise missiles, each one of which had four times the power of the atomic bomb that obliterated Hiroshima. Various tactics of the women-only protestors made international headlines highlighting their refusal to leave, even in the face of police brutality, arrests, imprisonment and fines; their persistent destruction of large parts of the perimeter fence and break-ins to the base; and large-scale demonstrations around the base, such as that in 1983 conducted by 50,000 women. The peace camp inspired

FIGURE 3.5: Women protestors sitting at gateway to Greenham Common Airbase, England. Trinity Mirror / Mirrorpix / Alamy Stock Photo.

women in other places in the United Kingdom and the world to use similar tactics, and is credited with adding pressure for the 1986 Intermediate Nuclear Forces Treaty between the United States and USSR. The experience led many of the women activists in the United Kingdom and other countries to campaign on other issues such as for women's rights and against patriarchy; environmental protection; and workers' rights (Harford, 1984).

Women's hopes of equality were often a cause of tension within mixed-sex peace movements in the 1960s although that period witnessed a major shift in the social locations of young people and women (Cockburn, 2012). Women joined politically active groups (later referred to as the "second wave of feminism") and successfully challenged many of the old stereotypes of them as inferior to men in intellect and strength. They pursued legal rights in issues including reproduction, domestic violence, and divorce law. Women's movements have emerged all over the world since then, developing both practical and strategic interests of women (Molyneux, 1985; Moser, 1989) during moments of war and of peacebuilding (Cockburn, 2012). They were often met with outright opposition and violence, but gradually achieved change.

After the Cold War, the focus of peace protests and activism shifted to the new wars that emerged in Europe and parts of the Global South. Most were civil wars and/or including transnational actors rather than interstate conflicts. They featured very complex delineations of enemies and allies, and often pitted relatives against each other, a situation which made it very challenging for women seeking to make common cause as peacebuilders. Nonetheless, across the world, women came to be strongly associated with activism to stop or prevent violent conflict. In many political movements for peace (whether against war, colonialism, occupation, or dictatorship) images of women, and particularly mothers, have been deployed with great potency by women activists. Nonviolent tactics sometimes achieved a momentary check in violence and oppression. The cross-cultural respect for the "mother" as a concept, if not an actual person, has also enabled singularly brave women to stand in front of armed men, tanks, and armored cars, and bring them to a halt. In some parts of the world the evocation of a female elder, or "grandmother," has had the same impact echoing the pre-colonial protests (Tripp, 2015). For example, in 2003 in Liberia women formed the Mass Action for Peace, to bring an end to war threatening to implement a "sex strike" and to remove their clothes in public (Gbowee, 2009).

Celebrated stories of handfuls of courageous women are internationally famous. For instance, in Somalia during the conflict in the 1990s, women travelled between warring clans to act as mediators, urging men to stop fighting and negotiate, while risking their own safety. They deployed their multiple memberships in different clans, as wives, mothers, daughters etc. (where men are only members of one clan). By exerting pressure on their clansmen, a small number of women were allowed to observe internationally supported peace talks. Women-led civil society organizations helped to disempower the warlords, reduce the significance of clan affiliation, ensure civil society representation at peace and reconciliation processes, and make progress on the participation of women in politics (Gardner and El Bushra, 2004).

Powerful effective actions such as those of marginalized Somali women challenge narratives of the ultra-dominance of the warrior, even humanizing armed men as they are seen to be paying attention to, and respecting, the views of mature women. In some cases, women activists were subsequently persecuted, and their heroism celebrated while they were in prison or dead and the halt in violence was temporary. But the images created and deployed of women standing up to life-threatening power, using their gendered characteristics, rather than "imitating men," continue to link women strongly with ideas about stopping violence and building peace. There are mixed views about the reasons why women use these images of themselves in this way. Many women activists have testified that innate qualities as mothers force them to work for peace in ways that men do not. But other courageous women have stated that they use the status and imagery of mothers simply because it is effective peacemaking strategy.

Heroic peacebuilding efforts by women have become global stories disseminated by electronic news media. For instance in 2001, as part of International Alert's Women Building Peace campaign, the United Nations Development Fund for Women (UNIFEM) awarded a Millennium Peace Prize for Women, "They had built peace through resistance to violence, and through the creation of space in which dialogue could take place across ethnicities. They were responsible for holding the fabric of society together, and for rebuilding trust across fractured communities." (www.un.org/press/en/2001/unifembriefing.doc.htm, accessed April 9, 2017). The awards were for groups, as well as individuals including *Ruta Pacifica de las Mujeres*, which is a coalition of women's organizations working towards conflict-resolution in Colombia. *Women in Black*, a worldwide network of women against war, violence and militarism, which organizes women-only, non-violent, silent demonstrations and protests, often in places which are prone to high levels of violence, is one such recipient. In addition, since 2000 fifteen women have been awarded the Nobel Peace Prize, and the last six were all from the Global South.[4] Such recognition has reinforced cultural linkages between images of women as pacific and peacebuilding as something natural for women to be involved with, rather than a political choice made by a minority of women.

Internationally, the association of women with peacebuilding peaked at the end of the twentieth century primarily due to the long-term partnership between many women's organizations from all over the world (including those with a wider remit than peace and anti-war), and the UN, which sponsored four World Conferences on Women between 1975 and 1995 (Marsh, 2006).[5] These conferences were remarkable gatherings of women activists, politicians, and academics. Each conference initiated new campaigns, but one theme, peace and security, persisted. They created meaningful global networks, increasingly enabled through new communication technologies, and brought together women from a wide range of societies, including women from India campaigning for land rights and well-educated feminists from the powerful countries of the Global North. The Convention on the Elimination of all Forms of Discrimination Against Women was adopted in 1979 by the United Nations General Assembly. It has been ratified by all but five UN member states (including the United States), and continues to be an important instrument for change. Perhaps the most dramatic impact was on the UN itself.

In 2000, the UN General Assembly held a special session "Women 2000: Gender Equality, Development, and Peace for the Twenty-First Century" in New York, to consider how to implement the 1995 Beijing World Conference commitments. This dramatic achievement showed that women's activism for peace was now taken seriously at the highest level. It formally recognized that its resolutions resulted from long-term campaigns of international feminists, expressed in the recommendations from the UN-sponsored conferences which argued that: (a) women have vulnerabilities during war which are distinct from men's; and (b) women have special qualities and abilities and that it would be efficacious for them to play a more equal role in negotiating and building peace. Since then the UN Security Council began to put gender issues at the heart of military peacekeeping operations, and subsequent UN-supported efforts at peacebuilding.

GENDERED PEACEBUILDING

Women and men experience conflict differently and therefore understand peace differently.
www.un.org/en/peacekeeping/issues/women/, accessed April 9, 2018

At the international level remarkable progress has been made: in establishing women's legal rights; in the identification of GBV as a potential war crime; and in some women's abilities to access such legal frameworks. The UN intervened at the highest level in security terms, via the Security Council, in a series of resolutions beginning in 2000, which were explicitly defined by gender issues and founded on assumptions about the "nature of women." Resolution 1325 called for an overhaul in attitudes and training of UN personnel; to promote women to prominent positions in "peace activity"; and included the need to work closely with local women. It highlighted the need to protect women and girls from violence in conflict settings and re-stated relevant UN positions on human rights. The Security Council's focus on these issues has been widely attributed to international publicity about the widespread rape and sexual torture of women during the Rwanda and Yugoslav wars. In the late twentieth century global public opinion had changed about the conduct of war and global responsibility to intervene, but also in what was understood about women's gender.

The killing and torturing of women in war continued, as did the almost complete absence of women from peace talks and peacebuilding policy forums. New Security Council Resolutions were passed that recognized the lack of real change. Resolution 1820 (2008) condemned sexual violence as a weapon of war and declared rape and other forms of sexual violence to be war crimes. Five further UN Security Council Resolutions followed (1888/2009, 1889/2009, 1960/2010, 2106/2013, 2122/2013). All sought to bring about the policy changes in Resolution 1325 that had not yet been implemented. Together these resolutions are referred to as the "UN Women, Peace and Security" (WPS) agenda, or framework. This policy agenda emanating from the heart of the UN was mainly a product of sustained actions by women's organizations that led to the Beijing Declaration and continued afterwards.

These resolutions have been much studied. There are many case studies that show highly varied impacts on the ground. Several themes in this literature are worth noting. First, the political timing that brought the views of feminist activists into conferences with influential UN officials was critical. Second, the resolutions give extremely powerful leverage to activists and politicians who may be able to take advantage of the opportunities they present usually with the support of international women's movements. Third, they have had some unintended consequences. The emphases on women as victims, and as having special qualities to broker peace, reinforced essentialist views of women which are not always helpful in reducing gender inequality. Fourth, the resolutions have not as yet actually produced in most member states the desired transformation of gender politics. This failure is perhaps not surprising because of the essentialist view of women embedded in them; whereas in their localities people know that women, and men, are more varied than the gender stereotypes.

However, there have been some, much heralded, examples of change such as bringing small numbers of women into negotiations; training peacekeeping forces in gender awareness; and involving greater numbers of women in peace negotiations and peacebuilding such as occurred in the preparation for the peace agreement in Sudan 2006 (www.c-r.org/accord/sudan/guests-table-role-women-peace-processes, accessed April 9, 2018). Colombia's peace process was the first to explicitly include a gender approach, and women comprised about half of those consulted in the peace process. The UN still boldly reaffirms this commitment on its various websites, arguing for its efficacy: "When women are included in peace processes there is a 20 per cent increase in the probability of an agreement lasting at least 2 years, and a 35 per cent increase in the probability of an agreement lasting at least 15 years" (www.unwomen.org/en/what-we-do/peace-and-security/facts-and-figures, accessed April 9, 2018). But the UN directives are by no means implemented effectively everywhere. UN Secretary-General Ban Ki-moon commented recently that,

> In failing to include women and girls in peacemaking and peacebuilding processes, we are not only failing women and girls . . . We are failing the world . . . I am ashamed of the many atrocities that continue to be committed against women and girls, including by some of our own peacekeepers . . . I am angered by the continued political exclusion of women.
>
> www.un.org/press/en/2016/sc12561.doc.htm, accessed April 9, 2018

Many critics suggest that the changes are not as significant as the UN claims above. Certainly, the call to put women at the table for peace negotiations and peacebuilding planning has not been fully implemented. In addition to highlighting this continued discrimination against women and a widespread lack of commitment to the goals of the UN resolutions, critics also suggest that for women to make effective contributions to peace in many parts of the world, the inequality between women and men, particularly in terms of education and "legal literacy" must be effectively reduced (Walsh, 2012).

The increasingly negative publicity generated by UN peacekeepers who have committed acts of gender-based violence has prompted reforms. The genocide in Rwanda and the wars in the break-up of the former Yugoslavia provoked a new era of UN and other international military interventions in conflicts in the Global South (especially in Africa 2000–10, and since then in the Middle East) resulting in a very steep increase in the numbers of soldiers, police and civilians donning blue helmets and becoming peacekeepers. Many cases of peacekeepers committing acts of sexual violence and exploitation against women and children, when they became news stories, have been met with severe public reprobation. Now, as part of WPS, all UN peacekeepers have to undergo gender-specific training. This training should have a greater impact. Research on the training behavior of peacekeepers has shown that some GBV transgressions committed by men in these trusted positions have been severely condemned, but that these publicized cases are not typical (Duncanson, 2016). One response to the problem has been to recruit more women as peacekeepers, with a famous example being a unit of Indian women police deployed in Liberia for a decade (https://news.un.org/en/story/2016/02/522102-feature-hailed-role-models-all-female-indian-police-unit-departs-un-mission, accessed April 9, 2018).

THE GENDERED POSTWAR PEACE

At the end of all wars in the modern era women have been confronted by what has come to be termed a "backlash" against wartime changes in gender relations. After World War II, this backlash occurred in the United States and Europe where legislation and social action removed women from jobs that were given to men returning from fighting. As a result many women lost the social status, as well as income, they had earned during wartime. Postwar backlash has since occurred in different countries and cultures across the world. Sometimes governments used state apparatus to push women "back" into "kitchens and fields," even if they had joined guerrilla armies as children (Cockburn 2004:40). The backlash discourse has often mixed new and old cultural norms and been accompanied by imagery that is a culturally specific equivalent to Pierson's (1989) concept of a "beautiful soul" strongly associating women with tradition, motherhood, and peace.

Sometimes backlash attacks on women became violent, both in public (committed by police, soldiers, peacekeepers, gang members) and in private (committed by husbands, partners, or other men in the household). Sometimes the level of violence, particularly "domestic violence" reached higher levels than before, or even during, wartime, and included new forms of GBV (Meintjes et al., 2001; Jacobs and Howard, 1987; Luciak, 2012). In camps for refugees and displaced people, and in areas where livelihood systems have collapsed, women continue to be forced to sell sex as a means of economic survival. Women also commonly find their contributions to the war and peace efforts marginalized in both official and popular accounts of war, as happened in Europe after both World Wars. There seems to be an attempt to deny that changes in gender relations were required for women to take on their wartime roles, and by implication, that such changes will actually be possible (Kelly, 2000:62; Pankhurst, 2012).

The considerable variety in the force and longevity of the backlash cannot be explained at a general level. Many so-called explanations are educated guesses, not based on sustained analysis of empirical data. The phenomenon can be so dramatic that it seems self-evident that it has something to do with gender relations and what, at that moment, is perceived by many men to be the correct behavior and social status of women. Observers often describe the backlash as a clash between genders that erupted when women who took on men's roles during wartime gained "too much" status and power for men to accept afterwards. This re-defining of gender relations after war ends has become associated with building peace in many places, albeit often very much to women's disadvantage. At the same time young men in poor countries often retain their weapons and, as they fail to find gainful employment, continue lives of violence, assaulting and killing each other and women. This particular legacy of warfare partly explains why Latin America has the world's highest homicide rate (Rivera, 2015; Pearce, 2010).

Public outcries against the predatory behavior of former combatants and peacekeepers, whether they are from poor countries of the Global South or the wealthy North (particularly Canada) go to the heart of questions about "what it is to be a soldier." Most of the commentary remains highly condemnatory with very muddled "explanations" given for the legal and social transgressions committed. Yet, prosecutions of soldiers for war crimes, and for peacekeepers' crimes against local populations are still weak and questioned by government officials. The WPS framework has focused official attention on the behavior of peacekeepers (Higate and Henry, 2004) and some militaries have developed new codes of behavior (Duncanson, 2016).

There is also growing public concern about what even the wealthiest countries expect from and do to their combat troops. The way their combat deaths have been memorialized in the United Kingdom reflects this change. Public support for and participation in the commemoration of "Remembrance Day," originally to mark the end of World War I, but later extended to remember all deceased service personnel, has been revived after waning in the 1980s. Commemoration of the actual moment the Armistice was signed in 1918 with a two-minute silence was reintroduced in 1995, and the parades and ceremonies of Remembrance Sunday make it a more significant custom than in previous decades when many people regarded these activities as supporting militarism and war and did not participate. Now the suffering endured by (mostly male) forces is highlighted, in some tension with national pride.

Similarly, Veterans Day in the United States has different meanings for different people. Veterans of the unsuccessful Vietnam War, often with anti-establishment views, receive recognition from the public along with veterans of other US wars. Many other countries hold "Heroes' Day" commemorations or similar events, where the politics of who is included reflect the tensions of contemporary political power. All these commemorations have in common a celebration of the male warrior in much the same vein as described by Pierson (1989). In some countries where activists have tried to make the commemoration of wartime sacrifices as inclusive as possible, women soldiers are also included, re-defining the conflict that is commemorated. Nonetheless these commemorations are mostly about the sacrifices made during a "just war" by young male warriors, an ideal masculinity to which only a minority of men conform.

In the Global North, public recognition and concerns about the well-being of serving and retired forces has become a political issue. These concerns include physical injuries and mental health problems (primarily depression and PTSD), but also high rates of drug and alcohol abuse and addiction, homelessness and unemployment, and a predilection to violence. Failure to provide adequate support and care for men who have served also raises issues about societies' preferred gendered identities. How should "real men" behave in war and peacetime? Is it possible for them to switch easily between military and civilian identities? Emerging scientific research helps explain why these transitions are problematic for some individuals, but since transition experiences vary, we also need social science and humanities to understand them. Public concerns for veterans' health are played down by governments in the rich countries that now face difficulties recruiting national forces and budgetary challenges resulting from post 9/11 wars that have expanded the geography and purposes of their military interventions (Pankhurst, 2016).

Female members of armed forces remain in the minority everywhere and do not receive the same public attention as male soldiers. They are often still regarded as an aberration, and individuals are singled out in the negative news stories especially in the United States that have highlighted, for example, women soldiers involved in ill-treatment of Iraqi prisoners and mothers serving on the front line said to be "abandoning their children". These cases demonstrate the persistence of starkly gendered binary stereotypes even in a country that has enacted some of the most advanced equalities legislation in the world.

Recovery from war and securing peace also requires political processes to deal with issues of justice regarding potential war crimes, and agreements about future legal rights. At least twenty-five post-conflict Truth Commissions (TCs) have been convened since 1974 (Hayner, 2002). TCs take many different forms, seeking sometimes to find out information about "the disappeared," as in Argentina, Uganda, and Sri Lanka; at other times working towards truth and justice as in Haiti and Ecuador; or truth and reconciliation as in Chile, South Africa, the Federal Republic of Yugoslavia, East Timor, and Peru. All truth commissions have been highly gendered. The most common underreported abuses in all of them were those suffered by women. TCs, including some held long after the crimes were committed, have developed over time ways to improve the conditions under which women will testify (Walsh, 2012). For instance, women's groups in Japan and neighboring countries came together to hold a War Crimes Tribunal in 2000, to look at sexual slavery by the Japanese army during World War II (Walsh, 2012). This Tribunal lacked official status, yet even though more than half a century had passed women still testified because they felt so strongly about unacknowledged wartime injustices. Justice for "comfort women" remains an issue for Korean activists today.

After the Cold War, governments and NGOs often made the establishment of democracy as evidenced by multi-party elections a high priority. Although advocates hoped for high levels of women's participation in new elections, it has proved difficult to realize this goal. Even where the political and legal apparatus was in place to allow women to take part in political life, their level of political participation tended to remain lower than men's. The key problems are both practical and cultural. Educational requirements for voter registration, and long distances to voting booths for women with no transport or childcare have been unexpected barriers to women's participation. Cultural obstacles against women standing for office and voting have included family and community pressures, sometimes backed by religious doctrine. Government interventions to overcome these obstacles in poor countries have nonetheless sometimes exceeded what is allowed in the Global North. For instance, seats for women were guaranteed in local and national government in Uganda at the same time that the use of women's quotas for political parties was deemed illegal in the United Kingdom (Tamale 1999; Tripp, 2005).

The greatest opportunities for building peace, however, are generally agreed to be in economic recovery and development. A thriving economy is widely considered a "peace dividend" that provides strong insurance against a return to conflict. In practice, compared to men, women have consistently lost out in terms of postwar economic land reforms, support for trade and industry, education and health care, and workers' rights and benefits (Pankhurst, 2012b). Perhaps increased input by women at peace talks and subsequent constitutional negotiations will lead to improvements. Over the past few decades, gender equality in economic development has been difficult not only because of continued discrimination against women, but also because there are global ideological divisions about the best way to improve economic performance and development. Since the late 1990s, UN Development Programs as well as INGOs on the ground have all agreed that effective state bureaucracies that maintain law and order, social services, education, and health care are necessary to ensure human security. Yet the economies of all recent "postwar" countries have been subject to the policies set by global financial institutions. They have been (and remain) strongly influenced by neo-liberal philosophies that consider state intervention and the development of large state bureaucracies as inhibitors to growth and development, even though the rich nations of the Global North do not operate their own economies on this basis. On the one hand postwar countries have embraced the need to reduce gender inequality for the sake of peace and prosperity, but the application of neo-liberal principles to economic strategy has remained gender blind. How this contradiction is worked out will have serious implications for women, and for peace.

CONCLUSION

The stereotypes about women and men outlined at the beginning of this chapter have been flexed in different wars during the modern era. Women have been fighters alongside men, have risen high in military structures, and undertaken new roles to support war efforts. Men have acted as peace negotiators, conscientious objectors and war-resisters. Against a backdrop of cultural norms about women and men—what they are able to do, what is in their biological nature, and what is right—wars have spurred massive social change between genders and what it means to be a man or a woman. Knowledge of these experiences ought to have dispelled any strong association between biology and the dominance of men, yet it has not.

Wars can be viewed with nostalgia for giving women (and men) unprecedented opportunities, whether they wanted them or not, particularly after a postwar social and political backlash against those same changes. Highlighting positive change during wartime has not been a common political strategy followed by women's organizations that generally have shunned war and violence. Instead organized women have sought throughout the world to be associated with peace and the protection of people and the planet from man-made disaster. Whether they were women campaigning with white poppies against a repeat of World War I, anti-nuclear demonstrators during the Cold War, or women in African civil wars seeking to get a seat at the negotiating table, women have often used their identities as mothers and carers to force political leaders to listen.

Such strategies have pushed the world's most powerful international security organization into identifying women not just as victims of war, but also as peace activists who are needed to end wars. This unexpected UN policy has had the unintended effect of reinforcing some gender stereotypes. A gap persists between the UN and other international organizations' goals of promoting gender equity that highlights women's vulnerability and their potential contributions for peace, and what has actually happened on the ground. In response, some feminists today argue that the WPS approach moved international action towards peace too far away from *gender analysis*, and overly focused the solution on women (Davies and True, 2015). In the meantime, more men die and kill in wars without much interrogation of *their* gender, an identity that predisposes so many to respond with violence to political and personal conflicts. War and violent conflict will persist until many more millions of men see that it is in their interest to resist certain types of masculinity and patriarchy.

For peace activists and scholars, the analysis of genders and how they are formed, maintained and changed over time provides great insights into people's lives during times of war and peace. In its absence the stereotypes of gendered war experiences persist; the variation in men and women's real war experiences is eclipsed; and significant potential for resolving conflict through non-violent means is lost. Learning from the history of the modern era provides us with a challenge to re-define heroism and virility as being non-violent and peace-oriented. This challenge will require effort and engagement from men as well as women, but is at the heart of our chances of establishing enduring peace.

CHAPTER FOUR

Peace, Pacifism, and Religion

Just War Traditions, Nonviolence, Peace Building, Social Justice, Human Rights, Sustainable Development, and Interfaith Dialogue

TOH SWEE-HIN (S.H. TOH)

Throughout history, warfare and organized violence have sometimes set peoples belonging to different religions against each other. Religious sects and religious faiths have often been blamed for promoting violence within and between societies. Early exemplars of these kinds of conflicts include the Crusades, the territorial expansion of Islam, the Inquisition in Europe, and the European colonialism that often included coerced conversions, ethnic cleansing, and systematic exploitation of indigenous peoples. Since the end of the Cold War, a conflict frequently described as between "godless Communism" and Western civilization, global politics has been reconfigured, and religious extremism again seems the greatest threat to world peace. Since the 9/11/2001 terror attacks by militant Islamists on New York City and Washington, DC, the idea that strong religious belief motivates terrorists has been widely disseminated by many governments that proclaimed a "war on terrorism" and by the global news media that have framed Islam as the most important contemporary breeder of extremism, hatred, and terrorist violence. The framing of Islam as a violent religion has promoted widespread Islamophobia and militant nationalism in most Western nations.

The Middle East, home of three important monotheistic religions, has often been perceived as an arena of religious-inspired violence. Political conflict between mostly Sunni Arabs and settler Jews in Palestine started during the 1920s and continues to the present day. The Arab–Israeli conflict, Middle Eastern civil wars, and terrorist attacks by regional non-state groups have often been presented by scholars and news media as exemplifying what Samuel Huntington called a "clash of civilizations" (1993). Since then, ancient civilizational hatreds have been invoked to explain outbreaks of terrorism, communal violence, and ethnic cleansing in the Balkans, and many other countries including India, Sri Lanka, Myanmar, Thailand, Niger, Mali, and Nigeria.

The global proliferation of these types of political violence since 9/11 has for many reinforced the idea that strong religious belief is the leading cause of terrorism and war. Proponents of this view include many Western atheists who argue that humanity would be less violent if organized religion were abolished. Militant atheists, notably Richard Dawkins (2006), Christopher Hitchens (2007), and Sam Harris (2005) have rejected tolerance for religion. They maintain that scientific naturalism is supreme in understanding reality. In their view, all religions promote "mindless faith" that is a source of "evil" and "violence."

However, religion per se does not necessarily motivate extremism and organized violence. Careful analysis of the dynamics and complexities of most conflicts, as well as of the doctrinal bases and practices of leading faith traditions by scholars such as Karen Armstrong (2011) and William Cavanaugh (2009) has challenged the "myth of religious violence."

Of course, many religious doctrines including those presented in holy texts and the teachings of founders and prophets have been, and still are, regarded by some of their believers as justification for violence and war. Yet clearly the core values and principles of all leading religions promote the cultivation of peaceable relationships and nonviolence in daily life. Whether or not religions motivate believers to act with violence or nonviolence depends on how individuals and groups interpret specific religious teachings. Thus, the potential for exclusionist interpretations of religious "truths" that promote discrimination and violence against nonbelievers always exists. However, much worldwide evidence indicates that religious belief alone is insufficient explanation for violent groups that proclaim "holy wars" and execute terrorist attacks. Specific wars and outbreaks of communal violence erupt out of the specific social, cultural, psychological, economic, and political conditions in specific places. The context and root causes of violence organized as religious conflict need to be clearly understood before we assess the role of faith political violence (Armstrong, Ibid.; Cavanaugh, Ibid.; Jurgensmeyer, 2003; British Academy, 2015; Sacks, 2015).

Many scholars in disciplines including history, political science, sociology, economics, and philosophy study the causes of political violence. Thousands of experts work in the hundreds of peace research and conflict resolution centers that have been established around the world since 1920. For modern peace researchers achieving peace requires long, complicated processes that eliminate structural violence in society, not just an ending of warfare. Peace researchers and peacebuilders who often work for non-governmental organizations have developed programs to create this holistic concept of peace. And through trial and error, effective peacebuilding methods have emerged in the twenty-first century (Pilisuk and Nagler, 2011; Darby and McGinty, 2003; van Tongeren, Brenk, Hellema and Verhoeven, 2005). Many international, national, regional, and local peacebuilding efforts have been inspired by diverse religious believers who see their faith as a motivation for working to establish peace (Little, 2007; Mun, 2007; Smock, 2008; Matyok et al., 2014; Gopin, 2000; Omar and Duffey, 2015; Hudo and Marshall, 2013; Coward and Smith, 2004).

This chapter first briefly reviews historical links between religion and violence and war, paying special attention to religious justifications of war. Then, it develops in greater detail how the teachings about nonviolence and humanity found in religions have been implemented by groups of believers. In the twenty-first century, religious convictions motivate millions of people who work every day to prevent war, resolve violent conflicts, and build peaceful societies after violent conflict ceases. Peacebuilding in an increasingly networked world has contributed to an expanding interfaith/interreligious dialogue movement. Peacebuilding has become a counterforce to those who see in religious diversity only inevitable "clashes of civilizations."

JUST WAR TRADITIONS

It is certainly true that the holy texts of major organized religions include doctrinal teachings and exhortations that literally justify physical force by believers against enemies, unbelievers, wrongdoers, and "others" (Renard, 2012; Selengut, 2017; Ellens, 2007; Jurgensmeyer and Kitts, 2011; Smith-Christopher, 2007; Pratt, 2017). Examples abound. In the Jewish Torah and in the Christian Old Testament, an angry God prescribes violence, death, and destruction for idolaters and enemies. Early Hindu sacred texts contain epics celebrating holy wars and violence by kings and warriors. Passages of the Koran exhort violent *jihad* towards disbelievers and enemies (Hussain, 2012).

Even Buddhism, widely regarded in the West as the exemplary pacifist religion, has promoted violence. Theravada Buddhism's Mahavamsa or Great Chronicle of Sri Lanka tells of a king who felt remorse for having killed many Hindus in a war, but received comforting advice from Buddhist monks who viewed the Hindus as unbelievers deserving of death (Deegale, 2014). In the past, in China, Buddhist monk leaders sometimes led thousands of followers in bloody wars, while Thai monks supported their kingdom's wars against neighboring countries (Burns, 2008: 20). During World War II, Zen priests and temples actively supported Japan's war machine by providing meditation training for soldiers (Victoria, 2006).

Major religions have long supported the idea that some kinds of killing are moral. Older religions, including Hinduism, Judaism, and Buddhism already in antiquity allowed leaders to wage wars to defend their peoples from enemies and destruction. What later became known as the "just war doctrine" was developed in the Catholic Church by leading theologians including Augustine and Thomas Aquinas. The medieval Church's principles and guidelines for the initiation and conduct of "just wars" are the basis for many secular and religious formulations of the "just war" tradition in the modern era (Mary, 2006; Evans, 2005). Three main pillars of modern international law—the Hague Conventions, Geneva Conventions, and the United Nations Charter—each have embedded in them principles of just war doctrine designed to strictly limit the use of violence by nation-states.

Self-defense has always been widely accepted as a moral reason for warfare, but attempts to go beyond this justification have been controversial. In the modern era, the only other legitimate reason for war is an authorization to use force voted by the United Nations Security Council. In the late twentieth century many Catholic clergy in Latin America preached a "liberation theology" that asserted that armed force may be needed to overthrow dictators and military rulers who use violence to maintain grossly unjust societies. This form of liberation theology was strongly rejected by Pope John Paul II (Ratzinger, 1984). However, other leaders of liberation theology who called for nonviolent strategies to overcome social injustices or structural violence, such as Bishop Helder Camara (1971) in Brazil were not sanctioned by Rome.

Just war doctrine was the focus of global political debates following the 9/11 attacks. In 2002, the United States government proclaimed a right to wage war to pre-emptively eliminate potential threats to national security, and announced it would invade Iraq to destroy threats posed by Saddam Hussein's regime. The US claim that Iraq possessed weapons of mass destruction was not confirmed by UN inspectors and has since been discredited, while US geostrategic motivations for the invasion have been clarified (Hinnebusch, 2007). During the week before the US and British invasion in 2003, tens of millions of people demonstrated around the world denouncing the war plan as unjust aggression. In the United States, the number of Christian leaders and communities justifying the war outweighed those who opposed it (Morrisey, 2018). But the multitudes of protesters who filled city streets around the world in early 2003 included followers of many different religions, all of whom considered the US-UK invasion of Iraq as an unjust war.

NONVIOLENCE

The global responses of religious believers to the Iraq war reflected longstanding disagreements about the meaning of "a just war." These disagreements stem from the fact that all major religions stress the responsibility of believers to practice nonviolence. Depending on how scriptures are read and doctrines interpreted, it is possible to find in them both the legitimation and refusal of war (Hogan, 2009). Believers who use their faith as justification for violence often share a conviction that their religious truth is absolute and superior to all others, blind loyalty to leaders, and a belief that moral ends can justify any means, including killing. However, there are many millions of religious people who reject the idea that killing is ever justified, who oppose as a matter of belief the mass killing always involved in warfare. As several religious scholars have recently noted, there are competing motifs of the "warrior and the pacifist" in faiths such as Buddhism, Judaism, Christianity and Islam (Kurtz, 2018).

Ahimsa means nonkilling or non-injury and non-harming. It is an ancient value of the religions that developed in South Asia: Jainism, Hinduism, and Buddhism and a principle that governs daily life and relationships. Those who embrace *ahimsa* not only reject physical violence, but also conduct themselves in ways that do not cause social, economic, cultural, and psychological harm. *Ahimsa* is rooted in the belief that all people and parts of the universe manifest the same cosmic divinity. *Ahimsa* upholds the "Golden Rule" of treating others as you would wish to be treated. As Shastri and Shastri (2007: 63) noted, the Mahabharata sees *ahimsa* as the "highest form of religion, virtue and duty." In the modern era, Mahatma Gandhi integrated *ahimsa* into his private life and the nonviolent struggle for India's independence (Merton, 1965).

In Jainism, an ancient religion that emerged in India, *ahimsa* remains an ultimate principle that requires followers to practice nonviolence towards even the smallest forms of life (Chapple, 2007). For Buddhists too *ahimsa* is a key precept for daily life as well as social action. The values of compassion and loving-kindness inform Buddha's calls for nonviolence towards all beings and his strategies for overcoming hatred, greed, and delusion (Queen, 2007). In Daoism, the classic text Dao De Jing upholds the way of refraining from using force and violence to rule, and to solving problems through peaceful means (Mitchell, 1988; Tam, 2007).

Undoubtedly Hindu scriptures and holy texts contain justifications for violence, revenge, and exclusion. Militant Hindus have inhibited peacebuilding in modern South Asia seeing in their sacred texts inspiration for Hindu nationalism (Appleby, 2000, pp. 118–94; Bose, 2009), a historical memory-based attitude to revenge, and support for the caste system. However, as Rajmohan (2004: 45–68) shows, these obstacles to peacebuilding can be overcome by a critical contextualized reading of the scriptures.

Mahatma Gandhi's life and work remain exemplary. His vision, principles, and nonviolent campaigns for India's independence and for non-discrimination and equality continue to inspire new generations of peacebuilders worldwide (Vinthagen, Ibid.).

Despite the passages in the Bible and Koran exhorting violence and doctrines that support "just war" and jihad in self-defense, the Abrahamic religions endorse nonviolence as moral wisdom that should be integrated in daily life and all social and political relationships. The peace or "shalom" that is consistently emphasized within the Rabbinic texts includes not just the absence of violence in physical terms but also acting according to the values of justice, truth, integrity, love, and respect. In the Christian Bible, the message of nonviolence is clearly present in the sermons of Jesus Christ that call on believers to be peacemakers, love their enemies, resist evil nonviolently, and practice forgiveness and reconciliation (Helmick and Petersen, 2001; Kurian, 2011). In the three main "Peace Churches" (Mennonites, Church of the Brethren, and Quakers), this Gospel of Peace remains institutionalized in explicit commitments to pacifism that unconditionally upholds nonviolence (Kleiderer and Mossa, 2006: 96–106). However, most Christians who generally practice nonviolence are not strict pacifists even though they believe the character of modern warfare has rendered just war doctrine no longer valid.

In Islam, there is also a growing commitment to drawing out the teachings of nonviolence in the holy texts as a response to militant Islamist radicals who use those texts to recruit fighters and terrorists. While acknowledging that the use of force (only one form of *jihad*) may be necessary as a last resort for self-defense against those who seek to attack the Islamic faith and community or to liberate people from oppression and tyranny, these modern scholars stress that the Prophet's teachings impose various restraints on violent *jihad*, including nonaggression and not harming innocents, children, women, the elderly, or the environment (Shah-Kazemi, 2009). Moreover, they argue that the more important *jihad*, waging an inner struggle to overcome spiritual failings, should be prioritized.

Islamic advocates of nonviolence believe the holy teachings strongly commend Muslims to build a peaceful world based on the sacredness of human life, social and economic justice, equality for all people, solidarity, love, kindness, compassion, patience, forgiveness, mercy, cooperation, and reconciliation (Abu-Nimer, 2003; Abu-Nimer and Badawi, 2011; Abdel Haleem, 2010; Kadayifci-Orellana, 2013: 443). They reject the decontextualized, manipulative and selective interpretations of selected passages of holy texts that justify extremist violence and exclusivism that have been propagated by Islamic theorists like Sayyid Qubt and the al-Qaeda leader Osama bin Laden (Appleby, Ibid.: 91–5,104–9; Brokopp, 2002). The Thai Muslim peace scholar-advocate, Chaiwat Satha-Anand (2018) has also clarified how nonviolent alternatives can replace the violence of terrorism pursued by some Muslim individuals and groups.

Despite the unceasing Arab–Israeli conflict and a recent resurgence of European anti-Semitism that encourages Jewish believers to read sacred texts as justifying armed defense of the "chosen people," scholars such as Marc Gopin (2000) have clearly identified Judaism's nonviolent social ethics, sacred stories, symbols, values, teachings, and practices which serve as resources for peacebuilding. Many Jews recognize that Middle East peace will require a just distribution of land and resources. Gopin goes further, urging Arabs and Jews to simultaneously adopt shared mourning of what has been lost, purposeful acts of humility, active empathic listening, social justice, confession of wrongdoing, and responsibility to heal the suffering of others.

The diverse and growing number of believers and leaders committed to the practice of nonviolence reveals one important way religious institutions and believers contribute to

FIGURE 4.1: Mohandas Ghandi. Wikimedia Commons (Public Domain).

"positive peace," or a holistic concept of peace. Globally Mahatma Gandhi's principles, strategies, and tactics have informed numerous successful nonviolent revolutions, as well as many movements dedicated to preventing war and building peace by guaranteeing social justice, human rights, and sustainable futures (Gandhi, 1999; Klostermaier, 2014; Vinthagen, 2015; Da Silva, 2001; Nojeim, 2004).

In India, Gandhi's disciple and spiritual successor, Sri Vinoba Bhave, founded the *Bhoodan* (land gift) and *Gramdan* (village gift) Movement that redistributes rich landowner-donated land to the rural poor (S.K.,1958; Shewan, Akela and Sharma, 2011). Hindu peacebuilders have also worked to establish social justice and domestic peace by challenging dam construction and practices of transnational corporations that threaten rural communities (Shiva, 2005; Lokashakti, n.d.).

PEACE BUILDING

Christian believers, churches and peacebuilding organizations have actively joined campaigns for nuclear and conventional disarmament, ending armed conflicts and wars that have produced so much death, suffering, and destruction of habitat, and so many refugees and internally displaced people. Successive Popes have advocated against wars, nuclear weapons, and militarism. Paul VI passionately appealed for "War No More, War Never Again" at the United Nations in 1965. John Paul II declared that the Iraq War would be "a defeat for humanity which could not be morally or legally justified." And Francis recently warned that "humanity risks suicide" with the increased danger of nuclear war between the United States and North Korea (Winfield, 2017; Zwick, n.d.; Paul VI, 1965).

In 1999, the World Council of Churches (1999) initiated a Decade of Nonviolence encompassing activities and programs to raise awareness and commitment to nonviolence, conflict transformation, peacemaking, and reconciliation. In his 2017 World Day of Peace Message, Pope Francis declared that "peace building through active nonviolence is the natural and necessary complement to the Church's continuing efforts to limit the use of force by the application of moral norms" (Schlabach, 2018). In questioning just war doctrine, American bishops have repeatedly emphasized virtues such as faith, hope, courage, compassion, humility, and patience inherent in nonviolent peacemaking (Macarthy, 2011).

The inspirational exemplar, Martin Luther King, showed how a Christian's deep commitment to non-violence so powerfully galvanized the civil rights movement in the United States (Carson & Shepard, 2001). One Jesuit priest, John Dear, together with other Christian peace activists, willingly accepted imprisonment and other punishment for protests at nuclear weapons bases and efforts to end US-led military interventions (Dear, 2001). Individual Christian and Jewish peacemakers have spent many courageous years helping to end violent conflicts in Northern Ireland, Bosnia, Kosovo, Ethiopia/Eritrea, Sudan, and Israel/Palestine. Drawing on their pacifist roots, the Mennonites, Quakers, and other "peace churches" have longstanding traditions of engaging in nonviolent peacebuilding, including gaining Congressional approval in the US of a conscientious objectors exemption from conscription for their members. Mennonites, using their Central Committee and Conciliation Services (Appleby, Ibid.:143–9), have become leaders in conflict mediation and transformation though concrete projects and skills development programs, including the well-known conciliation and training work of John Paul Lederach (2005). Christian Peacemaker Teams jointly organized by the Mennonite, Brethren and Quaker churches have conducted nonviolent interventions in many conflicts including Colombia's civil war and the Arab-Israeli conflict (Kleiderer, Minaert, and Mossa, 2006: 100–5).

In the early 1990s the Catholic Sant'Egidio Community founded in Rome as a lay association patiently gathered representatives of the Mozambique Government, insurgent armed groups, and Mozambican church leaders for peace talks that eventually ended the long bloody civil war. Since then, the Community has also mediated peace processes in numerous conflicts, including Mozambique, the Great Lakes Region in Africa, the Balkans, Colombia, North Uganda, and Darfur (Giro, 2008; Tyler, 2010; Appleby, Ibid.: 155–64). In Northern Ireland, Catholic and Protestant leaders facilitated the nonviolent resolution of armed conflict (Fitzduff, 2002; Berkeley Center for Religion, Peace & World Affairs, 2013; Ganiel, 2017; Little, 2007: 53–96). In West Papua, Rev. Benny Giay has worked tirelessly to establish a Zone of Peace for his people who have been struggling against Indonesian authorities for freedom, democracy, and human rights (Little, 2007: pp. 402–28). Project Ploughshares, initiated by the Canadian Council of Churches in 1976, and international Christian groups such as Pax Christi have campaigned for nuclear disarmament and the abolition of the arms trade, and raised public awareness on the deadly consequences of armed conflicts.

FIGURE 4.2: Palestinians remove a roadblock while a member of the Christian Peacemaker Team stands behind them. Wikimedia Commons (Public Domain).

In the Philippines, many Church leaders and millions of believers played an inspiring role in the historic nonviolent people power revolution that overthrew the Marcos dictatorship in 1986 (Goss-Mayer, 2011). Most recently, responding to President Duterte's deadly "war on drugs" in which several thousand people have been killed by police and vigilantes, the Catholic Church has condemned extrajudicial killings and called for democratic rule of law that guarantees all citizens a right to a fair trial (CBCP, 2017). Some clergy and churches have offered sanctuary to families of the victims and those who fear becoming a victim. Rather than a violent "war on drugs," the Filipino Catholic Church urges treating drug addiction as a health and social problem exacerbated by poverty and inequality.

Similarly, Buddhist teachings on *ahimsa* motivate believers to practice principles of nonviolence and seek social justice. Born into the lowest caste Dalits in India, Bhimrao Ramji Ambedkar courageously organized nonviolent campaigns for the rights and equality of Dalits (Mun, 2007). In Japan, the founder and leader of the lay Buddhist organization, Sokka Gakkai, was imprisoned in the 1940s for opposing Japan's war campaign. Since the war other Buddhist leaders such as Reverend Niwano have worked for disarmament, world peace, and interfaith cooperation (Mun, Ibid.: 41–4). In the 1960s, Vietnamese Buddhist monks and laypersons led by the Zen monk, Thich Nhat Hanh, organized protests against the escalation of the war (Hanh, 2007; Mun, Ibid.).

After going into exile in North America and Europe, Thich Nhat Hanh (1987; 2003) has actively promoted nonviolent conflict resolution and peacebuilding. Venerable Maha Ghosananda in Cambodia is another inspirational Buddhist leader who led lay Buddhists

FIGURE 4.3: Thich Nhat Hanh in Paris, 2006. Wikimedia Commons (Public Domain).

in an annual Walk for Peace and Reconciliation (*dhammayietra*) across conflict zones to urge the various political groups vying for power in post-Khmer Rouge Cambodia to cease fighting and build a peaceful society (Appleby, Ibid., pp. 123–8). His Holiness the Dalai Lama has repeatedly appealed for a nonviolent struggle for autonomy and freedom for his people and proposed that Tibet be recognized as "a sanctuary of peace and nonviolence where human beings and nature can live in peace and harmony" (Dalai Lama, 1987).

In the United States, Joanna Macy has inspired fellow Buddhists and peoples of other faiths to overcome despair in the face of the great crises facing humanity, and to actively work to build personal and social lives dedicated to compassion, justice and sustainable futures (Macy and Brown, 1998). These exemplary Buddhists have inspired the movement now referred to as "engaged Buddhism" that maintains that Buddhist principles of karma, understanding of suffering, interdependence and compassion require personal transformation and active contributions to a nonviolent, compassionate, just and sustainable world (Queen, 2000).

In Islam, Muslims who advocated or are engaged in nonviolent peacebuilding have gained greater recognition in recent decades. A well-known example is the Pashtoon leader Khan Abdul Ghaffar Khan (1969) who joined Gandhi in the nonviolent struggle for Indian independence. More recent Muslim peacebuilders include the late Dekha Ibrahim Abdi (Kadayifci-Orellana, Ibid.). With other women she founded the Wajir Peace and Development Committee (WPDC) in Kenya that brought government, parliamentary, clan, and religious leaders together to implement a peace agreement that ended a bloody conflict over water and livestock in her region.

Fatwas against terrorism and violent extremism have also been issued by Islamic leaders such as Imam Tahir ul-Qadri in Pakistan who leads the Minhaj-ul-Quran International (Kadayifci-Orellana, Ibid.: 440). In their study of thirty Muslim peacebuilders in the Balkans and the Great Lakes regions of Africa, Abu-Nimer and Kadayifci-Orellana (2008) showed that peacebuilders drew on Islamic values such as the unity of all humankind, compassion and mercy, justice, forgiveness, social responsibility, as well as indigenous conflict mechanisms and traditional respect for religious elders to reconcile conflicting parties, heal traumas, and challenge traditional structures that promote conflict and injustices.

Jewish efforts to build positive peace have usually been ignored in the global news media. For example, the religious Zionist peace camp "utilized the universalist and peace symbols associated with the holiday of Sukkot, Tabernacles, and the actual booth that every religious Jew constructs outside his or her house, to be a place of Israeli/Arab encounter" (Gopin, 2004). Since 2000, Jews and Muslims have also engaged in a ritual form of reconciliation by chanting *Shalom* and *Salaam* simultaneously every Friday above the area of their respective holy sites. A prominent Jewish organization established in 1998, Rabbis for Human Rights, has mobilized rabbis from diverse traditions to condemn human rights violations in Israel, including house demolitions, land evictions, and curfews experienced by Palestinians (Aschermann, 1999).

FIGURE 4.4: Rabbi Arik Ascherman of Rabbis for Human Rights who campaign to stop house demolitions on the West Bank, October 2012. Wikimedia Commons (Public Domain).

Newer religions have also drawn on their principles, doctrines and beliefs to build a culture of peace. In Sikhism, for example, the values and principles of sharing, selfless service, non-discrimination, and social justice, enunciated by the Gurus, are reflected in the provision of *langar* or free food to everyone. Sikh leaders and followers have also been inspired by Guru Nanak's devotion to interfaith understanding, and participate actively in interfaith dialogue organization and activities (see below).

The Baha'i faith has also actively promoted peacebuilding based on its key belief in the unification of all the peoples of the world in one universal family and the parallel concept of world citizenship (Universal House of Justice, 1985). Baha'i followers worldwide have therefore undertaken grassroots local and international peacebuilding and peace education projects (Gervais, 2004). These include school-based community development in war-ravaged areas of Bosnia; training Guyanese youth groups to prevent alcohol and drug abuse, suicide, HIV/AIDS and domestic violence; eliminating corporal punishment in Haitian schools; and training peer educators to teach street children nonviolence and conflict resolution.

The Soka Gakkai International (SGI) is the world's largest lay Buddhist organization. Inspired by the humanistic philosophy of Japan's Nichiren Buddhism, SGI "promotes peace, culture and education centered on respect for the dignity of life" and "a commitment to dialogue and nonviolence." In this century SGI President Daisaku Ikeda has published peace proposals for nuclear abolition, environmental protection, and strengthening the United Nations. SGI has collaborated with numerous faith institutions and civil society organizations for a nuclear-free world in conferences, symposia, exhibitions, and by lobbying governments and the United Nations (SGI, 2016).

This brief and selective sampling of the multitude of ways that believers have contributed to peacebuilding demonstrates that, contrary to the widespread public view of religions as a major cause of extremism, ethnic violence, terrorism, and war, more often than not, faith communities and organizations as well as religious individuals have been building a more peaceful world in the modern era. The "peace" these modern peacebuilders seek to achieve is much more than a world without warfare. A holistic concept of peace requires social justice, sustainable development, and nonviolent methods of resolving serious political conflicts. Like their secular counterparts with whom they often work, religious peacebuilders have been creating alternatives to political orders that employ force and the threat of violence to resolve all types of conflict from those arising out of interpersonal relationships to disputes between nations.

SOCIAL JUSTICE

A multi-dimensional and holistic concept of peace also means a world where all other forms of political, economic, social, cultural, and environmental violence are overcome. One metaphor of a culture of peace represents peace as a six-petal flower, comprised of six themes for building peace: dismantling a culture of war; living with justice and compassion; promoting human rights and responsibilities; building intercultural understanding; respect and solidarity; and living in harmony with the earth and cultivating inner peace (Toh, 2004).

As this image of peace suggests, in the twenty-first century, peacebuilding involves much more than opposition to war and dismantling a culture of militarism. Diverse religions and faiths teach a moral duty to seek justice and act with compassion. As Christians often affirm, there can be no peace without justice. Christ's Sermon on the

Mount is just one of many biblical passages affirming the central principle of social justice: that everyone should be able to meet their basic needs with dignity (DeYoung, 2012). Over the past century, various papal and church teachings have called for social justice (Dorr, 2013). Pope Leo XIII's *Rerum Novarum* focused attention on the exploitation of workers. Pius XI's *Quadragesimo anno* called on capitalists to promote social justice. Pope John XXIII laid the foundations for establishing a preferential "option for the poor." Pope Paul VI's *Populorum Progressio* significantly reconsiders the Western development model in order to address the root causes of poverty. Latin American bishops and clergy who catalyzed the emergence of liberation theology clearly articulated the preferential option for the poor, arguing the necessity of overcoming structural injustices and the conscientization of the poor to transform local, national, and global socio-economic systems (Gutierrez, 1988; Boff and Boff, 1987). Pope Francis emphatically reiterated the social teachings of the Catholic Church at the World Economic Forum, stating:

> We cannot remain silent in the face of the suffering of millions of people whose dignity is wounded, nor can we continue to move forward as if the spread of poverty and injustice has no cause. It is a moral imperative, a responsibility that involves everyone, to create the right conditions to allow each person to live in a dignified manner. By rejecting a "throwaway" culture and a mentality of indifference, the entrepreneurial world has enormous potential to effect substantial change by increasing the quality of productivity, creating new jobs, respecting labour laws, fighting against public and private corruption and promoting social justice, together with the fair and equitable sharing of profits.
>
> —2018

Judaism also upholds justice at the core of its teachings, and together with compassion, requires all Jews to share resources to uphold the dignity of all peoples (Schwarz, n.d.; Yanglowitz, 2014). Similarly, Buddha emphasized the need for all members of a society to receive sufficient remuneration for their work in order to live at a sufficient material level (Buddhadasa Bhikkhu et al., 2010). The principle of non-attachment includes rejecting greed (over-consumption or over-consumerism in modern terms) to enable equitable sharing of the world's resources among all peoples. In Islam, believers should develop a commitment to social justice and equality, including equitable distribution of wealth, among all members of a community (Baidhawy, 2012). Recognizing the principle of social justice shared by diverse faiths, the International Labour Office (2012) mobilized many religious institutions in a campaign to promote the rights of workers and social justice.

Regrettably, even though sustained economic growth and advanced technologies have enabled a minority of the world's population to enjoy "high" consumption lifestyles, the majority still suffer from poverty, hunger, and great inequalities within and between nations (Cavanagh & Mander, 2004; Shiva, 2013; Bello, 2009; OXFAM, 2017). Unjust economic and social systems, which reflect the problem of structural violence, disproportionately benefit elite owners of land and capital and wealthy consumers in the Global North and South. Powerful nation states and international financial organizations like the IMF and World Bank play key roles in promoting corporate-led globalization, profit-maximization, and unlimited growth (Shiva, Ibid.; Bello, Ibid.). However, there are increasingly hopeful signs in grassroots struggles, especially in the Global South, that challenge structural violence of dominant development policies by building communities based on social justice principles among rural and urban poor and indigenous peoples (Fisher and Ponniah, 2003; Sen & Waterman, 2009; Mander and Tauli-Corpuz, 2006; Shiva, 2005).

Social justice principles have inspired the resistance of many peoples of diverse religions and faiths. Faith leaders have also increasingly critiqued the dominant paradigm of corporate-led globalization. Pope John Paul II (2001) insisted that "globalization must serve solidarity and the common good." Pope Francis has called for decisive action to "put the economy at the service of people. Human beings and nature must not be at the service of money. Let us say NO to an economy of exclusion and inequality, where money rules, rather than serves" (Francis, 2017). Engaged Buddhists like Sulak Sivaraksa (2009) offer a Buddhist economic philosophy and framework for alternative just people-centered forms of sustainable development.

The Basic Christian Communities and nonviolent liberation theology movements have helped rural and urban poor peoples in the Global South to gain land, adequate housing, dignified work, basic social services, and other social needs (Padilla, 1987; Nessan, 2012). Social justice-oriented Christians have also been involved in prominent campaigns to forgive international debts, monitor the ethics of transnational corporations, initiate fair trade agreements that allow Global South producers and workers an equitable share of revenues, and convince citizens of the Global North to support policies aimed at making the economic world order just (Jones, 2013; Reed, 2001). Similarly, engaged Buddhists, Hindus, Jains, Daoists, Jews, and Muslims moved by religious principles of justice and compassion also participate in these campaigns. Notably, engaged Buddhism emphasizes overcoming the materialism embedded in the consumption-driven economic paradigm. Hence, while challenging global inequalities engaged Buddhists contest the ideology of powerful transnational corporations and institutions (Pyles, 2005; Mcleod, 2006). The

FIGURE 4.5: Environmental activist Vandana Shiva, 2013. Amanda Edwards / Contributor / Getty Images.

eco-feminist Hindu peacebuilder, Vandana Shiva (2005) has drawn on her religious values of sharing resources and earth democracy to mobilize India's rural poor in nonviolent conflicts with agribusiness giants and local elites aimed at building more just, self-reliant, and sustaining communities.

Another Hindu reform activist, Swami Agnivesh (2005) has worked for decades to overcome the discrimination of India's untouchability and caste system, while championing women's equality, religious tolerance, and reconciliation with Muslims. In Sri Lanka, the NGO called Sarvodaya Shramadama draws inspiration from teachings of the Buddha and Mahatma Gandhi to provide grassroots community development and conflict resolution programs in over 3,000 villages based on the principles of truth (*satya*), nonviolence (*avihimsa*) and selflessness (*pararthkami*) (Bond, 2005).

SUSTAINABLE DEVELOPMENT AND FUTURES

It is now widely recognized by people and governments around the world that humanity faces an unprecedented ecological crisis that, if not soon resolved, threatens our survival and that of many other species (Union of Concerned Scientists, n.d.; Klein, 2014; Shiva, 2013; Worldwatch Institute, 2017). Pollution, soil degradation, desertification, deforestation, ozone depletion, and loss of biodiversity are now compounded by accelerated climate change that brings increasing temperatures, weather extremes, and rising sea levels. Building peace also means living peaceably with our environment and all other species and not committing ecological violence. Religions and faith communities worldwide are inspiring and mobilizing their followers to contribute to the building of sustainable futures. They are reawakening the environmental conscience of their religions and faiths, revitalizing traditions that can be described as ecological wisdom and green theology.

There is considerable common ground among religions and faiths with respect to the principle of interdependence among all parts of the universe (Alliance of Religions & Conservation, n.d.; Edwards, 2006; Gardner, 2006; Barnhill & Gottleib, 2001; Toh & Cawagas, 2010). Indigenous spiritual traditions embodied in the wisdom of elders have promoted sustainable relationships between people and all other parts of Mother Earth for many thousands of years (Grim, 2001; Knudtson and Suzuki, 1992). Hindu believers recognize the integral connectedness of all beings and parts of the universe which must be accorded deep respect and compassion (Prime, 2006; Chapple and Tucker, 2000). Similarly, Jains are taught to practice *ahimsa* and compassion towards all beings in the universe, while Daoists must live simply in harmony with nature (Chapple, 2003; Miller n.d.; Giradot, Miller and Liu, 2001).

For Buddhists, the core principle of interdependence of all beings is linked to compassion and loving kindness that shapes humanity's peaceful and caring relationship with the environment (Kaza and Craft, 2000; Kaza, 2008; Tucker and William, 1998). Judaism emphasizes the divine interconnectedness of humanity with nature that needs to be protected and sustained (Yaffe & Allen, 2001; Tirosh-Samuelson, 2003). In Christian communities worldwide, the principles of green theology are increasingly affirmed (Berry, 1988; Bernstein, 2005; Bullmore, 1998). In 1979, John Paul II named St. Francis of Assisi the "Patron of Ecology" recognizing his deep love and respect for nature. His namesake Pope Francis issued *Laudato Si* (2015), a papal encyclical that describes care for the environment as a moral responsibility for Catholics. Most importantly, both Christians and Jews have been replacing the old ethics of human "dominion" over the environment that encouraged unsustainable development with a moral duty of ecological stewardship.

Muslims are also increasingly looking to the Prophet's practice of conservation, sustainable development, and resource management as a model for an ecological ethic based on four principles, including *Khalifa* or the responsibility principle of trusteeship (*amanah*) for the well-being of humanity and all nature (Foltz, Denny and Baharuddin, 2003; Dien, 2000). Among Sikhs and Baha'i, doctrines of environmental care are being fostered by doctrines, individual and institutional practices, and sustainable development projects (Grewal, 2014; Singh, 2011; Dahl, n.d.; Landau, 2002). Furthermore, among many believers, renewed traditions of environmental stewardship have been strengthened by other principles that contribute to sustainability such as living simply and searching for inner peace in Hinduism and Jainism; overcoming greed and attachments in Buddhism; and seeking to live frugally with moderation and harmony with nature in Daoism.

In recent decades, motivated by "green" theology and ecological sensitivity, diverse religious organizations and communities have developed nonviolent strategies and programs to save planet Earth and promote sustainable futures. For example, Christians, Jews, Buddhists, and Hindus have acted in solidarity with indigenous peoples worldwide to challenge corporate-led and national or local elite-controlled mining, logging, and agribusiness operations that destroy local environments and disrupt the lives of local, especially indigenous, communities. In India, Vandana Shiva and fellow environmental activists have taught marginalized rural communities to draw on Hindu and indigenous beliefs and practices to build a just and sustainable "Earth Democracy" that rejects globalized, corporate-led agribusiness-controlled monocultures and export-oriented systems of food production. Muslim communities and NGOs have enhanced sustainable development via organic farming, preserving island marine parks for eco-fishing, issuing *fatwas* to stop illegal logging, forest burning and mining, and establishing zero waste/carbon habitats (Kaitlin, 2008). In many countries, programs to establish Church-controlled green spaces and infrastructure are addressing climate change. The Living Churchyards and Cemetery Project (UK) redesigns churchyards and cemeteries to benefit wildlife, and the Canadian Faith and the Common Good "Greening Sacred Spaces program" rejects plastics and promotes recycling, renewable energy, and fair trade products (Faith and the Common Good, 2008).

HUMAN RIGHTS

A holistic culture of peace promotes the human rights of all people. Peaceable relationships among individuals and groups depend on shared commitments to protect human rights from the indignities and pain of violations. However, it is clear that during the modern era there have been frequent instances in which religious doctrines and faith traditions have been invoked to promote and justify violations of human rights. Today, as we have already seen, many religions and faith communities are committed to social justice and sustainable economic development. Similarly, many faith communities are drawing on core beliefs and values to challenge violations of civil and political rights that include extrajudicial killing, torture, cruel punishments, and the death penalty, as well as war-related violence against civilians. These efforts are relatively uncontroversial. But when it comes to recognizing the full human rights of women, as well as lesbians, gay, bisexual, and transgendered people (LGBT), and the right to abortions and birth control, serious conflicts and even violence have erupted within religious communities around the world.

Undoubtedly, the dominant interpretations of sacred texts in many religious and faith traditions have often supported patriarchal attitudes and social relationships. Even when acknowledging the core principle of human equality, discrimination against women has been and continues to be supported by scriptures and religious institutions (Crandall, 2012; Furlan, 2009; Engineer, 2008; Shukla-Bhatt, 2009). Patriarchy has sometimes led believers to reject their own institutional affiliation. However, there are expanding groups of women and feminist theologians who question their faith's patriarchal structures and relationships and who advocate for gender-justice transformations, especially through critical re-interpretations of scriptures and holy texts, as well as by campaigning for reform of religious laws and prevention of gender-based violence (Sunder, 2012; Tahmasesebi, 2012; Reuther, 1992; Gross, 1996; Barlas, 2001; Salem, 2013; Anwar, 2001; Kaybryn and Nidadavolu, 2012). In some countries, discrimination experienced by women religious or clergy within some faith communities, such as preventing women's ordination in some Christian churches or the proscription on full ordination of nuns in some Buddhist traditions (e.g. Theravada, Tibetan), has become a public issue. Gradually, while still facing many obstacles, women religious with the support of male counterparts and new interfaith networks have been empowering themselves in ways that are consistent with core faith principles of equality and justice (Ehrlich, 2017; International Network of Engaged Buddhists, 2013; Women's Ordination Conference, n.d.; Johnson, 2011).

Volatile tensions between religious communities and secular proponents of human rights have been rising over recent extensions of human rights protections to LGBT people, including the affirmation of LGBT rights by the UN Human Rights Council

FIGURE 4.6: Asia-Pacific Interfaith Symposium: Women, Faith, and a Culture of Peace; Multi-Faith Centre, Griffith University, Brisbane, Australia February 2008. Toh Swee-Hin photo collection.

(Human Rights Watch, 2016). The doctrines of many religions reject homosexuality and LGBT gender identities resulting in prejudices, exclusions, and even violence. There are, however, still emerging movements within these faiths for theological and institutional respect for sexual and gender diversity (Siker, 2006; Haverluck, 2017; Mackenzie, Falcon and Rahman, Martin, 2017; Jama, 2013; Murphy, 2012). Witte and Green (2012) have shown that various faiths or religions possess beliefs and principles, as well as ethical, moral and spiritual guidelines that complement universal human rights. Nonetheless, overcoming resistance to gender and sexual discriminations will be a long and difficult task. Clearly, an open dialogue between secular human rights discourses and religion or faith-based understandings and practices is necessary in order for the tensions to be resolved peaceably. Increasingly too, the problem of sexual abuse of children by clergy, most notably the Catholic Church, has highlighted the urgent need for its leaders to take action to protect young believers and to hold offending clergy accountable for their crimes (Terry, 2015; Goodstein and Otterman, 2018).

A peaceful society and world requires religious freedom that is practiced in ways that do not violate the freedom of religious belief or non-belief of others. There are still in the twenty-first century many places where believers are not allowed freely to practice their faith. Violations include blocking access to places of worship, restrictions on religious dress and symbols, denying persons the freedom to leave a faith or convert without coercion, discrimination in public places, and vilification in public pronouncements (Taylor, 2012; Evans, 2012; Ghanea, 2012; Lerner, 2012). Societies that demean the religions of some of their own citizens may also frame war in religious terms. In a century when we still hear wars called "crusades" and "jihads," all faiths and religions need to promote those core principles and values within their doctrines that accept diversity and inclusiveness and reject all forms of discrimination.

INTERFAITH DIALOGUE

Finally, when exploring the links between peace, nonviolence, and religions, it is important to examine whether and how different religions and faiths can interact with each other based on the principles of nonviolence, respect, understanding, openness, inclusiveness, love, kindness, and compassion found in their doctrines and teachings. In the modern era, many conflicts involving different faiths and religions grow out of a lack of understanding and from prejudices that encourage mistrust, discrimination, enmity, and even hatred. The growing modern movement known as interreligious dialogue, or more often as interfaith dialogue, addresses this serious problem (Cornille, 2013; Chia, 2016; Smock, 2002). A leading interfaith dialogue theologian, Hans Kung (2008) has made the stakes clear. "There will be no peace among the nations without peace among the religions," Kung wisely observes, and "There will be no peace among the religions without dialogue among the religions."

The United Nations has been an important player in the promotion of interfaith dialogue. UNESCO's Barcelona Declaration on the Role of Religion in the Promotion of a Culture of Peace states, "In human history, religious traditions and ethical ideals have frequently been used to justify wars and injustices, but the real message behind religious and ethical beliefs is unerringly directed at peace and fraternity" (UNESCO, 1994). Since 1994, the United Nations General Assembly has approved resolutions and sponsored meetings calling for interreligious dialogue, including in 2007 the first "High-Level Dialogue on Interreligious and Intercultural Understanding and Cooperation for Peace" that supported "the promotion of tolerance, understanding and universal respect on matters of freedom of religion or belief and cultural diversity." Since 2010, the first week of February has been designated the UN's World Interfaith Harmony Week. Today many religious or faith-based NGOs and civil society groups are highly visible actors at the United Nations (Carrette and Miall, 2017).

Interfaith dialogue contributes to peacebuilding first by facilitating interactions among peoples of different religions or faiths that promote mutual understanding based on the values of trust, respect, goodwill, and harmony. Clearly, participants engage in interfaith dialogue because they share an openness to listening to others, and hold an inclusive rather than an exclusivist view of their religious beliefs. Interfaith dialogue requires acknowledgment and critical respect for differences in doctrine and practices. The experience of interfaith dialogue worldwide shows that believers of diverse religions have been able to find common ground in terms of values, principles and spirituality. In practice, four levels or forms of interfaith dialogue have been developed: the dialogue of theological exchange; the dialogue of religious experience (e.g. visiting, observing and/or participating in rituals and practices in places of worship); the dialogue of life (e.g. informal gatherings, sharing human concerns, problems, joys, and sorrows); and the dialogue of action (collaborative activities for "integral development and liberation of people" (Pontifical Council for Interreligious Dialogue, Dialogue and Proclamation, 1991). Certainly, the first three forms of dialogue contribute to building greater harmony and peaceful relationships between peoples of different religions. But it is the fourth form, the dialogue of action, which can have a direct substantive impact on peacebuilding. When people of different religions or faiths find common or shared values, they are able to move from dialogue to action joining hands, heart and spirit in cooperative activities aimed at overcoming cultures of violence, injustice, discrimination and unsustainability.

Interfaith dialogue has required the development of appropriate methodologies and guidelines (Abu-Nimer, 2002; Swidler, 2004) and led to the organization of global institutions. The first official gathering of different religions from various countries to share their visions and philosophies was the 1893 World's Congress of Religions hosted by Chicago's churches (World's Parliament of Religions, 1893). It was not until a century later that this historic interfaith gathering was revived in Chicago as the first Parliament of the World's Religions (PWR). The PWR was "created to cultivate harmony among the world's religious and spiritual communities and foster their engagement with the world and its guiding institutions in order to achieve a peaceful, just, and sustainable world." (Parliament of the World's Religions, n.d.). Since then the PWR has convened five times (in Capetown, Barcelona, Melbourne, Salt Lake City, and Toronto). The PWR gathers members of diverse religions, faiths, and spirituality traditions to learn from each other's wisdom, overcome religious fears, hatred, and religiously motivated violence, act on common religious principles to build a "global ethic" promoting economic and social justice, nonviolence, reconciliation, and promote sustainable futures (Parliament of the World's Religions, 1993).

Prior to the first PWR in 1993, several major religions and faiths had already organized the international interfaith organization called Religions for Peace with the vision of respecting religious differences while celebrating a common humanity. Religions for Peace has created multi-religious partnerships for helping to resolve armed conflicts, promote democracy and freedom, heal HIV/AIDS sufferers, protect the environment, and empower youth and women in peacebuilding projects. Among its many initiatives, Religions for Peace has sponsored a mediation dialogue among warring factions in Sierra Leone, reconciliation efforts in Iraq, and assistance to children affected by Africa's AIDS pandemic. Its Global Women of Faith Network increases the agency of women of faith working to stop warfare, prevent gender-based violence against women and girls, and ending female poverty (Religions for Peace, n.d.). Religions for Peace holds a world assembly about every five years. The Eighth Assembly in Kyoto focused on the theme of "shared security" in which all sectors of every society acknowledge common vulnerabilities and assume collective responsibility to address them (Religions for Peace, 2006). Religious communities are also called to resist and confront any misuse of religion for violent purposes; become effective participants in conflict transformation, foster justice and sustainable development; and hold governments accountable for the commitments they make to improve the lives of their citizens.

In 2000, activists formed a network of grassroots-based interfaith cooperation circles calling it the United Religions Initiative (URI). URI now involves hundreds of interfaith "cooperation circles" in over seventy countries. They engaged in peacebuilding projects such as a fair trade cooperative of Jewish, Muslim, and Christian coffee farmers in Uganda; a summer training workshop program on Muslim–Christian dialogue for nation building in the Philippines; an interfaith encounter group of Muslim and Jewish mothers and daughters in Israel; and a Peruvian interfaith cooperation and organic food production workshop (United Religions Initiative, n.d.).

Apart from the work of these global interfaith organizations, there are many other positive local, national, regional, and international exemplars of interfaith dialogue contributing to peacebuilding outcomes. The global campaign to abolish nuclear weapons promoted by concerned member states of the United Nations and a wide range of civil society organizations and NGOs also has the support of many faith, ecumenical, and interfaith organizations including the World Council of Churches, Soka Gakkai International (SGI), Pax Christi, Quakers UK, and Religions for Peace. Other Buddhist and Muslim organizations have also collaborated with the International Campaign to Abolish Nuclear Weapons (ICAN) (World Council of Churches, 2015; SGI, 2014). The awarding of the Nobel Peace Prize for 2017 to ICAN affirmed the contributions of numerous groups to the campaign for a nuclear-free world, including diverse faiths and interfaith organizations (Finh and Thurlow, 2017). Many faith and interfaith organizations have also cooperated to support the global Arms Trade Treaty that, although limited in its restrictions on conventional weapons, finally entered into force in December 2014 (United Nations, 2013). The Inter-faith Perspective in Realizing the Role of Women Peacemakers in the Implementation of UNSCR 1325 met in Jakarta in 2014 to advance the implementation of UN Security Council Resolution 1325 that had been approved in 2000 to affirm the important role of women in the prevention and resolution of conflicts and in peacebuilding (Regional Interfaith Network, 2014).

In 2008, the former Saudi King Abdullah Bin Abdulaziz initiated a World Conference on Dialogue in Madrid attended by nearly 300 religious, political, and cultural leaders from fifty different countries. It called for interfaith dialogue to "defeat extremist viewpoints, find common cause and foster a spirit of peace" (Initiative for Interfaith Dialogue, 2011). This meeting was followed in 2012 by the establishment of the International Centre for Interreligious and Intercultural Dialogue in Vienna (KAICIID, n.d.).

Asia-Pacific Regional Interfaith meetings have been exemplary. The meetings have convened seven times since 2004 in various Asia-Pacific countries to promote peace and cooperation throughout this huge and diverse region. The 2009 meeting in Perth led in 2010 to the creation of a more permanent Regional Interfaith Network to sustain the dialogue between major gatherings (Regional Interfaith Network, n.d.).

The Multi-Faith Centre (now the Centre for Interfaith Cultural Dialogue) of Griffith University in Australia, established in 2002, also promotes interfaith dialogue that promotes a culture of peace. It sponsors numerous forums, workshops, conferences, exhibitions, sacred music concerts, training of adults and youth, and the integration of interfaith understanding in school curricula. The Centre has consistently emphasized the need for interfaith dialogue that builds a holistic culture of peace that overcomes Islamophobia, expresses solidarity with refugees and indigenous peoples, and promotes gender equality. It organizes interfaith commemorations of United Nations International Days, and active collaborations for disarmament, local/global justice, human rights, cultural respect, sustainable futures, and cultivating inner peace (Toh and Cawagas, 2006).

Many other interfaith organizations, networks or groups at local and national levels have undertaken actions to resolve and transform bloody conflicts and build more peaceful societies. For example, the Acholi Religious Leaders for Peace Initiative worked to mediate the conflict in Northern Uganda, during which the Lord's Resistance Army had forced thousands of children and youth to become child soldiers or sex slaves (Ochola, 2006). In Nigeria, former armed enemies Imam Muhammad Ashafa and Pastor James Wufe agreed to cease fighting and started a Muslim–Christian interfaith dialogue center to build peace in a region that had seen hundreds of Muslims and Christians killed (Ashafa and Wuye, 1999).

The Silsilah Dialogue Movement has for over three decades brought Christians and Muslims into dialogue that develops understanding of their respective religious traditions and cooperation in building a just and sustainable peace on the southern Philippine island of Mindanao. Its projects have included helping each other rebuild destroyed churches or schools and the creation of interfaith social enterprises to promote traditional medicines (D'Ambra, 2008). Yehuda Stolov founded the Interfaith Encounter Association in Israel in 2001 to involve Christian, Jewish, and Muslim Israelis and Palestinians in dialogues to understand their faiths and transcend mutual prejudices and fears in the context of lived experiences in the Israeli–Palestine conflict (Furnan, 2011). In January 2002, more than a dozen senior Christian, Jewish and Muslim leaders from the Holy Land met in Alexandria, Egypt and concluded an unprecedented joint declaration pledging to work together for a just and lasting peace (United States Institute of Peace, 2002).

In the United States, numerous grassroots interfaith groups and NGOs have helped to enhance public understanding of faith diversity, creating collaborative actions to build a more peaceful society. Exemplars include the Interfaith Center of New York that "works to overcome prejudice, violence, and misunderstanding by activating the power of the city's grassroots religious and civic leaders and their communities," and the Interfaith Youth Core which seeks to build "an ecosystem of people and campuses designed to make interfaith cooperation the norm, while creating the next generation of interfaith leaders" (Patel & Meyer, 2015).

As noted earlier, contemporary peacebuilders identify as structural violence the ever-growing gap between rich and poor that produces the poverty, hunger and a lack of basic necessities that afflict billions of people around the world. Many interfaith groups have been trying to alleviate suffering and eliminate these forms of structural violence. They have been especially active in regions where people suffer inordinately from a lack of resources that would improve their lives. Interfaith groups have succeeded in raising awareness and initiated projects to help people suffering from the HIV/AIDS pandemic (Global AIDS Interfaith Alliance, n.d.; Ecumenical Advocacy Alliance, n.d). An Interreligious Campaign in Mozambique has reduced malaria and developed programs

FIGURE 4.7: Imam Muhammed Ashafa and Pastor James Wuye of Nigeria at the eighth annual gala of the We Are Family Foundation, New York City, October 2010. Jerritt Clark / Contributor / Getty Images.

for children and maternal health (Inter-Religious Program Against Malaria, n.d.). Interfaith groups have also created alliances for integrity against corruption (Browne, 2004). The Global Network of Religions for Children initiated by Arigatou International has mobilized different religions and faiths to work on overcoming child poverty and protecting children's rights. There is also an International Interfaith Investment Group which seeks to contribute to a just and sustainable society by "promoting faith-consistent investments in the spirit of interfaith and international dialogue and cooperation" (Marshall and Van Saanen, 2007).

Interfaith organizations and networks have been at the forefront of local and global campaigns for addressing the crisis of climate change. For example, the Alliance of Religions and Conservation (ARC) has been helping the major religions to develop environmental programs based on their own core teachings, beliefs, and practices while creating alliances between faith communities and conservation groups. ARC has also developed a partnership with UNDP to facilitate major faiths in designing their Seven and Eight Year Plans for Generational Change on climate change and the environment. Many interfaith organizations have collaborated when lobbying national governments and international agencies to take decisive actions to overcome the climate crisis (The Forum on Religion and Ecology at Yale, n.d.; Toh & Cawagas, 2010).

In sum, through interfaith dialogue many religious and faith communities worldwide have been contributing to expanding and strengthening the role of religious people in building peace through activist nonviolent strategies. Of course, much work remains to be accomplished. The religious influence in many conflicts is complex and even contradictory. Interfaith dialogue on its own should not be seen as a panacea. As Braybrooke (1998), Kadayifci-Orellana (2013) and other interfaith dialogue proponents have noted, a number of obstacles still need to be overcome in practicing interfaith dialogue. One challenge is that not all leaders and believers are convinced that their religion needs to be open to dialogue and mutual respect for other faiths. "Traditionalists" and "exclusivists" still resist efforts to bring them into the interfaith dialogue circle. Minority voices and spirituality movements also need to be recognized, and dialogue with atheists encouraged. Gender disparities are another significant challenge. Women should equitably contribute their perspectives and wisdom in interfaith dialogue and peacebuilding. Most importantly, due to varying interpretations of religious doctrines, truths, and perspectives, sensitivity to differences among believers needs to be a foundation for interfaith dialogue. However, as this chapter has emphasized, such sensitivity will need to be underpinned by values and principles of peace, active nonviolence, justice, sustainability, and human rights and dignity.

CONCLUSION

This chapter has shown that religion and faith have played complex parts in war and violent conflicts and in peacemaking and peacebuilding. Religion and faith have been directly or indirectly complicit in promoting war and violence in the modern era, but they have also played a very important role in creating a holistic framework for a global culture of peace. There is a deep pool of principles, values, and teachings that have inspired and enabled religious and faith communities to build a culture of peace and nonviolence. In the twenty-first century there are now growing numbers of diverse examples of the peacebuilding visions, missions, and practices of believers and faith-based organizations. The challenges of creating a world based on principles of peace, justice, human rights, inclusivity, sustainable futures, and a spirituality embedded in both inner peace and social peace are undeniably great. All peoples, communities, and nations as well as civil society organizations and movements need to be engaged in this task. The good news is that a growing number of peoples of faith, religion and spirituality traditions are affirming with their minds, heart, and spirit the vital responsibility to be an "engaged" part of this project for the well-being of humanity and planet Earth.

CHAPTER FIVE

Representations of Peace

RUNE OTTOSEN AND RONALD EDSFORTH

This chapter differs significantly from its counterparts in the other volumes of this collection that focus on representations of peace, because it has been written in the historical era on which it is focused. Thus, like all the other chapters in Volume 6, it does not (because it cannot) benefit from a long historical perspective and the accumulated scholarly work of earlier generations. However, historians of our modern era like us have access to immense and unprecedented quantities of data and scholarship about their subject matter thanks to modern archival techniques and the ever-greater efficiencies of global communications networks. These data include countless modern representations of peace, many of them still produced in older forms like hand-drawn and printed pages, prayers, poetry, pamphlets, posters, drawings and cartoons, as well as paintings, sculpture, and architecture; and many more in modern media including photographs, audio recordings, film, and video, as well as in uniquely modern additions to the built environment like peace museums and peace parks.[1]

I. REPRESENTATIONS OF PEACE IN "THE GLOBAL COMMONS"

Since 1920 activists and artists produced countless representations of peace for local, national, and global peace organizations, movements, education programs, as well as anti-war protests, disarmament demonstrations, and non-violent political movements. Global flows of representations of peace peaked during the early Cold War and 1980s when fears of nuclear warfare between the United States and Soviet Union were rising, and just before and during international wars like those in Indochina 1961–75 and Iraq in 2003–2007. Overall, the sheer number and diversity of representations of peace produced and archived since 1920 is without precedent. Moreover, the impact of many of these representations has been multiplied many times over because they have been reproduced, widely disseminated, and continue to be in circulation in global political networks, in national and local news media, as well as on social media networks with billions of users.

Scholarly mastery of all these modern representations of peace seems to us an impossible task. Yet if you are modern consumers of the news like us, you will surely recognize and understand the meaning of many of these images because they have become key parts of

FIGURE 5.1: Peace sign designed by Gerald Holtom for Ban the Bomb March London to Aldermaston, April 1958. Bentley Archive / Popperfoto / Contributor / Getty Images.

a symbolic language that identifies and links peace activists around the world. The peace symbol originally designed by Gerald Holtom that is so often displayed during non-violent anti-war protests and peace demonstrations is one such representation.

During Easter 1958 the recently organized Campaign for Nuclear Disarmament (CND) led a small march fifty-two miles from Trafalgar Square in London to the Atomic Weapons Research Establishment in Aldermaston. Gerald Holtom, an artist, offered the CND sketches of a logo he wanted the marchers to place on banners and signs. Holtom's simple design combines the semaphore signals for N and D inside a circle. It appeared in photographs of the CND disarmament march in newspapers at the time. Soon, Holtom's design and increasing numbers of variations of it began appearing in anti-nuclear weapons and peace demonstrations throughout the world. During worldwide protests against America's war in Vietnam in the late 1960s, it became known as simply "the peace symbol" (Rigby 1998). It remains today perhaps the world's most widely recognized sign of public commitment to peace politics.

Visual images of people marching in nonviolent opposition to war and nuclear weapons and demonstrating for democracy, human rights, and social justice are among the most important and inspiring modern representations of peace. Sociologist Charles Tilly has described how in the twentieth century successful social movements developed different combinations of an ever-growing repertoire of non-violent political actions that build "concerted public representations of WUNC: worthiness, unity, numbers, and commitment" (2004: 3–5). Over time, many public displays of WUNC—such as sober demeanor, presence of dignitaries, marching with banners, singing, presenting petitions, braving bad weather, and standing up to police and troops—became transnational signs understood

FIGURE 5.2: Philippines President Corazon Acquino salutes the crowd celebrating the victorious People Power Revolution, March 2, 1986. The Asahi Shimbun / Contributor / Getty Images.

by people all over the world. In the early 1980s these and other signs of WUNC were prominently represented in photographic, video, and film images of Solidarity in Poland, the nuclear freeze movement in North America and Western Europe, and the nonviolent "People Power" revolution in the Philippines. At the time stirring images of the multitude confronting tanks in People Power demonstrations were disseminated worldwide in newspapers, magazines, and television news broadcasts. They undoubtedly inspired and informed the strategies and tactics used by the non-violent revolutionaries that toppled Communist regimes from Czechoslovakia to Mongolia a few years later (Karantnycky 2005; Schock 2005: 56–90; Ackerman and Duvall 2000: 421–68). And they continue to circulate in uniquely modern global communications networks.

The expansion of the Internet and the World Wide Web in this century has enabled the creation of distributed network structures located in what is popularly identified "cyberspace" and "virtual reality," and that has been somewhat controversially described as a new "global commons" (Hardt and Negri 2000: 300–303).[2] In this new virtual commons, people sharing affinities and concerns find each other and create networked communities without ever meeting in an actual physical place. The politics and moral character of these virtual communities are as varied, wonderful, and frightening as the people in them. Peace, human rights, democracy, sustainable development, and nonviolent political strategies are the bases for some of these networks, but so too are the promotion of all forms of violence, terrorism, racism, sexism, and environmental destruction. Although the companies and governments that promoted the rapid development of internet access, online businesses, and social media promoters promised the new communications technology would empower people, spread and strengthen democracy, and thus make the world more peaceful, we now recognize that this "cyber-utopian" promise was just one of many possible outcomes (Morozov 2011: xii–xvii; Silverman 2015: 5–7).

Nonetheless, as synchronization of massive global anti-war protests in 2003 demonstrated, it seems something we might call *a global peace culture* has been forming in the new global commons.[3] Global peace culture is represented in a host of interconnected networked progressive movements for disarmament and demilitarization, democracy, racial and gender equality, social and economic justice, and environmental protection. Peace is the umbrella under which they gather because as Hardt and Negri have noted, "The grievance against war tends in fact to become the summary of all grievances . . . Peace is the common demand and necessary condition to address global problems" (Hardt and Negri 2004: 284). Certainly that is what the visual content of global news seems to have been telling us.

In the new media-rich environment of the twenty-first century, "peace and war reflect and follow a discourse that is to a large extent shaped by images" (Moll 2008: 102). One reason is simply that we remember visual impressions better than verbal ones (Magnussen and Greenlee: 1999). When most of us recall recent conflicts, visual representations of news media coverage of warfare are usually more salient and detailed than what we read in texts, and the narrative of war they form clearer and more prominent than the narrative of peace. The Associated Press (AP) photographer Nick Ut's picture of Phan Thi Kim Phuc, the nine-year-old girl running screaming along a road after being hit by American napalm on June 8, 1972, is an example of an iconic image that informs our understanding of the Vietnam War. Newspapers around the world printed this AP photograph the next

FIGURE 5.3: Children fleeing their homes, Phan Thi Kim Phuc on right, after napalm bombing of Trang Bang, South Vietnam, June 8, 1972. Bettmann / Contributor / Getty Images.

day. It was widely viewed again when it was awarded the Pulitzer Prize and when it was named World Press Photograph of the Year, and it continues nearly a half-century later to generate interest and controversy as the image of "the napalm girl" that circulates in the global commons.[4]

With its focus on the pain and suffering of the most innocent of civilian victims, a child, Ut's photo seemed to capture what had become by 1972 the essential character of America's long war in Vietnam. In this image the war appears as a high-tech assault on a peasant country in which civilians suffer the worst casualties. Susan Sontag suggests that press photographs like that of "the napalm girl" even have a "deeper bite" than movies or television since they "freeze-frame" events in a single image. "In an area of information overload," Sontag writes, "the photograph provides a quick way of apprehending something and a compact form of memorizing it" (Sontag 2003). Sontag underlines the role of photography in our collective memories:

> The problem is not that people remember through photographs, but that they remember only through photographs. This remembering through photographs eclipses other forms of understanding and remembering. To remember is, more and more, not to recall a story but to be able to call up a picture.
> —Sontag 2003: 89

In her book *Regarding the Pain of Others*, Sontag discusses how widely circulated visual images of war's victims can mobilize support for anti-war peace policies. She regards publication of Robert Capa's photographs of the Spanish Civil War and World War II in *Life* magazine as an important turning point in the history of photojournalism. The Hungarian born Capa, Henri Cartier-Bresson, and several other prominent photographers founded the photo cooperative Magnum Photos in Paris in 1947. They were drawn together by a commitment to what we recognize in the twenty-first century as an ethical position of peace journalism: Magnum members should be committed to document contemporary conflicts free from chauvinist prejudices (Ottosen 2007).

Magnum Photo's ethics stood against the still common practice of using photographs, cartoons, and other visual elements to bolster the messages of official propaganda in war reporting (Ottosen 1995). Michael Griffin underlines the importance of visual images in the framing of stories in an essay comparing photographs in *Time*, *Newsweek*, and *US News & World Report* published during the 1991 Gulf War, the 2001 invasion of Afghanistan, and the 2003 invasion of Iraq (Griffin 2004). His conclusion stresses the ethnocentric and militaristic framing of these images:

> Photo coverage in the US news-magazines routinely supported Washington's "official" version of events. The American President was prominent in the pictorial coverage, appearing in pictures as a strong and confident leader. US troops, weapons, and military hardware dominated the deceptions, providing an image of a powerful and determined nation ready and able to vanquish its enemies. The enemy itself was reduced to stereotypical emblems. And the subtleties and complications of global economics and foreign affairs remained invisible. Finally, the human and economic costs of war were largely absent from news portrayals.
> —Griffin 2004: 399

Griffin's last point is important: photographic images in themselves will not create attention to human sufferings and create empathy with the victims of war. Representational legitimacy remains tied to power, and mainstream visual images of new wars are still more likely to fit into preexisting patriotic war narratives than contribute to peace-oriented narratives that open opportunities for nonviolent resolutions of conflicts (Ibid.: 400).

An image-driven discourse between narratives of peace and war developed incrementally since the late nineteenth century, but has recently been greatly accelerated by the rapid extension of new decentralized communications and media technologies. Today most of us accumulate in our mind's "pictorial memory" not just the images of remembered personal experiences (like those now also stored on people's smartphones), but also huge and growing reservoirs of mediated images. Frank Moll explains these mediated "representations depict memories of experience rather than experience itself." He continues, "every representation is influenced by the representations of previous events that we are already carrying with us as memories" (Moll: 100–2). In other words, the newest mediated images usually find their meaning as they fit into preexisting narrative frames. Sometimes those images that directly challenge official and mainstream media framing of a war, like that of "the napalm girl," make it into news and because they are subversive, they become an important part of peace politics.

The modern journalistic practice, summed up by American reporters in the phrase "If it bleeds it leads," usually insures war news (along with news of violent crimes, riots, plane crashes, and other bloody events) will be headlined. Nonetheless, fed by different flows of images, we also develop in our expanding pictorial memories narratives of peace. These visual narratives refute longstanding assumptions that most often inform mainstream war reporting including: (a) "our side" is good and the enemy "bad;" (b) the end justifies the means; (c) violence is always significant and decisive in serious political conflicts; and (d) that to think otherwise is naïve. Against these assumptions, the huge increase in the number and diversity of representations of peace work and peace politics now in circulation around the world represents a growing global awareness that modern war is seldom justifiable because it always produces enormous human suffering, and growing global belief that peaceful relations between nations and people are possible and attainable by peaceful means. The video images and photographs of the tens of millions of people who poured into the streets of cities around the world in February and March 2003 to peacefully protest the planned US and British invasion of Iraq displayed the growing geographic extent of these beliefs. Similarly, millions of people earned worldwide respect by showing WUNC and their commitment to nonviolence during the Green Revolution in Iran in 2009 and the Arab Spring revolts two years later, remarkable events that showed how representations of nonviolent People Power politics continued to shape serious political conflicts in some of the world's most repressive countries.

Although the Green Revolution and Arab Spring revolutions failed everywhere but Tunisia, nonviolent revolutions have, since 1945, been far more successful than violent revolutions. Between 1945 and 2005 more than fifty nonviolent revolutions succeeded in replacing governments with more democratic regimes, most of them since 1989 when images and voices of the nonviolent revolutionaries in action were frequently first broadcast (from the Berlin Wall, the Maidan Square in Kiev, etc.) in real time to global audiences and then circulated in global news media. Indeed, creating memorable images and theatrical displays of resistance to authorities for the news media has since Gandhi's day been a standard practice of nonviolent movements (Chenoweth and Stephan 2011: 3–29; Roberts and Ash eds. 2009: 372–84; Schock 2005: 56–90).

People in twenty-first century peace and nonviolent action networks strategically share mediated representations of anti-war politics and peace work. For example, leaders from Otpor!, the nonviolent group in Belgrade that led a successful revolt against Serbian

President Slobodan Milosevic in 2000, taught local Arab Spring leaders how to quickly attract greater numbers of supporters by circulating on social media photographs and video images of small carefully staged theatrical demonstrations (Williams 2012). Today, the ever-growing repertoire of nonviolent strategies and tactics is taught in seminars and posted on the websites of many organizations like the International Center on Nonviolent Conflict (ICNC). Since the 1930s when millions of movie goers around the world watched newsreels showing Gandhi's nonviolent armies resist British authorities, nonviolent activists have been valorized in countless mediated representations of their politics, their courage and sacrifices magnified especially in those images where they are confronted by armed police and troops who attack them with clubs, dogs, gas, rubber bullets, and sometimes deadly force. And leaders of nonviolent movements have received highly visible global honors such as the Nobel Peace Prize, suggesting that their stories, like the stories of traditional heroic warriors, may well endure in the words of Shakespeare's Henry V "from this day until the end of the world."

II. THE NOBEL PEACE PRIZE

The outlines of an emerging global peace culture can be seen reflected in the history of the Nobel Peace Prize, a modern honor of great global significance. The Peace Prize's history illustrates how changes in the definition of peace have enlarged the scope of peace work creating in the process interconnected global networks of scholars, organizations, activists, and policy makers dedicated to eliminating violent conflict in their own societies as well as warfare between nations. The annual announcement of the Nobel Peace Prize and the ceremony in Oslo that honors the new laureate is always an important global news story. Together these stories form a long series of representations of peace encompassing the whole modern era. The Nobel Peace Prize was awarded fifty two times between 1901 and 1972. It has been awarded every year since 1973.[5] By 2017, 131 individuals and twenty-seven organizations had become Nobel Peace Prize laureates.

The history of the Nobel Peace Prize establishes a rough chronology for the evolution of the definition of peace in the modern era. It shows what is recognized and represented as peace work has significantly changed in the modern era.[6] In 1895 Alfred Nobel's will set up a fund that would generate cash prizes for "those who, during the preceding year, shall have conferred the greatest benefit on mankind." Nobel had originally thought to limit the annual prizes to the fields of physics, chemistry, medicine, and literature; but an old friend and leading figure in the contemporary European peace and disarmament movements, Baroness Bertha Von Suttner, convinced him to add peace to the list of fields eligible for Nobel Prizes.[7] Nobel's final will distinguished the Peace Prize from the other Swedish Nobel Prizes, stipulating that a committee named by Norway's parliament, the Storting, would select "the person who shall have done the most or the best work for fraternity between nations, for the abolition or reduction of standing armies, and for the holding and promotion of peace congresses" (www.nobelprize.org/alfred_nobel/will-full.html), and a Norwegian committee has done so ever since. But especially in recent decades the Peace Prize committee has honored many people whose achievements lay in fields that Alfred Nobel and his contemporaries would not have recognized as peace work—including human rights, strategic nonviolence, promoting democracy, economic development, and environmental protection.

Indeed, as a Norwegian lawyer and peace activist, Frederick Heffermehl argues, the Peace Prize committee has frequently violated its legal responsibilities. With its explicit descriptions of just three types of peace work, Nobel's will seems very clear about what he intended to honor. "The prize Nobel established was not for peace in general," Heffermehl insists, it was meant to honor only "work toward the establishment of a peaceful, demilitarized international community through negotiations between nations" (2010: 38–9). Of course, given the fact that a committee appointed by the Norwegian Parliament (Stortinget) makes the award, it is perhaps not surprising that Peace Prize awards have often reflected Norway's foreign policy, particularly since the rules governing selection of members were changed in 1948 to give major political parties control of the five-member committee (Ibid.: 86–9).[8] Since then, the reformed Peace Prize committee has clearly deviated from Alfred Nobel's description of "champions of peace." It has brought new definitions of peace and peace work into its annual deliberations, and increasingly looked beyond Europe and North America.

The Nobel Peace Prize has reflected the increasing integration of old nations and the newer nations that have emerged from the old colonies of the West and Soviet Union, independent nations that did not exist when Nobel wrote his will. Since 1972, thirty Nobel Prize winners have been honored for peace work done in Africa, Asia, Latin America, and the Pacific region. The changing geographic distribution of the Peace Prize laureates reflects some of the most important political developments of the modern era. These include decolonization, movements to empower women in their homelands and secure human rights, democracy, and social justice in every society.

The presentation speeches, the laureates' lectures, the photographs and videos of the annual ceremony reveal other important long-term patterns of Nobel Peace Prize history. The first is a frequent renewal of the Nobel's original commitments to honor and encourage those people and groups that have used diplomacy and negotiations to prevent wars or bring them to an end, promoted disarmament or abolition of certain kinds of weapons, expanded international organizations and international law, and created movements and nongovernmental organizations committed to international peace. Before 1960 there were only a few significant deviations from the pattern of honoring peace work specifically mentioned in Nobel's will. During the eleven years when the World Wars raged, the Nobel Committee awarded only two Peace Prizes, in 1917 and 1944. Both times the honor was bestowed on the International Committee of the Red Cross for its work with prisoners of war.[9] The 1922 Peace Prize laureate was Fridtjof Nansen, who as the League of Nations High Commissioner for Refugees had directed the repatriation of prisoners of war and displaced persons after the Great War and then international humanitarian relief efforts in Russia during its civil war and related famine. In 1938, the Nansen International Office for Refugees of the League of Nations was honored for carrying on Nansen's work, but the 1938 Peace Prize also represented a vote of support for the League at a time when it was failing to counter fascist aggression. These four Peace Prizes show that the Nobel committee has since World War I considered humanitarian work, an activity not specified in Nobel's will, to be eligible for the Peace Prize.

The Peace Prize has often been shared by peace organizations and individuals or associated with the work of those organizations. The 2001 Peace Prize was a good example of this type of pairing. That year the world's most important intergovernmental peace organization, the United Nations, and its General Secretary, Kofi Anan, were named Peace Prize laureates. This kind of joint award recognizes how much individuals have contributed to the peace institutions that have empowered them. Only twice has the Peace Prize been split three ways. In 1994, Yasser Arafat, Simon Peres, and Yitzhak Rabin were selected for their attempts to establish peace in the Middle East by negotiating the

Oslo Accords—a type of peace work that Nobel clearly intended to honor and support. However, the same cannot be said about the 2011 Peace Prize that was split between three laureates—Ellen Sirleaf Johnson and Leymah Gbowee of Liberia, and Tawakkol Karman of Yemen. They received the Peace Prize for, in the words of the presentation, "their nonviolent struggle for the safety of women and for women's rights to full participation in peace building work" (www.nobelprize.org/nobel_prizes/peace/laureates/2011/).

The 2011 laureates are three of only sixteen women to be awarded a Nobel Peace Prize. For many decades after its establishment, the Peace Prize was awarded almost exclusively to men who had founded and led peace organizations, peace organizations themselves, and political leaders who had used their power to prevent war or bring armed conflicts to an end via negotiations, mediation, and arbitration. Disarmament, or at least attempts to control the development and proliferation of new weapons of war, have also been frequently honored by Peace Prizes. Baroness Von Suttner, who was famous for her novel *Lay Down Your Arms* and her efforts to stop Europe's arms race, was awarded the Peace Prize in 1905. She was the first and only woman to be so honored until Jane Addams, a founder and long-time leader of the Women's League for International Peace and Freedom (WILPF) was named a Peace Prize laureate in 1931. Emily Greene Balch, another American leader of the WILPF was awarded the Peace Prize in 1946. Thirty years later Betty Williams and Mairead Corrigan were honored for creating a grassroots nonviolent movement to bring peace to Northern Ireland. The Nobel Peace Prize committee's recognition of women's contributions to peace has expanded in recent decades as new ideas about positive peace were incorporated into their annual deliberations. Since 1976, eleven other women have been awarded Nobel Peace prizes.

The Nobel Peace Prize committee took a long time to begin honoring peace work accomplishments outside of Europe and North America. In 1935 Carlos Saavedra Lamas, the foreign minister of Argentina who helped promote the Kellogg-Briand Pact and the League of Nations in Latin America, and who led a conciliation commission that ended a long war between Bolivia and Paraguay, was honored. But it was not until 1960 that another person from the Global South was awarded a Peace Prize. Since then, scores of former European colonies have won their independence, some through armed revolt and others by nonviolent rebellions. Many of these former colonies have experienced protracted civil wars. The Nobel committee has in recent years more frequently honored individuals and nonviolent political organizations and movements that have worked in postwar peacebuilding projects aimed at ending all too familiar "cycles of violence" that prolong civil conflicts. Even in the modern era it seems, the ancient ethic of the warriors' honor still informs the common practice of rhetorically and visually representing battle deaths in religious terms as blood sacrifices that must be honored by spilling more blood so that, as Abraham Lincoln proclaimed in his Gettysburg Address, "these dead shall not have died in vain" (Ehrenreich 1997: 18–21).

In the early 1960s, the Nobel Prize committee signaled with two unprecedented awards its readiness to recognize and encourage nonviolent revolutions seeking to establish racial equality, democracy, and social justice *within a single society* as modern forms of peace work. They selected Albert Lutuli, a founder of the African National Congress and leader of the non-violent struggle against apartheid in South Africa, as the 1960 Peace Prize laureate. And in 1964 they awarded the Prize to Martin Luther King Jr. for his leadership of the nonviolent struggle for racial equality in the United States. By selecting these black men as laureate the Peace Prize committee broke down the Nobel Peace Prize committee's longstanding color barrier. They also signaled a new willingness to consider the elimination

FIGURE 5.4: Zulu Chief and President of the African National Congress Albert Lutuli accepts the 1960 Nobel Peace Prize. Bettmann / Contributor / Getty Images.

of what contemporary peace researchers were starting to call "structural violence" as forms of peace work necessary to establish true and lasting international peace.

In an unusually long presentation speech, Gunnar Jahn (chairman of the Peace Prize committee from 1941 to 1966) proclaimed in December 1961 what amounted to a radical new interpretation of Nobel's will saying, "Albert John Lutuli's fight has been waged within the borders of his own country; but the issues raised go far beyond them. He brings a message to all who work and strive to establish respect for human rights both within nations and between nations" (www.nobelprize.org/nobel_prizes/peace/laureates/1960/press.html).

Three years later Chairman Jahn reasserted this recently made connection between struggles to protect human rights within a single country and international peace. While acknowledging the geographic limits of Dr. King's work, Jahn explained, "Though Martin Luther King has not personally committed himself to the international conflict, his own struggle is a clarion call to all who work for peace." Stressing the global significance of King's widely publicized nonviolent campaigns for racial equality and social justice, Jahn continued:

> He is the first person in the Western world to have shown us that a struggle can be waged without violence. He is the first to make the message of brotherly love a reality

in the course of his struggle, and he has brought this message to all men, to all nations and races.

www.nobelprizes.org/nobel_prizes/peace/laureates/1964/press.html

Although we cannot know exactly how much widely published photographs and television news coverage of the violent repression by authorities of nonviolent anti-apartheid activists in Sharpeville, South Africa in 1960 and of civil rights workers in the American South in the early 1960s influenced the Peace Prize committee's deliberations, it is significant that Jahn specifically mentioned these events in his presentations of the Nobel Peace Prize to Lutuli and King. Since 1964, the scope of what the Nobel Prize committee considers "the most or best work to encourage fraternity among nations" has been enlarged further to honor and encourage those people and groups who have led nonviolent revolutions, assert and protect all persons' human rights, end poverty, and promote sustainable development. As it has done so, the Nobel Prize committee has created a legal controversy in Norway and some global confusion about the meaning of peace; but it has also been creating and depositing in the global commons a valuable history and visual representation of the evolution of the modern definition of "positive peace."

III. WAR JOURNALISM

In the modern era, consuming "the news" has long been a daily habit of the world's ever-growing urban populations. This habit spread in the early twentieth century when greater literacy levels and new printing technologies enabled the mass production of cheap illustrated newspapers. In the middle decades of the twentieth century, what the BBC always called "sound broadcasting" (radio) extended the news habit to poor and often illiterate populations in less developed rural regions. Movie newsreels, and then after 1950 television greatly enriched the visual content of the news. Although audiences for the daily news grew strongly during the Cold War, news providers for the most part remained the same private and public companies that generally supported governments' military policies (Briggs and Burke 2009: 196–211).

Since 2000, the Internet and the massive production and distribution of personal computers and smart phones has offered billions of people around the world access to vast quantities of news stories and images. The proliferation of new platforms disseminating information has also undermined the authority of long-established news sources that adhere to basic standards like checking sources and getting verification before publication. Today consumers of the news are increasingly linked to other like-minded people who shared their favorite news sources with them regardless of the sources' professionalism. This trend has eroded public confidence in the truthfulness of what the news media presents as factual. US President Donald Trump has demonstrated no faith in the truthfulness of the news media ever since he launched his political career in 2011 with repeated assertions that Barrack Obama was born in Africa. President Trump makes daily news by attacking journalists and media, frequently dismissing news critical of him and his administration as "fake news," even as he cites as factual stories that are not true. Pretending to protect the press, Trump threatens journalists saying "When the media lies to people I will never ever let them get away with it" (Ottosen 2017).

The new technologies used by consumers of daily news have no predetermined political trajectories. The meaning of the latest news is provided by the content providers who may or may not be committed to disseminating truthful information and providing access to a range of views on important issues like making a war and making peace. Especially when reporters rely exclusively on official sources speaking for one side engaged in conflict, war news can easily become propaganda. But there are more subtle ways war journalism so often achieves the same effect.

Robert Entman explains how the most important of these methods, framing, works:

> To frame is to elect some aspects of a perceived reality and make them more salient in a communicating text, in such a way as to promote a particular problem definition, causal interpretation, moral evaluation, and/or treatment recommendation.
> —Entman 1993: 52

Even though every conflict has its unique characteristics, the framing of wars by major news media often follows long-established patterns (Nohrstedt and Ottosen 2014). We know media framing of any violent conflict plays a crucial role in shaping how people understand and ultimately deal with it. In the twenty-first century national military policies, and presentations of them in national news media, continue to be shaped by the ideas of the most influential philosopher of war, Carl von Clausewitz (1780–1831), a Prussian officer who had experienced battle during the Napoleonic wars. Clausewitz's major treatise, *On War* (1832), remains today required reading in military academies all over the world. It defines war as a rational and powerful option for policy makers (Raporto 1968: 14). Clausewitz is best remembered for axioms like "War is a Mere Continuation of Policy with Other Means"[10] and that war is "an act of violence intended to compel our opponent to fulfill our will" (Clausewitz 1968: 101–22, 399–410). All the military planners who have followed Clausewitz believe careful estimates of probable costs and benefits must be calculated before deciding to make war. For them the mass murder of other human beings (for this is, after all, what war always involves) is never defined as a problem in itself, moral or otherwise, however much they may wish to minimize casualties.

Clausewitz, like "realists" before and after him, was indebted to the fourth-century Roman General Publius Flavius Vegetius Renatus for the maxim: "if you want peace, prepare for war."[11] Such preparations have gone on continuously in most nations around the world for centuries, creating in the modern era complex symbiotic relationships between the armed services, research universities, and almost every industry, including two of the most important producers of the images of war: Hollywood and the computer gaming industry (Turse 2008: 103–46). Today, Clausewitz's ideas retain their power among NATO and Western leaders (Rappoport 1968: 67). William Blum's overview of US-initiated wars since 1945 demonstrates the continued strong influence of Clausewitz's thinking on policy formation in the nation possessing the world's most powerful military, the United States (2001: 145–68).

After World War II, Western historians and political scientists found in their own recent past "lessons of Munich" that include the presumptions that you can never appease an aggressor, and that aggressors are never satisfied. These two presumptions guided US Cold War policy and informed the way Western, and especially US, news media framed serious international conflicts that in many other countries were framed very differently as struggles for national independence. The lessons of Munich were literally re-presented in the news media and classrooms on maps showing global patterns of Communist aggression whenever the United States launched its wars against Communist aggressors in Korea, Vietnam, and Central America, and later when it deployed massive military forces

FIGURE 5.5: Prime Minister Neville Chamberlain waves to the crowd at Heston Airport and declaims, "Peace in our Time," after returning from signing the Munich Agreement, September 1938. Hulton-Deutsch Collection / CORBIS / Corbis via Getty Images.

against Iraq, the country reportedly led by "the worst dictator since Hitler" in the Persian Gulf War (Dowd 1991).

The lessons of Munich also informed how the Cold War's nuclear arms race was framed in Western news. In the late 1960s, the US policy of Mutual Assured Deterrence (MAD) required building at enormous expense a nuclear arsenal that could achieve "overkill," or in other words, the ability to literally make our species *extinct*. All the major Western news media framed MAD as a rational peace policy called deterrence. The fearful insanity of this particular lesson of Munich—that the only effective response to threatened violence short of war is a more forceful display of threatened violence—was most memorably satirized in Stanley Kubrick's film, *Dr. Strangelove or: How I learned to Stop Worrying and Love the Bomb* (1964) that ends with images of a nuclear Armageddon.

Like so many of his contemporaries, Kubrick was frightened by both the Cold War's nuclear arms race and the way it had been normalized by both government policy makers and the major news media that covered military policy and international relations. The kind of close cooperation between the major print and broadcast news media and national governments that generated public support in Western nations for MAD was nothing new. It had been a norm in wartime since the advent of mass-circulation newspapers and magazines in the mid-nineteenth century. Phillip Knightley´s book *The First Casualty: From the Crimea to Vietnam: The War* is a perceptive history that explores the reasons why truth remains the first casualty in modern war reporting. Of course the most obvious reason is that modern governments engaged in war have often taken over, or at least heavily censored, all wars news. But propaganda and direct government control of the news is not really Knightley's subject. Instead he shows how the national identities of war journalists and the power of patriotism have consistently shaped war reporting.

Knightley takes as his point of departure the story of William Russell, a correspondent for *The Times* of London who covered the Crimean War (Knightley 1986). Russell was an archetypal male correspondent, reporting from the frontline with British soldiers in a war zone where he experienced first hand the bonding that so often transforms a small group of soldiers into a "band of brothers." Russell's loyalties were clearly aligned with the power elite and the educated middle class who formed the main readership for *The Times* (Høiby and Ottosen 2016). Russell framed his reports from the field in moral terms: the British imperial troops were good guys protecting civilization from their bad Russian opponents. Although ostensibly a correspondent for an independent newspaper that published objective reports about the war, Russell effectively framed the news from the viewpoint of the British government. As Knightley shows, this kind of patriotic framing of war news became standard practice among professional Western journalists in the modern era.

No government making a war in the modern era can escape skepticism about the truthfulness, legality, and morality of its case for war. The proclamation that the United States had a right to conduct pre-emptive and regime change wars issued in 2002 by President George W. Bush prepared the way for the US invasion of Iraq in 2003 (Office of the President: 2002). Bush and his top advisors tried to justify the invasion by reporting false claims made by US officials that Saddam Hussein's regime represented a global threat because it had weapons of mass destruction (WMDs). Official repetitions of this and other lies, like the highly charged claim that Iraq had collaborated with the 9/11 terrorists, were headlined in the major news media in the United States. At the same time numerous reports that uncovered the lies about WMDs, including many filed by United Nations' inspection teams in Iraq, were either marginalized or ignored altogether in America's news media. In many other countries, however, the falsehoods in the Bush Administration's case for war were a staple of the international news for many months. Thus, George W. Bush failed to build a global coalition of allies as his father had done for the first Gulf War in 1991. In fact, the biggest global anti-war protests ever were staged during the week before the United States and the United Kingdom attacked Iraq in March 2003.

The NATO bombing of Libya in 2011 provides another example of how Western leaders and most Western journalists shared the assumption that military action would be a decisive political tool, despite the fact that they knew that the unintended consequences of warfare cannot be controlled. Norway dropped a total of 588 bombs on Libya, more than any other NATO country. The bombardment of Libya forced a regime change that plunged the country into a long civil war that produced increased refugee flows into southern Europe. This bombardment was a misuse of UN Resolution 1973 that had authorized the use of force to protect the people of Benghazi with a no-fly zone, as well as an arms embargo and other sanctions on Libya.

By 2011, the unjustifiable and illegal US-British aggression had already left Iraq in ruins as a failed state, and the whole region engulfed in a widening conflict (Nohrstedt and Ottosen 2005). The forcible regime changes in Iraq and Libya had increased the bloodshed in those countries, and clearly paved the way for the rise of the so-called Islamic State (IS) and its violent jihad across the region. Yet major news media in both the

United States and Norway made no effort to highlight the connection between the NATO bombing in Libya and its failed state and the continuation of the brutal civil war in Syria, even though radical Islamists were bringing weapons from Libya into Syria (Ottosen and Øverbø 2016). Before 2003, al-Qaeda and other Islamist militants had no effective presence in Iraq or Libya (Ottosen et al. 2013). In fact, prior to these wars, the authoritarians Saddam Hussein and Muammar Gaddafi had firm control over their own territory. Saddam's Iraq had actually received military assistance from the United States during its long bloody war against Iran in the 1980s. More recently, both Iraq and Libya were even for a while regarded as allies against militant Islamist groups by Western powers (Campbell 2013). This recent history was not presented as a relevant context in the major Western news media reports when plans to attack these countries were announced. Once again it was war journalism: good "us" versus evil "them," a bloody conflict that offered no possibilities of a negotiated peace.

During these recent conflicts in the Middle East and North Africa, as in so many other serious crises of the modern era, war journalism only infrequently represented peace, and then only as a promise that would be realized after victory was achieved. On the other hand, war was well represented in the major new media's videos, photographs, interviews, and stories, while the possibility of finding a peaceful resolution was generally ignored in their war journalism. Journalistic representations of the modern era's warfare seem confirmation of William James' famous observation that "History is a bath of blood," as well as his acute prediction that the mass circulation of visual images of bloody casualties and the devastation created by modern warfare would not necessarily undermine the psychological power of the underlying patriotic, moral, and emotional narratives that government's deploy to justify their wars (1911: 1) However, there has emerged in recent years a challenge to the longstanding symbiotic relationship between governments making war and the journalists who report those wars. It is an important reform movement within the community of Western journalists called Peace Journalism.

IV. PEACE JOURNALISM

Peace Journalism is the offspring of Peace Research, a modern concentration within the general academic discipline, International Relations (IR). Peace Research emerged in northern Europe and North America after the mind-numbing slaughter and global devastation of World War II and the subsequent making of the nuclear arms race and Cold War convinced a few younger social scientists that policies built upon variations of the "realism" that prevailed in their profession would continue to reproduce the patterns of "bath of blood" history. The Peace Research Institute Oslo (PRIO), the first of many modern peace research centers, was founded in 1959 by a team of Norwegians who believed that a systematic study of peace and of political violence would open paths to nonviolent resolutions of serious conflict. Directed by the sociologist Johan Galtung, these first peace researchers rejected defining peace in simple negative terms as the absence of war or a threat of aggression.

In the 1960s, PRIO began publishing the policy-oriented the *Journal of Peace Research* that disseminated new ideas about peace as a complex positive process that includes *peacemaking*: moving parties in serious political conflict towards a peaceful resolution of their political differences, a process in cases of ongoing warfare that requires negotiated or mediated ceasefires. Another step in the process, *peacekeeping* in zones governed by ceasefires was already widely recognized as a UN policy that allowed negotiations for a

FIGURE 5.6: Johan Galtung in 1989 when he was a Professor of Peace Studies at the University of Hawaii. Fairfax Media Archives / Contributor / Getty Images.

more durable peace to proceed after fighting was halted.[12] The final and longest stage of this positive peace process, known today as *peacebuilding*, has evolved over many decades of "experiments" by local and national governments, intergovernmental organizations, and non-governmental organizations. Peacebuilding begins by attempting to reestablish old connections that have been broken by violence, and by trying to make new connections among former enemies.

As the 1960s ended, peace researchers, again inspired by Johan Galtung, began identifying forms of "structural violence" that they saw as the deeper causes of both intrastate and interstate bloodshed (Galtung 1969). Fifty years later, most peace researchers agree that enduring positive peace requires the order, justice, and social harmony that follows the elimination of structural violence including institutionalized racism and patriarchy, gross economic inequalities of income, and unsustainable "development" that threatens human habitats. Peace research is now established in academic and policy-oriented think tanks around the world. PRIO, and the Stockholm International Peace Research Institute (SIPRI) created in 1966, remain the world's leading policy-oriented peace research centers. Today there are across the world many other independent and government-supported peace research institutes, as well as hundreds of university based degree programs offering peace studies and conflict resolution studies. All of these institutions, as well as all of their journals, published reports, and policy recommendations are representations of a growing global peace culture.

Peace journalism is still very much a minority movement within its profession. Yet it is growing in influence. Peace journalists have since the turn of this century been trying to reform the ways serious political conflicts are reported. They critique mainstream war journalism, and try to teach different ways of framing wars and the establishment of peace. Peace journalism is now well represented in schools of journalism and in the journalism and peace studies departments of major universities around the world. Still, most reporters who work for major news media do not identify themselves as peace journalists even when they practice, as John Pilger, Robert Fisk, and Nicholas Kristof so often do, what peace journalism teaches. Nonetheless, the influence of peace journalism is represented every time we read or see an official account of warfare challenged by a focus on civilian casualties, the suffering of refugees, or interviews with people from different sides in a conflict and representatives of NGOs like Human Rights Watch and Médecins Sans Frontières.

Peace journalism extends Johan Galtung's work on structural violence and conflict resolution. His model of peace journalism builds on the dichotomy between what he calls "war journalism" and "peace journalism" (Ottosen 2010). It includes four major points which contrast the two approaches: war journalism is violence-oriented, propaganda-oriented, elite-oriented and victory-oriented. The war journalist's approach, as in sports journalism, often begins with a presumption that war is a zero-sum game where the winner takes all. A potential consequence of this presumption is that war journalism contributes to escalating and prolonging bloody conflicts by reproducing propaganda, often in the manner Knightley has described. When journalists echo officials and presume victory is the only way to end a conflict, they actually promote more warfare (Galtung 2002). Galtung has remained a touchstone for those in the movement. "Indeed," as the international relations specialist Richard Falk has noted,

> peace journalism owes much to Galtung's seminal work, and can be understood as an extension to journalism of his leadership in the founding and development of "peace studies" as an academic and activist field of study intended to offset the existing emphasis on "war studies".
>
> —Foreword in Lynch 2008: vii

Galtung recently compiled the following list of questions that journalists covering wars should answer:

1. What is the conflict about? Who are the parties including the parties beyond the conflict arena where the violence, if any, takes place?

2. What are the deeper structural and cultural roots, and history, of the conflict?

3. What kind of ideas exist about outcomes other than one party imposing itself on the other, particularly creative, new ideas? Can such policy ideas prevent violence?

4. If violence occurs, what are its less visible effects such as trauma and hatred and desires for revenge and for more glory?

5. Who is working to prevent violence, what are their visions of conflict outcomes, their methods? How can they be supported?

6. Who initiates reconstruction, reconciliation and resolution? Who merely reaps benefits like reconstruction contracts? (Galtung 2017)

Peace journalism in practice is defined by the choices editors and reporters make about what to report and how to report it, choices that should "create opportunities for society at large to consider and value nonviolent responses to conflict" (Lynch and McGoldrick 2005: 5). Peace journalists are wary of being seduced by government and military information strategies, such as the embedding of reporters in combat units that took place during the Anglo-American invasion of Iraq in 2003. They do not represent one side in a conflict. Peace journalists working in a war zone are people-oriented. They focus their attention on the victims of warfare (soldiers yes, but more often noncombatant casualties). Thus peace journalists give voice to the voiceless, including those people in the war zone who are working to open up nonviolent paths to peace. Peace journalism is not advocacy but very much a truth-oriented form of reporting. It reveals untruth *on all sides* and criticizes propaganda as contributing to continued bloodshed (Nohrstedt and Ottosen 2011).

Peace journalism originated in a debate among journalists and scholars at a conference convened by Transcend reporter Jake Lynch at Taplow House in London in August 1997 during which Galtung himself coined the term "peace journalism." (Lynch 2008: xi). Galtung wanted reporters to embrace peace journalism as a counter to what he labeled "war journalism." In former Sky News reporter Jake Lynch, he found a reporter already exploring ethical and theoretical questions about the responsibilities of journalists who reported from war zones. Jake Lynch has since then made the Peace Journalism program at the University of Sydney a world leader. Other leading academic proponents of peace journalism like Lynch have themselves been reporters.

Today, peace journalists seek to incorporate their approach into the standard practices of reporters assigned to war coverage, and in the curriculum of schools of journalism and journalism courses of universities and colleges around the world.

Steve Youngblood, editor of the magazine *Peace Journalist*, regularly documents the progress of peace journalism. His book, *Peace Journalism Principles and Practices*, offers many descriptions of scholarly research and academic courses, as well as a fair assessment of the impact of peace journalism's discourse on public debates and reporting about serious conflicts. Worldwide, at least forty-three universities offer Masters degrees in peace journalism, while many specialized organizations promote peace journalism's practices. A partial list of the most important institutional supporters of peace journalism includes Johan Galtung's Transcend Media Services (International), Jake Lynch's Centre for Peace and Conflict Studies (Australia), the Center for Global Peace Journalism (US), the Media Association for Peace (Lebanon), the Center for Media, Democracy, and Peace at Rongo University (Kenya), the Peace Journalism Foundation of East Africa (Uganda), the Institute for War and Peace Reporting (UK), Internews (UK), Corresponsal de Paz (Mexico), the Uganda Media Development Foundation, Mediothek (Germany), Common Ground News Service (International), International Media Support (Denmark), Peace Talks Radio (USA), and the US Institute of Peace (Youngblood 2016).

Peace journalism in general, and particularly Galtung's model of it, has many critics. BBC reporter David Loyn is the best-known critic within the community of reporters who have covered recent wars. His views are aired in a special issue of the journal *Conflict & Communication* (2007) that presented a debate between critics and defenders of peace journalism. In his article, Loyn criticizes peace journalists for imposing a political litmus test on reporters. Loyn prefers to use terms such as "truthfulness" and "objectivity" as journalistic guidelines, even though he acknowledges the limitations inherent in those terms. He states, "if we accept that objectivity is at least a worthy aspiration, even though not a tool to achieve the 'whole truth', then peace journalism fails a key test by imposing other expectations onto journalists" (Loyn, 2007: 5 in Nohrstedt and Ottosen 2008). Loyn is disturbed by Galtung's original war and peace model because its categories, its "war journalism" or "peace journalism" are too dualistic. He seems offended at being categorized as a war journalist by Jake Lynch and Annabel McGoldrick. Loyn says about their book, *Peace Journalism* (2005):

> They tend to lump everyone else together—those (like myself) who insist on objectivity, including a commitment to neutrality, along with the journalists of attachment who want to be able to name evildoers. For them we are all "war journalism". This single-minded contempt is allied with name-calling: "Otto the objective Ostrich", digging his head in the sand in the face of all glittering evidence collected by peace journalism to change his mind.
>
> —Loyn: 6

Loyn presents his own experiences as a reporter who covered the conflicts in Northern Ireland, Kosovo and Rwanda as evidence suggesting that had the peace journalism approach been preferred by the reporters covering those conflicts, their outcomes would have been worsened. In Northern Ireland, he claims using peace journalism's principle of transparency (what Galtung describes as "exposing untruth on all sides, and uncovering all cover-ups") would have made the secret negotiations between the parties impossible. In the case of Kosovo, Loyn came very close to the "journalism of attachment" promoted by Martin Bell and others during the civil war in the former Yugoslavia that framed military intervention by NATO forces as the only realistic solution to Milosevic's atrocities against the civilian population (Søvaag, 2005: 10).

To his credit, however, Loyn recognizes many of the mainstream media's reasons for failing to present truthful and complete pictures of world events. He observes,

> In the world of press conferences and the media opportunities which surrounds us, the only reporting which matters is off piste—finding out what really is going on. And there is simply not enough of it around. The business of reporting foreign news is under threat from many sources. The deep cut is in commercial revenues and the drive for audience makes it harder to report a wide agenda on mainstream outlets. The collapse of serious documentary-making cuts away another prop for those who want to understand world issues. The tyranny of the satellite dish tends to encourage quantity, sometimes at the expense of quality, on live 24 news channels.
>
> —Loyn, 2007: 10

In our opinion, Loyn ends his discussion on the limitations of objectivity where it should begin. The most important weakness in Loyn's arguments is the lack of context. We agree with Jake Lynch that if reporters fail to factor in propaganda and the media strategies of the parties in the conflict when gathering information, they will be unable to discern the truth of what is actually happening in a war zone.

Another critic of peace journalism, the media researcher Thomas Hanitzch, argues that peace journalism's proponents underestimate the material conditions for modern news reporting, and overestimate the possibilities for journalists to contextualize their stories as Lynch and others suggest. He thinks that a complex model like Galtung's is unfitted for the highly standardized narrative schemes required by modern news producers, and that promoting peace is inherently no nobler than the public relations campaigns and the "journalism of attachment" that promoted military intervention to stop ethnic cleansing in the Balkans. Even though Hanitzch is sympathetic to many aspects of peace journalism, such as the exposure of lies, the uncovering of cover-ups, and reporting the atrocities of war and the suffering of civilians, he suggests that they might better be labeled simply as "good journalism" (Hanitzch, 2007: 7; Nohrstedt and Ottosen, 2014).

Jake Lynch claims that Loyn, Hanitzch and other critics of peace journalism underestimate the willingness and ability of governments in the Western world to manipulate the media. He reminds us of the truth about the public explanations governments and their leaders offered for the "humanitarian interventions" in the Balkans in the 1990s, and of the Bush Administration's case for the invasion of Iraq in 2003 that included, in addition, stopping the now infamous (non-existent) threat from "weapons of mass destruction," the establishment of a democracy and a free market economy that would serve as model for other Arab nations. Lynch and other leading peace journalists argue that propaganda should be identified and presented in the context of other framings of a conflict. To do this reporters have to avoid being seduced by the patriotic appeals embedded in the rhetoric and images deployed by governments when they are making preparations for war, or making war itself; and they must recognize that uncritical adoption of the vocabulary of government official themselves may inhibit their desire and their ability to give voice to different sides of a conflict (Nohrstedt and Ottosen 2008: 11; Becker, 2008).

Jake Lynch and most peace journalists know that peace journalism is not support for a specific peace initiative or a particular peace strategy. Rather, they understand it as a realistic response to the complexity of practicing modern journalism in wartime. Its bloodshed and destruction, and especially the emotions it generates, make war an environment in which it is difficult to adhere to the journalistic ethic of "objectivity." Peace journalists have articulated guidelines designed to bring out more aspects of what is actually happening in wartime, and during those sometimes long periods of negative peace (like the Cold War of the last century and the confrontation between the United States and China in the South China Sea in this century) when governments engage in ceaseless preparation for war. Today, the news media's actual reporting of threats of war, war fighting and its victims, as well as of efforts to make peace and attempts to achieve reconciliation reflect the growing influence of peace journalism.

V. CONCLUSION

In his provocative study, *Why Nations Fight: Past and Future Motives for War* (2010), Richard Ned Lebow finds the majority of interstate wars since 1648 have been fought over issues of standing rather than fear, interest, or revenge. Lebow concludes his analysis with the observation that in the twenty-first century the global standing of nations is no longer based primarily on military power and control of other countries. Moreover, he argues that aggression in this century is generally viewed as not just illegitimate in international law, but as shameful and therefore not as capable of producing the kind of honor and standing that was once bestowed upon war. Memories and mediated visual representations of modern warfare have surely contributed to this ethical development.

So too have the ever-increasing representations of positive peace, peace work, and nonviolent revolutions and movements for human rights and social justice that circulate in the new global commons. Today, looking back over the modern era and into our pictorial memories of it, we still see all too frequently baths of blood. But we also see the making of a global peace culture, hopefully just in its formative stages, that will in time make warfare a rare exception to ways that people and nations resolve serious political conflicts.

CHAPTER SIX

Peace Movements

CECELIA LYNCH[1]

Peace movements from 1920 to the present have been extremely significant, controversial, and frequently messy, affairs. They have reflected their times and moved normative and ethical-political barometers (often in impressive ways). Yet they have inevitably fallen short of achieving all of their political goals. Modern peace movements have run the gamut from strict pacifism to militant non-violent resistance. They have demonstrated experimentation with forms of active non-violent resistance to war, militarism and often also economic, racial, and gender oppressions. With their expanded agendas, modern peace movements have been recognized as promoting forms of positive as well as negative peace.[2] Though they waxed and waned with the salience of militaristic approaches to international relations, peace movements have become more or less institutionalized features of transnational culture and politics in the twentieth and twenty-first centuries. Many modern peace movements have also reflected an underlying tension between achieving an end to war ("negative peace") and forms of "justice" that demonstrate the difficulty of achieving both negative and positive peace. More specifically, attempts to recognize racism, imperialism, and economic exploitation as forms of structural violence that are often embedded in warring societies have also informed and produced tensions within modern peace movements. This chapter discusses these features of peace movements, especially noting their incorporation of new ideas, strategies, and tactics over time.

Peace movements themselves, but also their historiography, should be interrogated by scholars and activists because numerous academic fields are only now expanding their intellectual and normative scope to include visions of peace beyond their European and American-centric origins. There have been important reasons for the original geographic and temporal boundaries placed on peace studies and peace history: in my own examination of interwar peace movements (Lynch 1999), a primary objective was to question the realist/idealist debate that long dominated western international relations theory and diplomatic history. Still, such geographic and temporal delineations had become seen as normative instead of heuristically navigated boundaries. The question becomes, then, what other regional and cultural perspectives and movements are slighted, if they are even known? While this chapter cannot purport to be all-inclusive, it addresses a range of western and non-western movements over the course of the past century, and suggests that still other movements around the world must continue to be investigated.[3]

PEACE MOVEMENTS, MILITARISM, AND CONFLICT

Modern peace movements arose from a distrust of the state's ability to protect its citizens from harm, and a belief that more equitable, inclusive and deliberative international institutional forms could be created that would curb the tendency of military powers to wage aggressive wars. It is difficult to exaggerate the anxiety, mistrust, and determination to be involved in future decisions about war and peace that the unexpectedly long and bloody conflict between the Great Powers produced. From 1920 onward, old and new peace movements reacted to the militarism and bloodshed of the Great War by pushing for collective security, disarmament, and arbitration; as well as various forms of "equality of status" among nations and peoples.

In the view of peace movement activists, arms races fed by greed and the growing global weapons trade were a special danger that kept the world at the precipice of war. In their view, the Great War had been unnecessary. It was made possible and encouraged by unchecked competitive weapons development and military rivalries. Peace activists believed disarmament could curb governments' militarist tendencies and, if complemented by new means to arbitrate disputes, realize the slogan that the Great War had indeed been "the war to end all wars." Arbitration had also been a major goal of the prewar peace movement. The Hague Conferences of 1899 and 1907 established a Permanent Court of Arbitration that still exists. After the war, peace activists wanted stronger efforts to settle international political disputes threatening war by compulsory arbitration, which they hoped would enable the development of nonviolent political solutions, thus preventing the kind of overreaction to real and perceived grievances that had helped to produce the Great War. Finally, peace movement activists advocated in favor of some type of "equality of status" among nations and peoples, although their debates on this issue were riven by pro- and anti-imperialist stances.

Peace movements were not, however, monolithic in their views or goals. In the United States and many parts of Europe (especially Britain), interwar peace movements drew support from important segments of society, including factions within major political parties. For example, peace policies had support among both Republicans and Democrats in the United States, and members of the Labour Party, the Conservative Party, and the Liberal Party in the United Kingdom. In both of these countries, as well as others, peace movements also included socialists and communists. Although the majority of peace activists were middle to upper-middle class, the various national movements also included some working-class members. The French peace movement resided primarily in the parties of the Left, although many of the Christian Democrats of the post-World War II era would later see themselves as peace advocates, especially regarding peaceful collaboration between France and Germany.

But in the United States and the United Kingdom, the strength of post-World War I peace movements lay in civil society rather than political parties. Women's groups, Christian and non-Christian pacifist groups, and League of Nations societies were especially active. Umbrella networks in both countries—the National Council for the Prevention of War (NCPW) in the United States and the National Peace Council (NPC) in the United Kingdom—attempted to maintain centrist postures that coordinated policy positions among various constituent organizations, although differing positions on the use of force and the economic causes of war frequently made this impossible. As the NPC admitted in retrospect, "the lowest common denominator of agreement" reduced "policy at times to a platitudinous level" (NPC 1959; Lynch 1999: 31).

Outside of North America and Europe, peace activism existed in parts of East and South Asia and among advocates of racial equality and decolonization in Africa and the African diaspora. In Japan, mostly middle and upper class women's peace activists organized and collaborated with transnational (primarily Western) groups. Taeko Shibahara argues that as they emerged from Japan's late-nineteenth century modernization process, "Japanese feminists negotiated a humanitarian space within Japan's expansion as a nationalist, militarist, imperialist, and patriarchal power" (Shibahara 2015: 1). Even during Japan's militaristic expansion, some activists maintained a pacifist stance, including Uchimura Kanzo, who, according to David Cortright, is often considered "Japan's most distinguished pre-World War II pacifist" (Cortright 2008: 29). In India, a succession of nonviolent resistance movements led by Mohandas Gandhi undermined British authority, and were closely observed by Western peace activists who were inspired by them to take up "nonviolent action in a large-scale political situation" (A.J. Muste, in Henthoff 1982: 191).

Pan-African movement leaders and civil rights activists in the United States, including W.E.B. DuBois and Ida B. Wells, founders of the National Association for the Advancement of Colored People (NAACP), and A. Philip Randolph, the leader of the Brotherhood of Sleeping Car Porters, critically described the racism that enabled both colonialist rationales for the world wars and US military interventions in the Americas. Anti-imperialist movement groups in North America collaborated with counterparts in Latin America to oppose US military interventions. As Randolph and Chandler Owen wrote,

> So long as African territory is the object of unstinted avarice, greed and robbery, while its people with dark skins are considered as just subjects of exploitation—now here and there in slavery, enforced labor, peonage and wage slavery—just so long will the conditions smolder and brew which needs must inevitably be prolific in the production of future war.
>
> —Bennett and Howlett 2014: 166–7

In addition to leftist political parties, groups that combined anti-imperialism and peace activism during the period included the Anti-Imperialist League, the American Civil Liberties Union (ACLU) and the Women's International League for Peace and Freedom (WILPF) (Bouvier 2002: 15; Foster 1995).

The WILPF, provides one of the most interesting cases of transnational peace activity that also attempted (though only partially) to address racial injustice and economic inequality (Foster 1995; Blackwell 2004; Confortini 2012). As Joyce Blackwell has pointed out, WILPF early on included both black and white members, although a number of the white members did not initially want to encourage the participation of black women. WILPF was a consistent voice in favor of rectifying economic injustices, but at the same time, its own members (whether black or white) tended to come from the upper classes, since they had to pay their own way to national and international conferences (Blackwell 2004: 46). WILPF, along with Christian pacifists and socialists, also spent considerable time and effort opposing US interventions in Latin America as well as supporting independent nations in Africa and the Caribbean such as Ethiopia, Liberia, and Haiti (Blackwell 2002:115).

One of the more fascinating aspects of interwar movements was their strong rootedness in the arts and humanities. The Harlem Renaissance in the United States produced literature, music, and theater that connected racial equality and peace. While "peace" was not a primary concern for Harlem Renaissance artists, they did see racism as one of

FIGURE 6.1: Margaret Bondfield addresses Women's International League for Peace and Freedom rally at the World Disarmament Conference 1932. Wikimedia Commons (Public Domain).

the causes of war. Other well-known writers specifically concerned with promoting peace during the interwar era included philosopher Bertrand Russell, the Bloomsbury Group in London, and socialist novelists in many countries. *All Quiet on the Western Front*, novelist Erich Maria Remarque's searing presentation of the suffering, survival, and disillusionment of young Germans in the trenches, became an international bestseller. Transformed into a feature film, it won the first ever Academy Award for Best Picture in 1930.

The horrors of modern war inspired popular artists. Dystopic fiction published in the interwar period, including chilling visions of totalitarian futures by H.G. Wells and Aldous Huxley, proved to have enduring appeal. Picasso's *Guernica* forever memorialized the Spanish Civil War and became perhaps the period's best-known visual rendition of the sufferings and violence of war. As at least a partial corrective, the necessity of incorporating women into decision making (e.g. in Virginia Woolf's *A Room of One's Own*), infused the arts and resonated throughout contemporary peace movements.

FIGURE 6.2: King Felipe VI of Spain and Barack Obama view *Guernica* in the Reina Sofía Museum in Madrid, July 2018. Handout / Handout / Getty Images.

Peace movements during this period focused a great deal of energy and activity on promoting global international organization in the form of the League of Nations. This support was especially characteristic of liberal, women's, and some religious groups including the League of Nations Societies of various countries, the US National Committee on the Cause and Cure of War, and the World Alliance for International Peace through the Churches. Socialists in groups like the No More War Movement of the United Kingdom decried the power politics of the League and its emphasis on *nations* rather than *peoples*, although they still supported some of the League's initiatives on disarmament. The idea of creating an institutional structure to prevent war through collective security and manage international conflict had grown out of the nineteenth-century transnational legal movements that culminated in the Hague Conferences of 1899 and 1907 that had produced international conventions regulating warfare and established a Permanent Court of Arbitration. In the 1920s, arbitration was the major area of agreement among widely disparate peace groups. There was no consensus on the degree to which such organizations should also take on imperialism and economic equality.

The League of Nations, as a result, became a primary locus of peace movement pressures. The proposals aimed primarily to achieve negative forms of peace in the short and medium terms (decommissioning of troops and prohibitions on submarines, bombers, and chemical weapons), along with implementation of mandatory arbitration to prevent the outbreak of future wars. But because the US Senate had rejected League membership, the movement acquiesced in extra-League measures as well, such as the 1928 Kellogg-Briand Pact that was supposed to "outlaw" aggressive war (Josephson 1979).

The groundswell of support for Kellogg-Briand in the United States was indicative of the ability of interwar movements, especially those in America and Britain, to mobilize large numbers of people in support of disarmament and arbitration proposals. The League of Nations societies claimed to represent hundreds of thousands of adherents. Their leaders tended to be establishment figures (such as Lord Robert Cecil in the United Kingdom) who moved in and out of governments. League support organizations were not the only ones to mobilize huge numbers of people, however. Women's groups led the effort to collect millions of signatures to pressure governments to reduce naval armaments at the London Naval Conference of 1930, which included the three major naval powers of the time: Britain, the United States, and Japan (Lynch 1999). During this period, peace movements in the West, particularly the United States and the United Kingdom, definitively put to rest the idea that ordinary citizens should not participate in debating decisions of "high politics," including foreign and defense policy because, as the total warfare of 1914–18 demonstrated, the result of such decisions could have an enormous impact on their lives.

A persistent issue that divided peace movements during this period, however, was how to address economic, racial, and political oppression in the form of continued colonialism and League of Nations mandates in the Middle East and Africa. Before World War I, Gandhi's first experiments with nonviolence in South Africa in order to gain rights for Indians had ignored the plight of the black majority in that country.[4] Nevertheless, as pointed out earlier, many peace activists in other parts of the world learned of his nonviolent campaigns against British rule in India, connecting them to their own peace projects, and seeing strategic nonviolent activism as an extension of pacifism. Moreover, the fact that Gandhi himself promoted both independence from a colonial power and nonviolent political struggle helped to introduce new issues into peace movement debates, including whether efforts for peace should also play a role in overturning colonialism. Some conservative and liberal movement members supported the alleged "mission civilisatrice" of either colonialism or the mandate system. For example, General Jan Smuts of South Africa became an ardent advocate of the League of Nations, even while he upheld racial segregation and oppression in his own country. Smuts was instrumental in designing the League's mandate system, including giving South West Africa a "C" mandate designation to denote a "least-developed" category of territories that were allegedly in most need of paternalistic supervision (Grovogui 1996: 214). Many of the League of Nations Union leaders in Britain, including Lord Robert Cecil and Gilbert Murray, were similarly supporters of British imperialism. They embraced the concept of "enlightened patriotism," a kind of global imaginary in which the British Empire, with its multiplicity of peoples, went hand in hand with League collective security principles (McCarthy 2011: 133). Still others, including socialist and communist peace group members, along with some religious pacifists, strongly opposed colonialism by both the European powers in Africa and Asia and the United States in Latin America and the Philippines. The Women's International League, for example, frequently decried the repeated US interventions in Central America during the period (Foster 1995). Some peace movement members in the United States began taking racial issues more seriously, including young activists in the WILPF and the Fellowship of Reconciliation (FOR). Bayard Rustin, a young pacifist and FOR activist in the 1930s, exemplified this new direction. Rustin would later become one of the leading strategists of both the black civil rights and gay rights movements.

FIGURE 6.3: Bayard Rustin 1964. Wikimedia Commons (Public Domain).

TENSIONS BETWEEN PEACE AND JUSTICE

The rise of fascism in Italy, Germany, Japan, and Spain provoked tensions within peace movements over the degree to which strictly pacifist positions could respond adequately to increasingly militaristic and authoritarian regimes. Nevertheless, the peace movement became increasingly transnational in the 1930s, not only with regard to women's groups such as the WILPF and the League of Nations societies, but also through transnational faith-based peace activism. The World Fellowship of Faiths, for example, met in London in 1937 to promote "peace and progress through world fellowship," and included the Emperor Haile Selassie of Ethiopia as well as delegates from the East Indies, Ceylon, Germany, the Netherlands, Hungary, India, and Mexico, as well as the United States and Britain (Terrell 1980: 403).

Peace movements after 1920, and throughout the interwar period, became the subject of trenchant critiques by the late 1930s and during and after World War II, including those written by historian and British Labour Party activist E.H. Carr and theologian Reinhold Niebuhr, although these critiques have themselves been shown to be deficient and frequently inconsistent (Lynch 1999). Peace movement groups demanded inclusion in debates over questions of war and peace, and policies regarding defense and security, law and international organization. In addition to proclaiming the idea that average citizens should not be included in official debates regarding foreign policy, war and peace, public critics of peace movements often disparaged and denigrated the social components of the movement itself, including women who were also at that time agitating for the right to vote in numerous countries. Perhaps one of the most significant legacies of this era, however, is that women's groups such as the WILPF, as well as some of the smaller pacifist groups such as the War Resisters League (WRL) and the International Fellowship of Reconciliation (IFOR) not only survived the lean years of World War II and its aftermath, but continue to be active in peace movements to this day (Confortini 2012).

PEACE MOVEMENTS DURING THE COLD WAR

Peace groups working in the interwar period continued to promote the normative basis of global international organization, even after their numbers declined with the onset of World War II. Many groups strategized in favor of the incipient UN and attended the San Francisco Conference where the UN Charter was signed in June 1945. While League of Nations Associations and transnational church organizations (such as the Federal Council of Churches in the United Nations) took the lead in pressing for the continuation of global international organization after the war, other groups that had declined during the war also actively participated. Thus, peace groups that were founded during and after World War I continued throughout World War II to agitate for a new global international organization.

The planning commission that worked on the creation of the UN, along with the US Department of State, developed a broad list of pacifist as well as non-pacifist peace groups to contact during this process. They included the Quakers, as well as other Protestant, Catholic, and Jewish peace committees, and numerous women's groups. Most of the peace groups contacted were included as "consultants" in preparations for the 1945 San Francisco conference, which established the UN (Lynch 1999: 197, 202). Their role in San Francisco previewed the consultative status granted "nongovernmental organizations" in the UN's Economic and Social Council (ECOSOC) after 1945. As a result, despite the movement's overall decline in numbers during the war years, numerous peace groups became gradually institutionalized as part of the UN's ongoing collaborations with civil society actors around the world. Most of these nongovernmental organizations (NGOs) opposed great power control of the UN, and specifically the charter's provision for a great power veto in the Security Council. In the aftermath of the world war, many of them also worked on refugee issues and human rights. The UN's Universal Declaration of Human Rights, approved by the General Assembly in 1948, was a milestone achievement that laid out an agenda for incorporating human rights protections into international law.

Thus, while many groups that gained consultative status favored the liberal internationalist postwar order led by the United States, other groups such as the FOR and WILPF challenged the inequalities and militarism of postwar liberalism. Moreover, students who had been involved in activist groups on the Left during the 1930s increasingly turned their energies to work for racial equality during the war years. Pacifists from the Fellowship of Reconciliation founded the Congress of Racial Equality (CORE) in Chicago in 1942. By 1961 there were fifty-three chapters of CORE across the United States that provided highly committed nonviolent activists, like the Freedom Riders, to the civil rights movement. Their challenges to establishment policies made increasingly strong connections between racism at "home" (in places like the United States) and abroad, especially in colonized areas of Africa and South Asia, and in Indochina where the US war was escalating.

By the 1960s, the global geopolitical situation was altered in important ways. The mass movement for racial equality in the United States, decolonization in Africa and Asia, and broader support for social and economic as well as civil and political conceptions of human rights continued, but fear of radiation from above-ground nuclear testing added to the concerns that the Cold War arms race between the United States, its allies, and the former Soviet Union was causing untold harm to populations around the globe. Peace activists began to focus on the irrationality of nuclear deterrence, the growing number of nuclear powers (the United States, the former Soviet Union, China, the United Kingdom and France), and the irresponsibility and harmful radiation effects of open nuclear testing. New antinuclear groups arose, including the National Committee for a Sane Nuclear Policy (SANE), founded in 1957 in the United States, and Physicians for Social Responsibility (PSR), founded in 1961 (the latter group developed by 1980 into the International Physicians for the Prevention of Nuclear War (IPPNW)). These groups gained some policy successes, first in forcing most nuclear weapons testing underground and second in promoting controls on the spread of nuclear weapons through the Nuclear Non-Proliferation Treaty (NPT) of 1968, which began the series of arms-control measures that were to be negotiated throughout the Cold War. Nevertheless, most arms-control treaties placed ceilings on the growth in certain kinds of weapons, rather than reducing their overall numbers. Peace movement groups included those calling for additional arms-control measures, but also included others insisting on complete nuclear disarmament.

The antinuclear movement's moral soul, however, resided in Japan, where the only two nuclear bombs ever to be used as weapons in wartime had instantly killed between 60,000 and 80,000 people in Hiroshima and 40,000 more in Nagasaki in August 1945, and continued killing, shortening lives, and producing birth defects for many years thereafter. As a result of these bombings, Japan developed a strongly antimilitarist and especially antinuclear peace culture, which continues to challenge renewed forms of Japanese militarism to this day.

Moreover, the *hibakusha,* or survivors of the atomic bombings, along with others in the Japanese peace movement, engaged in forms of activism that presented the evidence of nuclear horrors to populations around the world. One interesting example concerned a 1964 joint effort by Japanese movement activists and black activists in Harlem to counter nuclear testing and nuclear proliferation (Intondi 2015). Malcolm X helped to organize this event, while W.E.B. DuBois, after the Hiroshima and Nagasaki bombings, "traveled to Japan and consistently criticized the use of nuclear weapons" (Intondi 2015). In addition, Bayard Rustin, who had worked with the FOR since the 1930s and was a founder of CORE (which advocated for racial justice and peace together), also went to Ghana "to try to prevent France from testing its first nuclear weapon in Africa" (Intondi 2015). These activists and many others linked opposition to racism and colonialism, just settlements of postcolonial conflicts, and the abolition of nuclear weapons in a transcontinental movement that spanned Japan, West Africa, and the United States.

At this time, national liberation movements added to peace concerns in several ways. European powers engaged in bloody wars to keep control of colonial territories. France in Algeria, Belgium in the Congo, Britain in India and then Kenya, and Portugal in

FIGURE 6.4: Hiroshima's first Peace Festival, 1948. Carl Mydans / Contributor / Getty Images.

Mozambique and Angola used force in bloody attempts to retain overseas colonies. The United States tried to replace French influence in Vietnam, and continued its frequent interventions in Latin America during and after the Cuban revolution. Nevertheless, between 1957 and 1962, most countries in Africa became independent (except for today's Angola and Mozambique, Zimbabwe and Namibia, which became independent in 1975, 1980, and 1990, respectively). Many of the anti-colonial movements, such as Kenya's Mau Mau, used armed force against extremely violent repression. Other liberation groups like the movement led by Kwame Nkrumah in Ghana achieved national independence nonviolently. However, in this increasingly postcolonial Cold War world, peace activists made important linkages between "proxy" wars against communist powers such as the US war in Vietnam, US interventions in Latin America, and European interventions in Southeast Asia and Africa, and numerous injustices against "third world" populations.

In the United States, as a result of this mixing of issues, "Americans concerned with peace and social justice might work for a nuclear test ban in 1963, civil rights legislation in 1964, and to stop military escalation in Vietnam in 1965" (Meyer 1993: 457). Consequently during the late 1960s and early 1970s in the United States, as well as many other countries, "peace" movements transformed into "antiwar" movements. Students for a Democratic Society (SDS) led numerous marches and demonstrations on many American college campuses. The transnational movement against the war in Vietnam

FIGURE 6.5: Dutch artists protest in Amsterdam against the Vietnam War, December 1966. Wikimedia Commons (Public Domain).

became what David Cortright calls "the largest, most sustained, and most powerful peace campaign in human history" (2008: 157), as well as the largest anti-colonial effort of the era, gaining adherents not only in the United States, but also across Europe, Japan, and Southeast Asia. The movement included, among numerous other elements, contacts between women in Vietnam and the United States who worked in favor of "antiwar diplomacy" (Frazier 2017). It was also supported in the United States by movements for racial equality. Martin Luther King, Jr., spoke out against the Vietnam War in a famous 1967 speech at Riverside Church in New York City. But peace movements were not the only anti-colonial actors: Frantz Fanon, who joined the National Liberation Front in Algeria, was among a number of activists who fought with rebel movements against colonial and postcolonial impositions of power by Western nations.

During the 1980s, many peace groups turned their attention to other issues as the last struggles for national liberation outside Soviet-controlled Eurasia ended. Countering a new round of the nuclear arms build-up, and opposing American interventions in support of dictatorships in Central and South America were the paramount peace issues in the United States. Additionally, numerous transnational peace groups in the United States and Europe actively supported the South African anti-apartheid movement (Klotz 1995). Many, including the WILPF, also became increasingly concerned with the ongoing conflict in the Middle East, and especially the continuing occupation of Palestinian territories seized by Israel in the 1967 war (Confortini 2012).

The arms race between the United States and the former Soviet Union, as well as the spread of nuclear weapons to additional countries, provided a frequent source of peace movement mobilization and critique throughout the Cold War. In the 1970s, the United States and USSR negotiated two Strategic Arms Limitation (SALT) Treaties. The antinuclear movement revived and quickly grew by the early 1980s to include millions of people around the world. Two policy changes then signaled problems for SALT diplomacy. In 1979, the North Atlantic Treaty Organization (NATO) agreed to deploy new American-made intermediate-range Cruise and Pershing II nuclear missiles in Europe to "modernize" its arsenal, and in 1981 US President Ronald Reagan authorized the development of new generations of nuclear weapons along with new, allegedly "limited" nuclear war-fighting strategies. The antinuclear peace movement, motivated by new fears of the actual use of these weapons of mass destruction, exploded into action. New, large-scale groups took off urging opposition to nuclear escalation, especially a "nuclear freeze" first articulated by activist and peace researcher Randall Forsberg. Forsberg's nuclear freeze idea catalyzed more than a million people to join a 1982 march to UN headquarters in New York City to press for an immediate halt to the nuclear arms build-up (Meyer 1990; Wittner 2009). In 1983 and 1984 hundreds of thousands demonstrated against the deployment of intermediate-range nuclear weapons in the European capitals of London, Brussels, and Paris. A new East-West European peace group formed, organizing itself as the European Nuclear Disarmament (END) movement. END tried with some success to link West European concerns about peace with East European concerns about human rights. Activists in this movement, including Adam Michnik, E.P. Thompson, Mary Kaldor, and Vaclav Havel, worked overtly and covertly to create trans-European dialogue in ways that assisted the eventual process that brought down the Berlin Wall, and eventually the bipolar Cold War world system (Kaldor 1991; Rochon 1988).

Peace movements during the 1980s also increasingly protested the transfer of arms and other military assistance to governments and pro-government militias in El Salvador, Guatemala, Honduras, Chile, and Argentina, and to right-wing, anti-government militias in Sandinista-controlled Nicaragua. The militias and authoritarian governments violently suppressed both rebel groups and nonviolent activists in all of these countries and used fear of communism to maintain US support. Activists in these countries engaged in innovative forms of protest, such as weekly vigils by the Mothers of the Disappeared in Buenos Aires to draw attention to the systematic repression of students and others opposed to the Argentinian dictatorship. They, along with religious leaders such as Archbishop Oscar Romero of El Salvador, who steadfastly insisted on advocating nonviolent strategies of resistance in the bloody Salvadoran civil war, became symbols of the courage of Latin American forces for justice and peace.

Opposition to Latin American dictatorships and US government policies in support of them also became a transnational cause. The Committee in Solidarity with the People of El Salvador (CISPES) remained noncommittal on nonviolence, while the Solidarity movement advocated joining Central American activists in putting their bodies in areas where mass killings were occurring as a form of nonviolent resistance. These and other groups, including the FOR and War Resisters League, organized numerous demonstrations and acts of civil disobedience in the United States against Reagan administration policies in Central America. The religious Sanctuary movement also mobilized to help refugees from the Central American civil wars settle in North America and Europe, along the lines of the nineteenth-century "underground railroad" (Coutin 1993).

Peace movement groups took up the cause of transnational racial injustice at this time by supporting the resistance to the apartheid system in South Africa. Peace groups tended to support the African National Congress (ANC) movement and political party, even though they disagreed about whether the ANC's position in favor of a wide range of tactics against apartheid, including the use of violence, was justified. Many peace groups also became increasingly outspoken backers of the Palestinian cause during the 1970s and 1980s (Confortini 2012). Not only transnational peace groups and Arab states, but also many peace activists in Israel such as Rabbis for Human Rights and B'Tselem (both founded in the late 1980s), supported Palestinian calls for an end to Israel's occupation and the establishment of a secure Palestinian state (Omer 2013).

As in previous periods, cultural manifestations of peace sentiment, including of the nuclear arms race, decolonization and anti-apartheid struggles, the Vietnam War, and civil wars in Central America produced numerous artistic, musical and popular culture renderings. It is impossible to provide even a partially comprehensive survey in this chapter. Several of note either for their impact or cultural innovation include Stanley Kubrick's famous 1964 film, *Dr. Strangelove or: How I Learned to Stop Worrying and Love the Bomb,* which became the iconic representation of satirical response to nuclear anxieties. The Bread and Puppet Theater, founded in 1963, used striking, larger-than-life puppets to dramatize peace and economic justice concerns, becoming a standard fixture in peace marches throughout the period. African and South Asian writers memorialized independence struggles in novels and plays (e.g. Ngugi and Micere 1976), and Central American folk art pieces, coffee, and other products began to be sold through niche peace and justice movement markets, which have since burgeoned through the development of the "fair trade" movement for economic and environmental justice throughout the world (Raynolds and Bennett 2015).

Peace scholarship also became a cottage industry during the Cold War, and peace and conflict studies centers proliferated from their Norwegian origins and the path-breaking work of Johan Galtung to the other Nordic countries (Sweden, Denmark, and Finland), as well as in most other parts of the world (India, the United States, Canada, Japan, and Germany among many other countries). Some of these peace research centers focus more on methodologies; some on the causes of conflict and conflict resolution; some on both. Quantitatively oriented peace research centers aligned themselves with the post-1945 "behavioral revolution" in the social sciences, developing "a concern for theoretical development and empirical testing" in order to be taken seriously as policy-oriented academics (Wallensteen 2011: 6). Peace research was a post-World War II counterpart to the international law movement of the pre- and post-World War I eras. Both attempted to reason through the causes of war and decipher technical metrics (and thereby the mechanisms) for creating the conditions for peace. In addition to more historically and/or critically-oriented scholarship, these studies provide a wide range of perspectives on which students of peace and peace activists base their analyses.

PEACE AND HUMANITARIAN INTERVENTION IN THE POST-COLD WAR ERA

Toward the end of the 1980s, mass-based peace movements declined in the West. The 1987 Intermediate Range Nuclear Forces Treaty between the United States and the former Soviet Union reduced or eliminated the newer weapons deployed in Europe, and moved toward even greater reductions of strategic weapons in both superpower countries. Between 1989 and 1991, the Cold War ended, at least in part due to East-West peace movement activism, as mentioned previously. By the early 1990s, civil wars in El Salvador and Nicaragua had ended in negotiated cease-fires and elections. Thus, two of the major peace issues of the 1980s in the Western Hemisphere, nuclear weapons and militarized support of oppressive Latin American dictatorships, lost much of their salience. Many groups directed their peace activism into other areas, including humanitarianism (by groups such as the American Friends Service Committee), the creation of an International Criminal Court (especially by lawyers' organizations and foreign policy groups), environmental protection (by groups such as Greenpeace), and transnational development and social welfare (by women's rights and anti-poverty groups).

At the same time, new violent conflicts erupted, generating new issues for peace scholars and activists to address. The post-Cold War wars in a wide range of sites including Somalia, the Balkans, and Rwanda, provoked intense debate about the responsibility of the "international community" to intervene in ways that went further than longstanding UN peacekeeping roles. A number of prominent policy makers came together under the auspices of the Canadian government to outline a new normative guideline called the "Responsibility to Protect," or R2P. This concept has two major components: the responsibility of states to protect their populations, and in the event that they cannot or will not do so, the responsibility of the international community to step in, through a range of measures from incentives and diplomatic pressure to sanctions and even military interventions (ICISS 2001). Since its articulation in 2001, R2P has been criticized by some peace advocates who believe it too easily provides justification for military interventions. But centrist, internationalist scholars and policy makers espouse R2P arguing it provides the means to check crimes against humanity that include ethnic cleansing and genocide (O'Connell 2010; Doyle 2011).

In addition to elite elaboration of measures for international conflict management, other peace and nonviolence proponents have engaged in "bottom-up" peace initiatives.

FIGURE 6.6: Liberian women demand peace in front of ECOMIL headquarters in Monrovia, August 28, 2003. PIUS UTOMI EKPEI / Stringer / Getty Images/.

The Christian and Muslim women of Liberia who came together to found Women of Liberia Mass Action for Peace exemplified this kind of grassroots initiative. Those women pressed their respective political leaders for peace during the second Liberian civil war, and it was ended in 2003 largely because of their efforts. Leymah Gbowee, one of the leaders of this movement, was a co-winner of the Nobel Peace Prize in 2011, and continues to speak around the world in favor of women's peace activism.

In this century, the idea of peace has become increasingly parsed to include not simply citizen and official diplomacy and nonviolent action to promote peace during conflict, but also the development of a host of "post-conflict" measures generically called "peacebuilding." Perhaps the most prominent mechanism for increasing measures of trust in post-conflict societies has taken the form of Truth and Reconciliation Commissions, in some places simply called Truth Commissions. The South African TRC led by Archbishop Desmond Tutu gained worldwide attention with the idea that perpetrators of violence on all sides should come forward and acknowledge their roles, ideally asking for and obtaining forgiveness from their victims. Numerous proponents extol these commissions, while critics point out first that forgiveness is not always either sought or obtained, nor should it necessarily be expected; and secondly that the division of populations into perpetrators and victims is too rigid and simplistic, creating categories that do not fully account for all the nuances of political struggles for justice (Leebaw 2011). Nevertheless, such commissions, as well mechanisms like the local "gacaca courts" that were set up to adjudicate the Rwandan genocide, continue to be created and also to be debated among advocates of peacebuilding (Chakravarty 2006).

Peace advocacy and peace research have developed in many different directions after 1991 without a central core issue like the Cold War nuclear arms race. However, the militant responses of President George W. Bush's administration to the al-Qaeda terror attacks on New York City and Washington, DC in September, 2001—invasions of Afghanistan in 2001 and especially Iraq in 2003—demonstrated that the era of global mass-based peace movements was far from over. Once again, numerous new groups, including United for Peace and Justice and the Act Now to Stop War & End Racism (ANSWER) coalition, were organized and joined with long-established and still-active organizations such as the FOR, Quaker peace groups, and WILPF. This new global peace movement gained strength after the invasion of Afghanistan, as the United States government made false claims about weapons of mass destruction in Iraq to set the stage for an invasion of that country. Mass demonstrations filled city streets not only in the United States, but also across Europe, the Middle East, and Australia during the months when the George W. Bush administration made its case for a regime change war against Saddam Hussein's Iraq. This movement to prevent war culminated in "what was by some accounts the largest single coordinated protest in history," when "[r]oughly 10 million to 15 million people . . . assembled and marched in more than 600 cities" around the world (Tharoor 2013). The United States and its ally the United Kingdom still invaded Iraq in March 2003, but activists across the world became emboldened to collaborate and communicate in new ways, particularly on social media sites.

In late 2010, Mohamed Bouazizi, a twenty-six-year-old Tunisian fruit vendor, immolated himself to protest police brutality, igniting the phenomenon which became known as the "Arab Spring" across the Middle East and North Africa. Large-scale civil society demonstrations—both nonviolent and violent—rapidly spread as young Arab democracy activists used new social media to spread their ideas and tactics during the next two years. In Yemen, Syria, Libya, and Bahrain, nonviolent attempts failed. However,

FIGURE 6.7: Prisoner liberated by crowd in Kasserine during People Power revolution in Libya 2010. Antoine Gyori - Corbis / Contributor / Getty Images.

Tunisia's movement successfully used strategic nonviolence to bring to power an enduring democratic government. In Egypt, the initial successes of the nonviolent movement were reversed, and in both Syria and Libya long and bloody conflicts resulted.

Arab and non-Arab peace advocates carefully studied these campaigns for lessons regarding nonviolent revolution, as well as for the pros and cons of enacting the Responsibility to Protect (Hallward and Norman 2015). The Syrian uprisings soon turned into full-scale civil war against Bashar Al-Assad. As of this writing, Syria's civil war has displaced millions of people renewing vociferous debates among peace advocates about whether armed intervention to stem the violence is justified, whether intervention would increase the body count but fail to change the regime, or whether it would stem the violence and lay the groundwork for lasting peace. Peace advocates, including religious organizations such as the Palestinian Sabeel, numerous Christian denominations, Jewish Voice for Peace, and Rabbis for Human Rights, also remain focused on opposing the Israeli occupation of Palestine that they see as a major cause of instability and political violence in the Middle East.

THE ROLE OF PEACE MOVEMENTS IN INTERNATIONAL POLITICAL CULTURE

Peace movements, along with other social movements, have been an established nongovernmental feature of international political culture since 1920. In this modern era, questions of justice, including racial, economic, and gender justice, and freedom from political oppression, have consistently entered into debates about peace. Addressing such questions has prompted differing stances on the means and goals of positive peace, as well as ways of securing negative forms of peace. In the twenty-first century, interstate warfare is rare, but almost none of the issues addressed in this chapter have been resolved despite significant normative and policy successes. All classes of weapons, including nuclear weapons, continue to be modernized. New generations of nuclear weapons again blur the meaning of deterrence. Nuclear weapons have been added to the arsenals of more countries, even as other countries (e.g. South Africa, Brazil) abandoned their nuclear weapons development. Nuclear proliferation has been slowed by the NPT, as well as by related antinuclear normative "taboos" promoted by peace activists and the work of government/elite coalitions (Solingen 2009; Tannenwald 2008). Other kinds of weapons continue to be bought and sold in a flourishing international arms market that is subsidized by major powers, but also includes the legal and illegal reselling of older weapons in poorer nations.

Arbitration mechanisms remain relatively weak in the twenty-first century. However the formation of the International Criminal Court (ICC), created by the Rome Statute of 1998, has institutionalized the concept of individual responsibility for war crimes and crimes against humanity (Struett 2008). The civil society gains of the Arab Spring that raised hopes for establishing genuine democracies have been reversed in most of the Middle East. Economic inequalities have increased within the Global North and between the Global North and Global South. Both peace and war continue to be gendered in important ways, although activists' efforts have now resulted in UN Security Council Resolution 1325, mandating women's inclusion in peacebuilding processes (Shepherd 2008; Basu 2016). Peace movements continue to be comprised of both "liberal" and "radical" factions: the former desiring to establish institutional and normative restrictions on weaponry and war, and the latter attempting to enact forms of economic redistribution that would, in their view, establish the bases for more permanent forms of positive peace.

One concept that has emerged from this debate concerns the idea of "justpeace." Articulated by John Paul Lederach and other peacebuilding scholar/activists, this concept reconfigures peace to insist on its positive form, which can only be attained according to its proponents along with establishment of political, social, and economic justice. Still, different proponents put varying weights on the degree of structural transformation, gender, economic, and racial equality, and reconciliation mechanisms necessary to obtain a justpeace (Lederach 2010; Philpott and Powers 2010; Omer, Appleby and Little 2015). The tensions that have arisen in peace movements over the past century demonstrate the difficulty and the necessity of achieving both peace and justice. This history shows that the major challenges for peace movements in the past will remain salient in the future.

CHAPTER SEVEN

Peace, Security, and Deterrence

JOHN MUELLER

Leading or developed countries, reversing the course of several millennia, no longer envision major war as a sensible method for resolving their disputes. Indeed, international war of all kinds has, in recent decades, been remarkably rare. Although there is no physical reason why such wars cannot recur, they often seem to be obsolescent, if not completely obsolete (Mueller 1989, 2004; Ray 1989; Fettweis 2010; Pinker 2011 Horgan 2012).

On May 15, 1984, the countries in Europe, once the most warlike of continents, had substantially managed to remain at peace with each other for the longest continuous stretch of time since the days of the Roman Empire (Schroeder 1985: 88; see also Luard 1986, 395–99; Sheehan 2008; Pinker 2011: 249–51). That rather amazing record has now been further extended, and today one has to go back more than two millennia to find a longer period in which the Rhine remained uncrossed by armies with hostile intent (de Long 2004).

"All historians agree," observed Leo Tolstoy in *War and Peace* in 1869, "that states express their conflicts in wars" and "that as a direct result of greater or lesser success in war the political strength of states and nations increases or decreases" (1966: 1145). Whatever historians may currently think, this notion, it certainly appears, has become substantially passé. Prestige now comes not from prowess in armed conflict, but from economic progress, maintaining a stable and productive society, and, for many, putting on a good Olympics or sending a rocket to the moon. This remarkable development suggests that a significant cultural shift in attitudes toward war has taken place. It has its origins in the early years of the modern age: in the aftermath of World War I.

THE IMPACT OF WORLD WAR I

European attitudes toward war changed profoundly at the time of World War I. This change can perhaps be quantified in a rough sort of content analysis. Before that war it was very easy to find serious writers, analysts, and politicians in Europe and the United States exalting war as beautiful, honorable, holy, sublime, heroic, ennobling, natural, virtuous, glorious, cleansing, manly, necessary, and progressive while finding peace to be debasing, trivial, and rotten, and characterized by crass materialism, artistic decline, repellant effeminacy, rampant selfishness, base immorality, petrifying stagnation, sordid frivolity, degrading cowardice, corrupting boredom, bovine content, and utter emptiness (Mueller 1989: ch. 2; Stromberg 1982). After the war, such people become extremely rare, though the excitement of the combat experience continued (and continues) to have its fascination for some.

This suggests that the appeal of war, both as a desirable exercise in itself and as a sensible method for resolving international disagreements, diminished markedly on that once war-racked continent. In an area where war had been accepted as a standard and permanent fixture, the idea suddenly gained substantial currency that war was no longer an inevitable or necessary fact of life and that major efforts should be made to abandon it.

This change has often been noted by historians and political scientists. Arnold Toynbee points out that World War I marked the end of a "span of five thousand years during which war had been one of mankind's master institutions" (1969: 214). In his study of wars since 1400, Evan Luard observes that "the First World War transformed traditional attitudes toward war. For the first time there was an almost universal sense that the

FIGURE 7.1: *I Didn't Raise My Boy to be a Soldier*, Sheet Music USA 1915. Wikimedia Commons (Public Domain).

deliberate launching of a war could now no longer be justified" (1986: 365). Bernard Brodie points out that "a basic historical change had taken place in the attitudes of the European (and American) peoples toward war" (1973: 30). Eric Hobsbawn concludes, "In 1914 the peoples of Europe, for however brief a moment, went lightheartedly to slaughter and to be slaughtered. After the First World War they never did so again" (1987: 326). And K.J. Holsti observes, "When it was all over, few remained to be convinced that such a war must never happen again" (1991: 175). Or as A.A. Milne recalls, "In 1913, with a few exceptions we all thought war was a natural and fine thing to happen, so long as we were well prepared for it and had no doubt about coming out the victor. Now, with a few exceptions, we have lost our illusions, we are agreed that war is neither natural nor fine, and that the victor suffers from it equally with the vanquished" (1935: 9–10). Obviously, this change of attitude was not enough to prevent the cataclysm of 1939–45 or the many smaller armed conflicts that have taken place since 1918. But the existence of these wars should not be allowed to cloud an appreciation for the shift of opinion that occurred during World War I.

What was so special about World War I? There seem to be several possibilities. The first is the most obvious: the war was massively destructive. But in a broader historical perspective, the destructiveness of the war does not seem to be all that unique. A high estimate of the death rate would suggest that about 4.1 percent of the European population

FIGURE 7.2: American delegates arrive in the Netherlands for Women's Peace Congress, April 1915. Library of Congress / Contributor / Getty Images.

perished in the war (Sivard 1987: 29–31). A war in which one in twenty-five dies is calamitous, but there had been hundreds, probably thousands, of wars previously in which far higher casualty rates were suffered. According to Frederick the Great, Prussia lost one-ninth of its population in the Seven Years War (Luard 1986: 51). This was a proportion higher than almost any suffered by any combatant in the wars of the twentieth century (Small and Singer 1982: 82–99). Holsti calculates that, "if measured in terms of direct and indirect casualties as a proportion of population," the Thirty Years War was Europe's most destructive armed conflict (1991: 313). Moreover, there was a substantial belief that many of the wars had been even more horrible than they actually were. For example, a legend prevailed for centuries after the Thirty Years War holding that it had caused Germany to suffer a 75 percent decline in population (Wedgwood 1938: 516). Yet disastrous experiences and beliefs like this had never brought about a widespread revulsion with war as an institution, nor did they inspire effective, organized demands that it be banished. Instead war continued to be accepted as a normal way of doing things.

Nor was World War I special in the economic devastation it caused. Many earlier European wars had been fought to the point of total economic exhaustion. By contrast, within a few years after World War I, most of the combating nations had substantially recovered economically: by 1929 the German economy was fully back to prewar levels, while the French economy had surpassed prewar levels by 38 percent (Overy 1982: 16).

World War I toppled several political regimes—in Germany, Russia, and Austria-Hungary—but it was hardly unusual in this respect. And to suggest that World War I was new in the annals of warfare in its tragic futility and political pointlessness would be absurd—by most reasonable standards huge numbers of previous wars would rival, and often surpass, it on those dimensions. One of the most famous wars in history, after all, was fought over an errant wife with the result that, as one of Shakespeare's characters rather ungraciously observes, "For every false drop in her bawdy veins a Grecian's life hath sunk; for every scruple of her contaminated carrion weight, a Trojan hath been slain: since she could speak, she hath not given so many good words breath as for her Greeks and Trojans suffer'd death."

Actually, in some respects World War I could be seen to be an *improvement* over many earlier wars. Civilian loss, in the West at least, was proportionately quite low, while earlier wars had often witnessed the destruction of entire cities. And a wounded soldier was far more likely to recover than in earlier wars where the nonambulatory wounded were characteristically abandoned on the battlefield to die in lingering agony from exposure and blood loss. Disease was also becoming much less of a scourge than in most earlier wars.

World War I is often seen to be unusual because it was so unromantic. But if that is so, it is because people were ready to see, and to be repulsed by, the grimness of warfare. Mud, filth, leeches, and dysentery were not invented in 1914, but are standard accompaniments of warfare.

For Europeans, the Great War was special in that it followed a century characterized by phenomenal economic growth, something that was in part facilitated by the century of near-total peace that the continent had just undergone (Gat 2017, ch. 6). However, the growth by itself did not change attitudes toward war. Even as they were enjoying the benefits of peace they continued to assume war to be a normal fact of life and as most continued to thrill at the thought of it. Moreover, the United States had also undergone an enormous period of economic growth (and freedom from significant war) before its Civil War, and in its own terms that war was as brutal and horrible as World War I. Yet the experience did not bring about a rejection of war among the American people—indeed quite soon Americans were romanticizing about war just like Europeans who had not yet undergone the experience of "modern" war (Linderman 1987: 266–97; Mueller 1989: 30–2, 38–9).

World War I was unique in that it raised the specter that through some combination of aerial bombardment and gas or bacteriological poisoning the next large war could lead to world annihilation—the destruction of winner and loser alike. But wars of annihilation and wars in which civilians were slaughtered were hardly new: history is filled with examples. Moreover, it seems likely that this phenomenon was more a result of antiwar feeling than its cause: that is, people opposed to war in a sense *wanted* everyone to believe the next one would be cataclysmic in the desperate hope that this belief would make it less likely to occur. This is suggested by the fact that the apocalyptic literature about the next war for the most part emerged in the 1930s, when the danger of another war was growing, not in the 1920s as a direct result of World War I (Clarke 1966: 169–70).

In the end, the war seems to have been quite unique in one important respect: it was the first war in history to have been preceded by substantial, organized antiwar agitation. The idea that war ought to be abolished as a way of doing business in the developed world was rapidly growing in the two or three decades before the war. Peace societies were proliferating, famous businessmen were joining the fray, various international peace congresses were being held and governments were beginning to take notice and to participate. Political liberals and feminist leaders were accepting war opposition as part of

FIGURE 7.3: Children of farm workers in Kent, England have their gas masks checked, August 29, 1939. George W. Hales / Stringer / Getty Images.

their intellectual baggage (Patterson 1976: 129). And many Socialists were making it central to their ideology (Wank 1988: 48–52). Although it was still very much a minority movement and largely drowned out by those who exalted war, the gadfly arguments were persistent and unavoidable. The existence of the movement probably helped Europeans and Americans to look at the institution of war in a new way when the massive conflict of 1914–18 entered their experience. They were at last ready to begin to accept the message. Within half a decade, war opponents, once a derided minority, became a decided majority: everyone now seemed to be a peace advocate.

World War I served, therefore, essentially as a catalyst. It was not the first horrible war in history, but because of the exertions of the prewar antiwar movement it was the first in which people were widely capable of recognizing and being thoroughly repulsed by those horrors and in which they were substantially aware that viable alternatives existed.

INTERNATIONAL WAR SINCE WORLD WAR I

The peacemakers of 1918 adapted many of the devices antiwar advocates had long been promoting, at least in part. A sort of world government, the League of Nations, was fabricated. Aggression—the expansion of international boundaries by military force—was ceremoniously outlawed. Legal codes and bodies that might be able to deal peacefully with international disputes were also set up, and quite a bit of thought went into the issue of arms control, in part because of the theory that the Great War, like lesser ones before it, had principally been caused by the greed of munitions makers. For many, then, the real threat and the true enemy had become *war itself*, and the preservation of international peace became a prime national interest goal.

Since World War I, industrialized countries in the developed world have participated in four wars or kinds of war: first, the cluster of wars known as World War II; second, wars relating to the Cold War; third, various wars in their colonies; and fourth, policing wars—assorted applications of military force, particularly after the Cold War, to pacify civil conflicts and to topple regimes deemed to be harmful.

World War II

In Japan, a distant, less developed state that had barely participated in World War I, many people could still enthuse over war in a manner than had become largely obsolete in Europe: it was, as Alfred Vagts points out, the only country where old-style militarism survived the Great War (1959: 451). By the 1920s the new Japanese army had become the center of a militant, romantic ideology that stressed nationalism and expansion. Scorning materialism—which they associated with the classes they despised as well as with the nation they found most threatening, the United States—the ideologues latched onto the mystical notion that it was Japan's historic mission to expand into East Asia, thereby securing peace in the area and preserving their hundreds of millions of fellow Asians from imperialist oppression. War, the Japanese war ministry proclaimed, was "the father of creation and the mother of culture" (Luard 1986: 368). The Japanese were willing to risk major war rather than give up on their grand schemes (Brodie 1973: 272). It took a cataclysmic war for the Japanese to learn the lessons Europeans had garnered from World War I. But the Japanese were to learn the lesson well.

The war in the Pacific, then, while not inevitable, was clearly in the cards due to Japan's general willingness to risk all to achieve its extravagant ambitions. In Europe, by contrast, it appears that only one man embraced such sentiments, but he proved to be crucial. That is to say, but for Germany's leader, Adolf Hitler, the war there would likely never have come about.

This conclusion, although shunned by those who dismiss all "great man" interpretations of the past, has been accepted by a significant number of prominent historians. For example, Gerhard Weinberg notes, "whether any other German leader would indeed have taken the plunge is surely doubtful, and the very warnings Hitler received from some of his generals can only have reinforced his belief in his personal role as the one man able, willing, and even eager to lead Germany and drag the world into war" (1980: 664). F.H. Hinsley noted: "Historians are, rightly, nearly unanimous that ... the causes of the Second World War were the personality and the aims of Adolf Hitler ... [I]t was Hitler's aggressiveness that caused the war" (1987: 71–2). Similarly, William Manchester observes that the war Hitler started was one "which he alone wanted" (1988: 197). John Lukacs

FIGURE 7.4: Adolf Hitler addressing a meeting in Berlin, January 1, 1937. Hulton Archive / Stringer / Getty Images.

finds that World War II "was inconceivable and remains incomprehensible without him" (1997: xi), while John Keegan notes that "only one European really wanted war: Adolf Hitler" (1989). And Donald Cameron Watt concludes:

> What is so extraordinary in the events which led up to the outbreak of the Second World War is that Hitler's will for war was able to overcome the reluctance with which virtually everybody else approached it. Hitler willed, desired, lusted after war . . . In every country the military advisers anticipated defeat, and the economic advisers expected ruin and bankruptcy.
>
> —1989: 610[1]

In order to bring about another continental war it was necessary for Germany to desire to expand into areas that would inspire military resistance from other major countries and to be willing and able to pursue war when these desires were so opposed. Although the general theme of eastern expansion had been around for quite a while and while it was still in the air after World War I, Hitler seems to have been important, and probably crucial, for its incorporation not only into effective German foreign policy, but also into Nazi ideology. That is, it was neither obvious nor natural that it would emerge as an important theme in German politics after 1920 (Stoakes 1986: 216). In fact, Hitler's own political tactics suggest the expansionary theme was *not* significantly popular: he found it tactically wise to mellow and downplay this element of his thinking as he neared and then attained office (Rich 1973: xi).

As it happens there is quite a bit of information about German public opinion during the Nazi era. An analysis of this mass of material has led Ian Kershaw to conclude that the German population, like that in other areas of Europe, was "overwhelmingly frightened of the prospect of another war" and approached the prospect of "another conflagration" with "unmistakable dread" (1987: 2, 143). Another analyst of German public opinion characterizes it as "dead set" against major war (Steinert 1977: 50). As Manchester has put it, "the German people hated war as passionately as their once and future enemies" (1988: 307). Nor was there notable enthusiasm for continental war within the military. The military leaders were among that near-consensus in Germany which, as Weinberg puts it, "could conceive of another world war only as a repetition of the last great conflict" (1980, 18–19; see also Gat 2001, 83).

Thus, in his aggressive policy of eastward expansion—the issue that was to trigger continental war in Europe—Hitler was playing on old themes. But while these themes had support from some Germans, there was nothing remotely natural or inevitable about the process by which they came to dominate German foreign policy in the 1930s. Moreover, to get his policies adopted, Hitler had not only to mislead his own public, but he also had to override the objections of some of his most important cronies and co-workers, some of whom opposed aggressive eastward expansion and tried to divert Hitler's policy. As Hitler stated in 1938, "Circumstances have forced me to talk almost exclusively of peace for decades" (Fest 1974: 536).

Throughout, Hitler was in total and personal control. As Rich puts it, "The point cannot be stressed too strongly; Hitler was master of the Third Reich" (1973, 11). Or, in Fest's words, "From the first party battle in the summer of 1921 to the last few days of April, 1945 . . . Hitler held a wholly unchallenged position; he would not even allow any principle, any doctrine, to hold sway, but only his own dictates" (Fest 1974: 8).

There was simply no one else around who had these blends of capacities. Most of the other top German leaders were toadies or sycophants, and certainly none could remotely arouse the blind adulation and worship Hitler inspired. As Weinberg suggests, Hitler was "the one man able, willing, and even eager to lead Germany and drag the world into war" (1980: 664). And Hitler was well aware of this. As he told his generals in 1939, "essentially all depends on me, on my existence, because of my political talents" (Alexandroff and Rosecrance 1977: 416–17). He was, he boasted, "irreplaceable. Neither a military man nor a civilian could replace me" (*Documents on German Foreign Policy, 1918–1945*, Series D, Vol. VIII, United States Government Printing Office, 1954: 443).

Clearly, if, against all odds, history's greatest manmade cataclysm came about only because one spectacularly skilled, lucky, and determined man willed it into existence, this circumstance has substantial implications. It suggests, for example, that World War II in Europe was not a continuation of World War I which, in many respects, can be seen as a sort of "natural" war: it was on the cards and likely to emerge one way or another out of the various conflicts of the war-anticipating—even war-eager—contestants. It also suggests that the 1920s and 1930s were not peculiarly unstable. Nor did World War II grow out of the depression of the 1930s. The experience further suggests that totalitarianism neither requires war to function, nor does it necessarily lead to war. Many postwar thinkers, including George Orwell in his famous novel, *1984*, tended to associate the two. However, but for Hitler's maniacal expansionary zeal and extreme willingness to accept risk, even a totalitarian Nazi Germany would not have gone to war.

World War I shattered what some have called the "war-like spirit" in Europe and North America and made large majorities there into unapologetic peace-mongers. World War II, it appears, reinforced that lesson in those places (probably quite unnecessarily), and it converted the previously militaristic Japanese in Asia. When bodies were buried, surviving prisoners freed, and the rubble had settled, the appeal and wisdom of a direct war between developed industrialized nations had been thoroughly discredited.

Lessons about the strategy and tactics of peace were also gleaned from the experience. To opt out of a war system there were (and still are) two central paths a war-averse country could take. One is the pacifist (or Chamberlain) approach: be reasonable and unprovocative, stress accommodation and appeasement, and assume the best about one's opponent—an approach that might have worked with just about any German leader except Adolf Hitler. The chief error was to assume that Hitler could not possibly be so daft as to be willing to risk a repetition of a continental war like World War I. And to help with that misperception, Hitler went out of his way in every foreign policy speech to stress how much he abhorred war—it was perhaps his biggest lie (Mueller 1989: 69).[2] The other path is the deterrence (or Churchillian) approach: arm yourself and bargain with trouble makers from a position of military strength.

The chief lesson garnered by the end of the 1930s—in particular by the experience with Hitler—was that, while the pacifist approach might work with some countries, an approach stressing deterrence and even confrontation was the only way to deal with others. To that degree, war remained part of the political atmospherics even for the war averse.

The Cold War

In the late 1940s, after the annihilation of the aggressive regimes that had started history's most destructive war, the United States and the Soviet Union rose to central international prominence. Wary wartime allies, the two big countries—superpowers, they were quickly labeled—gradually became contesting and often hostile opponents.

On one level, the Soviet Union was essentially content with the postwar status quo—indeed, except for the dismemberment of Germany, even a war-exhausted Hitler might have been satisfied with the empire his archenemy Josef Stalin controlled. On another level, however, the Soviets were viscerally opposed to that status quo. According to the ideology on which the regime had been founded in 1917, world history is a vast, continuing process of progressive revolution. Steadily, in country after country, the oppressed working classes would violently revolt, destroying the oppressing capitalist classes and aligning their new regimes with other like-minded countries. Eventually the world would be transformed, class and national rivalries would vanish, and eternal peace and utopian harmony would inundate the earth.

In general, the capitalist West adopted two policies to deal with the Communist threat: deterrence and containment. Communist states were willing at times to use military force—that is, aggression—to advance their interests. Most importantly, in 1950 the Soviets and the new Communist regime in China approved an invasion of South Korea by Communist North Korea, a distant war of expansion by a faithful ally that was expected to be quick, risk-free, and cheap (Khrushchev 1970, 370; Simmons 1975, 163). For the most part, however, leaders in the West viewed the war in Korea as confirming their worst fears. Rather than seeing it for what it was—a limited, opportunistic probe in an area of seemingly peripheral interest, President Harry Truman maintained that "If this was allowed to go unchallenged it would mean a third world war, just as similar incidents had brought on the second world war" (1956: 333). Meanwhile, a National Security Council document darkly suspected Korea to be "the first phase of a general Soviet plan for global war," and the CIA authoritatively opined that, "in the belief that their object cannot be fully attained without a general war," the "Soviet rulers may deliberately provoke such a war" before 1954 (Trachtenberg 1991, 112–13; see also Mueller 2012).

Such alarmist anxieties obviously proved to be over-wrought, but at the time they inspired an extended exercise in what Robert Johnson has called "nuclear metaphysics" (1997; see also Mueller 1988, 1995: ch. 5, 2010a: ch. 3). In this, it was assumed that the Soviet Union needed to be deterred from launching a direct war against the United States or Western Europe. However, it seems clear that, although the USSR and other Communist states did subscribe to an aggressive agenda that involved support for class warfare, revolutionary civil wars, and subversion in capitalist countries, they were extremely wary of any experience that might lead to a conflict like World War II. Their ideology never envisioned direct Hitler-style aggressive warfare, whether nuclear or not, as a sensible method for pursuing the process of world revolution. As Robert Jervis notes, "The Soviet archives have yet to reveal any serious plans for unprovoked aggression against Western Europe, not to mention a first strike against the United States" (2001: 59). And Vojtech Mastny concludes that "The strategy of nuclear deterrence [was] irrelevant to deterring a major war that the enemy did not wish to launch in the first place" (2006: 3). That is, the extravagant alarmism that inspired the Cold War arms race was essentially based on nonsense, not sound intelligence. In the process, however, the United States spent somewhere between 5.5 and 10 trillion dollars on nuclear weapons and delivery systems—enough to purchase everything (or about half of everything) in the country except for the land (Rhodes 2007: 306). All this, primarily to confront, to deter, and to make glowering and menacing faces at, a perceived threat of direct military aggression that, essentially, didn't exist. In all, it was the stuff of comedy—or, more accurately, farce (Mueller 2010a, 2011c: 127–9).

In addition to deterrence, anti-Communists stressed the policy of containment—keeping Communism from coming into power in additional countries through revolution, civil warfare, or subversion. In complicity with the neighboring Soviet Union, the Communist Party in democratic Czechoslovakia alarmingly fomented a coup in 1948, taking over the country and bringing it into the Soviet camp. There was great fear that a similar process might take place elsewhere in Europe, especially in Italy and France where Communism seemed to have a substantial attraction. But its appeal waned fairly quickly on that continent. However, international Communism could cast its eye with more pleasure on the less-developed areas of the world where dozens of new nations were emerging, most of them carved out of European colonial empires that were gradually dismantled in the postwar era. Communism could be advanced in the third world, as it came to be called, through example, aid, persuasion, and perhaps, as in Czechoslovakia, a bit of judicious subversion. Thus, successful anticolonial wars brought a Communist regime to North Vietnam in 1954 and potentially congenial regimes to Indonesia in 1949 and to Algeria in 1962. And Cuba joined the camp after Fidel Castro's victory there in 1959.

Dealing with subversion, revolution, and revolutionary civil war in the third world was seen as an important containment challenge. The process underwent its bloodiest development in South Vietnam. By 1965, insurgents there, increasingly aided and supported by Communist North Vietnam, appeared to be on the verge of victory, and it seemed that the only way to rescue the situation was to send large numbers of American troops. Vietnam was seen to be an important testing ground of the efficacy of such wars. As Defense Secretary Robert McNamara put it at the time, the conflict was "a test case of US capacity to help a nation meet a Communist 'war of liberation'" (*Pentagon Papers* 1971, Vol. 3: 500, see also 50–51). And North Vietnamese leaders agreed: "South Vietnam is the model of the national liberation movement of our time. If the special warfare that the United States imperialists are testing in South Vietnam is overcome, then it can be defeated anywhere in the world" (Fulbright 1966: 169). An extensive effort to wear Communist forces down militarily began but after a long costly struggle it was the American will that broke, and so, although it did not come out the way American strategists had planned, the war did represent a triumph for the strategy of attrition (Mueller 1980).

After the substantially abandoned and ill-led South Vietnamese forces collapsed to the Communists in 1975, the United States spent a few years in a sort of containment funk. For the most part it stood idly by while the Soviet Union, in what seems in retrospect to have been remarkably like a fit of absent mindedness, opportunistically collected an overseas empire of nine or ten unimportant countries. These included Vietnam, Cambodia, and Laos in Southeast Asia; Angola, Mozambique, and Ethiopia in Africa, South Yemen in the Middle East; Grenada and Nicaragua in Latin America; and Afghanistan in Asia. The "correlation of forces," the Soviets came happily to believe, had magically and decisively shifted in their direction (Breslauer 1987: 436–7; Hosmer and Wolfe 1983: 12).

However, all of these Soviet allies reacted by almost instantly becoming economic and political basket cases, and often military ones as well, and by turning expectantly to the Soviet Union for the political equivalent of maternal warmth and sustenance. The Soviets concluded that they would have been better off contained, and under Mikhail Gorbachev they soon abandoned their threateningly expansionist ideology and their devotion to impelling ideas about the global class struggle. Most impressively, Gorbachev matched deeds to words particularly by withdrawing Soviet troops from Afghanistan. With that change, the whole premise upon which containment policy rested was shattered, and the Cold War came to an end (Mueller 2011a: ch. 5). During its course, it generated crises and surrogate wars, but direct war between the main contestants seems never to have been close, and it became less likely as time passed (Mueller 1989, ch. 7).

Colonial Wars

Throughout the last two centuries there have been many wars resulting from the efforts of imperial countries to gain, and then to maintain, their hold on distant, or sometimes attached, colonial territories. Indeed, fully 199 of the 244 wars Luard identifies as having taken place between 1789 and 1917 were wars of colonization or decolonization (1986: 52, 60). Another analysis enumerates 149 colonial and imperial wars waged between 1816 and 1992 (Ravlo et al. 2001). One of the great, if often undernoted, changes during the Cold War was the final demise of the whole idea of empire—previously one of the great epoch-defining constants in human history (Crawford 2002, Ray 1989: 431–2, Keeley 1996: 166–7). Colonialism's demise has meant, of course, an end to its attendant wars.

Policing Wars

Having substantially abandoned armed conflict among themselves, the highly developed countries became free to explore various devices and avenues for managing the world if they so desired. Some of these devices are diplomatic, social, or economic, but the judicious application of military force—in ventures that might be called "policing wars"—has also been available. In particular, the former "great powers" could expand their efforts and collaborate on international police work to deal with civil wars and with destructive domestic regimes. The opportunities in the post-Cold War world are considerable. Most recent civil warfare, though certainly not all, can readily be policed because the aggressions are chiefly perpetrated by poorly coordinated, often savage, thugs. Moreover, many of the most vicious governments are substantially criminal regimes that could be readily toppled by coordinated forces sent from outside. Since the end of the Cold War, there have been a number of instances in which developed countries have applied military force in other countries in an effort to correct conditions they consider sufficiently unsuitable.

For the most part, however, civil warfare and vicious regimes have not actually inspired a great deal of alarm in the developed world except when they seem to present a direct threat—as in the cases of some rogue states and in cases where countries in which non-state global threats like al-Qaeda and ISIS have been based. To a degree, the wars in Yugoslavia of the 1990s might also be included because at the time alarmists tended, incorrectly, to envision the widespread expansion of such "ethnic" armed conflicts.[3] Most of the interventions were successful in that they ended civil conflicts and/or deposed contemptible regimes at low cost after which the intervening forces withdrew in short, or fairly short, order turning the countries over to governments that were very substantial improvements over what had been there before and that continued to govern comparatively well. In several cases, however, the ventures successfully changed the regime in the short term but failed in the longer term when the country soon devolved into costly civil armed conflict (Somalia, Afghanistan, Iraq, Libya), or when the new governments established proved to be scarcely better than those that had been deposed (Haiti, and perhaps Kosovo).

However, in this century policing wars are likely to become unusual because there is, overall, little stomach for such operations for at least three key reasons. To begin with, there is little or no political gain at home from success in such ventures. In addition, there is a low tolerance for casualties in such applications of military force, for example, the loss of a couple of dozen soldiers in the Blackhawk down incident in Somalia in 1993 led the mighty United States to withdraw from the country. Moreover, the experience with policing wars has been accompanied by an increasing aversion to the costs and difficulties of what is often called nation-building. Thus, absent an extreme provocation comparable to the 9/11 attacks, it is much more likely that such policing ventures will not be undertaken. Indeed, in its defense priority statement of January 2012, the Defense Department firmly emphasized (i.e. rendered in italics) that *"US forces will no longer be sized to conduct large-scale, prolonged stability operations."*[4] Or, as David Sanger puts it, America is "out of the occupation business" (2012: 419).

Thus, particularly with the experience of Afghanistan and Iraq behind them, calls to send troops to wage such interventions are unlikely to find a very receptive audience. Rather, they are likely to come up against an effective Iraq/Afghan syndrome built on a clear and overwhelming dictum, "let's not do that again" (Mueller 2005, 2011a: 209–10, 217–19, 2011b, 2011c, 2014).

INTERNATIONAL WAR AND PEACE SINCE WORLD WAR II

Not only have developed countries, including the Cold War superpowers, managed to stay out of war with each other since World War II, but there have also been remarkably few international wars of any sort since 1945. Although armed contests between the Israeli government and Palestinian rebels have frequently erupted, no Arab or Muslim country has been willing since 1973 to escalate the contest to international war by sending its troops to participate directly. And after a series of international wars, India and Pakistan have not really waged one since 1971. The only truly notable exception in the last forty years (and it is an important one) was the bloody war between Iran and Iraq that lasted from 1980 to 1988. In addition, there were border skirmishes and conflicts in the 1970s between China and Vietnam and between Ethiopia and Somalia; regime-changing invasions by Tanzania of Uganda in 1978–79 and by the United States of tiny Grenada in 1983 and of Panama in 1989; and a brief armed disputation between Britain and Argentina in 1982 over some remote and nearly barren islands in the South Atlantic.

After the Cold War, there have been some policing wars in the Middle East—one in 1991 to push invading Iraq out of Kuwait, and later a set of post-9/11 wars which mainly degenerated into extended civil conflict in the area. There have also been armed conflicts between Israel and substate groups on its borders. But of the international wars waged since the end of the Cold War in 1989, there was only one that fits cleanly into the classic model in which two countries have it out over some issue of mutual dispute, in this case territory: the almost unnoticed, but quite costly, conflict between Ethiopia and Eritrea that transpired between 1998 and 2000.

It should also be noted that there was a considerable expansion over the last half-century in the number of independent states. When these states were colonies, they could not, by definition, engage in international war with each other. It is particularly impressive that there have been so few international wars during a period in which the number of entities capable of conducting them has increased so greatly. Meanwhile, outside the Cold War, developed countries enjoyed relations that were, by historical standards, so amicable that it actually sounds strange and banal even to suggest that they displayed a notable "unwillingness for war" with each other. It is of considerable significance that, for well over half a century now, no one in France or Germany in any walk of life has advocated a war between these two once war-eager countries. The most notable and striking statistic in the history of warfare is zero: the number of wars conducted between developed states since the end of World War II (Pinker 2011: 249–51). "Given the scale and frequency of war during the preceding centuries in Europe," notes Luard, "this is a change of spectacular proportions: perhaps the single most striking discontinuity that the history of warfare has anywhere provided" (1986: 77).[5] The fact that scarcely anyone ever even bothers to comment on this phenomenon (or non-phenomenon) may be even more impressive.

Indeed, it seems likely that had Adolf Hitler gone into art rather than into politics; had he been gassed a bit more thoroughly by the British in the trenches in 1918; had he succumbed to the deadly influenza of 1919; had he, rather than the man marching next to him been gunned down in the Beer Hall Putsch of 1923; had he failed to survive the automobile crash he experienced in 1930; had he been denied the leadership position in Germany; or had he been removed from office at almost any time before September 1939, Europeans might today be celebrating a century of freedom from international war in their area.

It has occurred to some that a potential cure for most war—at least international war—would be to disallow territorial expansion by states. And, after a certain amount of shuffling around, that is what the peacemakers of 1945 set out to do. Building on efforts conducted after World War I, international boundaries were declared essentially to be sacrosanct—that is, unalterable by the use or threat of military force—no matter how illogical or unjust some of them might seem to interested parties. And the peoples residing in the chunks of territory contained within them would be expected to establish governments which, no matter how disgusting or reprehensible, would then be dutifully admitted to a special club of "sovereign" states known as the United Nations. Efforts to change international frontiers by force or the threat of force were pejoratively labeled "aggression" and sternly declared to be unacceptable and illegal according to the United Nations' charter.

Rather amazingly, this process has, for various reasons and for the most part, worked. Although many international frontiers were in dispute and although some of the largest states quickly became increasingly enmeshed in a profound ideological and military rivalry known as the Cold War, the prohibition against territorial aggression has been astoundingly successful. In the decades since 1945, there have been many cases in which countries split through internal armed rebellion (including anti-colonial wars), and there have been many border disputes. However, reversing the experience and patterns of all recorded history, there have been remarkably few substantial alterations of international boundaries through force. Indeed, the only time one UN member tried to conquer another to incorporate it into its own territory was when Iraq "anachronistically"—to apply Michael Howard's characterization (2000: 92)—invaded Kuwait in 1990, an act that inspired almost total condemnation in the world and one that was reversed in 1991 by military force.[6]

CIVIL WAR AND TERRORISM

In many respects, then, the institution of war, like slavery before it, has shown evidence of being in notable decline in many of its forms, including and especially the one that has traditionally been the most examined, discussed, and feared—international war. What is left is civil war, and a number of these rage in the Middle East—almost all of them exacerbated by extended intervention by outside countries. However, by 2016 some five-sixths of the world's population lived in areas (including the entire Western hemisphere) with little or no war of any kind (Pinker and Santos 2016).

Extrapolating wildly from 9/11, a terrorist event ten times more destructive than any other in history, terrorism has repeatedly been presented as a massive, even existential, threat to the West. But al-Qaeda, a fringe group of a fringe group, has done remarkably little since it got horribly lucky in 2001. Terrorism has remained a rare phenomenon except in war zones where, by deft definitional shift, what would previously have been called insurgency is now being labeled terrorism. This shift is particularly the case with the Islamic State group that emerged in western Iraq and eastern Syria in 2014 (Mueller and Stewart 2017, Cronin 2015).

In the United States, Islamist terrorism has inflicted some six deaths per year since 2001. This low number may be due to a deterrence element—terrorism simply does not recommend itself because it generally proves to be not only unproductive but actually counterproductive. However, the low number of casualties is unlikely to be the result of security measures. There have been scores of terrorist plots rolled up in the United States by the authorities but, looked at carefully, the culprits left on their own do not seem to have had the capacity to increase the death toll very much. As Brian Jenkins puts it, "Their numbers remain small, their determination limp, and their competence poor" (Jenkins 2011: 1; see also Mueller and Stewart 2016a: ch. 3). Nor can security measures have deterred terrorism. Some targets, such as airliners, may have been taken off the list, but potential terrorist targets remain legion (Mueller and Stewart 2016a, 2016b).

THE CONSEQUENCES OF A CULTURE OF PEACE

Over the twentieth century, particularly within the ever-expanding developed world, something that might be called a culture of peace, or an aversion to war, has been established with regard to how countries relate to each other. The process suggests that war is merely an idea, an institution or invention that has been grafted onto human existence (Mead 1964, Mueller 1989, 1995: ch. 8, 2011a: ch. 4, Horgan 2012). It is not a trick of fate, a thunderbolt from hell, a natural calamity, a systemic necessity, or a desperate plot contrivance dreamed up by some sadistic puppeteer on high. The culture of peace has come about, it seems, without changing human nature; without creating an effective world government or system of international law; without modifying the nature of the state or the nation-state; without fabricating an effective moral or practical equivalent; without enveloping the earth in democracy or prosperity; without devising ingenious agreements to restrict arms or the arms industry; without reducing the world's considerable store of hate, selfishness, nationalism, and racism; without increasing the amount of love, justice, or inner peace in the world; without altering the international system; without establishing security communities; without improving the competence of political leaders; and without doing much of anything whatever about nuclear weapons. The institution of war, particularly at the international level, seems to be in pronounced decline because of the way attitudes toward it have changed, roughly following the pattern by which the ancient and once-formidable formal institution of slavery became discredited and then obsolete.

FIGURE 7.5: Memorial for Fallen Soldiers World War I, in Ohlsdorf, Germany overlooks graves of 3,400 Germans, 230 Russians, 6 Serbs, 6 Poles, 2 Romanians, and 1 French soldier. Age Fotostock / Alamy Stock Photo.

Steven Pinker is not comfortable with this sort of explanation. He suggests that "the most satisfying explanation of a historical change is one that identifies an exogenous trigger," and, although he does acknowledge that "new ideas" can sometimes have such an impact, he yearns for "a causal story with more explanatory muscle than 'Developed countries stopped warring because they got less warlike'" (2011: xxiii, 278). Similarly, Jack Levy and William Thompson acknowledge that, while "ideas are not unimportant," they do not "drop from the sky." Rather, "they emerge from and coevolve with more material changes" (2011: 204–5). However, as Ernest Gellner has put it, "A great deal can happen without being necessary and without being inscribed into any historic plan" (1988).[7] The remarkable rise of war aversion and of the culture of peace seems to be a case in point.

Moreover, while war aversion does not seem to have been "caused" by some grander or more material changes, the establishment and maintenance of a culture of peace, or freedom from international war, may cause, or at least productively facilitate, other developments (Mueller 2010b). The twentieth century saw a great expansion of international trade, interdependence, and communication, but this is more likely to be the consequence of peace than the cause of it. International tensions and the prospect of international war have a strong dampening effect on trade because each threatened nation has an incentive to cut itself off from the rest of the world economically in order to ensure that it can survive if international exchange is severed by military conflict. By contrast, if a couple of countries that have previously been in a conflict relationship lapse into a comfortable peace and become extremely unlikely to get into war, businesses in both places are likely to explore the possibilities for mutually beneficial exchange.

The same process may hold for the rise of international institutions and norms. They often stress peace, but like expanded trade flows, they are not so much the cause of peace as its result. Many of the institutions that have been fabricated in Europe—particularly ones like the Coal and Steel Community that were so carefully forged between France and Germany in the years following World War II—have been specifically designed to reduce the danger of war between erstwhile enemies. However, it is difficult to see why the institutions should get the credit for the peace that has flourished between those two countries for the last three quarters of a century.[8] They are among the consequences of the peace, or the culture of peace, that has enveloped Western Europe since 1945, not its cause.

Peace may also furnish countries with the security and space in which to explore and develop democracy because democracy and democratic idea entrepreneurs are more likely to flourish when the trials, distortions, and disruptions of war—whether international or civil—are absent. Countries often restrict or even abandon democracy when domestic instability or external military threat seems to loom. By the same token, when people are comfortably at peace, they may come to realize that they no longer require a strongman to provide order and can afford to embrace the benefits of democracy.

CHAPTER EIGHT

Peace as Integration

GENEVIÈVE SOUILLAC

This chapter charts manifestations of peace as integration during the twentieth century. It investigates the normative power of ideas that have shaped the century and underpinned the growth of international organizations, international law, and movements for social justice, ecology and peace. Its main claim is that the late-modern era's contribution to peace was successful insofar as its institutional development featured a coherent theoretical commitment to positive peace promoting the normative, political, and social features of a flourishing and just collective human life. While the twentieth century saw fragile bonds of civility repeatedly broken by wars, genocides, and enduring neocolonial legacies, interstate cooperation and social mobilization sustained the cause of peace with justice. Since the inception of modern peace movements, social mobilization has built upon existential concerns to affirm peace, justice, and respect for the environment as core social, political, and cultural values within modernity. The moral force of these ideas has sustained the integration of institutional processes of cooperation and accountability and celebrated a diverse and inclusive view of humanity. Such forms of peace as integration to this day find their origin and their motivational force in the critical struggle against divisive forms of nationalism, dehumanization, and morbid legacies left unresolved. As the chapter argues, the aspirational power of peace as integration contained in its moral force continues to motivate the recovery of the public space heralded by political modernity, democratic republicanism, and cosmopolitan liberalism, but it remains fragile and requires sustained revitalization.

The chapter explores three areas where peace as integration has provided the answer to the twentieth century's existential concerns. The first section of the chapter turns to the beginnings of institutional thinking about cooperation and world peace. The growth of militarist nationalism and the modern advent of war on a global industrial scale revitalized historical critique and pacifist conceptions of moral agency. As two world wars shattered the Enlightenment's faith in rational progress, emergent views on peace internationalism that resisted perceived regressions of civilization were charged with prophetic significance. Realistic doubts about the moral capacity of nation-states renewed trust in human mobilization in the name of peaceful ideals, and legal institutionalism became the means of constraining claims to absolute sovereignty. The second section examines how an innovative global order continued to affirm the goal of morally shaping the historical destiny of states. While the Cold War, the threat of nuclear annihilation, and decolonization contradicted the smooth path of Western notions of progress, international organizations and normative frameworks such as the UN and the EU were successfully established. These institutionalized limits on the territorial aims of nations and enshrined equal respect for the self-determination of peoples. Supported by the emergence of transnational civil forces, and aided by the growth of the media's international scrutiny, these institutions and norms also facilitated the postcolonial critique of the West and of its civilizing mission. As the third section analyzes, the force of the idea of peace for regional and local social integration strengthened with the rising awareness of the direct and structural violence spawned by empire and neocolonial geopolitics and expressed in local conflicts. The leadership provided by movements and policies accentuating the socially integrative role of peace motivated the commitment to developing knowledge about the transformation of conflict and the conditions for peace in an era of complexity.

Overall, the chapter traces the sustained moral gravitas of peace and human rights norms within a globalized historical context where the rapid growth of international law pursued pacifism's legacy aiming to delegitimize militarism and extreme forms of nationalism. Social constructivist accounts of the relations between states, cosmopolitan theories of norm dynamics, as well as transnational advocacy, contributed in practical and theoretical ways to psychosocial insights into collective processes of repair for communities shattered by structural injustice and violence. These conceptually innovative frameworks reflect and support the institutional building of peace and the empowerment of actors and communities towards social integration as an antidote to further division along political, ethnic, cultural, and religious lines that constitute the fertile ground for nationalism, militarism, and the political passions of populism. Ultimately, they break down the classical divide between realist politics and peace-oriented idealism, showing that peace can be practically built at a variety of levels from the critique of injustice and emphasis on the democratic rule of law, to conflict resolution and conflict transformation mechanisms. These responses to existential threats innovate by integrating complexity with a view to both learning from the past and creating the future. Negotiating contested collective narratives has become crucial for the long-term processing of legacies of violence and injustice. As this chapter emphasizes, the epistemic role of history and critique and the socially integrative force of peace gleaned by visionaries over a century ago have become once again a core issue for citizens and leaders.

PEACE AS MORAL FORCE: THE POWER OF IDEAS AGAINST THE DESTRUCTION OF WAR

The rise of peace as a moral force for politics emerges from the secular legacy of the Enlightenment and its faith in reason (Bok 1995). Early modern advocates for peace such as Erasmus, the Abbé de Saint-Pierre, and Kant grappled with questions of practical morality, political power and human nature inherited from Antiquity. In the emerging opposition between "realism" and "idealism," differing views about the place of morality in political relations and the human propensity for violence paved the way for the ideological impact of nationalism in nineteenth-century Europe, where love of country emerged as a new source of social and political cohesion (Gellner 2009; Anderson 2016). Ethno-nationalist discourses grounded in race, culture, and language conflicted with civic nationalism. In his lecture of March 11, 1882 at the Sorbonne, entitled "What is a Nation?" Ernest Renan (2018) famously proposed to ground the spirit of nationhood in civic voluntarism rather than in a static ethnic and cultural conception of a people frozen in history. How did the idea of peace and global cooperation emerge against this backdrop of ideas? How did a second wave of internationalism, building upon erudite Enlightenment cosmopolitanism, take shape in the West at the turn of the twentieth century?

The intellectual legacy of rationalism and the rise of nationalism paradoxically combined to fashion the contradictions of the early twentieth century. Towering intellectual figures of the early twentieth century such as Jean Jaurès and Henri Bergson grappled with the atmosphere of nationalism and impending war that characterized its first two decades. While nationalism expressed longing for identity and country, the belief in the civilizing role of reason and history also prevailed even as World War I ushered in a tragic consciousness of history. Emergent nationalist ideologies fueled the outbreak of World War I, leading to the catastrophe of war on an industrial scale and challenging notions of progress and of history. The French Catholic philosopher Yves Simon (1941) observed that the intellectual atmosphere at the time of his arrival in Paris from a French province in 1920 was striking in its intense focus on international peace, to the detriment of discussions on domestic politics. Encapsulated first in nationalist, then in totalitarian ideologies, reason appeared to defeat itself, posing new limits to human agency, and requiring further institutional and normative approaches to support liberal notions of autonomy and social action.

Both Jean Jaurès and Henri Bergson shared a dynamic view of humanity's creative renewal and a strong belief in the power of ideas, exhibiting parallel paths of intellectual and practical engagement for peace. In 1878, both succeeded brilliantly at the entrance exam for the *École Normale Supérieure*, while later in 1881, they achieved the *agrégation* of philosophy. Unlike Bergson, Jaurès chose political activism rather than a formal academic career, becoming a renowned parliamentarian and defender of social justice, and writing and publishing extensively for *L'Humanité* and other newspapers. Jaurès, a prophet of social mobilization for justice, echoed the growth of other social movements of the time (Tilly and Wood 2012; Martin 2008). At the Basel Congress of the Second International on November 24–25, 1912, he recast the workers' cause as a tool for peace. He keenly observed the effects of capital and industry, and saw how ideologies such as nationalism exacerbated existing forms of imperialism and underscored unchecked monopolies of economic power in a context of rapid industrialization and exploitation. Shocked by the sheer number of combatant deaths during the Balkan wars of 1912–13, Jaurès also saw in the new, industrial scale of modern wars a warning of catastrophes to come. Ten days before the beginning of World War I, Jaurès referred to the nightmare of the several armies of millions of soldiers that would perish should a conflict break out between the European powers. In the intensely patriotic mood of the time, Jaurès prophetically rejected nationalism. On the evening of July 31, 1914 in Paris, he was assassinated by a right-wing nationalist fanatic before he could write what he intended to be a seminal article for *L'Humanité* on behalf of an integral vision of social justice (Souillac 2016).

Meanwhile, Henri Bergson's popularity and influence as a professor, intellectual and diplomat was widening. Bergson won the Nobel Prize for Literature in 1927. His philosophical body of work included reflections on perception, memory, evolution and ethics and emphasized the *élan vital* (Kreps 2016). Towards the end of his life in 1935, Bergson published *The Two Sources of Morality and Religion* (1977) in which he defended the potential for an inclusive society oriented towards creative emergence. Earlier, in 1917, French Prime Minister Aristide Briand had sent Bergson to Washington, DC to

FIGURE 8.1: Memorials honoring soldiers who were killed in World War I, like this one in Saint Cyprien, Dordogne are located in villages and towns in France. D. P. Fry photo collection.

persuade US president Woodrow Wilson to renounce US neutrality and enter the war raging in Europe. Accounts differ on the precise nature of the mutual influence between Wilson and Bergson. Wilson's suspicions about the Continent resonated with Bergson's doubts about the readiness of the world to take on a League of Nations (Tooze 2015). But their ideas of global cooperation and of the federating power of institutions converged, and Bergson returned to France hopeful that with the help of the United States, the building of peace could begin after an Allied victory. Bergson's work alongside President Wilson in designing the League of Nations reflects, as Soulez and Worms (2002) argue, his practical investment in the power of ideas through international cooperation and institution building. Later, from 1921 to 1926, Bergson became the President of the International Commission for Intellectual Cooperation, the precursor of UNESCO.

The lives and work of Jaurès, Bergson and Wilson reflect the contradictions at the heart of a dawning twentieth century (Soulez 1989; Soulez and Worms 2002). Caught in the intensely patriotic atmosphere of their time, and only a few days after the assassination of Jean Jaurès, Bergson justified the war in a speech on August 8, 1914, as a struggle for civilization and against the forces of German militarism. On December 12, 1914, Bergson's annual public speech as President of the *Académie des Sciences Morales et Politiques* denounced German war crimes. Despite the turn of the century's innovation in the sciences, the humanities and the arts (Compagnon 2015), historians concur on the frequent recourse to notions of civilization and even race in the propaganda of World War I (Audoin-Rouzeau & Becker 2003). For Caeymaex (2012) as for Soulez (1989), the seeds of Bergson's later defense of universal peace lay in his elaborate theory of the creative evolution of humanity as well as in his personal outrage at the war. Overall however, the sheer moral devastation imposed by the war stifled philosophical endeavor and the voice of rationalism, argues Claudine Tiercelin (2015), who highlights the value of the era's dissenting voices.

Jaurès, Bergson and Wilson were highly influential thinkers who were ambivalently caught in the fraught ascent of conflicting notions of progress and civilization, identity and technology, blatant nationalistic power and new forms of democratic legitimacy. The convergent critiques of nationalism, militarism, and expansionism prophetically underscored values such as freedom and equality, dialogue, and democratic participation to challenge narrowly established and exclusivist ideologies and identities. The Fourteen Points famously devised by Wilson to negotiate the end of World War I included free trade, open agreements, democratic values and the principle of sovereignty and self-determination, preempting the liberal international order that followed World War II. Wilson was significantly influenced by anti-militarist and antiwar activism in the United States (Kazin 2017), and understood that rapidly growing peace movements (Cortright 2008; Ceadel 1980, 2017) held moral force and constituted a vehicle for the principled mediation of historical violence. The France-US led Kellogg-Briand pact of August 1928 (1929: 57–64) also boldly (or foolishly for its critics) established the groundwork for an international legal framework to renounce war as an instrument of national policy (Hathaway and Shapiro 2017). This principle is embedded in the UN Charter. Notably, the US relinquished the renunciation of war as an instrument of national policy in the *National Security Strategy* (2002) issued by the White House in September 2002. This move foreshadowed the justification of the US invasion of Iraq in March 2003 as both a preventive and a preemptive option to adapt the use of military force to the policy's identification of new forms of imminent threat.

Visionary political and civil society actors pursued their attempts to integrate politics and ethics in order to forge the overlapping conceptual and institutional, legal and moral architectures that we now take for granted as the building blocks of positive peace. Yet despite prophetic actors, the disconnect between the catastrophes of history and the narrative of the progress of civilization remained in place. Further, increasingly sterile debates between liberal internationalist and realist perspectives have haunted politics and defied peace throughout the modern era. The belligerent and volatile context of the early twentieth century was a continuation of a nineteenth century marked by colonial expansion and wars of empire, and posed new ethical conundrums with regard to difference, and universality. These have still not been resolved after a second world war, the Cold War, and now several decades of power politics. Nevertheless, the legacy of early twentieth-century thinkers and doers is to have invoked an alternative path of peace with passion and sophistication. This legacy runs through the twentieth century and into the twenty-first. It reflects the achievement of a structure of international norms in its design to guide cooperation between states and empower grassroots mobilization for peace with justice, despite social and political pressures to undermine it ever since.

INTEGRATING INSTITUTIONS AND IDEAS FOR PEACE: OBSTACLES AND ALTERNATIVES

World War I yielded a new awareness of the catastrophic consequences of historical forces, of which nationalism appeared as the most divisive. Further, the systematic extermination of ethnic and social categories not fitting into Nazi definitions of superior race has stood out since the end of World War II as an affront to human conscience. America's atomic bombing of Hiroshima and Nagasaki to end the war in the Pacific also shocked the world because the sheer industrial and scientific prowess of modernity was exploited to kill instantly on an unprecedented massive scale. The idea of peace emerged in this context of accumulated man-made catastrophes as a humanist counterforce for the moralization of a modern age that had been structured by states, empires, nationalist ideologies, and increasingly, industry at the service of war. The United Nations Charter of 1945, and, in 1948, both the Universal Declaration of Human Rights (UDHR) and the signing of the Convention Against Genocide, powerfully signaled a halt to the dehumanization wrought by Great Power expansionism and challenged other classical forms of state behavior. The Universal Declaration of Human Rights, supported by the UN Commission on Human Rights established in 1946 (the Human Rights Council since 2006), and later, by the Office of the High Commissioner for Human Rights (the OHCHR, established in 1993), pioneered the global architecture of human rights by shaping one of the most inclusive and audacious philosophical anthropologies, one that integrated the core rights of the liberal tradition with the civic democratic rights inherited from the French Revolution of 1789, and social and cultural rights (Moyn 2012; Souillac 2005; Hunt 2008; Glendon 2001; Morsink 1997).

The formation of the EU was a milestone experiment in internationalism in response to the horrors of war. Grounding security in cooperative, rather than defensive state behavior was new for European countries traumatized by invasion and occupation. The project was nurtured by generations of visionary leaders from France and Germany, Jean Monnet at the outset, then De Gaulle, Adenauer, Mitterrand, and Kohl, and more recently, French President Emmanuel Macron and German Chancellor Angela Merkel. UK voters narrowly approved an unprecedented withdrawal from the EU in a June 2016 referendum. Withdrawal was initially scheduled to take place March 29, 2019. Until then, the European Union had kept growing on a continent repeatedly divided by war and celebrated for its cultural, ethnic and linguistic diversity. The Treaty of Paris in 1951 initially established the European Coal and Steel Community (ECSC) as a supranational organization aimed at preventing future war by integrating through trade its six founding members, namely France, West Germany, Belgium, Luxembourg, the Netherlands and Italy. After a proposal for federating Europe through a defense and political community was rejected, the European Economic Community (EEC) and the European Atomic Energy Community were created by treaties signed in Rome in 1957. The integration of additional member states began in the 1970s with the inclusion of Denmark, Ireland, and the United Kingdom, and continued in the 1980s with the addition of Greece, Spain, and Portugal. A form of political integration of EEC members through shared institutions including a parliamentary assembly and a judicial system was achieved in 1979. The EU

FIGURE 8.2: Poster by Alain Carrier in 1991 by the United Nations to celebrate the Universal Declaration of Human Rights. Personal copy, D. P. Fry photo collection.

is now a political and economic union of twenty-eight member states and over five hundred million people, the source of significant amounts of foreign aid, and the recipient of the Nobel Peace Prize in 2012.

Led by Jean Monnet and supported by Robert Schuman, the utopian project of European unity after the two world wars generated unprecedented diplomatic innovations aimed at integration at multiple levels. Even a minimal degree of transfer of sovereignty in a postwar context soured by humiliation and defeat made any attempt at generating regional institutions seem like a pipe dream. Yet following his conceptualization and drafting of what would be called the Schuman Plan, Jean Monnet became the first president of the European Coal and Steel Community. He persevered throughout his life in his belief in the practical and moral worth of European unification (Monnet 1978; Duchêne 1994; Fransen 2001). Hurt feelings and trauma could not disappear, but European leaders nonetheless worked on building trust through new forms of cooperation for prosperity. As Monnet evocatively writes in his memoir about his first meeting with Chancellor Adenauer of Germany on May 23, 1950, described by François Fontaine as "the true birth of Franco-German reconciliation, and of the European Community founded on equality of rights" (Brinkley and Hackett 1991: 43):

I already had some idea of how Adenauer looked, with his rigid figure and impassive face ... The man before me was not self-assured, but anxious to know what I was going to say, and unable completely to conceal a degree of mistrust. Clearly, he could not believe that we were really proposing full equality; and his attitude was still marked by long years of hard negotiation and wounded pride. Our conversation lasted for an hour and a half. As it progressed, I saw the old man gradually relax and reveal the emotion that he had been holding back.

—Monnet 1978: 309

Certainly, Monnet understood the importance of shared institutions. But beyond functionalist theories, for which Monnet had little interest, commentators and friends agree that Monnet's approach was unique and perhaps best encapsulated in his own defiant belief that "(w)ar was in men's imagination, and (it) had to be opposed by imagination" (Monnet 1978: 290). As George Ball writes, "with his usual perspicacity, Monnet recognized that the very irrationality of the scheme would compel progress and might then start a chain reaction" (Brinkley and Hackett 1991: xiii).

Monnet's tireless work shows that mere functionalist institutionalism misses the historical and symbolic role of institutions. "Coal and steel," he writes, "were at once the key to economic power and the raw materials for forging weapons of war," a "double role (which) gave them immense symbolic significance, now largely forgotten" (Monnet 1978: 293). Monnet's negotiating skills, learned as a representative of his family's business, had led him to hold an important role during, and after World War I when he became Deputy Secretary-General of the League of Nations from 1919 to 1923. Monnet challenged elite notions of commerce and empire with the common sense of someone familiar with the land, and pursued a humanist pragmatism, understanding the importance of seizing the moment and making creative connections (Fransen 2001). For Monnet, who was not ideologically motivated but included in his long-term vision a careful understanding of the human crafting process, institutional resilience through history is both shaped and shared by all because, as he writes, "(n)othing is possible without men: nothing is lasting without institutions" (Monnet 1978: 304–5). As he comments in his Memoirs, "(i)t was less a question of solving problems, which are mostly in the nature of things, than of putting them in a more rational and human perspective, and making use of them to serve the cause of international peace" (Monnet 1978: 297). Ultimately, Monnet believed in "the power of simple ideas expressed plainly and unvaryingly, over and over again" (Monnet 1978: 331). The "permanent dialogue" between national governments and common institutions was "part of a civilizing process whereby nation-states were coming to accept the supremacy of law, as fellow citizens do" (Mayne 1991: 121).

Monnet's lesson of a strong institutionalism backed by the symbolic power of ideas resonates in the twenty-first century. His faith in the potential of institutions to federate human emotions and hope adds a uniquely innovative feature to the European experiment in peace as integration. The enduring appeal of this experiment lies in Monnet's investment in the psychosocial dimensions of peace. Monnet's "slow and unspectacular" work, in his words, of forging the unity of Europe went by a "fundamental choice of a method for continual and psychological integration" (Monnet 1978: 300). The *amitié franco-allemande*, sealed in 1963 by de Gaulle and Adenauer with the *Traité de l'Elysée*, was not an epiphenomenon of Europe's economic and political integration. Instead, Franco-German friendship was conceived as the core engine of European integration. Franco-

FIGURE 8.3: Reading Jean Monnet, the author's book collection. D. P. Fry photo collection.

German reconciliation was a long-term historical process which now serves as a model of conflict resolution and reconciliation thanks to its political, social, and psychological complexity (Ackermann 1994). The outpouring of appreciation and homage for Helmut Kohl and Simone Veil, who both died in June of 2017, testifies to the persuasive impression the EU has made on the regional landscape. Simone Veil, a Holocaust survivor who became France's Minister of Health, was the first president of the newly elected European Parliament in 1979. Veil attributed her enduring belief and commitment to European integration to her mother whom she saw die in the concentration camp Bergen Belsen; her mother who had always insisted on the vital importance of forgiveness and reconciliation.

The integration of ideational concerns such as peace with the necessary pragmatism of institutionalism and a subtler understanding of the motivations of human behavior no doubt has greatly influenced the history of peace as integration in the modern era despite conceptual and practical difficulties. Despite criticisms and impediments, the growth of the EU to include twenty-eight member states (as of this writing) left an unprecedented impression illustrating how institutions and values shape actors' interests, and influencing theories from intergovernmentalism to environmentalism (Selin and Van de Veer 2015). The enduring affirmation of sovereignty in the international system has often functioned against cooperation, with the UN Security Council veto provision a most important case because it limits the application of the doctrine of collective security that is present in the UN Charter (Danchin and Fischer 2010). Still, regional integration continued in the decades following World War II. Classic military defense organizations such as the North

Atlantic Treaty Organization (NATO), and intergovernmental institutions such as the Organization of American States, the African Union, and the Association of South East Asian Nations have been establishing varying types and degrees of economic, political, and legal integration. As Goertz, Diehl and Balas (2016) note, empirical evidence indicates that a complex institutional world now prevents classical wars of territorial acquisition through norms that constrain sovereignty claims, encourage the mediation of international conflict, and increase the costs of blatant territorial conquest. Even in cases of secretive or underhand movements by states, sanctions exist; and increasingly today, the scrutiny of global public opinion may act as a deterrent. Overall, institutional integration modified conceptions of security in the modern era, with notions of collective, and later of human security integrating defense, development, the responsibility to protect, and global and environmental justice more generally as issues of common concern.

Scholarly analyses during the Cold War typically generated balance of power theories framed by realist and neorealist accounts of international anarchy, state behavior, and human nature (Morgenthau 1963; Bull 2012; Waltz 2001). Subsequent schools of thought that contest purely realist frameworks stress the integration of global governance, international law, soft power, and civil society (Keohane 1986, 2005; Goldstein and Keohane 1993; Keohane and Nye 2011). The growing impact of norms on the motivations of state actors in a post-Westphalian era (Linklater 1999, 2007; Wendt 1999; Mapel and Nardin 1998) are explained as reflecting the deepening social interaction of states and

FIGURE 8.4: The expansion of the UN as a forum for cooperation on matters of common interest is evidence of a new institutional global order. D. P. Fry photo collection.

challenge prior accounts of the international system and of diplomacy. As the role of norms in shaping political motivation has become clearer, our understanding of these institutional developments continue to extend our understanding of agency. The expansion of the UN as a forum of international cooperation on matters of common interest, standard-setting and international treaty law, especially in human rights, humanitarian, and environmental law, structures another level of the global order (Frost 1986; Linklater 1999, 2007). Its policy guidelines address what are increasingly seen as regional and global challenges to humanity such as environmental degradation, public health threats, endemic poverty, and armed conflicts. Although love of country is still encouraged by enduring power rivalries and domestic politics, transnational ideals and alliances have drawn the contours of a global public space where both justice and the institutionalization of cooperation and dialogue by multiscalar actors have become synonymous with the promotion of peace.

Nevertheless realism's assumption of an anarchic interstate structure produces a pervasive ideological bias against peace as irenic idealism. In the realist world-view, international organizations such as the UN and EU, and civil society mobilizations in nongovernmental organizations constitute additional layers of soft power on a resolutely brutal and anarchic international system. These accounts often draw from mythical narratives of violence and war as the natural condition of humanity and perpetuate classical views of an international order that is in a chronic state of delayed or potential war. The plethora of narratives about aggression, war, and violence still advocated by some scholars in primatology, economics, evolutionary psychology, and other disciplines accept and play on the hackneyed dichotomy between civilized and uncivilized (Chagnon 2013; Bowles 2009; Wrangham and Peterson 1996). They support triumphalist accounts of an evolutionary progress from so-called archaic societies to an era of global governance and Western institutions (Pinker 2011). Despite the long and varied cultural history of international society (Watson 2009), it is customary to see in the international order the normative product of Western civilization since the *jus gentium*, or law of nations, was elaborated by early modern thinkers in response to the rivalries and expansion of European princes (Brown, Nardin and Rengger 2002). This emancipatory narrative assumes the perennial nature of dominant state power and remains focused on building negative peace without problematizing the existing system or situating it in a critical history of modernity.

The proliferation of scholarly interest in medieval, early modern and modern theologies of just war (Elshtain 1992; Holmes 2016) throughout the decades of the Cold War has testified to the prevalence of this cultural orientation. While Just War theories provided reasonable objections to pacifist positions deemed untenable in the case of the Allied victory against Nazi Germany (Walzer 2015), they did not explore further alternatives beyond the hackneyed opposition between war and pacifism. On the other hand, successful nonviolent regime change as in India and the Philippines, nonviolent movements for reform like the US Civil Rights movement in the 1960s, as well as protests against the Vietnam War and the 2003 Iraq War illuminated forms of civic action that spoke to alternative ways of understanding domination and war and that questioned their prevalence in modernity (Chenoweth and Stephan 2012). Essentialist narratives about human nature undergirding explanatory theories about world order perpetuate the view that peace in a Westphalian order of states cannot exist outside of an international order dominated by Western civilization. They have also affirmed policy shifts by states from wars of conquest to wars of defense, making other peace policy alternatives appear absurd. These accounts misconstrue emancipation as requiring violence and conflict, perpetuate and glorify patriarchal narratives about the struggle of civilization in taming a presumed human appetite for violence and brutality. Crucially, they avoid the critical function of the peace paradigm with its disruptive effects on power, violence, and empire. Thus, Jaurès and Bergson at different times questioned the apparently seamless connection between political power, the state's war machine, and dogmatic moral definitions of civilization. The moral force of peace from the grassroots, they argued, was not the result of a civilizing morality but of the critique of a modern world that had lost its soul, dried up by industrialization, mechanization, and homogenization.

INTEGRATING INSTITUTIONS, PEOPLE AND PRACTICE: BUILDING LASTING PEACE

Binary approaches pitting idealism against realism overlook alternatives that take the pragmatic features of positive peace seriously. Critics of international cooperation and of multilateralism ultimately reinforce the culture of war, its assumptions of Western supremacy, and its attendant narratives of a clash of civilizations (Huntington 1996), even as the rapid transformation of geopolitics and demographics challenge Western economic and political dominance. Yet the sheer destruction of two World Wars followed by the ideological simplifications of the Cold War and its many bloody proxy wars fought amid the threat of nuclear annihilation, highlight the relationship of human agency to history. Ethical questions regarding human civilization, modernity and violence thus often remain influenced by unexamined epistemologies and the rationalizations of human progress regarding harm, including the scourge of war. The critique of the West provoked by decolonization and inspired by social and antimilitarist ideals and nonviolent movements generated new debates on civilization and progress. The objectification of "archaic" societies by Western epistemologies is symptomatic of the growth of modern institutional knowledge in the context of Western expansion and colonialism. As noted by Elise Boulding (2000) and Douglas Fry (2006, 2007), rather than problematizing inherited controversies about the violence or peacefulness of human nature, such epistemologies reinforce the "war-nurtured identity of Western civilization" (Boulding 2000: 13) based on an essentialized view of human behavior at individual and group levels. Instead, peace and security necessitate a complex appraisal and disclosure of historical events and patterns of violence that reproduce the humiliation of groups and nations (Moïsi 2010; Linklater 2011, 2017; Souillac 2012, 2015; Souillac and Fry 2016).

Exploring the critical force of peace as integration in theory and practice reverses scholarly accounts and public discourse that overlook the breadth and depth of the positive peace architecture built in the twentieth century. During the Cold War, decolonization processes combined with new forms of nationalism gained momentum, while in 1991 the collapse of the Soviet Union brought an end to the ideological division between the Eastern and Western blocs, and seemingly affirmed the triumph of liberal democracy. However, since this post-Cold War turning point emphasized human rights norms sourced at the core of Western democracy, it also witnessed the flourishing of civil society actors as well as renewed calls for increased cooperation to address issues of planetary concern from human rights to the environment. Agencies such as ECOSOC and the legal provision for nongovernmental actors in the UN Charter authorized the role of civil society actors in their scrutiny of state behavior in the areas of peace, justice and human rights. This new political sphere has enhanced the global exchange of information and ideas and shaped activist goals in the field of social justice, associating them with matters of cosmopolitan concern (Falk 1995, 2000, 2016; Souillac 2012, 2015). As Andrew Linklater (2011) argues, cosmopolitan harm conventions (CHCs) and the normative debates surrounding them depend on critical reflexivity and considerations of alterity. They should enable deliberative discussion about rules of inclusion, exclusion, and coexistence (Linklater (2007: 56). Since the end of the Cold War, the underlying structures of inequality, poverty, domination, and exploitation that were standard features of both totalitarianism and of empires are being scrutinized with renewed vigor, yielding intersectional critiques of the global system that were initiated by decolonization.

The democratization of the international society of states under the auspices of the UN facilitated the critical scrutiny necessary for the ongoing integration of peace with human rights, democratization and development goals. A consolidation of the discursive and normative connections between human rights, conflict, and peace can be traced from the UN's Geneva and Genocide Conventions (1949) through subsequent UN Conventions that have: (a) *defined* universal civil and political rights (1966), and economic, social, and cultural rights (1966); (b) *defined* the rights of particular classes of people: children (1989), migrant workers (1990), and the disabled (2006); and (c) *outlawed* racial discrimination (1965), discrimination against women (1979), torture (1984), and enforced disappearances (2006). Especially after the Cold War, the rights discourses that produced these international conventions show the claims of culture gaining increasing relevance (Alston and Goodman 2012; Goodhart 2016).

The application of these principles can be observed in humanitarian and development policy. With a shift from national security to human security and a focus on the vulnerabilities faced globally by humans (Kaldor 2003, 2007). The change was announced in the UN Development Program's groundbreaking *Human Development Report* in 1994. Its scope was elaborated in *Human Security Now* (2003) produced by the UN Commission on Human Security that was chaired at the time by Nobel Prize winning economist Amartya Sen and former High Commissioner for Refugees, Sadako Ogata. *Human Security Now* examines a wide range of issues including postconflict recovery, political freedom, food security, migration flows, and gender-based violence that have built on the UN's Millennium Development Goals (MDGs) and become the basis for regional human development programs. Critics of the human security school point to the vagueness arising from its inclusiveness and to the difficulties in translating its ideals into concrete policies for states to implement. However, its emergence in the global normative discourse has had the merit of drawing attention to broader structures of geopolitical inequality within neo-imperial realities.

Development and human security concerns sustain the human rights, peace and cooperation agendas by integrating them into a coherent set of overarching public policy goals that can be institutionally iterated regionally, thus reinforcing their reach and influence. When US President Franklin D. Roosevelt's 1941 Four Freedoms Speech expressed the concern with freedom from fear, freedom from want, and the freedoms of speech and faith, it also opened a pathway for the integration of human security with the provision of basic rights, sustainable development, and positive peace, within a post-Cold War era. The substantial body of human rights law and standard-setting documents negotiated within intergovernmental organizations from the Council of Europe to the Organization of American States and the African Union exemplify these trends. The Council of Europe's Court of Human Rights has generated a substantial body of case law and jurisprudence due to its unique structure and powers, as well as controversy with regard to some of its judgments that keep the public debate on human rights alive and well (Clarke 2017; Christoffersen and Madsen 2013). Meanwhile, the Inter-American Commission on Human Rights monitors and promotes the human rights defined in the American Convention on Human Rights by examining petitions, and the African Commission on Human and People's Rights undertakes studies and disseminates information for the promotion and protection of human rights through its main instrument, the *African Charter on Human and People's Rights*, and the African Court on Human and People's Rights.

Further, normative integration (Souillac 2004) shaped peacekeeping and peacebuilding mandates at the end of the Cold War, when UN mandates expanded to include human rights and democratic institution and nation building. Such mandates included demobilization, the repatriation of child soldiers, election monitoring, and the mainstreaming of gender and human security perspectives (Miall, et al. 2015; Schirch 2013; Bellamy 2010; Mertus and Helsing 2006). The application of global institutional discourses on peace, human rights and humanitarian work across intergovernmental and nongovernmental agencies eventually led to further critique (Richmond 2011, 2016; Bell and Coicaud 2006). As Oliver Richmond (2014) argues, the reconstruction of political communities under the auspices of the international community is often limited by the legitimacy deficit of liberal peace projects. Following the controversy regarding the universal nature of international human rights in the 1990s (Bell and Bauer 1999; Dunne and Wheeler 1999), anthropology inquired into the local application of human rights agendas (Goodale 2008, 2009, 2014). Finally, the convergence of responsibility to protect with promotion of democratic regime change in the 1990s led to vigorous debates on the morality and legality of humanitarian intervention on human rights grounds (Weiss 2016; Scheid 2014; Moyn 2014; Chandler 2006; Whelsh 2006; Walzer 2004; Finnemore 2004; Holzgrefe and Keohane 2003; Wheeler 2003). Ultimately, peace as integration in the era after the end of the Cold War showed that if the double standards historically evidenced by the *mission civilisatrice* were to be exposed, and globalization still to define our normative universe, then global policy must always be contextualized geopolitically, including in the case of policies for humanitarian and development aid (Brauman 1995, 2000; Klein 2002).

Overarching norms such as human rights are undergirded by the civic values of participation, cooperation, and dialogue. These values serve the connected causes of political critique, human security, and peace by informing nonviolent practices that challenge powerful establishments, and by expressing a concern for a culturally inclusive approach that allows for the development of complex identities (Souillac 2004, 2012). Contemporary legal, moral and normative dimensions of international life have had transformative effects on accountability both in domestic and global political arenas, illustrating how public deliberation about global norms redefines civilized behavior. Global norm dynamics highlight new forms of legitimacy that consolidate new norms affirming peace and human rights not only internationally but, crucially, domestically as well (Keck and Sikkink 1998; Risse, Ropp and Sikkink 1999; Risse and Ropp 2013). The shaming induced by global scrutiny that is enhanced by unprecedented digital and satellite communications networks encourages political change by creating the social, political, and psychological conditions necessary for the socialization of state actors while also encouraging civil society actors and transnational solidarity. Human rights monitoring from Kenya to Indonesia and Morocco has delivered a degree of compliance which has impacted the global image of these states (Risse and Ropp 2013), enabling changes in

FIGURE 8.5: Medieval city hall Frankfurt am Main, displaying (right to left) the flags of Frankfurt, Germany, and the EU. D. P. Fry photo collection.

political identity as societies question themselves and face transitions after conflict and trauma. In the emblematic case of South Africa, apartheid was dismantled and new norms regarding race were negotiated domestically in the face of growing isolation from the international community (Klotz 1999).

Peace as integration in the late-modern era thus harnesses grassroots mobilization and the legally mediated solidarity of international human rights law to deal with the many legacies of violence and the struggles against impunity (Roht-Ariazza 1995, 2006). The institutional growth of international criminal law, including case law developed by the ad hoc international tribunals to prosecute war crimes and crimes against humanity in the former Yugoslavia (ICTY) in 1993, and *génocidaires* in Rwanda (ICTR) in 1994, applies humanitarian and human rights conventions, changing both local and global perceptions of criminal responsibility with regard to conflict and its consequences. While the new International Criminal Court (ICC) that began its work in 2003 has met with criticism as a suspicious continuation of Western-led geopolitics (Bosco 2014; Cryer 2003) and also from the United States as a threat to national sovereignty, it is now widely recognized that the global public sphere requires a balancing act between the critique of geopolitical interests and the rights of victims (Sikkink 2011, 2017). Resolution of many ethical, diplomatic, and legal issues in both official and people's war crimes tribunals remains elusive. Nonetheless, these legal bodies contribute to the development of public knowledge about the nature of war crimes, justice, and the positive peaceable resolution of violent conflict. Wider theoretical descriptions of the institutional, ideational, and psychosocial landscapes that explain violence and conflict indicate that peace is most sustainable when it integrates a variety of concerns from justice to democracy, to the recovery of memory and the fostering of reconciliation (Philpott 2006; Volkan 2006; Fitzduff and Stout 2006). Multi-track diplomatic endeavors (Diamond 1999), in coordination with local and transnational actors, enable a complex approach to conflict transformation with a view to repairing broken social cohesion and collectively facing the past, present, and future.

Transitional processes demonstrate how multifaceted peace as integration becomes in practice. Restorative justice mechanisms like commissions set up to publicly reveal the truth about conflicts and use it to promote reconciliation have been used in transitional democracies to deal with the legacies of ideological and state-sponsored violence in countries such as Argentina, Chile, Peru, Guatemala, El Salvador, and Morocco (Hayner 2010; Roht-Ariazza and Mariezcurerena 2006), and to aid recovery in post-conflict and post-genocidal societies from Northern Ireland to South Africa, Cambodia, Indonesia, Rwanda and Mozambique. These mechanisms exemplify peace as integration by offering a repertoire of tools from which to model peacebuilding tasks while enshrining participatory values and reframing peace as a collective long-term endeavor that requires careful re-crafting of social relationships. Restorative justice balances forgiveness, amnesty and justice, and memory with the need to move forward after violent conflicts (Sullivan and Tifft 2007; Sriram and Pillay 2010). Combining local and global institutional tools to deal with the varied dimensions of healing and reconstruction (Tutu 2000; Manning 2014), they also locate responsibility at the political level of the community through a variety of social and cultural rituals of narration, commemoration, and symbolization. Here, anthropological sensitivity to cultural context is essential. Peacemakers on the ground resource local knowledge in the form of traditional, religious, and indigenous methods of conflict resolution to supplement global mechanisms and empower local actors (Souillac and Fry 2014; Souillac and Fry 2016; Schirch 2005; Lederach 1995, 1997). While every effort to produce restorative justice has experienced difficulties, many cases testify at least to the partial success of complementary approaches to peacebuilding that integrate the recognition of the psychological consequences of trauma and combine retributive and restorative justice with a sensitivity to the particularities of local context (Roht Ariazza and Mariezcurrena 2006; Llewellyn and Philpott 2014; Helmick and Petersen 2002; Sullivan and Tifft 2007).

Ultimately, a culture of peace (Daniel Bar-Tal 2007, 2009) requires "extensive changes in the socio-psychological repertoire of group members" (Bar-Tal 2009: 363–5). Conflict transformations that harness people power (Francis 2002), echoing the paradigm-changing UN reports on human security, integrate past, present, and future in a transgenerational approach to justice that relies on the transmission of critical knowledge about oppression to future generations. Normative solidarity was consolidated in Germany and Europe after 1945 out of public democratic debates about collective responsibility with regard to "repugnant legacies" such as the Holocaust, demonstrating how "constitutional patriotic bonds can develop and be renewed in the medium of politics itself" (Habermas 2006: 77). As in the case of European unification, universal norms forge constitutional identities that contribute additional layers to local and territorial belonging and harness collective responsibility regarding historical legacies of violence (Souillac 2012; Souillac and Fry 2015). In addition, these rituals generate alternative, pluralist spaces in which all may democratically participate (Souillac 2012). Such secular spaces also support the resolution of the religious dimensions of conflict that call for

FIGURE 8.6: Kristof Wodiczko's *Arc de Triomphe, Institut mondial pour l'abolition de la guerre*, Abolition of War Exhibition, Kuntsi Musen of Modern Art, Vaasa, Finland, 2014. D. P. Fry photo collection.

renewed investment in inter-faith dialogue fostering forgiveness (Gopin 2010; Llewellyn and Philpott 2014; Helmick and Petersen 2002); and in reconciliation as outcome and process (Bar-Tal and Bennink 2004). Peacebuilding processes grounded in people power give concrete form to positive conceptions of peace, expanding our moral imagination (Lederach 2005) and what Robert Jay Lifton (2017) calls our "imaginative resources" for survival.

CONCLUSION

In this twenty-first century, new challenges to peace as integration and to a liberal, humanist international order based on inclusive, democratic norms and values have emerged. These challenges include the call to hospitality posed by recent waves of migration, increasing economic inequality, the rise of populist ethno-nationalism, and the protection of the environment. They come with growing knowledge that peaceful solutions can only be found in the keen awareness of complexity. This chapter affirms the ideational component of peace as integration in the modern era. Rather than the "soft" link in an anarchic international system in which peace is based on military power, the modern legacies of peace as integration constitute the moral force necessary for the gains of the twentieth century to be further developed in the twenty-first. Historical and theoretical accounts that presume an anarchic international system miss the pertinence of a broader, positive conception of peace for the prevention of structural and direct forms of violence. Moving further towards peace as integration will depend on maintaining moral and normative continuity with the modern institutions, norms and actions for peace discussed in this chapter. Our melancholy and frustrations need not validate the modernist theme of the "implosion of civilization," but can redefine instead what constitutes civilized processes (Souillac 2015). As Richard Falk (1982:14–15) comments, exemplifying the synergistic spirit called for by peace as integration:

> We require a special sort of creativity that blends thought and imagination without neglecting obstacles to change. We require, in effect, an understanding of those elements of structure that resist change, as well as a feel for the possibilities of innovation that lie within the shadowland cast backward by emergent potential structures of power. Only within this shadowland, if at all, is it possible to discern "openings" that contain significant potential for reform, including the possibility of exerting an impact on the character of the emergent system.

Will the modern peace project that began in the nineteenth century withstand these geopolitical challenges and lead to further integration in the collective global imagination? Only time will tell.

NOTES

Introduction

1. Unless noted otherwise, all statistics without citations used in this Introduction like these world population estimates are drawn from the website ourworldindata.org, which is produced by a team of experts led by Max Roser, director of the Oxford Martin Programme on Global Development, Oxford University.
2. In August 2008, Russia and Georgia engaged in a border war that lasted just twelve days. Russia's annexation and occupation of Crimea in 2014 did not result in a major war, although it was not recognized by the UN and the US and EU imposed sanctions.
3. John Mueller has effectively challenged this simplistic interpretation by highlighting the war aversion created in Germany by World War I, and stressing the key role of Adolf Hitler in reversing it by organizing the politics of revenge and the restoration of Germany's military glory and empire (2004: 54–65).
4. We now know that the Japanese successfully negotiated the condition that the Emperor be allowed to retain his throne, before their surrender.
5. It is not, however, true that during the twentieth century the percentage of civilians killed in warfare rose from 10 percent in World War I to 90 percent during recent decades, as many peace advocates have argued. Peace research scholars have shown that the typical ratio of military–civilian deaths in wars since 1990 is probably closer to what it was in World War II, 50:50 (Goldstein 2011: 258–61).
6. Al Gore, a former vice president of the United States, was also named a Nobel Peace Prize winner in 2007 for his work, including his book *Earth in the Balance* (1992) and his documentary film *An Inconvenient Truth* (2006), dedicated to raising public awareness of the dangers of global climate change.
7. The unprecedented character of drone warfare and how it undermines and mocks the public morality of the United States is thoroughly described and critiqued in the late Norman Pollack's recently published *Capitalism, Hegemony and Violence in the Age of Drones* (2018).

Chapter 1

1. In a private communication several years ago, Johan Galtung related how the distinction between "positive" and "negative" peace was "in the air" in the 1960s, and that he was one of several popularizers of it.
2. See *Positive Peace Report* (2015), issued by the Institute for Economics and Peace in Sydney, Australia. Available online: http://visionofhumanity.org/#/page/mews1264; and the *Global Peace Index (2016)*, also issued by the Institute for Economics and Peace and also available online: http//visionofhumanity.org/gpi-data.

Chapter 2

1. Warfare results in murders, injuries, and destruction, but war is more than a lot of violence. War is organized violence for purposes defined by political authorities (leaders of groups, bands, tribes, nations, empires, etc.).

Chapter 3

1. UNDP also produces four additional indices each year that are based on public data from the majority of the world's countries. Indices of countries' conflict status are also publicly available (e.g. Fund for Peace produces a Fragile States Index, http://fundforpeace.org/fsi/).
2. This research constitutes a very large canon of work and highlights are listed in the Bibliography.
3. The poppy was an American invention in 1920, later taken up by other Allied countries. The symbolism of the poppy representing the dead (as they grew in abundance in the ground churned up by warfare and field cemeteries) has persisted, but amid controversy about the meaning of the remembrance acts.
4. They were: 2003: Shirin Ebadi, Iran; 2004: Wangari Muta Maathai, Kenya; 2011: Ellen Johnson Sirleaf, Liberia; 2011: Leymah Gbowee, Liberia; 2011: Tawakel Karman, Yemen; 2014: Malala Yousafzai, Pakistan.
5. In Mexico City in 1975, Copenhagen in 1980, Nairobi in 1985, and Beijing in 1995, followed by a crescendo of activity taking up the Beijing recommendations between 1995 and 2000.

Chapter 5

1. There are today at least fifty peace museums, the majority in Europe and Japan; and 147 peace parks, all but ten created since 1920 (Aspel 2016; peace.maripo.com/p-parks.htm).
2. The term "global commons" had been used for two decades by environmentalists to describe the total stock of natural resources upon which human survival depends when Hardt and Negri expanded it to include the global stock of intellectual resources.
3. Peace cultures, as Elise Boulding has explained, produce "peaceable diversity," an interconnected but diverse mosaic of peaceable life ways (2000: 3–6).
4. Facebook underestimated the iconic power of this particular image when it censored it in the summer following its new policy of not showing nude bodies. After the editor of *Aftenposten*, Norway's biggest newspaper, published an open letter in protest, Facebook promised to reconsider its policy regarding important historical pictures (*Aftenposten* September 9, 2016).
5. No Peace Prizes were awarded in 1914–16, 1918, 1923, 1924, 1932, 1939–43, 1948, 1955, 1956, 1966, 1966, and 1972.
6. The series of short biographies, presentation speeches, and laureate lectures produced by the Nobel Prize organization document in detail these changes in the definitions of peace and peace work. www.nobelprize.org/nobel-prizes/peace/laureates/.
7. The sixth Nobel Prize, in economic sciences, was not established by Alfred Nobel. It was created in 1968 with a donation from the Swedish National Bank.
8. Heffermehl is particularly critical of the alignment of many Peace Prizes with US foreign policy, and with what he sees as the distortions of Nobel's intent that stem from Norway's active participation in NATO.

9. The ICRC's adherence to a policy of strict political neutrality (to insure unfettered access to victims of warfare) during World War II and in more recent conflicts has been sharply criticized especially by human rights organizations and Médecins Sans Frontières, as a form of complicity with cruel and repressive regimes.
10. English translations of the phrase have commonly rendered the phrase "war is a continuation of policy *by* other means." A better translation of the original German is "a continuation of policy *with* other means" because it is consistent with Clausewitz' belief that all diplomatic and other interactions between belligerents do not necessarily cease when armed combat begins.
11. Classic realists citing the Melian Dialogue in Thucydides' *Peloponnesian War* as their founding principle, assert might makes right, and shun moral arguments. Modern neo-realists admit moral concerns may play a role in foreign policy, but the anarchic character of the nation-state system requires constant readiness for war.
12. Canada's foreign minister, Lester Pearson, had famously persuaded the UN to deploy peacekeepers in Egypt to permit British, French, and Israeli forces to withdraw and negotiators to achieve a peaceful resolution of the Suez Crisis in 1956. Pearson was awarded the 1957 Nobel Peace Prize for those efforts.

Chapter 6

1. I would like to thank Yesenia Guitierrez for her important assistance with the images in this chapter.
2. Johan Galtung first used the terms "negative peace" and "positive peace" in 1964 to distinguish between the absence of violent hostilities that had long been accepted by scholars and political leaders as the definition of peace, and the existence of justice that ensures peace within and between societies. These and other definitions of peace are discussed at length in Chapter One of this volume.
3. The list of Nobel Peace Prize winners, particularly since 1960, provides one demonstration of the global nature of peace activism. Laureates include Jane Addams and Martin Luther King, Jr., Mother Teresa, Aung San Suu Kyi, Nelson Mandela, Shirin Abadi, Wangari Maatthai, Leymah Gbowee, and Rigoberta Menchu.
4. Indeed, Gandhi's campaigns in South Africa were based in part on the premise that Indian South Africans were different from (and superior to) "natives." As a result, activists today in Ghana have protested against a statue of Gandhi on the campus of the University of Ghana at Legon. See (www.cihablog.com/petition-gandhis-statue-university-ghana-must-come/), accessed September 27, 2016.

Chapter 7

1. This passage is quoted approvingly by another distinguished historian, Gordon A. Craig, in a review of the Watt book (1989: 11). See also Kershaw 2000: 841; Bullock 1993: 973.
2. For a compilation, see *Hitler on Peace*, politicalscience.osu.edu/faculty/jmueller/hitpeace.pdf.
3. For a discussion, see chapter 6 in Mueller (2004). For assessments stressing that interventions tend to be carried more for national interest reasons than for humanitarian ones, see Menon 2016, DiPrizio 2002.
4. For more extensive description of the policy change see the full text of the announcement at www.defense.gob/news/Defense_Strategic_Guidance.pdf.
5. There are a few potential exceptions. The most likely one is perhaps the Soviet suppression of a rebellion in its satellite, Hungary, in 1956, although in many respects this seems more

like a colonial war. The conflict between Greece and Turkey over Cyprus in 1974 could also conceivably be an exception, even though the two countries never came directly into violent conflict with each other. There are some aspects of the Croatian offensive in neighboring Bosnia in 1993–94 during the chaotic civil war that are sometimes seen to be essentially international in scope. And NATO's rather bizarre "war" over Kosovo in 1999 might also be considered an exception, as might conflicts between Russia and Georgia in 2008 and between Russia and Ukraine in 2014.

6. For a discussion of the process and a detailed enumeration of territorial changes since 1945, see Zacher 2001. The recent Russian acquisition of Crimea may be an exception to this pattern.

7. Relevant may be an observation by Robert Dahl: "Because of their concern with rigor and their dissatisfaction with the 'softness' of historical description, generalization, and explanation, most social scientists have turned away from the historical movement of ideas. As a result, their own theories, however 'rigorous' they may be, leave out an important explanatory variable and often lead to naive reductionism" (1971: 182–3). See also Mueller 1999, 2011a.

8. As is done in Russett and Oneal 2001: 158, Ikenberry 2001: chapter 6. For the argument that effective business-regulating institutions tend to be put into place when the behavior they seek to foster has already become fairly common, see Mueller 1999: 95–8.

BIBLIOGRAPHY

Abdel Haleem, Muhammad A.S. (2010), "The Politics of Peace in Islam," in Linda Hogan and Dylan Lee Lehrke (eds.), *Religions and the Politics of Peace and Conflict* , 104–21, Eugene, OR: Pickwick.

Abrams, Irwin (1988), *The Nobel Peace Prize and the Laureates: An Illustrated Biographical History 1901–1987*, Boston: G. K. Hall.

Abu-Nimer, Mohammad and Badawi, Jamal A. (2011), "Alternatives to War and Violence: An Islamic Perspective," in Marc Pilisuk and Michael N. Nagler (eds.), *Peace Movements Worldwide*, 1: 151–70, Santa Barbara, CA: Praeger.

Abu-Nimer, Mohammed (2002), "The Miracles of Transformation through Interfaith Dialogue," in D.R. Smock (ed.), *Interfaith Dialogue and Peacebuilding*, Washington, DC: US Institute of Peace Press.

Abu-Nimer, Mohammed (2003), *Nonviolence and Peacebuilding in Islam*, Gainesville, FL: University Press of Florida.

Abu-Nimer, Mohammed and Kadayifci-Orellana, S. Ayse (2008), "Muslim Peacebuilding Actors in Africa and the Balkan Context: Challenges and Needs," *Peace & Change,* 33(4): 549–81.

Ackerman, Peter, and Jack Duvall (2000), *A Force More Powerful: A Century of Nonviolent Conflict*, New York: Palgrave.

Ackermann, Chantal (1994), "Reconciliation as a Peacebuilding Process in Post War Europe. The Franco-German Case," *Peace and Change*, 19(3): 229–49.

Adolf, Anthony (2009), *Peace: A World History*, Cambridge, UK: Polity Press.

African Rights (1995), *Not So Innocent: When Women Become Killers*. London: African Rights.

Agnivesh, Swami (2005), *Hinduism in the New Age*, Delhi: Hope India Publications.

Alexandroff, Alan, and Richard Rosecrance (1977), "Deterrence in 1939," *World Politics*, 29(3) April: 404–24.

Allen, Mark, and Terry Jones (2014), *Violence and Warfare among Hunter-Gatherers*, Walnut Creek, CA: Left Coast Press.

Al-Sadat, Anwar (1978), "Nobel Lecture," *Nobelprize.org*, December 10. Available online: www.nobelprize.org/nobel_prizes/peace/laureates/1978/al-sadat-lecture.htm.

Alston, Philip and Ryan Goodman (2012), *International Human Rights*, Oxford: Oxford University Press.

Aman, Kenneth, ed. (1988), *Border Regions of Faith*, Maryknoll: Orbis Books.

Anderlini, S. (2007), *Women Building Peace: What They Do, Why It Matters*, Boulder, CO: Lynne Rienner Publishers.

Anderson, Benedict ((1983) 2016), *Imagined Communities*, London: Verso.

Anwar, Zainah (2001), "The Struggle for Women's Rights Within the Religious Framework: The Experience of Sisters in Islam," in Colin Barlow (ed.), *Modern Malaysia in the Global Economy: Political and Social Change into the 20th Century*, Northampton, MA: Edgar Elgar Publishing.

Aoláin, Fionnuala Ní, Dina Francesca Haynes, and Naomi Cahn (2011), "Criminal Justice For Gendered Violence and Beyond," *International Criminal Law Review*, 11(3): 425–43.

Apicella, C., F. Marlowe, J. Fowler, and N. Christakis (2012), "Social Networks and Cooperation in Hunter-Gatherers," *Nature*, 481: 497–502.
Appiah, Kwame Anthony (2010), *The Honor Code: How Moral Revolutions Happen*, New York: Norton.
Appleby, R. Scott (2000), *The Ambivalence of the Sacred. Religion, Violence, and Reconciliation*, Lanham/Boulder/New York/Oxford: Rowman & Littlefield Publishers.
Aranburu, Xabier Agirre (2010), "Sexual Violence Beyond Reasonable Doubt: Using Pattern Evidence and Analysis for International Cases," *Law & Social Inquiry*, 35(4): 855–79.
Ardrey, Robert (1961), *African Genesis*, New York: Dell.
Ardrey, Robert (1966), *The Territorial Imperative*, New York: Atheneum.
Arendt, Hannah (1966), *Eichmann in Jerusalem: A Report on the Banality of Evil*. New York: Viking Classics.
Ariarajah, S. Wesley, "Religion and Violence: A Protestant Christian Perspective," *Ecumenical Review*, 55(2003): 136–43.
Arigatou International (n.d.), The Global Network of Religions for Children, https://gnrc.net/en/.
Arms Control Association (2018), *Fact Sheets*. Available online: www.armscontrol.org.
Armstrong, Karen (1993), *A History of God*, New York: Alfred A. Knopf.
Armstrong, Karen (2010), *Twelve Steps to a Compassionate Life*, Toronto: Vintage Canada.
Armstrong, Karen (2015), *Fields of Blood: Religion and the History of Violence*, New York: Knopf Doubleday.
Aron, Raymond (1966), *Peace and War: A Theory of International Relations*. Garden City, NY: Doubleday.
Asal, Victor and Beardsley, Kyle (2007), "Proliferation and International Crisis Behavior," *Journal of Peace Research*, 44(2): 139–55.
Aschermann, Arik (1999), "Rabbis for Human Rights: The Other Face of Judaism," *Palestine-Israel Journal*, 6(1).
Ashafa, Muhammad Nurayn and Wuye, James Movel (1999), *The Pastor and the Imam*, Lagos: Ibrash Publications.
Aspel, Joyce (2016), *Introducing Peace Museums*, London and New York: Routledge.
Audoin-Rouzeau, Stéphane and Annette Becker (2003), *Retrouver la Guerre*, 14–18, Paris: Folio.
Baaz, Maria Eriksson, and Maria Stern (2009), "Why Do Soldiers Rape? Masculinity, Violence, and Sexuality in The Armed Forces in The Congo (DRC)," *International Studies Quarterly*, 53(2): 495–18.
Baaz, Maria Eriksson, and Maria Stern (2013), *Sexual Violence as a Weapon of War?: Perceptions, Prescriptions, Problems in The Congo and Beyond*, London: Zed Books.
Babst, Dean V. (1964), "Elective Governments: A Force for Peace," *The Wisconsin Sociologist*, 3: 9–14.
Baggett, Blaine and Jay Winter (1996), *The Great War and the Shaping of the Twentieth Century: Episode 4 Slaughter*, PBS (Public Broadcasting Service).
Baidhawy, Zakiyuddin (2012), "Distributive Principles of Economic Justice: An Islamic Perspective," *Indonesian Journal of Islam and Muslim Societies*, 2(2): 241–66.
Balikci, Ansen (1970), *The Netsilik Eskimo*, Garden City, NY: Natural History Press.
Ball, George W. (1991), "Introduction," in Douglas Brinkley and Clifford Hackett, *Jean Monnet: The Path to European Unity*, xii–xxii, New York, NY: Saint Martin's.
Ban, K.M. (2014), *The Road to Dignity by 2030: Ending Poverty, Transforming All Lives and Protecting the Planet*, New York: United Nations.

Barash, David (2000), *Approaches to Peace: A Reader in Peace Studies*, New York and Oxford: Oxford University Press.
Barash, David (ed.) (2017), *Approaches to Peace: A Reader in Peace Studies*, 4th ed., New York and Oxford: Oxford University Press.
Barash, David and Webel, Charles (2018), *Peace and Conflict Studies*, 4th ed., Los Angeles: SAGE.
Barnhill, David, and Roger Gottlieb, eds. (2001), *Deep Ecology and World Religions: New Essays on Sacred Ground*, Albany, NY: SUNY.
Bar-Siman-Tov, Yaacov, ed. (2004), *From Conflict Resolution to Reconciliation*, Oxford: Oxford University Press.
Bar-Tal, Daniel (2009), "Reconciliation as a Foundation of Culture of Peace," in Joseph de Rivera (ed.), *Handbook on Building Cultures of Peace*, 363–77, New York City, NY: Springer.
Bar-Tal, Daniel and Gemma H. Bennink (2004), "The Nature of Reconciliation as an Outcome and as a Process," in Yaacov Bar-Siman-Tov (ed.), *From Conflict Resolution to Reconciliation*, 11–38, Oxford: Oxford University Press.
Basu, Soumita. (2016), "The Global South Writes 1325 (Too)," *International Political Science Review*, 37(3): 362–74.
Becker, Jörg (2004), "Afghanistan the War and the Media," in Norstedt, Stig A. and Ottosen, Rune (eds.) *US and the Others. Global Media Images and "The War on Terror,"* Gothenburg: Nordicom.
Beevor, Anthony (2002), "They raped every German female from eight to eighty," *The Guardian*, May 1, 2002.
Bell, Daniel A. and Jean-Marc Coicaud, eds. (2006), *Ethics in Action. The Ethical Challenges of International Human Rights Nongovernmental Organizations*, Cambridge: Cambridge University Press.
Bell, Daniel A. and Joanne R. Bauer, eds. (1999), *The East Asian Challenge for Human Rights*, Cambridge: Cambridge University Press.
Bellamy, Alex. J., et al. (2010), *Understanding Peacekeeping*, 2nd ed., Cambridge: Polity Press.
Bellier, Irène, and Thomas M. Wilson (2000), "Building, Imagining, and Experiencing Europe: Institutions and Identities in the European Union," in Irène Bellier and Thomas M. Wilson (eds.), *An Anthropology of the European Union*, 1–27, Oxford: Berg.
Bello, Walden (2009), *The Food Wars*, London: Verso.
Bello, Walden and Baviera, M. (2010), "Food Wars," in F. Magdoff and B. Tokar (eds.), *Agriculture and Food in Crisis*, 33–50, New York: Monthly Review.
Benedict XVI, Pope (2009), Encyclical Letter *Caritas in Veritate*.
Bennett, Clinton (2008), *In Search of Solutions. The Problem of Religion and Conflict*, London/Oakville: Equinox.
Bennett, Olivia, Jo Bexley, Kitty Warnock (1995), *Arms to Fight. Arms to Protect*, London: Panos.
Bennett, Scott H. and Charles F. Howlett, eds. (2014), "Terms of Peace and the Darker Races," *Antiwar Dissent and Peace Activism in World War I America: A Documentary Reader*, Lincoln: University of Nebraska Press.
Bergson, Henri (1977), *The Two Sources of Morality and Religion*, Southbend, IN: University of Notre Dame Press.
Bergson, Henri (1998), *Creative Evolution*, trans. Arthur Mitchell, Mineoloa, NY: Dover Publications.
Berkeley Center for Religion, Peace & World Affairs (2013), *Northern Ireland: Religion in War and Peace*, Berkeley: Berkeley Center for Religion, Peace & World Affairs.

Berndt, Ronald M. (1972), "The Walmadjeri and Gugadja," in M.G. Bicchieri (ed.), *Hunters and Gatherers Today*, 177–216, Prospect Heights, IL: Waveland.
Bernstein, Ellen (2005), *The Splendor of Creation: A Biblical Ecology*, Cleveland, OH: Pilgrim.
Berry, Thomas (1988), *The Dream of the Earth*, San Francisco: Sierra Books.
Bhagwati, Jaddish (2004), *In Defense of Globalization*, Oxford and New York: Oxford University Press.
Bibbings, Lois (2003), "Images of Manliness: The Portrayal of Soldiers and Conscientious Objectors in the Great War," *Social & Legal Studies* 12(3): 335–58.
Bicchieri, M. G. ed. (1972), *Hunters and Gatherers Today*, Prospect Heights, IL: Waveland.
Bielefeldt, Heiner (2011), "Report of the Special Rapporteur on Freedom of Religion or Belief," Heiner Bielefeldt, *United Nations General Assembly, Human Rights Council*. https://reliefweb.int/sites/reliefweb.int/files/resources/A-HRC-19-60_en.pdf.
Birdsell, Joseph B. (1971), "Australia: Ecology, Spacing Mechanisms and Adaptive Behaviour in Aboriginal Land Tenure," in R. Crocombe (ed.), *Land Tenure in the Pacific*, 334–61, Oxford: Oxford University Press.
Bjorklund, David F. and Anthony D. Pellegrini (2002), *The Origins of Human Nature: Evolutionary Developmental Psychology*, Washington, DC: American Psychological Association Books.
Blackwell, Joyce (2004), *No Peace Without Freedom: Race and the Women's International League for Peace and Freedom, 1915–1975*, Carbondale, IL: Southern Illinois University Press.
Blum, William (2001), *Rogue State*, London: Pluto Press.
Boehm, Christopher (1999), *Hierarchy in the Forest: The Evolution of Egalitarian Behavior*, Cambridge, MA: Harvard University Press.
Boff, Leonardo and Boff, Clodovis (1987), *Introducing Liberation Theology*, Maryknoll, NY: Orbis Books.
Bolt, Christine (2014), *The Women's Movements in the United States and Britain from the 1790s to the 1920s*, London: Routledge.
Bond, George D. (2005), *Buddhism at Work: Community Development, Social Empowerment and the Sarvodaya Movement*, Bloomfield, CT: Kumarian Press.
Bonta, Bruce D. (2013), "Peaceful Societies Prohibit Violence," *Journal of Aggression, Conflict, and Peace Research*, 5: 117–29.
Boraine, A. and S. Valentine, eds. (2006), *Transitional Justice and Human Security*, Cape Town: International Center for Transitional Justice.
Bosco, Daniel (2014), *Rough Justice. The International Criminal Court in a World of Power Politics*, Oxford: Oxford University Press.
Bose, Anuja (2009), "Hindutva and the Politicization of Religious Identity in India," *Journal of Peace, Conflict and Development*, 13, February. Available online: www.bradford.ac.uk/social-sciences/peace-conflict-and-development/archive/.
Boulding, Elise (2000), *Cultures of Peace: The Hidden Side of History*, Syracuse: Syracuse University Press.
Bouvier, Virginia M., ed. (2002). *The Globalization of US–Latin American Relations: Democracy, Intervention, and Human Rights*. Westport, CT: Praeger.
Bowles, Samuel (2009), "Did Warfare Among Ancestral Hunter-Gatherers Affect the Evolution of Human Social Behaviors?" *Science*, 324: 1293–98.
Brauman, Rony (1995), *Humanitaire. Le dilemme. Entretien avec Philippe Petit*, Paris: Textuel.
Brauman, Rony (2000), *L'Action humanitaire*, Paris: Flammarion.

Braybrooke, Marcus (1998), "The Interfaith Movement in the 20th Century." Available online: www.interfaithdialoguebasics.be/the%20interfaith%20movement%20in%20the%2020th%20century.htm.

Breslauer, George W. (1987), "Ideology and Learning in Soviet Third World Policy," *World Politics*, 39(3) April: 429–48.

Bridcut, John (1998), *People's Century: Total War 1939*, BBC.

Briggs, Asa and Peter Burke (2009), *A Social History of the Media: From Guttenberg to the Internet*, Cambridge: Polity Press.

Brinkley, Douglas and Clifford Hackett, eds. (1991), *Jean Monnet. The Path to European Unity*, New York: St. Martin's.

Brockopp, Jonathan E. (2008), "Jihad and Islamic History," in Bryan Rennie and Philip L. Tite, eds., *Religion, Terror and Violence: Religious Studies Perspectives*, 144–59. New York: Routledge.

Brodie, Bernard (1973), *War and Politics*, New York: Macmillan.

Brown, Chris, Terry Nardin, and Nicholas Rengger, eds. (2002), *International Relations in Political Thought. Texts from the Ancient Greeks to the First World War*, Cambridge: Cambridge University Press.

Brown, Donald E. (1991), *Human Universals*, New York: McGraw-Hill.

Browne, Evie (2014), "Faith-based Organisations, Conflict Resolution and Anti-corruption," Birmingham: GSDRC. Available online: www.gsdrc.org/docs/open/hdq1141.pdf.

Brownmiller, Susan (2013), *Against Our Will: Men, Women and Rape*, New York: Simon and Schuster.

Buddhadasa, Bhikkhu, Visalo, Pra Paisan, Swarin, Nalin, Khuankaew, Ouyporn, Loy, David R., Zin, Min, Santikaro, and Watts, Jonathan S. (2010), *Rethinking Karma: The Dharma of Social Justice*, Chiangmai: Silkworm Books.

Bull, Hedley (2012), *The Anarchical Society. A Study of Order in World Politics*. 4th ed., New York, NY: Columbia University Press.

Bullmore, Michael A. (1998), "The Four Most Important Biblical Passages for a Christian Environmentalism," *Trinity Journal*, 19(2): 139–62.

Bullock, Alan (1993), *Hitler and Stalin: Parallel Lives*, New York: Vintage.

Bunson, Matthew E. ed. (1997), *The Dalai Lama's Book of Wisdom*, London: Random House.

Buruma, Ian (2013), *Year Zero: A History of 1945*, New York: Penguin.

Burns, Charlene Embrey (2008), *More Moral than God: Taking Responsibility for Religious Violence*, New York: Rowman & Littlefield Publishers.

Buss, David M. (2005), *The Murderer Next Door: Why the Mind is Designed to Kill*, New York: Penguin.

Buss, Doris (2009), "Rethinking 'Rape as a Weapon of War'," *Feminist Legal Studies*, 17(2): 145–63.

Caeymaex, Florence (2012), "Bergson et la politique," in F. Caeymaex, A. Janvier and A. François (eds.), *Annales Bergsoniennes V. Bergson et la politique: de Jaurès à aujourd'hui*, 169–333, Paris: Presses Universitaires de France.

Camara, Bishop Helder (1971), *The Spiral of Violence*, London: Continuum International Publishing Group, Ltd.

Campbell, Horace (2013), *Global NATO and the Catastrophic Failure in Libya*, New York: Monthly Review.

Capdevilla, Luc, and Daniele Voldman (2006), *War Dead: Western Societies and the Casualties of War*, Edinburgh: University of Edinburgh Press.

Carrette, Jeremy and Miall, Hugh, eds. (2017), *Religion, NGOs and the United Nations: Visible and Invisible Actors in Power*, New York: Bloomsbury.

Carson, Clayborne & Shepard, Chris eds. (2001), *A Call to Conscience: The Landmark Speeches of Dr. Martin Luther King Jr.*, New York: Warner Books.

Catholic Bishops Conference of the Philippines (CBCP) (2017), "For I find no pleasure in the death of anyone who dies—oracle of the Lord God (Ezekiel 18:32)." *CBCP Pastoral Letter*, February 5. Available online: www.cbcpnews.com/cbcpnews/?p=91162.

Cavanagh, John and Mander, Jerry, eds. (2004), *Alternatives to Economic Globalization: A Better World Is Possible*, San Francisco, CA: Berrett-Koehler Publishers, Inc.

Cavanaugh, William T. (2009), *The Myth of Religious Violence*, Oxford: Oxford University Press.

Ceadel, Martin (1980), *Pacifism in Britain 1914–1945: The Defining of a Faith*, Oxford: Oxford University Press.

Ceadel, Martin (2017), "The London Peace Society and Absolutist-Reformist Relations Within the Peace Movement, 1816–1939," *Peace and Change. A Journal of Peace Research*, 42(4): 496–520.

Chagnon, Napoleon (2013), *Noble Savages: My Life Among Two Dangerous Tribes—the Yanomamö and the Anthropologists*, New York: Simon and Schuster.

Chakravarty, Anuradha. (2006), "Gacaca Courts in Rwanda: Explaining Divisions Within the Human Rights Community," *Yale Journal of International Affairs* (Winter-Spring): 132–145.

Chandler, David (2006), *From Kosovo to Kabul and Beyond. Human Rights and International Intervention*, London: Pluto Press.

Chapple, Christopher Key (2007), "Jainism and Nonviolence," in Daniel L. Smith-Christopher (eds.), *Subverting Hatred: The Challenge of Nonviolence in Religious Traditions*, 1–17, Maryknoll, NY: Orbis Books.

Chapple, Christopher Key and Tucker, Mary Evelyn, eds. (2000), *Hinduism and Ecology: The Intersection of Earth, Sky, and Water*, Cambridge, MA: Harvard University Press.

Chapple, Christopher Key, ed. (2003), *Jainism and Ecology: Nonviolence in the Web of Life*, Cambridge, MA: Harvard University Press.

Charles, J. Daryl (2005), *Between Pacifism and Jihad: Just War and Christian Tradition*, Downers Grove, IL: Intervarsity Press.

Chenoweth, Erica, and Maria J. Stephan (2012), *Why Civil Resistance Works: The Strategic Logic of Nonviolent Conflict*, New York: Columbia University Press.

Chia, Edmund Kee-Fook, ed. (2016), *Interfaith Dialogue: Global Perspectives*, New York: Palgrave Macmillan.

Christie, David, Wagner, R. and Winter, D. (2001) *Peace, Conflict, and Violence: Peace Psychology in the 21st Century*, Upper Saddle River, NJ: Prentice Hall.

Christoffersen, Jonas and Mikael Rask Madsen (2013), *The European Court of Human Rights Between Law and Politics*, Oxford: Oxford University Press.

Churchill, Winston ([1930] 1996), *My Early Life, 1874–1904*, New York: Simon & Schuster.

Clarke, I.F. (1966), *Voices Prophesying War, 1763–1984*, London: Oxford University Press.

Clarke, Robert (2017), *The "Conscience of Europe"? Navigating Shifting Tides at the European Court of Human Rights*, Les Sables d'Olonne: Kairos.

Clastres, Pierre (1972), "The Guayaki," in M.G. Bicchieri (ed.), *Hunters and Gatherers Today*, 138–74, Prospect Heights, IL: Waveland.

Clausewitz, Carl von (1968), *On War*, London: Penguin.

Coates, A.J. (1997), *The Ethics of War*, Manchester: Manchester University Press.

Cockburn, Cynthia (1998), *The Space Between Us: Negotiating Gender and National Identities in Conflict*, London: Zed Books.

Cockburn, Cynthia (2007), *From Where We Stand: War, Women's Activism And Feminist Analysis*, London: Zed Books.
Cockburn, Cynthia (2010), "Gender Relations as Causal in Militarization and War: A Feminist Standpoint," *International Feminist Journal of Politics*, 12(2): 139–57.
Cockburn, Cynthia (2012), *Antimilitarism: Political and Gender Dynamics of Peace Movements*, New York: Springer.
Cockburn, Cynthia (2013), "War and Security, Women and Gender: An Overview of the Issues," *Gender & Development*, 21(3): 433–52.
Cohen, Dara Kay (2013), "Explaining Rape During Civil War: Cross-National Evidence (1980–2009)," *American Political Science Review*, 107(3): 461–77.
Cohen, Stanley (2001), *States of Denial: Knowing about Atrocities and Suffering*, Cambridge: Polity.
Cohn, Carol (1987), "Sex and Death in the Rational World of Defense Intellectuals," *Signs: Journal of Women in Culture and Society*, 12(4): 687–718.
Cohn, Carol, ed. (2013), *Women and Wars: Contested Histories, Uncertain Futures*, Hoboken, NJ: John Wiley & Sons.
Compagnon, Antoine, ed. (2015), *Actes du Colloque de rentrée du Collège de France. Autour de 1914–1918: Nouvelles figures de la pensée*, 1995-221, Paris: Odile Jacob.
Confortini, Catia. (2012), *Intelligent Compassion: Feminist Critical Methodology in the Women's International League for Peace and Freedom*, Oxford: Oxford University Press.
Conklin, Harold C. (1954), "The Relation of Hanunóo Culture to the Plant World," PhD diss., Anthropology, Yale University, New Haven.
Cooper, John Milton Jr. (2009), *Woodrow Wilson: A Biography*, New York, NY: Knopf.
Cornille, Catherine, ed. (2013), *The Wiley-Blackwell Companion to Inter-Religious Dialogue*, New York: Wiley-Blackwell.
Cortright, David (2007), "The Movement Against the War in Iraq," *Nonviolent Social Change: The Bulletin of the Manchester College Peace Studies Institute*, 34.
Cortright, D. (2008), *Peace. A History of Movements and Ideas*, Cambridge: Cambridge University Press.
Coutin, Susan (1993), *The Culture of Protest: Religious Activism and the US Sanctuary Movement*. Boulder, CO: Westview Press.
Coward, Harold and Smith, Gordon S., eds. (2004), *Religion and Peacebuilding*, Albany: SUNY.
Craig, Gordon A. (1989), "Making Way for Hitler," *New York Review*, October 12: 11–16.
Crandall, B. (2012), *Gender and Religion*, London: Continuum.
Crawford, Neta C. (2002). *Argument and Change in World Politics: Ethics, Decolonization, and Humanitarian Intervention*, Cambridge: Cambridge University Press.
Crawford, Neta C. (2013). "Civilian Death and Injury in the Iraq War, 2003–2013," Cost of War Papers, Watson International Institute for International and Public Affairs.
Cronin, Audrey (2015), "ISIS is not a Terrorist Group," *Foreign Affairs*, March/April.
Cryer, Robert (2003), "Human Rights and the Question of International Criminal Courts and Tribunals," in Michael C. Davis, Wolfgang Dietrich, and Bettina Sholdan (eds.), *International Intervention in the Post-Cold War World. Moral Responsibility and Power Politics*, 60–79, London: Routledge.
D'Ambra, Sebastiano, PIME (2008), *Call to a Dream: The Silsilah Dialogue Movement*, Zamboanga City: Silsilah Dialogue Movement.
Da Silva, Anthony (2001), "Through Nonviolence to Truth," in Raymond G. Helmick and Rodney L. Petersen (eds.), *Forgiveness and Reconciliation*, 305–28, Radnor, PA: Templeton Foundation Press.

Dahl, Arthur Lyon (n.d.), The Bahá'í Faith and Ecology, Available online: http://fore.yale.edu/religion/bahai/.

Dahl, Robert A. (1971), *Polyarchy*, New Haven, CT: Yale University Press.

Dalai Lama, His Holiness the 14th (1987), "Five Point Peace Plan Address to the US Congressional Human Right's Caucus,". Available online: www.dalailama.com/messages/tibet/five-point-peace-plan.

Danchin, Peter G. and Horst Fischer, eds. (2010), *United Nations Reform and New Collective Security*, Cambridge: Cambridge University Press.

Darby, Roger and McGinty, Robert, eds. (2003), *Contemporary Peacemaking Conflict, Peace Processes and Post-war Reconstruction*, New York: Palgrave Macmillan.

Dart, Raymond A. (1953), "The Predatory Transition from Ape to Man," *International Anthropological and Linguistic Review*, 1: 201–18.

Darwent, John and Christyann M. Darwent (2014), "Scales of Violence across the North American Arctic," in Mark Allen and Terry Jones (eds.), *Violence and Warfare in Hunter-Gatherers*, 182–203, Walnut Creek, CA: Left Coast Press.

Davie, Maurice R. (1929), *The Evolution of War: A Study of Its Role in Early Societies*. New Haven: Yale University Press.

Davies, Sara and Jacqui True (2015), "Reframing Conflict-Related Sexual And Gender-Based Violence: Bringing Gender Analysis Back In," *Security Dialogue* 46(6): 495–512.

Dawkins, Richard (2006), *The God Delusion*, New York: Houghton Mifflin.

de Long, Bradford (2004), "Let Us Give Thanks (Wacht am Rhein Department)," November 12. Available online: www.j-bradford-delong.net/movable_type/2004-2_archives/000536.html.

de Mel, Neloufer, Samuel, Kumudini and Soysa, Champika K. (2012), "Ethnopolitical Conflict in Sri Lanka: Trajectories and Transformations," in Dan Landis and Rosita D. Albert (eds.), *Handbook of Ethnic Conflict: International Perspectives*, 93–118, New York: Springer.

De Waal, Frans (1995), *Our Inner Ape: A Leading Primatologist Explains Why We Are Who We Are*, New York: Riverhead.

De Waal, Frans (2013), "Foreword," in Douglas P. Fry (ed.), *War, Peace, and Human Nature: The Convergence of Evolutionary and Cultural Views*, xi–xiv, New York: Oxford University Press.

Dear, John (2001), *Living Peace*, New York: Doubleday.

DeBerri, Edward and Hug, James E., eds. (2003), *Catholic Social Teaching*, Maryknoll, NY: Orbis Books.

Deegalle, Mahinda (2014), "Is Violence Justified in Theravada Buddhism?," *Social Affairs*, 1(1): 83–94.

Deng Ming-Dao (1992), *365 Tao*, New York: HarperCollins.

Denkers, N., and Trew, J. (2007), "Galvanizing Communities to End Child Labor," *CARE*, 11: 1–37.

Des Lauriers, Matthew R. (2014), "The Spectre of Conflict on Isla Cedros, Baja California, Mexico," in Mark Allen and Terry Jones (eds.), *Violence and Warfare in Hunter-Gatherers*, 204–19, Walnut Creek, CA: Left Coast Press.

Deutsch, Morton (2006), "Justice and Conflict," in Morton Deutsch, Peter T. Coleman, & Eric Marcus (eds.), *The Handbook of Conflict Resolution*, 2nd ed., 43–68, San Francisco: Jossey-Bass.

DeVido, Elise Anne (2013), "Thich Nhat Hanh," in Sharon Henderson Callahan (ed.), *Religious Leadership: A Reference Handbook*, 613–18, New York: Sage.

DeYoung, Curtiss Paul (2012), "Christianity: Contemporary Expressions," in Michael D. Palmer and Stanley M. Burgess (eds.), *The Wiley-Blackwell Companion to Religion and Social Justice*, 61–76, Oxford: Blackwell.

Diamond, Louise (1999), "Multi-Track Diplomacy in the 21st Century," in *People Building Peace. Inspiring Stories from Around the World. European Centre for Conflict Prevention in Cooperation with IFOR and the Coexistence Initiative of State of the World Forum*, 77–86, Utrecht: European Centre for Conflict Prevention/International Books.

Dien, M.I. (2000), *The Environmental Dimensions of Islam*, Cambridge: Butterworth.

DiPrizio, Robert C. (2002), *Armed Humanitarians*, Baltimore, MD: Johns Hopkins University Press.

Dobkowski, Michael (2012), "A Time for War and a Time for Peace: Teaching Religion and Violence in the Jewish Tradition," in B.K. Pennington (ed.), *Teaching Religion and Violence*, 47–73, Oxford: Oxford University Press.

Dorr, Donal (2013), *Option for the Poor and the Earth*, Diliman: Claretian Publications.

Dovidio, J., Gaertner, S., & Kafati, G. (2000), "Group Identity and Intergroup Relations: The Common In-Group Identity Model," in S. Thye, E. Lawler, M. Macy, and Henry Walker (eds.), *Advances in Group Processes*, 17: 1–35, Bingley, UK: Emerald.

Dovidio, J., Gaertner, S., & Saguy, T. (2009), "Commonality and the Complexity of 'We': Social Attitudes and Social Change," *Personality and Social Psychology Review*, 13: 3–20.

Dowd, Ann Reilly (1991), "How Bush Decided," *Fortune* 123(3): 45–46.

Doyle, Michael W. (2011), "The Folly of Protection," *Foreign Affairs*. Available online: www.foreignaffairs.com/articles/Africa/2011-03-20/folly-protection.

Doyle, Michael, and Nicholas Sambanis (2006), *Making War & Building Peace: United Nations Peace Operations*, Princeton: Princeton University Press.

Dreher, Diane (1990), *The Tao of Inner Peace*, New York: Harper Collins.

Drinan, Robert F. (2001), *The Mobilization of Shame: A World View of Human Rights*, New Haven: Yale University Press.

Duchêne, François (1994), *Jean Monnet. The First Statesman of Interdependence*, New York, NY: W.W. Norton.

Duffey, Michael and Omar, Irfan, eds. (2015), *Peacemaking and the Challenge of Violence in Religion*, West Sussex: Wiley Blackwell.

Duncanson, Claire (2016), *Gender and Peacebuilding*, London: Polity Press.

Dunne, Tim and Nicholas J. Wheeler (1999), *Human Rights in Global Politics*, Cambridge: Cambridge University Press.

Dyble, Mark, Gul Deniz Salali, Nikhil Chaudhary, Abigail Page, Daniel Smith, James Thompson, Lucio Vinicius, Ruth Mace, and Andrea Migliano (2015), "Sex Equality Can Explain the Unique Social Structure of Hunter-Gatherer Bands," *Science*, 348: 796–8.

Ecumenical Advocacy Alliance (n.d.), "Religious Leadership in Response to HIV." Available online: www.e-alliance.ch/en/s/hivaids/summit-of-high-level-religious/.

Ednan, Aslan and Hermansen, Marcia (2017), *Religion and Violence*, Weisbaden: Springer.

Edwards, Denis (2006), *Ecology at the Heart of Faith*, Maryknoll: Orbis Books.

Ehrenreich, Barbara (1997), *Blood Rites: Origins and History of the Passions of War*, New York: Henry Holt.

Einstein, Albert (1932), "Albert Einstein and Sigmund Freud, Why War?" *Volume 6. Weimar Germany*, 1918/19–1933. July 30. Available online: http://germanhistorydocs.ghi-dc.org/pdf/eng/PROB_EINSTEINFREUD_ENG.pdf.

Einstein, Albert (1949), "Why Socialism," *Monthly Review*, 1(1), May.

Einstein, Albert (1984), *The World as I See It*, Secaucus, NJ: Citadel Press.

El Bushra, Judy (2000), "Transforming Conflict: Some Thoughts on a Gendered Understanding of Conflict Processes," in Susie Jacobs, Ruth Jacobson & Jennifer Marchbank, eds., *States of Conflict. Gender, Violence and Resistance*, London: Zed Books.

El-Bushra, Judy (2007), "Feminism, Gender, and Women's Peace Activism," *Development and Change*, 38(1): 131–47.

El Fadl, Khaled Abou; Ali, Tariq; Viorst, Milton; Esposito, John; et al. (2002), *The Place of Tolerance in Islam*, Boston: Beacon Press.

Elias, Norbert (2000), *The Civilizing Process: Sociogenetic and Psychogenetic Investigation*, Oxford: Blackwell.

Ellens, J. Harold, ed. (2007), *The Destructive Power of Religion. Violence in Judaism, Christianity, and Islam*, London: Praeger.

Elshtain, Jean Bethke (1987), *Women and War*, University of Chicago Press.

Elshtain, Jean Bethke (1998), "*Women and War*: Ten Years On," *Review of International Studies*, 24(4): 447–60.

Elshtain, Jean Bethke, ed. (1992), *Just War Theory*, New York: NYU Press.

Elster, John (2004), *Closing the Books. Transitional Justice in Historical Perspective*, Cambridge: Cambridge University Press.

Endicott, Kirk (1983), "The Effects of Slave Raiding on the Aborigines of the Malay Peninsula," in A. Reid (ed.), *Slavery, Bondage and Dependency in Southeast Asia*, 216–45, New York: St. Martin's.

Endicott, Kirk, and Karen L. Endicott (2008), *The Headman Was a Woman: The Gender Egalitarian Batek of Malaysia*, Long Grove, IL: Waveland.

Enloe, Cynthia (1993), *The Morning After: Sexual Politics at the End of the Cold War*, Berkeley: University of California Press.

Enloe, Cynthia (2000), *Maneuvers: The International Politics of Militarizing Women's Lives*, Berkeley: University of California Press.

Enloe, Cynthia (2010), *Nimo's War, Emma's War: Making Feminist Sense of the Iraq War*, Berkeley: University of California Press.

Enloe, Cynthia (2016), *Globalization and Militarism: Feminists Make the Link*, Rowman & Littlefield.

Enquist, Magnus, and Olof Leimar (1990), "The Evolution of Fatal Fighting," *Animal Behaviour*, 39: 1–9.

Entman, R.M. (1993), "Framing: Toward Clarification of a Fractured Paradigm," *Journal of Communication*, 43(4): 51–58.

Esposito, John L. (1992), *The Islamic Threat. Myth or Reality?*, Oxford: Oxford University Press.

European Centre for Conflict Prevention (1999), *People Building Peace: 35 Inspiring Stories from around the World*.

Evans, Carolyn (2012), "Religion and Freedom of Expression," in Witte, John Jr. and M. Christian Green (eds.), *Religion and Human Rights*, 188–203, Oxford: Oxford University Press.

Evans, Mark, ed. (2005), *Just War Theory: A Reappraisal*, Edinburgh: Edinburgh University Press.

Fahey, J. & R. Armstrong, eds. (1992), *A Peace Reader: Essential Readings on War, Justice, Non-Violence, and World Order*, Belmont, CA: Wadsworth.

Faith & the Common Good (2008), The Toronto School of Theology. Ten Community Profiles. Greening Sacred Spaces.

Falk, Richard (1981), "Introduction: The Grotian Quest," in C.S. Edwards, *Hugo Grotius. The Miracle of Holland. A Study in Political and Legal Thought*, Chicago: Nelson-Hall.

Falk, Richard (1995), "The World Order Between Inter-state Law and the Law of Humanity: The Role of Civil Society Institutions" in Daniele Archibugi and David Held (eds.), *Cosmopolitan Democracy*, Cambridge: Polity Press.

Falk, Richard (2000), *Human Rights Horizons. The Pursuit of Justice in a Globalizing World*, London/New York: Routledge.

Falk, Richard (2008), *Achieving Human Rights*, London/New York: Routledge.

Falk, Richard (2012), "Nuclear weapons as instruments of peace?," *AlJazeera*, April 9. Available online: www.aljazeera.com/indepth/opinion/2012/04/201249735749131.html.

Falk, Richard (2016), *Power Shift. On the New Global Order*, London: Zed Books.

Farrall, Jeremy (2009), "Impossible Expectations? The UN Security Council's Promotion of the Rule of Law after Conflict," in Brett Bowden, Hilary Charlesworth and Jeremy Farrall (eds.), *The Role of International Law in Rebuilding Societies after Conflict*, Cambridge: Cambridge University Press.

Ferguson, Niall (2010), *The War of the World: Twentieth-Century Conflict and the Descent of the West*, New York: Penguin.

Ferguson, R. Brian (2013a), "Pinker's List: Exaggerating Prehistoric War Mortality," in Douglas P. Fry (ed.), *War, Peace, and Human Nature: The Convergence of Evolutionary and Cultural Views*, 112–31, New York: Oxford University Press.

Ferguson, R. Brian (2013b), "The Prehistory of War and Peace in Europe and the Near East," in Douglas P. Fry (ed.), *War, Peace, and Human Nature: The Convergence of Evolutionary and Cultural Views*, 191–240, New York: Oxford University Press.

Fettweis, Christopher J. (2010), *Dangerous Times? The International Politics of Great Power Peace*, Washington, DC: Georgetown University Press.

Fihn, Beatrice and Thurlow, Setsuko (2017), *Nobel Lecture given by the Nobel Peace Prize Laureate 2017, ICAN, Oslo, 10 December 2017*. Available online: www.icanw.org/campaign news/ican receives-2017-nobel-peace-prize/.

Finnemore, Martha (2004), *The Purpose of Intervention. Changing Beliefs about the Use of Force*, Ithaca, NY: Cornell University Press.

Fisher, William F. and Ponniah, Thomas, eds. (2003), *Another World Is Possible*, London: Zed Books.

Fitzduff, Mari (2002), *Beyond Violence: Conflict Resolution Process in Northern Ireland*, Tokyo: United Nations University Press.

Fitzduff, Mari and Chris E. Stout, eds. (2006), *The Psychology of Resolving Global Conflicts: From War to Peace*, 1–3, Westport, CT/London: Praeger.

Flood, Gavin (1996), *An Introduction to Hinduism*, Cambridge: Cambridge University Press.

Foltz, Richard C., Frederick M. Denny, and Azizan Baharuddin, eds. (2003), *Islam and Ecology: A Bestowed Trust*, Cambridge, MA: Harvard University.

Fontaine, François (1991), "Forward with Jean Monnet," in Douglas Brinkley and Clifford Hackett (eds.), *Jean Monnet. The Path to European Unity*, 1–66, New York: St. Martin's Press.

Fornari, Franco (1976), *The Psychoanalysis of War*, Garden City, NY: Doubleday.

Forum on Religion and Ecology at Yale (n.d.), "Climate Change Statements from World Religions." Available online: fromfore.yale.edu/climate-change/statements-from-world-religions/interfaith/.

Foster, Carrie A. (1995), *The Women and the Warriors: The US Section of the Women's International League for Peace and Freedom, 1915–1946*, Syracuse, NY: Syracuse University Press.

Francis, Diana (2002), *People, Peace and Power: Conflict Transformation in Action*, London: Pluto Press.

Francis, Pope (2015), on "Care for our Common Home," in Encyclical Letter *Laudato Si'* of the Holy Father Francis, Vatican.

Francis, Pope (2017), "Message of His Holiness Pope Francis on the Occasion of the World Meetings of Popular Movements in Modesto (CA)," February 10. Available online: https://w2.vatican.va/content/francesco/en/messages/pont-messages/2017/documents/papa-francesco_20170210_movimenti-popolari-modesto.html.

Francis, Pope (2018), To Professor Klaus Schwab, Executive Chairman of the World Economic Forum. Prepared speech read at Davos. Available online: www.weforum.org/agenda/2018/01/the-pope-s-announcement-to-wef18/.

Frank, Jerome D. (1968), *Sanity and Survival: Psychological Aspects of War and Peace*, New York: Random House.

Fransen, Frederic J. (2001), *The Supranational Politics of Jean Monnet. Ideas and Origins of the European Community*, Santa Barbara, CA: Praeger.

Frazier, Jessica M. 2017. *Women's Antiwar Diplomacy During the Vietnam War Era*. Chapel Hill: The University of North Carolina Press.

Freud, Sigmund ([1930] 1961), *Civilization and Its Discontents*, trans. and ed. James Strachey, New York: W. W. Norton.

Freud, Sigmund (1932), "Albert Einstein and Sigmund Freud, Why War?" *Volume 6. Weimar Germany*, 1918/19–1933. September. Available online: http://germanhistorydocs.ghi-dc.org/pdf/eng/PROB_EINSTEINFREUD_ENG.pdf.

Freud, Sigmund. (1959), *Collected Papers, Volumes 4 and 5*, New York: Basic Books.

Frieden, Jeffry A. (2006), *Global Capitalism: Its Fall and Rise in the Twentieth Century*, New York: Henry Holt.

Friedman, Thomas L. (1999), *The Lexus and the Olive Tree*, New York: Farrar, Straus and Giroux.

Friedman, Thomas L. (2006), *The World is Flat: A Brief History of the Twenty-First Century*, New York: Farrar, Straus and Giroux.

Frost, Mervyn (1986), *Towards a Normative Theory of International Relations*, Cambridge: Cambridge University Press.

Fry, Douglas P. (1980), "The Evolution of Aggression and the Level of Selection Controversy," *Aggressive Behavior*, 6: 69–89.

Fry, Douglas P. (2005), *The Human Potential for Peace. An Anthropological Challenge to Assumptions about War and Violence*, Oxford: Oxford University Press.

Fry, Douglas P. (2006a), *The Human Potential for Peace: An Anthropological Challenge to Assumptions about War and Violence*, New York: Oxford University Press.

Fry, Douglas P. (2009), "Anthropological Insights for Creating Nonwarring Social Systems," *Journal of Aggression, Conflict and Peace Research* 1: 4–15.

Fry, Douglas P. (2009), *Beyond War. The Human Potential for Peace*, Oxford: Oxford University Press.

Fry, Douglas P. (2011), "Human Nature: The Nomadic Forager Model," in Robert W. Sussman and C. Robert Cloninger (eds.), *Origins of Altruism and Cooperation*, 227–47, New York: Springer.

Fry, Douglas P. (2012), "Life without War," *Science* 336: 879–84.

Fry, Douglas P. (2013a), "War, Peace, and Human Nature: The Challenge of Achieving Scientific Objectivity," in Douglas P. Fry (ed.), *War, Peace, and Human Nature: The Convergence of Evolutionary and Cultural Views*, 1–21, New York: Oxford University Press.

Fry, Douglas P. (2013b), "Cooperation for Survival: Creating a Global Peace System," in Douglas P. Fry (ed.), *War, Peace, and Human Nature: The Convergence of Evolutionary and Cultural Views*, 543–58, New York: Oxford University Press.

Fry, Douglas P., and Anna Szala (2013), "The Evolution of Agonism: The Triumph of Restraint in Nonhuman and Human Primates," in Douglas P. Fry (ed.), *War, Peace, and Human Nature: The Convergence of Evolutionary and Cultural Views*, 451–74, New York: Oxford University Press.

Fry, Douglas P., and Geneviève Souillac (2016), "Peace by Other Means," *Common Knowledge*, 22: 8–24.

Fry, Douglas P., and Patrik Söderberg (2013a), "Lethal Aggression in Mobile Forager Bands and Implications for the Origins of War," *Science* 341: 270–3.

Fry, Douglas P., and Patrik Söderberg (2013b), "Supplementary Material for Lethal Aggression in Mobile Forager Bands and Implications for the Origins of War." Available online: www.sciencemag.org/content/341/6143/270/suppl/DC1.

Fry, Douglas P., and Patrik Söderberg (2014), "Myths about Hunter-Gatherers Redux: Nomadic Forager War and Peace," *Journal of Aggression, Conflict and Peace Research* 6: 255–66.

Fry, Douglas P., Bruce Bonta, and Karolina Baszarkiewicz (2008), "Learning from Extant Cultures of Peace," in Joseph de Rivera (ed.), *Handbook on Building Cultures of Peace*, 11–26, New York: Springer.

Fry, Douglas P., Gary Schober, and Kaj Björkqvist (2010), "Nonkilling as an Evolutionary Adaptation," in J. Evans Pim (ed.), *Nonkilling Societies*, 101–28, Honolulu: Center for Global Nonkilling.

Fulbright, J. William (1966), *The Vietnam Hearings*, New York: Vintage.

Ferguson, Niall (2006), *The War of the World: Twentieth-Century Conflict and the Descent of the West*, New York: Penguin.

Fest, Joachim C. (1974), *Hitler*, trans. Richard Winston and Clara Winston, New York: Harcourt Brace Jovanovich.

Furlan, N. (2009), "Institutionalised Christianity and the Question of Gender Hierarchy." Available online: www.krcak.srce.hr/file/97853.

Furnan, Freida Kerner (2011), "Religion and Peacebuilding: Grassroots Efforts by Israelis and Palestinians," *Journal of Religion, Conflict and Peace*, 4(2).

Galtung, Johan (1969), "Violence, Peace, and Peace Research," *Journal of Peace Research*, 6(3): 167–91.

Galtung, Johan (1996), *Peace by Peaceful Means: Peace and Conflict, Development and Civilisation*, Oslo: International Peace Research Institute.

Galtung, Johan (2017), "Peace Journalism: What, Why, Who, How, When, Where?," *TMS Peace Journalism*, January 2, 2017. Available online: www.transcend.org//tma/2017/01 (accessed March 21, 2017).

Galtung, Johan and MacQueen, Graeme (2008), *Globalizing God*, Oslo: Kolofon Press.

Galtung, Johan, Jacobsen, Carl, and Brand-Jacobsen, Kai Fritjof (2002), *Searching for Peace: The Road to TRANSCEND*, London: Pluto Press.

Galtung, Johan and Ikeda, D. (1995), *Choose Peace: A Dialogue between Johan Galtung and Daisaku Ikeda*, London: Pluto Press.

Gandhi, Arun (ed.) (1999), *World without Violence: Can Gandhi's Vision Become Reality*, Memphis, TN: M.K. Gandhi Institute for Nonviolence.

Gandhi, M.K. ([1951] 1969), *Non-Violent Resistance (Satyagraha)*, New York: Schocken Books.

Gandhi, M.K. (1968), *Satyagraha in South Africa*, in *The Selected Works of Mahatma Gandhi* Shriman Narayan (ed.), 109–10, Ahmedabad: Navajivan Trust.

Gandhi, Mahatma (1921), "Young India 6-10-21," in Mahatma Gandhi (1955), *My Religion*, 183, Ahmedabad: Navajivan Publishing.

Gandhi, Rajmohan (2004), "Hinduism and Peacebuilding," in Harold Coward and Gordon S. Smith (eds.), *Religion and Peacebuilding*, 45–68. Albany: SUNY.

Ganiel, Gladys (2017), Religion and Global Society. *Available online:* http://blogs.lse.ac.uk/religionglobalsociety/2017/08/how-evangelical-religion-contributed-to-peace-in-northern-ireland-and-what-we-can-learn-from-it/.

Gardner, G.T. (2006), *Inspiring Progress. Religions' Contributions to Sustainable Development*, New York: Norton.

Gardner, Judith and Judy El Bushra, eds. (2004), *Somalia-The Untold Story: The War Through The Eyes of Somali Women*, CIIR, 2004.

Gardner, Peter (2004), "Respect for All: The Paliyans of South India," in Graham Kemp and Douglas P. Fry (eds.), *Keeping the Peace: Conflict Resolution and Peaceful Societies around the World*, 53–71, New York: Routledge.

Gaspar, Karl, M. (1990), *A People's Option: To Struggle for Creation*, Quezon City: Claretian Publications.

Gat, Azar (2001), "Isolationism, Appeasement, Containment, and Limited War: Western Strategic Policy from the Modern to the 'Postmodern' Era," in Zeev Maoz and Azar Gat (eds.), *War in a Changing World*, 77–91, Ann Arbor, MI: University of Michigan Press.

Gat, Azar (2017), *The Causes of War and the Spread of Peace*, Oxford: Oxford University Press.

Gbowee, Leymah (2009), "Effecting Change Through Women's Activism in Liberia," *IDS Bulletin*, 40(2): 50–53.

Gellner, Ernest ((1983) 2009), *Nations and Nationalism*, Ithaca: Cornell University Press.

Gellner, Ernest (1988), "Introduction," in Jean Baechler, John A. Hall and Michael Mann (eds.), *Europe and the Rise of Capitalism*, 1–5, London: Basil Blackwell.

Gervais, Marie (2004), "The Baha'i Curriculum for Peace Education," *Journal of Peace Education*, 1(2): 205–24.

Ghanea, Nazila (2012), "Religion, Equality and Non-Discrimination," in Witte, John Jr. and M. Christian Green (eds.), *Religion and Human Rights*, 204–17, Oxford: Oxford University Press.

Ghiglieri, Michael P. (1999), *The Dark Side of Man: Tracing The Origins of Male Violence*, Reading, MA: Perseus.

Giles, Wenona and Jennifer Hyndman, eds. (2004), *Sites of Violence: Gender and Conflict Zones*, University of California Press.

Gioseffi, Daniela ed. (1988), *Women on War: Essential Voices for the Nuclear Age*, New York: Simon & Shuster.

Girardot, N.J., Miller, James and Liu Xiaogan, eds. (2001), *Daoism and Ecology: Ways within a Cosmic Landscape*, Cambridge, MA: Harvard University Center for the Study of World Religions.

Giro, Mario (1998), "The Community of Saint Egidio and its Peace-making Activities," *The International Spectator: Italian Journal of International Affairs*, 33(3): 85–100.

Gittings, John (2012), *The Glorious Art of Peace: From the Iliad to Iraq*, Oxford and New York: Oxford University Press.

Gittings, John (2016), "Peace in History," in Oliver P. Richmond, Sandra Pogodda, and Jasmin Ramović (eds.), *The Palgrave Handbook of Disciplinary and Regional Approaches to Peace*, 21–9, London: Palgrave/Macmillan.

Glendon, Mary Ann (2001), *A World Made New. Eleanor Roosevelt and the Universal Declaration of Human Rights*, New York: Random House.

Global AIDS Interfaith Alliance (n.d.). Available online: www.thegaia.org/.

Glover, Jonathan (1999), *Humanity: A Moral History of the Twentieth Century*, New Haven: Yale University Press.
Goertz, Gary, Paul F. Diehl and Alexandru Balas (2016), *The Puzzle of Peace. The Evolution of Peace in the International System*, Oxford: Oxford University Press.
Goldblatt, Betha and Meintjes, Sheila (1998), "South African Women Demand The Truth," in Meredeth Turshen and Clotilde Twagiramariya (eds.), *What Women Do In Wartime*, London: Zed Press.
Goldstein, Joseph (2002), *One Dharma*, New York: HarperCollins.
Goldstein, Joshua (2011), *Winning the War on War: The Decline of Armed Conflict Worldwide*, New York: Dutton.
Goldstein, Judith, and Robert O. Keohane (1993), *Ideas and Foreign Policy: Beliefs, Institutions and Political Change*, Ithaca: Cornell University Press.
Goodale, Mark (2009), *Surrendering to Utopia. An Anthropology of Human Rights*, Stanford: Stanford University Press.
Goodale, Mark, ed. (2008), *Human Rights. An Anthropological Reader*, Hoboken, NJ: Wiley-Blackwell.
Goodale, Mark, ed. (2014), *Human Rights at the Crossroads*, Oxford: Oxford University Press.
Goodhart, Michael (2005), *Democracy as Human Rights: Freedom and Equality in the Age of Globalization*, London and New York: Routledge.
Goodhart, Michael, ed. (2016), *Human Rights. Politics and Practice*, Oxford: Oxford University Press.
Goodstein, Laurie and Otterman, Sharon (2018), "Catholic Priests Abused 1,000 Children in Pennsylvania." Available online: www.nytimes.com/2018/08/14/us/catholic-church-sex-abuse-pennsylvania.html.
Gopin, Marc (2000), *Between Eden and Armageddon*, Oxford: Oxford University Press.
Gopin, Mark (2009), *To Make the Earth Whole. The Art of Citizen Diplomacy in an Age of Religious Militancy*, Lanham, MD: Rowman & Littlefield.
Gorbachev, Mikhail (1991), "Nobel Lecture," *Nobelprize.org*, June 5. Available online: www.nobelprize.org/nobel_prizes/peace/laureates/1990/gorbachev-lecture_en.html.
Gordimer, Nadine (2008), *Beethoven was One-Sixteenth Black*, New York, Penguin.
Goss-Mayr, Hildegard (2011), "When Prayer and Revolution Became People Power," in Marc Pilisuk and Michael Nagler (eds.), *Peace Movements Worldwide, Vol. 1 History and Vitality of Peace Movements*, 129–35, Santa Barbara: Praeger.
Grewal, Dalvinder Singh (2014), "Environmental Protection in Sikhism." Available online: www.sikhnet.com/news/environmental-protection-sikhism.
Griffin, Michael (2004), "Picturing America's 'War on Terrorism' in Afghanistan and Iraq: Photographic Motifs as News Frames," *Journalism*, 5(4): 381–402.
Grim, John. ed. (2001), *Indigenous Traditions and Ecology: The Interbeing of Cosmology and Community*, Cambridge, MA: Harvard University Press.
Gross, R. (1996), *Feminism and Religion*, Boston: Beacon.
Grossman, Dave (1995), *On Killing: The Psychological Cost of Learning to Kill in War and Society*, Boston: Little Brown.
Grossmann, Dave, and Bruce Siddle (2008), "Psychological Effects of Combat," in Lester Kurtz et al. (eds.), *Encyclopedia of Violence, Peace, and Conflict*, 2nd ed., 3(1): 796–1,805, New York: Elsevier/Academic.
Gusinde, Martin ([1937] 2003), *The Yahgan: The Life and Thought of the Water Nomads of Cape Horn*, Human Relations Area Files (eHRAF), Yahgan, Doc.1. New Haven, CT: HRAF.

Gusmao, Kay Rala Xanana (2003), "Challenges for peace and stability," *University of Melbourne's Chancellor's Human Rights Lecture*, April 7. Available online: www.unimelb.edu.au/__data/assets/pdf_file/0004/1727572/20030407-gusmao.pdf.

Gutierrez, Gustavo (1988), *A Theology of Liberation*, 15th ed., Maryknoll, NY: Orbis Books.

Gutman, Roy, and David Rieff, *Crimes of War: What the Public Should Know*, New York: W.W. Norton.

Haas, Jonathan (1996), "War," in David Levinson and Melvin Ember (eds.) *Encyclopedia of Cultural Anthropology*, 4: 1357–61, New York: Henry Holt.

Haas, Jonathan, and Matthew Piscitelli (2013). "The Prehistory of Warfare: Misled by Ethnography," in Douglas P. Fry (ed.), *War, Peace, and Human Nature: Convergence of Evolutionary and Cultural Views*, 168–190. New York: Oxford University Press.

Habermas, Jürgen (2006), *The Divided West*, trans. C. Cronin, Cambridge, MA: Polity Press.

Haidt, Jonathan (2012), *The Righteous Mind: Why Good People Are Divided by Religion and Politics*, New York: Pantheon.

Hallowell, A. Irving (1974), "Aggression in Saulteaux Society," in A. Irvin Hallowell (ed.), *Culture and Experience*, 277–90, Philadelphia: University of Pennsylvania Press.

Hallward, Maia Carter, and Julie M. Norman (2015), *Understanding Nonviolence: Contours and Contexts*, Cambridge: Polity Press.

Hamilton, Alexander, James Madison, and John Jay ([1788] 2008), *The Federalist Papers*, Oxford: Oxford University Press.

Hanh, Thich Nhat (1987), *Being Peace*, Berkeley: Parallax Press.

Hanh, Thich Nhat (2003), *Creating True Peace*, London: Rider.

Hanitszch, Thomas (2007), "Situating Peace Journalism in Journalism Studies: A Critical Appraisal," *Conflict & Communication*, 6(2).

Hapke, Laura (1997), *Daughters of the Great Depression: Women, Work, and Fiction in the American 1930s*, Athens, GA: University of Georgia Press.

Hardt, Michael and Antonio Negri (2000), *Empire*, Cambridge, MA: Harvard University Press.

Hardt, Michael and Antonio Negri (2004), *Multitude: War and Democracy in the Age of Empire*, New York: Penguin.

Harford, Barbara and Sarah Hopkins (1984), *Greenham Common: Women at the Wire*, London: Women's Press, 1984.

Harris, Sam (2005), *The End of Faith: Religion, Terror and the Future of Religions*, New York: W.W. Norton & Co.

Hart, Donna, and Robert W. Sussman (2009), *Man the Hunted: Primates, Predators, and Human Evolution*, Boulder, CO: Westview Press.

Harvey, Peter (1990), *An Introduction to Buddhism*, Cambridge: Cambridge University Press.

Hatchen, William A. and James F. Scoton (2016), *The World News Prism: Digital, Social and Interactive*, 9th ed., Oxford and Malden, MA: Wiley Blackwell.

Hathaway, Oona A. and Scott J. Shapiro (2017), *The Internationalists: How a Radical Plan to Outlaw War Remade the World*, New York: Simon and Schuster.

Haverluck, Michael F. (2017), "150 'queer' UMC clergy demand LGBT ordination," *OneNewsNow*, Monday April 24. Available online: https://onenewsnow.com/church/2017/04/24/150-queer-umc-clergy-demand-lgbt-ordination.

Hayner, Priscilla (2002), *Unspeakable Truths: Confronting State Terror and Atrocity*, Routledge.

Hayner, Priscilla B. (2010), *Unspeakable Truths: Transitional Justice and the Challenge of Truth Commissions*, London/New York: Routledge.

Hazen, Pierre (2007), *Judging War, Judging History: Behind Truth and Reconciliation*, Stanford: Stanford University Press.

Heffermehl, Frederik S. (2010), *The Nobel Peace Prize: What Nobel Really Wanted*, Santa Barbara, CA: Praeger.

Heft, James (2014), *Beyond Violence: Religious Sources of Social Transformation in Judaism, Christianity and Islam*, New York: Fordham University Press.

Helmick, Raymond G. and Rodney L. Petersen, eds. (2002), *Forgiveness and Reconciliation: Religion, Public Policy, and Conflict Transformation*. Templeton Foundation Press.

Helmick, Raymond G., and Petersen, Rodney L., eds. (2001), *Forgiveness and Reconciliation*, Radnor, PA: Templeton Foundation Press.

Hendricks, Obery M. Jr. (2006), *The Politics of Jesus*, New York: Doubleday.

Henthoff, Nat. 1982. *Peace Agitator: The Story of A. J. Muste*. New York: A. J. Muste Memorial Institute.

Hertog, Kartrien (2010), *The Complex Reality of Religious Peacebuilding*, New York: Rowman & Littlefield.

Higate, Paul and Marsha Henry (2004), "Engendering (In) Security in Peace Support Operations," *Security Dialogue*, 35(4): 481–98.

Hinnebusch, Raymind (2007), "The US Invasion of Iraq: Explanations and Implications," *Critiquer: Critical Middle Eastern Studies*, 16(3): 209–28.

Hinsley, F.H. (1987), "Peace and War in Modern Times," in Raimo Väyrynen (ed.), *The Quest for Peace*, 63–79, Beverly Hills, CA: Sage.

Hitchens, Christopher (2007), *God Is Not Great: How Religion Poisons Everything*. New York: Twelve.

Hobsbawm, Eric J. (1987), *The Age of Empire 1875–1914*, New York: Vintage.

Hogan, Linda (2017), "Between Legitimation and Refusal: Jewish, Christian and Islamic Responses to Political Violence," in Linda Hogan and Dylan Lee Lehrke (eds.), *Religion and the Politics of Peace and Conflict*, ix–xxii, Eugene, OR: Pickwick Publications.

Høiby, Marte and Rune Ottosen (2016), "Reduced Security for Journalists and Less Reporting from Frontline," in Ulla Carlsson (ed.), *Freedom of Expression and Media in Transition: Studies and Reflections in the Digital Age*, 181–91, Gothenburg: Nordicom.

Holsti, Kalevi J. (1991), *Peace and War: Armed Conflicts and International Order 1648–1989*, Cambridge: Cambridge University Press.

Holzgrefe, J. L. and Robert O. Keohane, eds. (2003), *Humanitarian Intervention. Ethical, Legal and Political Dilemmas*. Cambridge: Cambridge University Press.

Honey, Maureen (1985), *Creating Rosie the Riveter: Class, Gender, and Propaganda During World War II*, Amherst: University of Massachusetts Press.

Horgan, John (2012), *The End of War*, San Francisco, CA: McSweeney's.

Horst Cindy (2017), "Implementing the Women, Peace and Security Agenda? Somali Debates on Women's Public Roles and Political Participation," *Journal of Eastern African Studies*, 11(3): 389–40.

Hosmer, Stephen T., and Thomas W. Wolfe (1983), *Soviet Policy and Practice toward Third World Countries*, Lexington, MA: Lexington Books.

Houge, Anette Bringedal (2015), "Sexualized War Violence. Knowledge Construction and Knowledge Gaps," *Aggression And Violent Behavior*, 25: 79–87.

Howard, Michael (2000), *The Invention of Peace: Reflections on War and International Order*, New Haven: Yale University Press.

Howell, Signe (1988), "From Child to Human: Chewong Concepts of Self," in G. Jahoda and I.M. Lewis (eds.), *Acquiring Culture: Cross Cultural Studies in Child Development*, 147–68, London: Croom Helm.

Howell, Signe (1989), "'To Be Angry is not to be Human, but to be Fearful Is": Chewong Concepts of Human Nature," in Signe Howell and Roy Willis (eds.), *Societies at Peace: Anthropological Perspectives*, 45–59, London: Routledge.

Howell, Signe, and Roy Willis (1989), *Societies at Peace: Anthropological Perspectives*, London: Routledge.

Hrdy, Sarah B. (1977), *The Langurs of Abu*, Cambridge, MA: Harvard University Press.

Hrdy, Sarah B. (2009), *Mothers and Others: The Evolutionary Origins of Mutual Understanding*, Cambridge, MA: Harvard University Press.

Huda, Qamar-ul and Marshall, Katherine (2013), "Religion and Peacebuilding," in Craig Zeliger (ed.), *Integrated Peacebuilding: Innovative Approaches to Transforming Conflict*, 151–72, Boulder, CO: Westview.

Hughbank, Richard J., and Dave Grossman (2013), "The Challenge of Getting Men to Kill: A View from Military Science," in Douglas P. Fry (ed.), *War, Peace, and Human Nature: Convergence of Evolutionary and Cultural Views*, 495–513, New York: Oxford University Press.

Hunt, Lynn (2008), *Inventing Human Rights. A History*, New York: Norton.

Huntington, Samuel (1996), *The Clash of Civilizations and the Remaking of World Order*, London: Penguin.

Hussain, Amir (2012), "Confronting Misoislamia: Teaching Religion and Violence in Courses on Islam," in B.K. Pennington (ed.), *Teaching Religion and Violence*, 118–48, Oxford: Oxford University Press.

Hynes, Samuel (1997), *The Soldiers' Tale: Bearing Witness to Modern War*, New York: Penguin.

ICISS/International Commission on Intervention and State Sovereignty (2001), *The Responsibility to Protect*. Ottawa, CA: International Development Research Centre.

Ikeda, Daisaku and Tehranian, Majid (2003), *Global Civilization. A Buddhist-Islamic Dialogue*, London: British Academic Press.

Ikenberry, G. John (2001), *After Victory: Institutions, Strategic Restraint, and the Rebuilding of Order after Major Wars*, Princeton: Princeton University Press.

IISS (International Institute for Strategic Studies) (2017), *Armed Conflict Survey 2017*.

ILO (International Labour Office) (2012), *Convergences: Decent Work and Social Justice in Religious Traditions*, Geneva: ILO.

Interfaith Center of New York (n.d.). Available online: http://interfaithcenter.org/.

Interfaith Youth Core (n.d.). Available online: www.ifyc.org/.

International Forum on Globalization (2002), *Alternatives to Economic Globalization*, Oakland, CA: Barrett-Koehler.

International Network of Engaged Buddhists (2013), "Asian Women's Interfaith Gathering," January 18–20, Wongsanit Ashram, Thailand. Available online: www.inebnetwork.org/images/stories/report/woman_gathering.jpg.

Inter-Religious Program Against Malaria. Available online: https://berkleycenter.georgetown.edu/organizations/inter-religious-program-against-malaria.

Intondi, Vincent, July 30, 2015. "W. E. B. DuBois to Malcolm X: The Untold History of the Movement to Ban the Bomb," *If We Knew Our History Series*, Zinn Education Project. Available online: https://zinnedproject.org/2015/07/web-dubois-malcolmx-ban-the-bomb/.

Iriye, Akira (2002), *Global Community: The Role of International Organizations in the Making of the Contemporary World*, Berkeley: University of California Press.

Jacobs, Susie and Tracey Howard (1987), "Women in Zimbabwe: Stated Policy and State Action," Haleh Afshar (ed.), *Women, State and Ideology*, 28–47, London: Palgrave Macmillan.

Jacobs, Susie, Ruth Jacobson and Jennifer Marchbank, eds. (2000), *States of Conflict. Gender, Violence and Resistance*, London: Zed Books.

Jama, Afdhere (2013), *Queer Jihad: LGBT Muslims on Coming Out, Activism and the Faith*, Oracle Releasing.

James, William (1910), "The Moral Equivalent of War." Available online: www.consitution.org/wj/meow.htm.

Jenkins, Brian Michael (2011), *Stray Dogs and Virtual Armies: Radicalization and Recruitment to Jihadist Terrorism in the United States Since 9/11*, Santa Monica: RAND.

Jerryson, Michael K. (2011), *Buddhist Fury: Religion and Violence in Southern Thailand*, New York: Oxford University Press.

Jervis, Robert (2001), "Was the Cold War a Security Dilemma?," *Journal of Cold War Studies*, 3(1) Winter.

John Paul II, Pope (2001), Address of the Holy Father to the Pontifical Academy of Social Sciences, 27 April. Available online: https://w2.vatican.va/content/john-paul-ii/en/speeches/2001/april/documents/hf_jp-ii_spe_20010427_pc-social-sciences.html.

Johnson, Elizabeth (2011), *She Who Is: The Mystery of God in Feminist Theological Discourse*, New York: Continuum.

Johnson, Robert (1997), *Improbable Dangers: US Conceptions of Threat in the Cold War and After*, New York: St. Martin's.

Johnston, Douglas, and Sampson, Cynthia, eds. (1994), *Religion, The Missing Dimension of Statecraft*, New York: Center for Strategic and International Studies, Oxford University Press.

Jones, Tim and Jubilee Debt Campaign (2013), *Jubilee Economics: Contents Biblical Teaching and Financial Crisis*, London: Jubilee Debt Campaign.

Josephson, Harold (1979), "Outlawing War: Internationalism and the Pact of Paris," *Diplomatic History*, 3: 377–90.

Juergensmeyer, Mark (2003), *Terror in the Mind of God*, Berkeley: University of California Press.

Juergensmeyer, Mark and Kitts, Margo, eds. (2011), *Princeton Readings in Religion and Violence*, Princeton: Princeton University Press.

Kaba, Marcel (2009), "Targeting the World: Assessing the Lawfulness of the Bush Doctrine," *The New Presence, Journal of Central European Affairs*, 2.

Kadayifci-Orellana, S. Ayse (2013), "Inter-Religious Dialogue and Peacebuilding," in Catherine Cornille (ed.), *The Wiley-Blackwell Companion to Inter-Religious Dialogue*, 149–67. New York: John Wiley.

Kaitlin (2008), "Eco-Islam Development. Inside Islam: Dialogues and Debates." Available online: https://insideislam.wisc.edu/2008/12/eco-islam/.

Kaldor, Mary (2003), *Global Civil Society. An Answer to War.* Cambridge: Cambridge University Press.

Kaldor, Mary (2007), *Human Security*. Cambridge: Polity.

Kaldor, Mary, ed. (1991), *Europe From Below: An East-West Dialogue*. Verso Press.

Kant, Immanuel (1983), *Perpetual Peace and Other Essays on Politics, History, Morals*, Indianapolis, IN: Hackett Publishing Company.

Karatnycky, Adrian, Peter Ackerman and Mark Y. Rosenberg (2005), *How Freedom is Won: From Civic Resistance to Durable Democracy*, Washington, DC: Freedom House.

Kaur, Jangroop (2005), "The Concept of Peace and the Guru Granth Sahib," *The Indian Journal of Political Science*, 66(3): 649–60.

Kaybryn, J. and Nidadavolu, V. (2012), "A Mapping of Faith-based Responses to Violence Against Women and Girls," Bangkok: UNFPA Asia and the Pacific Regional Office. *Available online:* www.unfpa.org/public/home/publications/pid/13190.

Kaza, Stephanie (2008), *Mindfully Green*, Boston: Shambhala.
Kaza, Stephanie, and Kraft, Kenneth, eds. (2000), *Dharma Rain: Sources of Buddhist Environmentalism*, Boston: Shambhala Publications.
Kaza, Stephanie, ed. (2005), *Hooked!*, Boston & London: Shambala.
Kazin, Michael (2017), *War Against War: The American Fight for Peace 1914–1918*, New York: Simon and Schuster.
Keck, Margaret E. and Kathryn Sikkink (1998), *Activists Beyond Border: Advocacy Networks in International Politics*, Ithaca, NY: Cornell University Press.
Keegan, John (1989), "Only One Man Wanted to Ignite World War II," *Los Angeles Times*.
Keeley, Lawrence H. (1996), *War Before Civilization: The Myth of the Peaceful Savage*, Oxford: Oxford University Press.
Kelly, Liz (2000), "Wars Against Women: Sexual Violence, Sexual Politics and the Militarised State," in Susie Jacobs, Ruth Jacobson & Jennifer Marchbank (eds.), *States of Conflict. Gender, Violence and Resistance: 45–65*, London: Zed Books.
Kelly, Raymond C. (2000), *Warless Societies and the Origin of War*, Ann Arbor: University of Michigan Press.
Kelly, Robert L. (1995), *The Foraging Spectrum: Diversity in Hunter-Gatherer Lifeways*, Washington, DC: Smithsonian Institution.
Kelman, Herbert C. (2004), "Reconciliation as Identity Change. A Social-Psychological Perspective," in Yaacov Bar-Siman-Tov (ed.), *From Conflict Resolution to Reconciliation*, 11–124, Oxford: Oxford University Press.
Kemp, Graham and Douglas P. Fry, eds. (2004), *Keeping the Peace: Conflict Resolution and Peaceful Societies Around the World*, New York: Routledge.
Keohane, Robert O. (2005), *After Hegemony. Cooperation and Discord in the World Political Economy*, Princeton, NJ: Princeton University Press.
Keohane, Robert O. and Joseph S. Nye (2011), *Power and Interdependence*, 4th ed., London: Pearson.
Keohane, Robert O., ed. (1986), *Neorealism and Its Critics*, New York: Columbia University Press.
Kershaw, Ian (1987), *The "Hitler Myth": Image and Reality in the Third Reich*, New York: Oxford University Press.
Kershaw, Ian. (2000), *Hitler 1936–45: Nemesis*, New York: Norton.
Khan Abdul Ghaffar Khan (1969), *My Life and Struggle; Autobiography of Badshah Khan*, Delhi: Hind Pocket Books.
Khrushchev, Nikita (1962), "Letters exchanged with President Kennedy," *Washington DC: US Department of State*, October 23. Available online: http://microsites.jfklibrary.org/cmc/oct26/.
Khrushchev, Nikita (1970), *Khrushchev Remembers*, Edward Crankshaw and Strobe Talbott (ed.), Boston: Little, Brown.
Kimball, C. (2003), *When Religion Becomes Evil*, San Francisco: HarperCollins.
King Abdullah bin Abdulaziz International Centre for Interreligious and Intercultural Dialogue. KAICIID Dialogue Centre Annual Report 2013–2014. Vienna: KAICIID.
King Jr., Martin Luther (1958), "Pilgrimage to Nonviolence," *Stride Toward Freedom*, Boston: Beacon.
King Jr., Martin Luther (1964), "Nobel Lecture: The Quest for Peace and Justice," *Nobelprize.org*, December 11. Available online: www.nobelprize.org/nobel_prizes/peace/laureates/1964/king-lecture.html.
King, S.B. (2009), *Socially Engaged Buddhism*, Honolulu: University of Hawai'i.

Kleiderer, John, Paul Minaert and Mark Mossa (2006), *Just War, Lasting Peace*, Maryknoll, NY: Orbis Books.
Klein, Naomi (2002), *Fences and Windows. Dispatches from the Front Lines of the Globalization Debate*, New York: Picador.
Klein, Naomi (2004), "Baghdad Year Zero," *Harper's Magazine*, September: 43–53.
Klein, Naomi (2014), *This Changes Everything: Capitalism vs the Climate*, New York: Simon & Schuster.
Kloestmaier, Klaus (2014), "Ahimsa," in Matyok, Thomas, Flaherty, Maureen, Tuso, Hamdesa, Senehi, Jessica and Byrne, Sean (eds.), *Peace on Earth: The Role of Religion in Peace and Conflict Studies*, 31–41, New York: Lexington Books.
Klotz, Audie (1999), *Norms in International Relations: The Struggle against Apartheid*, Ithaca: Cornell University Press.
Kluckholm, Clyde, and Fred L. Strodtbeck (1961), *Variations in Value Orientations*, Evanston, IL: Row and Peterson.
Knauft, Bruce (1991), "Violence and Sociality in Human Evolution," *Current Anthropology*, 32: 391–428.
Knightley, Philip (1982), *The First Casualty from the Crimea to Vietnam: The War Correspondent as Hero, Propagandist, and Myth Maker*, London: Quartet Books.
Knitter, P. (1995), *One Earth Many Religions*, Maryknoll, NY: Orbis Books.
Knitter, Paul, and Muzaffar, Chandra, eds. (2002), *Subverting Greed: Religious Perspectives on the Global Economy*, Maryknoll, NY: Orbis Books.
Knudtson, Peter and Suzuki, David (1992), *Wisdom of the Elders*, Toronto: Stoddard.
Kokko, Hanna (2013), "Conflict and Restraint in Animal Species: Implications for War and Peace," in Douglas P. Fry (ed.), *War, Peace, and Human Nature: Convergence of Evolutionary and Cultural Views*, 38–53, New York: Oxford University Press.
Konner, Melvin (2006), "Human Nature, Ethnic Violence, and War," in Mari Fitzduff and Chris E. Stout (eds.), *The Psychology of Resolving Global Conflicts: From War to Peace*, 1: 1–39, Westport, CT: Praeger Security International.
Korten, David (1995), *When Corporations Rule the World*, San Francisco: Berrett-Koehler Publishers & Kumarian Press.
Kotler, Arnold, ed. (1996), *Engaged Buddhist*, Berkeley: Parallax Press.
Kreps, David. (2016), *Bergson, Complexity and Creative Emergence*, London: Palgrave Macmillan.
Kubrick, Stanley (1972), "The Hechinger Debacle: Now Kubrick Fights Back." Available online: www.visual-memory.co.uk/amk/doc/0037.html.
Kumar, D. (2012), *Islamophobia and the Politics of Empire*, Chicago, IL: Haymarket Books.
Kumar, Satish (2002), *You Are Therefore I Am*, Devon: Green Books.
Kung, Hans (2008), "A New Paradigm of International Relations," in Bryan Rennie and Philip L. Tite (eds.), *Religion, Terror and Violence: Religious Studies Perspectives*, 103–15, London: Routledge.
Kurian, George Thomas (2011), "Forgiveness," in George Thomas Kurian (ed.), *The Encyclopedia of Christian Civilization*, Hoboken, NJ: Wiley Online Library.
Kurtz, Lester R. (eds.) (2018) *The Warrior and the Pacifist: Competing Motifs in Buddhism, Judaism, Christianity, and Islam*, New York: Routledge.
Lacina, Bethany, Nils Petter Gleditsch, and Bruce Russett (2006), "The Declining Risk of Death in Battle," *International Studies Quarterly*, 50(3): 673–80.
Lahiri, Mayanjot (2017), *Ashoka in Ancient India*. Cambridge, MA: Harvard University Press.

Lama, Dalai (1989), "Nobel Lecture," *Nobelprize.org*, December 11. Available online: www.nobelprize.org/nobel_prizes/peace/laureates/1989/lama-lecture.html.

Landau, Richard (2002), "The Baha'i Faith and the Environment," in Peter Timmerman (ed.), *Encyclopedia of Global Environmental Change*, 5: Social and Economic Dimensions of Global Environmental Change, New York: Wiley.

Laozi (2004), *Dao De Jing: The Book of the Way*, translated by Robert Moss, Berkeley, CA: University of California Press.

Lauren, Paul Gordon (2003), *The Evolution of International Human Rights: Visions Seen*, Philadelphia: University of Pennsylvania Press.

Leacock, Eleanor (1954) "The Montagnais 'Hunting Territory' and the Fur Trade, Memoirs of the American Anthropological Association," *American Anthropologist*, 56(2), part 2, memoir 78.

LeBow, Richard Ned (2010), *Why Nations Fight: Past and Future Motives for War*, Cambridge: Cambridge University Press.

Lederach, John Paul (1995), *Preparing for Peace: Conflict Transformation Across Cultures*, Syracuse, New York: Syracuse University Press.

Lederach, John Paul (1997), *Building Peace: Sustainable Reconciliation in Divided Societies*, Washington, DC: USIP Press.

Lederach, John Paul (2005), *The Moral Imagination: The Art and Soul of Building Peace*, Oxford: Oxford University Press.

Lee, Richard B. (1993), *The Dobe Ju/'hoansi*, 2nd ed., Fort Worth: Harcourt Brace.

Lee, Richard B. (2014), "Hunter-Gatherers on the Best-Seller List: Steven Pinker and the 'Bellicose School's' Treatment of Forager Violence," *Journal of Aggression, Conflict, and Peace Research*, 6: 216–28.

Leebaw, Bronwyn. (2011), *Judging State-Sponsored Violence, Imagining Political Change*, Cambridge: Cambridge University Press.

Lefebure, Leo D. (2000), *Revelation, the Religions and Violence*, Maryknoll, NY: Orbis Books.

Lefebvre, Alexandre and Melanie White, eds. (2012), *Bergson, Politics and Religion*, Durham & London: Duke University Press.

Lenin, Vladimir Ilyich *Prolelorshaya Revolulsia*, No. 5(28) in *Lenin Collected Works, Volume 2* (1974), 290–4, Moscow: Progress Publishers.

Lerner, Nathan (2012), "Religion and Freedom of Association," in Witte, John Jr. and M. Christian Green (eds.), *Religion and Human Rights*, 218–35, Oxford: Oxford University Press.

Levy, Jack S., and William Thompson (2011), *The Arc of War: Origins, Escalation, and Transformation*, Chicago: University of Chicago Press.

Lewis, Bernard (2003), "'I'm right, You're wrong, Go to Hell'. Religions and the Meeting of Civilizations," *The Atlantic*, 291(4).

Lifton, Robert Jay (2017), *The Climate Swerve. Reflections on Mind, Hope and Survival*, New York: New Press.

Linderman, Gerald F. (1987), *Embattled Courage: The Experience of Combat in the Civil War*, New York: Free Press.

Linklater, Andrew (1999), *The Transformation of Political Community. Ethical Foundations of the Post-Westphalian Era*, Columbia: University of South Carolina Press.

Linklater, Andrew (2007), *Critical Theory and World Politics. Citizenship, Sovereignty and Humanity*, London: Routledge.

Linklater, Andrew (2011), *The Problem of Harm in World Politics: Theoretical Investigations*, Cambridge: Cambridge University Press.

Linklater, Andrew (2017), *Violence and Civilization in the Western States-Systems*, Cambridge: Cambridge University Press.
Little, David, ed. (2007), *Peacemakers in Action*, Cambridge: Cambridge University Press.
Llewellyn, Jennnifer J. and Daniel Philpott, eds. (2014), *Restorative Justice, Reconciliation, and Peacebuilding*, Oxford: Oxford University Press.
Lokashakti Power of the People (n.d.), "Narmada Bachao Andolan(1989–)," *The Lokashakti Encyclopedia of Nonviolence, Peace, & Social Justice*. Available online: www.lokashakti.org/encyclopedia/groups/143-narmada-bachao-andolan.
Lopez, Donald S. Jr., ed. (2004), *Buddhist Scriptures*, London: Penguin Group.
Lowe, Keith (2012), *Savage Continent: Europe in the Aftermath of World War II*, New York: St. Martin's Press.
Loyn, David (2007), "Good Journalism or Peace Journalism," *Conflict & Communication*, 6(2).
Luard, Evan (1986), *War in International Society*, New Haven, CT: Yale University Press.
Luciak, Ilja (2012), "Joining Forces for Democratic Governance: Women's Alliance-Building for Post-War Reconstruction in Central America," Pankhurst, Donna *Gendered Peace*, 239–74, Routledge.
Lukacs, John (1997), *The Hitler of History*, New York: Knopf.
Lynch, Cecelia. (1999), *Beyond Appeasement: Interpreting Interwar Peace Movements in World Politics*, Ithaca: Cornell University Press.
Lynch, Jake (2008), *Debates in Peace Journalism*, Sydney: Sydney University Press.
Lynch, Jake and Annabel McGoldrick (2005), *Peace Journalism*, Stroud UK: Hawthorn Press.
Maathai, Wangari (2004), "Nobel Lecture," *Nobelprize.org*, December 10. Available online: www.nobelprize.org/nobel_prizes/peace/laureates/2004/maathai-lecture-text.html.
Macarthy, E.S. (2011), "Christian Social Teaching: Integrating the Virtue of Nonviolent Peacemaking," in Marc Pilisuk and Michael N. Nagler (eds.), *Peace Movements Worldwide*, 1, Santa Barbara, CA: Praeger.
Mack, Andrew (2005), "Human Security Report 2005: War and Peace in the 21st Century," *Die Friedens-Warte*, 80 (1/2): 177–91.
Mackenzie, Pastor Don Ted Rabbi Falcon, and Imam Jamal Rahman (2011), *Religion Gone Astray*, Woodstock: Skylight Paths Publishing.
Macnair, Rachel M. (2003), *The Psychology of Peace: An Introduction*, Westport: Praeger.
Macy, Joanna and Molly Y. Brown (1998), *Coming Back to Life: Practices to Reconnect our Lives, our World*, Gabriola Island, BC: New Society.
Madeley, John (2008), *Big Business, Poor Peoples*, London: ZED.
Magnussen, Svein, and Mark W Greenlee (1999), "The Psychophysics of Perceptual Memory," *Psychological Research*, 62(2–3): 81–92.
Malinowski, Bronislaw (1941), "An Anthropological Analysis of War," *American Journal of Sociology*, 46: 521–50.
Manchester, William (1988), *The Last Lion, Winston Spencer Churchill: Alone, 1932–1940*, Boston: Little, Brown.
Mander, Jerry and Tauli-Corpuz, Victoria, eds. (2006), *Paradigm Wars. Indigenous Peoples' Resistance to Globalization*, San Francisco: Sierra Club Books.
Manning, Peter (2017), *Transitional Justice and Memory in Cambodia: Beyond the Extraordinary Chambers*, London: Routledge.
Mapel, D.R. and T. Nardin, eds. (1998), *International Society. Diverse Ethical Perspectives*, Princeton: Princeton University Press.
Marlowe, Frank (2010), *The Hadza Hunter-Gatherers of Tanzania*, Berkeley: University of California Press.

Marshall, K. et al. (2011), "Women in Religious Peacebuilding," Washington: United States Institute for Peace. Available online: www.usip.org/publications/women-in-religiouspeacebuilding.

Marshall, Katherine and Van Saanen, Marisa (2007), *Development and Faith*, Washington, DC: World Bank.

Marshall, S.L.A. ([1947] 2000), *Men against Fire: The Problem of Battle Command*, Norman, OK: University of Oklahoma Press.

Martin, James (2017), *Building a Bridge: How the Catholic Church and the LGBT Community Can Enter into a Relationship of Respect, Compassion, and Sensitivity*, New York: Harper Collins.

Martin, William G. (2008), *Making Waves. Worldwide Social Movements, 1750–2005*, London: Routledge.

Mary, Br. Lawrence (2006), "Catholic Teaching Concerning a Just War," *Catholicism.org*. Available on www.cathilicism.org/Catholic-teaching-just-war.html.

Maschner, Herbert (1997), "The Evolution of Northwest Coast Warfare," in Debra L. Martin and David W. Frayer (eds.), *Troubled Times: Violence and Warfare in the Past*, 267–302, Amsterdam: Gordon and Breach.

Mastny, Vojtech (2006), "Introduction," in Vojtech Mastny, Sven G. Holtsmark, and Andreas Wenger (eds.), *War Plans and Alliances in the Cold War: Threat Perceptions in the East and West*, London and New York: Routledge, 2006.

Matera, Marc, et al. ([2011] 2012), *The Women's War of 1929: Gender and Violence in Colonial, Nigeria*, London: Palgrave MacMillan.

Mattelart, Armand (2000), *Networking the World 1794–2000*, Minneapolis: University of Minnesota Press.

Matyok, Thomas, Flaherty, Maureen, Tuso, Hamdesa, Senehi, Jessica and Byrne, Sean, eds. (2014), *Peace on Earth: The Role of Religion in Peace and Conflict Studies*, New York: Lexington Books.

Maynard Smith, John (1974), "The Theory of Games and the Evolution of Animal Conflicts," *Journal of Theoretical Biology*, 47: 209–21.

Maynard Smith, John, and G.R. Price (1973), "The Logic of Animal Conflict," *Nature*, 246: 15–8.

Mayne, Richard, "Gray Eminence," in Douglas Brinkley and Clifford Hackett, eds. (1992), *Jean Monnet. The Path to European Unity*, 114–28, New York: St. Martin's.

Mazlish, Bruce (2006), *The New Global History*, New York and London: Routledge.

McCarthy, Helen. (2011), *The British People and the League of Nations: Democracy, Citizenship and Internationalism, c. 1918–48.* Manchester: University of Manchester Press.

McCormick, Patrick (2006), "Violence: Religion, Terror, War," *Theological Studies*, 67: 142–63.

McLeod, Melvin, ed. (2006), *Mindful Politics: A Buddhist Guide to Making the World a Better Place*, Sommerville, MA: Wisdom Publications.

McTernan, Oliver (2007), *Violence in God's Name*, London: Darton, Longman & Todd.

McWilliams, Monica, and Avila Kilmurray (2015), "From the Global to the Local: Grounding UNSCR 1325 on Women, Peace and Security in Post Conflict Policy Making," *Women's Studies International Forum*, 51.

Mead, Margaret (1964), "Warfare is only an Invention—Not a Biological Necessity," in Leon Bramson and George W. Goethals (eds.), *War: Studies from Psychology, Sociology, Anthropology*, 269–74, New York: Basic Books.

Meggitt, Mervyn (1965), *Desert People: A Study of the Walbiri Aborigines of Central Australia*, Chicago: University of Chicago Press.

Meintjes, Sheila, Anu Pillay, and Meredeth Turshen (2001), *The Aftermath: Women in Post-Conflict Transformation*, London: Zed Books.

Menon, Rajan (2016), *The Conceit of Humanitarian Intervention*, New York: Oxford University Press.

Merton, Thomas (ed.) (1965), *Gandhi on Non-Violence*, New York: New Directions.

Mertus, Julie A. and Jeffrey W. Helsing, ed. (2006), *Human Rights and Conflict. Exploring the Links Between Rights, Law and Peacebuilding*, Washington, DC: US Institute of Peace.

Meyer, David S. (1990), *A Winter of Discontent: The Nuclear Freeze and American Politics*. New York: Praeger.

Meyer, David S. (1993), "Protest Cycles and Political Process: American Peace Movements in the Nuclear Age," *Political Research Quarterly* 46(3): 451–79.

Miall, Hugh, Tom Woodhouse, Oliver Ramsbotham and Christopher Mitchell, eds. (2015), *The Contemporary Conflict Resolution Reader*, Cambridge: Polity.

Miller, James (n.d.), "Daoism and Ecology, Forum on Religion and Ecology." Available online: http://fore.research.yale.edu/religion/daoism/index.html.

Milne, Alan Alexander (1935), *Peace with Honour*, New York: Dutton.

Minow, Martha (1998), *Between Vengeance and Forgiveness: Facing History after Genocide and Mass Murder*, Boston: Beacon Press.

Miqdad, Mohammad Ibrahim (2015), "Islam and the Rejection of Violence," *Palestine-Israel Journal of Politics, Economics & Culture*, 20–21(41): 33–9.

Mitchell, Stephen (1988), *Tao Te Ching: A New English Version*, New York: HarperCollins.

Mohamed, H. and Hoehne, M. (2013), "The Impact of Civil War and State Collapse on the Roles of Somali Women: A Blessing in Disguise," *Journal of Eastern African Studies*, 7(2): 314–33.

Mohanty, Chandra Talpade (2003), "'Under Western Eyes' Revisited: Feminist Solidarity Through Anticapitalist Struggles," *Signs: Journal of Women in Culture and Society*, 28(2): 499–535.

Moïsi, Dominique (2010), *The Geopolitics of Emotion. How Cultures of Fear, Humiliation and Hope are Reshaping the World*, New York: Anchor.

Möller, Frank (2008), "Imaging and Remembering Peace and War," *Peace Review: A Journal of Social Justice*, 20: 100–106.

Molyneux, Maxine (1985), "Mobilization Without Emancipation? Women's Interests, the State, and Revolution in Nicaragua," *Feminist Studies*, 11(2): 227–54.

Monnet, Jean (1978), *Memoirs*, trans. Richard Mayne, Garden City, NY: Doubleday.

Montagu, Ashley (1976), *The Nature of Human Aggression*, Oxford: Oxford University Press.

Montagu, Ashley (1978), *Learning Non-Aggression: The Experience of Non-Literate Societies*, Oxford: Oxford University Press.

Moore, Natasha (2015), "The Realism of the Angel in the House: Coventry Patmore's Poem Reconsidered," *Victorian Literature and Culture*, 43(1): 41–61.

Morgenthau, Hans ((1948) 1963), *Politics Among Nations: The Struggle for Power and Peace*, New York: Knopf.

Morozov, Evgeny (2011), *The Net Delusion: The Dark Side to Internet Freedom*, New York: Public Affairs.

Morrisey, Christopher, A. (2018), *Christianity and American State Violence in Iraq: Priestly or Prophetic?*, New York: Routledge.

Morrow, William (2012), "Violence and Religion in the Christian Tradition," in Brian K. Pennington (ed.), *Teaching Religion and Violence*, 94–117, Oxford: Oxford University Press.

Morsink, Johannes (2009), *Inherent Human Rights. Philosophical Roots of the Universal Declaration*, Philadelphia: University of Pennsylvania Press.

Moser, Caroline (1989), "Gender Planning in the Third World: Meeting Practical and Strategic Gender Needs," *World Development*, 17(11): 1799–1825.

Moser, Caroline and Fiona C. Clark (2001), *Victims, Perpetrators Or Actors?: Gender, Armed Conflict and Political Violence*, London: Zed Books.

Moyn, Samuel (2012), *The Last Utopia. Human Rights in History*, Cambridge, MA: Belknap Press.

Moyn, Samuel (2014), *Human Rights and the Uses of History*, London: Verso.

Mueller, John (1980), "The Search for the 'Breaking Point' in Vietnam: the Statistics of a Deadly Quarrel," *International Studies Quarterly*, 24(4) December: 497–519.

Mueller, John (1988), "The Essential Irrelevance of Nuclear Weapons: Stability in the Postwar World," *International Security*, 13(2) Fall: 55–79.

Mueller, John (1989), *Retreat from Doomsday: The Obsolescence of Major War*, New York: Basic Books.

Mueller, John (1995), *Quiet Cataclysm: Reflections on the Recent Transformation of World Politics*, New York: Harper Collins.

Mueller, John (1999), *Capitalism, Democracy, and Ralph's Pretty Good Grocery*, Princeton: Princeton University Press.

Mueller, John (2004), *The Remnants of War*, Ithaca and London: Cornell University Press.

Mueller, John (2005), "The Iraq Syndrome," *Foreign Affairs*, November–December, 44–54.

Mueller, John (2010a), *Atomic Obsession: Nuclear Alarmism from Hiroshima to Al-Qaeda*, New York: Oxford University Press.

Mueller, John (2010b), "Capitalism, Peace, and the Historical Movement of Ideas," *International Interactions*, 36 March: 169–84.

Mueller, John (2011a), *War and Ideas: Selected Essays*, London and New York: Routledge.

Mueller, John (2011b), "The Iraq Syndrome Revisited: US Intervention, From Kosovo to Libya," *foreignaffairs.com*, March 28.

Mueller, John (2011c). "Questing for Monsters to Destroy," in Melvyn Leffler and Jeffrey W. Legro (eds.), *In Uncertain Times: American Foreign Policy after the Berlin Wall and 9/11*, Ithaca: Cornell University Press.

Mueller, John (2012), "History and Nuclear Rationality," *nationalinterest.org*, November 19.

Mueller, John (2014), "Iraq Syndrome Redux: Behind the Tough Talk," *foreignaffairs.com*, June 18.

Mueller, John, and Mark G. Stewart (2016a), *Chasing Ghosts: The Policing of Terrorism*, New York: Oxford University Press.

Mueller, John, and Mark G. Stewart (2017), "Misoverestimating Terrorism," in Michael S. Stohl, Richard Burchill, and Scott Englund (eds.), *Constructions of Terrorism: An Interdisciplinary Approach to Research and Policy*, Berkeley, CA: University of California Press.

Mueller, John, and Mark Stewart (2016b), "How Safe Are We? Asking the Right Questions about Terrorism," *foreignaffairs.com*, August 15.

Mukta, Parita (2000), "Gender, Community, Nation: The Myth of Innocence," in Susie Jacobs, Ruth Jacobson & Jennifer Marchbank (eds.), *States of Conflict. Gender, Violence and Resistance*: 45–65, London: Zed Books.

Mun, Chanju (2007), "Buddhist Peacemakers in Modern Times," in Chanju Mun (ed.), *Mediators and Meditators: Buddhism and Peacemaking*, 1–48, Honolulu: Blue Pine Books.

Mun, Chanju, ed. (2007), *Mediators and Meditators: Buddhism and Peacemaking*, Honolulu: Blue Pine Books.

Murphy, Danny Pio (2012), "First Same-Sex Buddhist Wedding Held in Taiwan," *Spirituality Ireland Blog*, August 17. Available online: http://spiritualityireland.org/blog/index.php/2012/08/first-same-sex-buddhist-wedding-held-in-taiwan/.

Myers, Fred (1986), *Pintupi Country, Pintupi Self: Sentiment, Place, and Politics among Western Desert Aborigines*, Berkeley: University of California Press.

Nagler, Michael (2014), *The Nonviolence Handbook: A Guide for Practical Action*, San Francisco: Berrett-Koehler.

Nakao, Hisashi, Kohei Tamura, Yui Arimatsu, Tomomi Nakagawa, Naoko Matsumoto, and Takehiko Matsugi (2016), "Violence in the Prehistoric Period of Japan: The Spatio-Temporal Pattern of Skeletal Evidence for Violence in the Jomon Period," *The Royal Society: Biology Letters*, March 30, 2016. DOI: 10.1098/rsbl.2016.0028.

National Peace Council (1959), *The NPC: 1908–1958*, London: NPC.

Nepstad, Sharon Erickson (2004), "Religion, Violence, and Peacemaking," *Journal for the Scientific Study of Religion*, 43(2): 297–301.

Nepstad, Sharon Erickson (2008), *Religion and War Resistance in the Ploughshares Movement*, New York: Cambridge University Press.

Nessan, Craig L. (2012), *The Vitality of Liberation Theology*, Eugene, OR: Pickwick Publications.

New Annual Register or Repository of History, Politics, Arts, Sciences, and Literature for 1822 (1823), London: Longman, Hurst, Rees, Orme, and Brown.

Ngugi wa Thiong'o and Micere Githae Mugo (1976). *The Trial of Dedan Kimathi*. Waveland Press.

Niebuhr, Reinhold ([1932] 2013), *Moral Man and Immoral Society*, Louisville, KY: Westminster John Knox Press.

Nixon, Richard (1970), "First Annual Report to the Congress on United States Foreign Policy for the 1970s," online by Gerhard Peters and John T. Woolley, *The American Presidency Project*, February 18. Available online: www.presidency.ucsb.edu/ws/?pid=2835.

Nohrstedt, Stig A. and Rune Ottosen (2014), *New Wars, New Media and New War Journalism. Professional and Legal Challenges in Conflict Reporting*, Gotheburg: Nordicom.

Nohrstedt, Stig A. and Ottosen, Rune (2008), "War Journalism in the Threat Society: Peace Journalism as a strategy for challenging the mediated culture of fear?," *Conflict & Communication Online*. 7. Available online: www.cco-regener-online.

Nohrstedt, Stig A. and Ottosen, Rune (2011), "Peace journalism-critical discourse case study: media and the plan for Swedish and Norwegian defense cooperation," in Shaw, Ibrahim Seaga, Jake Lynch, Robert A Hackett (eds.), *Expanding Peace Journalism: Comparative and Critical Approaches*, 217–38, Sydney: Sydney University Press.

Nojeim, Michael J. (2004), *Gandhi and King: The Power of Nonviolent Resistance*, Westport, CT: Praeger.

Nordstrom, Carolyn (1997), *Girls and Warzones: Troubling Questions*, Oslo: Life & Peace Institute.

O'Connell, Mary Ellen. 2010, "Responsibility to Peace: A Critique of R2P," *Journal of Intervention and Statebuilding*, 4(1): 39–52.

Obama, Barack H. (2009), "Nobel Lecture: A Just and Lasting Peace," *Nobelprize.org*, December 10. Available online: www.nobelprize.org/nobel_prizes/peace/laureates/2009/obama-lecture_en.html.

Ochola, Robert Lukwiya (2006), "The Acholi Religious Leaders' Peace Initiative in the battlefield of Northern Uganda," *Diplomarbeit zur Erlangung des Magistergrades an der Theologischen Fakultät der Leopold-Franzens-Universität Innsbruck*. Available online: http://nointervention.com/archive/Africa/Uganda/ochola_diplomarbeit.pdf.

Office of the President of the United States (2002), *National Security Strategy of the United States of America*, Washington, DC: The White House.
Olsson, Louise and Theodora-Ismene Gizelis, eds. (2015), *Gender, Peace and Security: Implementing UN Security Council Resolution 1325*, Routledge.
Omar, Abdul Rasheid (2015), "Religious Violence and State Violence," in Abdul Rasheid Omar, R. Scott Appleby and David Little (eds.), *Oxford Handbook of Religion, Conflict, and Peacebuilding*, 236–58, Oxford: Oxford University Press.
Omer, Atalia, R. Scott Appleby, and David Little, eds. (2015), *The Oxford Handbook of Religion, Conflict and Peacebuilding*. Oxford: Oxford University Press.
Omer, Atalia. (2013), *When Peace is Not Enough: How the Israeli Peace Camp Thinks About Religion, Nationalism, and Justice*, Chicago: University of Chicago Press.
Osterhammel, Jürgen, and Niels P. Petersson (2005), *Globalization: A Short History* Princeton: Princeton University Press.
Otterbein, Keith F. (1970), *The Evolution of War: A Cross-Cultural Study*, New Haven, CT: Human Relations Area Files Press.
Ottosen, Rune (1995), "Enemy Images and the Journalistic Process," *Journal of Peace Research*, 32(1): 97–112.
Ottosen, Rune (2007), "Emphasizing Images in Peace Journalism: A Case Study from Norway´s Biggest Newspaper," in *Peace Journalism: The State of the Art*, Dov Shinar and Wilhelm Kempf (eds.), Berlin: Regener.
Ottosen, Rune (2010). "Galtung's Theory on Peace Journalism and Norwegian Journalism on Afghanistan," in Johansen, Jørgen Jones, John Y. (eds.), *Experiments with Peace. Celebrating Peace on Johan Galtung's 80th Birthday*, 258–66, Oxford: Pambazuka Press.
Ottosen, Rune (2010a). "The War in Afghanistan and Peace Journalism in Practice," *Media, War and Conflict*, 3(3): 261–78.
Ottosen, Rune and Øvrebø, Sjur (2016), "Who's to Blame for the Chaos in Syria? The Coverage of Syria in *Aftenposten* with Libya as Doxa," in Orgeret, Kristin Tayeebwa, William (Red.), *Journalism in Conflict and Post-Conflict Conditions. Worldwide Perspectives*, 63–80, Gothenburg: Nordicom.
Ottosen, Rune, Tore Slaatta, and Sigurd Øfsti (2013), "How they Missed the Big Story: Norwegian News Media and NATO's Military Operation in Libya," *Conflict & Communication*. Available online: www.cco-regener-online.
Overy, R.J. (1982), "Hitler's War and the German Economy: A Reinterpretation," *Economic History Review*, 35(2) May: 272–91.
OXFAM (2017), "An Economy for the 99%," Oxford: OXFAM.
Padilla, C. Rene (1987), "A New Ecclesiology in Latin America," *International Bulletin of Missionary Research*," Oct.: 156–64. Available online: www.internationalbulletin.org/issues/1987-04/1987-04-156-padilla.pdf.
Pain, Stephanie (2001), "The Great Tooth Robbery," *The New Scientist*, London: June 16.
Pankhurst, Donna, ed. (2012a), *Gendered Peace: Women's Struggles for Post-War Justice and Reconciliation*, Routledge.
Pankhurst, Donna (2012b), "Introduction: Gendered War and Peace," in Donna Pankhurst (ed.), *Gendered Peace: Women's Struggles for Post-War Justice and Reconciliation*, Routledge.
Pankhurst, Donna (2012c), "Post-War Backlash Violence Against Women: What Can 'Masculinity' Explain?," in Donna Pankhurst (ed.), *Gendered Peace: Women's Struggles For Post-War Justice And Reconciliation*, Routledge.
Pankhurst, Donna (2016), "'What is Wrong With Men?': Revisiting Violence Against Women in Conflict and Peacebuilding," *Peacebuilding*, 4(2): 180–93.

Parliament of the World's Religions (1993), "Declaration Toward a Global Ethic." Available online: https://parliamentofreligions.org/pwr_resources/_includes/FCKcontent/File/TowardsAGlobalEthic.pdf.

Parliament of the World's Religions (n.d.). Available online: https://parliamentofreligions.org/.

Patel, Eboo and Cassie Meyer (2015), "Youth and Interfaith Conflict Transformation," in R. Scott Appleby, Atalia Omer, and David Little (eds.), *The Oxford Handbook of Religion, Conflict, and Peacebuilding*, 470–87, New York: Oxford University Press.

Patterson, David S. (1976), *Toward a Warless World: The Travail of the American Peace Movement, 1887–1914*, Bloomington, IN: Indiana University Press.

Paul VI, Pope (1965), "Address of the Holy Father Paul VI to the United Nations Organization, 4 October 1965." Available online: https://w2.vatican.va/content/paul-vi/en/speeches/1965/documents/hf_p-vi_spe_19651004_united-nations.html.

Pearce, Jenny (2006), "Bringing Violence 'Back Home': Gender Socialisation and the Transmission of Violence through Time and Space," *Global Civil Society*, 2006–7: 42–61.

Pearce, Jenny (2010), "Perverse State Formation and Securitized Democracy in Latin America," *Democratization*, 17(2): 286–306.

Pennington, Brian K. (2012), "Striking the Delicate Balance: Teaching Violence and Hinduism," in Brian K. Pennington (ed.), *Teaching Religion and Violence*, 19–46, Oxford: Oxford University Press.

Pennington, Brian K. ed. (2012), *Teaching Religion and Violence*, Oxford: Oxford University Press.

Philpott, Daniel and Gerard F. Powers, eds. (2010), *Strategies of Peace. Transforming Conflict in a Violent World*, Oxford: Oxford University Press.

Philpott, Daniel and Gerard F. Powers, eds. (2010), *Strategies of Peace. Transforming Conflict in a Violent World*, Oxford: Oxford University Press.

Philpott, Daniel, ed. (2006), *The Politics of Past Evil. Religion, Reconciliation and the Dilemmas of Transitional Justice*, Southbend: University of Notre Dame Press.

Pierson, Roach R (1989), "Beautiful Soul or Just Warrior: Gender and War," *Gender and History*, 1(1): 77–86.

Pietersee, Jan Nederveen (2015), *Globalization & Culture: Global Melange*, Lanham, Maryland: Rowan & Littlefield.

Pilisuk, Marc and Michael N. Nagler, eds. (2011), *Peace Movements Worldwide*, Vol. 1 History and Vitality of Peace Movements, Santa Barbara, CA: Praeger.

Pinker, Steven (2011), *The Better Angels of Our Nature: Why Violence Has Declined*, New York: Viking.

Pinker, Steven, and Juan Manuel Santos (2016), "Colombia's Milestone in World Peace," *New York Times*, August 26: A19.

Plümper, Thomas, and Eric Neumayer (2006), "The Unequal Burden of War: The Effect of Armed Conflict on the Gender Gap in Life Expectancy," *International Organization*, 60(3): 723–54.

Pollack, Norman (2018), *Capitalism, Hegemony and Violence in the Age of Drones*, London: Palgrave Macmillan.

Pontifical Council for Interreligious Dialogue, Dialogue and Proclamation (1991), "Reflections and Orientations on Interreligious Dialogue and the Proclamation of the Gospel of Jesus Christ," May 19, 1991. Available online: www.vatican.va/roman_curia/pontifical_councils/interelg/documents/rc_pc_interelg_doc_19051991_dialogue-and-proclamatio_en.html.

Pope Francis (2015), *Laudato Si'*. Encyclical Letter of the Holy Father Francis on Care for our Common Home, Vatican. Available online: http://w2.vatican.va/content/francesco/en/encyclicals/documents/papa-francesco_20150524_enciclica-laudato-si.html.

Pope Francis (2016), "Pope says 'world at war because it has lost peace' but religion not to blame," *Japan Times*, July 28. Available online: www.japantimes.co.jp/news/2016/07/28/world/social-issues-world/pope-says-world-war-lost-peace-religion-not-blame/.

Popovic, Srdja, and Matthew Miller (2015), *Blueprint for Revolution: How to Use Rice Pudding, Lego Men and Other Nonviolent Techniques to Galvanize Communities, Overthrow Dictators, or Simply Change the World*, New York: Spiegel & Grau.

Porter, Elizabeth (2007), *Peacebuilding: Women In International Perspectives*, UK: Routledge.

Power, Samantha (2002), *A Problem from Hell: America in the Age of Genocide*, New York: Basic Books.

Pratt, Douglas (2017), *Religious Extremism*, London: Bloomsbury.

Prime, Ranchor (2006), *Hinduism and Ecology: Seeds of Truth*, London: Cassell & WWF.

Project Ploughshares (n.d.), "Overview." Available online: http://ploughshares.ca/about-us/.

Puchala, Donald J. (2003), *Theory and History in International Relations*, London: Routledge.

Putin, Vladimir (2015), "Meeting of the Valdai International Discussion Club," *Official Internet Resources of the President of Russia*, October 22. Available online: http://en.kremlin.ru/events/president/transcripts/50548.

Pyles, Loretta (2005), "Understanding the Engaged Buddhist Movement: Implications for Social Development Practice," *Critical Social Work*, 6(1). Available online: www.criticalsocialwork.com/units/socialwork/critical.nsf/8c20dad9f1c4be3a85256d6e006d1089/3e9b18c1f86ebce385256fd700634820?OpenDocument.

Pynn, Tom (2014), "The Dao De Jing on Cultivating Peace," *Peace Review: A Journal of Social Justice*, 26: 357–64.

Queen, Christopher S. (2007), "The Peace Wheel: Nonviolent Activism in the Buddhist Tradition," in Daniel L. Smith-Christopher (ed.), *Subverting Hatred: The Challenge of Nonviolence in Religious Traditions*, 14–37, Maryknoll, NY: Orbis Books.

Queen, Christopher S. ed. (2000), *Engaged Buddhism in the West*, Boston: Wisdom Publications.

Randolph, A. Philip., and Chandler Owen. (1917/2014), "Terms of Peace and the Darker Races," in Scott H. Bennett and Charles H. Howlett (eds.), *Antiwar Dissent and Peace Activism in World War I America*, 165–9, Lincoln: University of Nebraska Press.

Rapoport, Anatol (1968) "Introduction," in Clausewitz, Carl von, *On War*, London: Penguin.

Ratzinger, Joseph Cardinal (1984), "Instruction on Certain Aspects of the Theology of Liberation'," *Congregation for the Doctrine of the Faith*, Vatican. Available online: www.vatican.va/roman_curia/congregations/cfaith/documents/rc_con_cfaith_doc_19840806_theology-liberation_en.html.

Rauchhaus, Robert (2009), "Evaluating the Nuclear Peace Hypothesis," *Journal of Conflict Resolution*, 53(2): 258–77.

Ravlo, Hilde, Nils Petter Gleditsch, and Han Dorussen (2001), *Colonial War and Democratic Peace*, Oslo, Norway: PRIO.

Ray, James Lee (1989), "The Abolition of Slavery and the End of International War," *International Organization*, 43(3) Summer: 405–39.

Raynolds, Laura T. and Elizabeth A. Bennett, eds. (2015), *Handbook of Research on Fair Trade*, Northampton, MA: Edward Elgar Publishing.

Reed, Charles (2001), *Development Matters: Christian Perspectives on Globalization*, London: Church House Publishing.

Regional Interfaith Network (2012), "Sixth Regional Interfaith Dialogue," Semarang, Indonesia. Available online: http://regionalinterfaith.org.au/?page_id=110.

Regional Interfaith Network (2014), "Asian Women Peacemaker's Conference," August 1, 2010. Available online: http://regionalinterfaith.org.au/?p=122.

Regional Interfaith Network (n.d.), "Statements of Regional Interfaith Dialogues." Available online: http://regionalinterfaith.org.au/?page_id=77R (accessed May 11, 2015).

Reichhardt, Tony (2015), "The Deadliest Air Raid in History," *Air & Space Smithsonian*, May 9, 2015.

Religions for Peace (2006), "The Kyoto Declaration on Confronting Violence and Advancing Shared Security Religions for Peace, Eighth World Assembly," August 2006. Available online: https://rfp.org/wp-content/uploads/2017/09/Kyoto-Declaration-Final-Draft.pdf.

Religions for Peace (2008), *We Can Cooperate for Peace*, New York: Religions for Peace.

Religions for Peace (n.d.), "Global Women of Faith Network." Available online: https://rfp.org/connect/global-women-of-faith-network/.

Renard, John, ed. (2012), *Fighting Words: Religion, Violence and the Interpretation of Religious Texts*, Berkeley: University of California.

Rennie, Bryan and Philip Tite (2008), *Religion, Terror and Violence: Religious Studies and Perspectives*, New York: Routledge.

Rhodes, Richard (2007), *Arsenals of Folly: The Making of the Nuclear Arms Race*, New York: Knopf.

Rich, Norman (1973), *Hitler's War Aims: Ideology, the Nazi State, and the Course of Expansion*, New York: Norton.

Richmond, Oliver (2011), *A Post-Liberal Peace*, London: Routledge.

Richmond, Oliver (2014), *Failed Statebuilding. Intervention, the State, and the Dynamics of Peace*, New Haven: Yale University Press.

Richmond, Oliver (2014), *Peace: A Very Short Introduction*, Oxford: Oxford University Press.

Richmond, Oliver (2016), *Peace Formation and Political Order in Conflict Affected Societies*, Oxford: Oxford University Press.

Richmond, Oliver, Pogodda, Sandra, and Ramovic, Jasmin, eds. (2016), *The Palgrave Handbook of Disciplinary and Regional Approaches to Peace*, New York: Palgrave Macmillan.

Rigby (1998), "The Origins of the Peace Symbol," *Peace Review*, 10(3), 475–80.

Risse, Thomas, Stephen C. Ropp (2013), *The Persistent Power of Human Rights: From Commitment to Compliance*, Cambridge: Cambridge University Press.

Risse, Thomas, Stephen C. Ropp, and Kathryn Sikkink (1999), *The Power of Human Rights: International Norms and Domestic Change*, Cambridge: Cambridge University Press.

Rivera, Mauricio (2015), "The Sources of Social Violence in Latin America. An Empirical Analysis of Homicide Rates, 1980–2010," *Journal of Peace Research*, 53(1): 84–99.

Roberts, Adam and Timothy Garton Ash (2009), *Civil Resistance & Power Politics: The Experience of Nonviolent Action from Gandhi to the Present*, Oxford: Oxford University Press.

Rochon, Thomas R. (1988), *Mobilizing for Peace: The Antinuclear Movements in Western Europe*, Princeton: Princeton University Press.

Roht-Arriaza, Naomi (2006), *The Pinochet Effect. Transitional Justice in the Age of Human Rights*, Philadelphia: University of Pennsylvania Press.

Roht-Arriaza, Naomi and Javier Mariezcurrena, eds. (2006), *Transitional Justice in the Twenty-First Century. Beyond "Truth versus Justice,"* Cambridge: Cambridge University Press.

Roht-Arriaza, Naomi, ed. (1995), *Impunity and Human Rights in International Law and Practice*, Oxford: Oxford University Press.

Ronan, Marian (2007), "Ethical Challenges Confronting the Roman Catholic Women's Ordination Movement in the Twenty-First Century," *Journal of Feminist Studies in Religion*, 23(2): 149–69.
Roper, Marilyn K. (1969), "A Survey of the Evidence for Intrahuman Killing in the Pleistocene," *Current Anthropology*, 10: 427–59.
Roper, Marilyn K. (1975), "Evidence of Warfare in the Near East from 10,000–4,300 BC," in Martin A. Nettleship, R. Dalegivens, and A. Nettleship (eds.), *War, Its Causes and Correlates*, 299–340, The Hague: Mouton.
Roser, Max (2018), "War and Peace," Published online at OurWorldInData.org.
Roser, Max, and Mohamed Nagdy (2018), "Nuclear Weapons," Published online at OurWorldIn Data.org.
Rostami-Povey, Elaheh (2007), "Gender, Agency and Identity, The Case of Afghan Women in Afghanistan, Pakistan and Iran," *The Journal of Development Studies*, 43(2): 294–311.
Rotberg, Robert I and Dennis Thompson (2000), *Truth vs Justice. The Morality of Truth Commissions*, Princeton: Princeton University Press.
Russett, Bruce, and Oneal, John, (2001), *Triangulating Peace: Democracy, Interdependence, and International Organizations*, New York: Norton.
S.K. (1958), "The Land Gift Movement in India: Vinoba Bhave and His Achievement," *The World Today*, 14(11): 487–95.
Sacks, Jonathan (2015), *Not in God's Name: Confronting Religious Violence*, London: Hodder & Stoughton.
Safi, Omid, ed. (2003), *Progressive Muslims on Justice, Gender, and Pluralism*, Oxford: Oxford University Press.
Sagan, Scott and Benjamin A. Valentino (2017), "The Nuclear Weapons Ban Treaty: Opportunities Lost," *Bulletin of the Atomic Scientists*, July 16. Available online: http://thebulletin.org/nuclear-weapons-ban-treaty-opportunities-lost10955.
Sahlins, Marshall (2008), *The Western Illusion of Human Nature*, Chicago: Prickly Paradigm Press.
Salem, Sara (2013), "Feminist Critique and Islamic Feminism: The Question of Intersectionality," *The Postcolonialist*, 1(1). Available online: http://postcolonialist.com/civil-discourse/feminist-critique-and-islamic-feminism-the-question-of-intersectionality.
Sampson, Cynthia (1997), "Religion and Peacebuilding," in I. William Zartman and J. Lewis Rasmussen (eds.), *Peacemaking in International Conflict: Methods and Techniques*, 273–316. Washington, DC: US Institute of Peace Press.
Sanchez, Oscar Arias (1987), "Acceptance Speech," *Nobelprize.org*, December 10. Available online: www.nobelprize.org/nobel_prizes/peace/laureates/1987/arias-acceptance.html.
Sanger, David E. (2012), *Confront and Conceal: Obama's Secret Wars and Surprising Use of American Power*, New York: Crown.
Sarvodaya Shramadana Movement (n.d.). Available online: www.sarvodaya.org/.
Satha-Anand, Chaiwat (2018), "Transforming Terrorism with Muslims' Nonviolent Alternatives," in Lester Kurtz (ed.), *The Warrior and the Pacifist: Competing Motifs in Buddhism, Judaism, Christianity, and Islam*, New York: Routledge.
Scheid, Ron E., ed. (2014), *The Ethics of Humanitarian Intervention*, Cambridge: Cambridge University Press.
Schell, Jonathan (1982), *The Fate of the Earth*, New York: Knopf.
Schirch, Lisa (2005), *Ritual and Symbol in Peacebuilding*, Sterling, VA: Kumarian Press.
Schirch, Lisa (2013), *Conflict Assessment and Peacebuilding Planning. Toward a Participatory Approach to Human Security*, Sterling, VA: Kumarian Press.

Schlabach, Gerald (2018), "Pope Francis Shifting Catholics to Just Peacebuilding," *SYMPOSIUMETHICS*, Wednesday, April 25. Available online: http://symposiumethics.org/2017/01/06/pope-shifting-to-just-peacebuilding/.

Schock, Kurt (2005), *Unarmed Insurrections: People Power Movements in Nondemocracies*, Minneapolis: University of Minnesota Press.

Schroeder, Paul (1985), "Does Murphy's Law Apply to History?," *Wilson Quarterly*, 9(1).

Schwarz, Rabbi Sid (n.d.), "Judaism and Social Justice: Five Core Values from the Rabbinic Tradition." Available online: www.qscience.com/doi/pdf/10.5339/rels.2012.justice.10.

Sciegocki, J. (2008), "Neoliberal Globalization: Critiques and Alternatives," *Theological Studies*, 69: 321–339. Available online: cdn.theologicalstudies.net/69/69.2/69.2.5.pdf.

Selengut, Charles (2017), *Sacred Fury: Understanding Religious Violence*, 3rd ed., New York: Rowman and Littlefield.

Selin, Henrik and Stacy D. VanDeveer (2015), *European Union and Environmental Governance*, New York: Routledge.

Selin, Shannon (2016), "How were Napoleanic Battlefields Cleaned Up?" Available online: https://shannonselin.com/2016/07/napoleonic-battlefield-cleanup/.

Sen, Amartya (1999), "Democracy as a Universal Value," *Journal of Democracy* 1999, 10.

Sen, Jai and Waterman, Peter, eds. (2009), *World Social Forum Challenging Empires*, Montreal/New York/London: Black Rose Books.

Service, Elman R. (1966), *The Hunters*, Englewood Cliffs, NJ: Prentice-Hall.

SGI (2014), "Peace Activities Annual Report 2014." Available online: www.sgi.org/content/files/resources/ngo-resources/SGI_PEACE_ACTIVITIES_2014_ANNUAL_REPORT.pdf.

SGI (2016), "Peace Activities: 2016 Annual Report," Tokyo: SGI. Available online: www.sgi.org/content/files/resources/ngo-resources/sgi-peace-activities-2016-annual-report.pdf.

SGI (n.d.), "President Ikeda's Proposals." Available online: www.sgi.org/about-us/president-ikedas-proposals/

SGI (Soka Gakkai International) (n.d.), "Faith Communities Unite Against Nuclear Weapons at ICAN Civil Society Forum Issue Joint Statement." Available online: www.sgi.org/in-focus/2014/faith-communities-nuclear-weapons.html.

Sharma, Arvind, ed. (1994), *Religion and Women*, New York: State University of New York Press.

Sharp, Gene (2005), *Waging Nonviolent Struggle: 20th Century Practice and 21st Century Potential*, Boston: Porter Sargent Publishers.

Shastri, Sunanda Y. and Shastri, Yajneshwar S. (2007), "Ahimsa and the Unity of all Things: A Hindu View of Nonviolence," in Daniel L. Smith-Christopher (ed.) (2007), *Subverting Hatred: The Challenge of Nonviolence in Religious Traditions*, 57–75, Maryknoll, NY: Orbis Books.

Shay, Jonathan (1994), *Achilles in Vietnam: Combat Trauma and the Undoing of Character*, New York: Touchstone.

Sheehan, James J. (2008), *Where Have All the Soldiers Gone? The Transformation of Modern Europe*, Boston: Houghton Mifflin.

Shephard, Ben (2003), *A War of Nerves: Soldiers and Psychiatrists in the Twentieth Century*, Cambridge, MA: Harvard University Press.

Shepherd, Laura. 2008. "Power and Authority in the Production of United Nations Security Council Resolution 1325," *International Studies Quarterly*, 52, 2(1): 383–404.

Shewan, M.A., Akela, A.C., and Sharma, N.P. (2011), *Acharya Vinoba Bhave*, Mumbai: Himalaya Books.

Shibahara, Taeko. (2015), *Japanese Women and the Transnational Feminist Movement Before World War II*, Philadelphia: Temple University Press.

Shifferd, Kent D. (2011), *From War to Peace: A Guide to the Next Hundred Years*, Jefferson, NC: McFarland.
Shiva, Vandana (2005), *Earth Democracy*, Cambridge: South End Press.
Shiva, Vandana (2013), *Making Peace with the Earth*, London: Pluto.
Schock, Kurt (2005), *Unarmed Insurrections: People Power Movements in Nondemocracies*, Minneapolis: University of Minnesota Press.
Shukla-Bhatt, N. (2009), "A Reflection on the Challenges for Hindu Women in the Twenty-first Century," *Journal of Oriental Studies*, 19: 61–70. Available online: www.iop.or.jp/09198/shukla-bhatt.pdf.
Siker, Jeffrey S. (2006), *Homosexuality in the Church: Both Sides of the Debate (Movements)*, Santa Barbara, CA: Greenwood Publishers.
Sikh Missionary Society (n.d.), "A Sikh Approach to War and Peace." Available online: www.sikhmissionarysociety.org/sms/smsarticles/advisorypanel/gurmukhsinghsewauk/sikhapproachtowarandpeace.html.
Sikkink, Kathryn (2011), *The Justice Cascade: How Human Rights Prosecutions Are Changing World Politics*, New York: Norton.
Sikkink, Kathryn (2017), *Evidence for Hope: Making Human Rights Work in the 21st Century*, Princeton: Princeton University Press.
Silverman, Jacob (2015), *Terms of Service: Social Media and the Price of Constant Connection*, New York: Harper Collins.
Simmons, Robert R. (1975), *The Strained Alliance: Peking, Pyongyang, Moscow and the Politics of the Korean Civil War*, New York: Free Press.
Singh, Rajwant (2011), "Sikhism and Caring for the Environment in Practice." Available online: www.ecosikh.org/wp-content/uploads/2011/09/Sikhism-and-Caring-for-the-Environment-in-Practice.pdf.
Sivakumaran, Sandesh (2007), "Sexual Violence Against Men in Armed Conflict," *European Journal of International Law*, 18(2): 253–76.
Sivaraksa, Sulak (2001), *Seeds of Peace: A Buddhist Vision for Renewing Society*, Berkeley: Parallax Press.
Sivaraksa, Sulak (2009), *The Wisdom of Sustainability: Buddhist Economics for the 21st Century*, Kihei, HI: Koa Books.
Sivard, Ruth Leger (1987), *World Military and Social Expenditures 1987/88*, Washington, DC: World Priorities.
Sjøvaag, Hanne (2005), "Attached or detached? Subjective methods in war journalism," MA thesis, Department of Information Science and Media Studies, University of Bergen.
Skeat, W., and C. Blagden (1906), *Pagan Races of the Malay Peninsula*, London: Macmillan.
Skjelsbaek, Inger (2001), "Sexual Violence and War: Mapping Out a Complex Relationship," *European Journal of International Relations*, 7(2): 211–37.
Sluys, Cornelia M.I. van der (1999), "Jahai," in Richard B. Lee and Richard Daly (eds.), *The Cambridge Encyclopedia of Hunters and Gatherers*, 307–11, Cambridge: Cambridge University Press.
Small, Melvin, and J. David Singer (1982), *Resort to Arms: International Civil Wars, 1816–1980*, Beverly Hills, CA: Sage.
Smith-Christopher, Daniel L. (2007), *Subverting Hatred: The Challenge of Nonviolence in Religious Traditions*, Maryknoll, NY: Orbis Books.
Smock, David R. (2008), *Religion in World Affairs. Its Role in Conflict and Peace*, USIP Press.
Smock, David R. ed. (2002), *Interfaith Dialogue and Peacebuilding*, Washington, DC: USIP Press.

Söderberg, Patrik, and Douglas P. Fry (2017), "Anthropological Aspects of Ostracism," in Kipling D. Williams and Steve A. Nida (eds.), 258–72, New York: Routledge.

Soka Gakkai International (n.d.). Available online: www.sgi.org/our-story.html.

Solingen, Etel. (2009), *Nuclear Logics: Contrasting Paths in East Asia and the Middle East*, Princeton: Princeton University Press.

Somerville, John (1954), *The Philosophy of Peace*, New York: Liberty Press.

Sontag, Susan (2003), *Regarding the Pain of Others*, New York: Farrar, Straus, and Giroux.

Souillac, Geneviève (2004), "From Global Norms to Local Change: Theoretical Perspectives on the Promotion of Human Rights in Societies in Transition," in Shale Horowitz and Albrecht Schnabel (eds.), *Human Rights and Societies in Transition: Causes, Consequences, Responses*, 77–100, Tokyo, New York, Paris: United Nations University Press.

Souillac, Geneviève (2011), *The Burden of Democracy: The Claims of Cultures, Public Culture, and Democratic Memory*, Lanham, MD: Rowman & Littlefield/Lexington Books.

Souillac, Geneviève (2012), *A Study in Transborder Ethics: Justice, Citizenship, and Civility*, Brussels/Frankfurt/New York: Peter Lang.

Souillac, Geneviève (2015), "The Cosmopolitan Ideal and the Civilizing Process: Expanding Citizenship for Peace," in Sybille De La Rosa and Darren O'Byrne (eds.), *The Cosmopolitan Ideal: Challenges and Opportunities*, 137–56, London: Rowman & Littlefield.

Souillac, Geneviève (2016), "Jean Jaurès: A Man of Peace," *Peace Review: A Journal of Social Justice*, 28(1): 123–31.

Souillac, Geneviève, and Douglas P. Fry (2013), "The Relevance of Nomadic Forager Studies to Moral Foundations Theory: Moral Education and Global Ethics in the Twenty-First Century," *Journal of Moral Education*, 42: 346–59.

Souillac, Geneviève, and Douglas P. Fry (2014), "Indigenous Lessons for Conflict Resolution," in Peter T. Coleman, Morton Deutsch, and Eric Marcus (eds.), *The Handbook of Conflict Resolution: Theory and Practice*, 3rd ed., 602–22, San Francisco: Jossey-Bass.

Souillac, Geneviève, and Douglas P. Fry (2015), "The Human Quest for Peace, Rights, and Justice: Convergence of the Traditional and the Modern," in Johanna Seibt and Jesper Garsdal (eds.), *How is Global Dialogue Possible? Foundational Research on Values, Conflicts, and Intercultural Thought*, 225–49, Berlin: DeGruyter.

Souillac, Geneviève, and Douglas P. Fry (2016), "Anthropology: Implications for Peace," in Oliver P. Richmond, Sandra Pogodda, & Jasmin Ramović (eds.), *The Palgrave Handbook of Disciplinary and Regional Approaches to Peace*, New York: Palgrave Macmillan.

Souillac, Geneviève, and Douglas P. Fry (2017), "The Original Partnership Societies: Evolved Propensities for Equality, Prosociality, and Peace," *Interdisciplinary Journal of Partnership Studies*, 4(1): Article 4. Available online: http://pubs.lib.umn.edu/ijps/vol4/iss1/4.

Soulez, Philippe (1989), *Bergson politique*, Paris: Presses Universitaires de France.

Soulez, Philippe (1997), *Bergson. Biographie*, Paris: Flammarion.

Soulez, Philippe and Frédéric Worms (2002), *Bergson*, Paris: Presses Universitaires de France.

Sponsel, Leslie E. (2016), "The Anthropology of Peace and Nonviolence," *Diogenes*, 1–16.

Sponsel, Leslie E., and Thomas Gregor, eds. (1994), *The Anthropology of Peace and Nonviolence*, Boulder: Lynne Rienner.

Spretnak, Charlene (1991), *States of Grace*, New York: Harper Collins.

Sriram, Chandra Lekhas and Suren Pillay, eds. (2010), *Peace vs Justice? The Dilemma of Transitional Justice in Africa*, London/New York: Boydell & Brewer.

Staub, Ervin (1989), *The Roots of Evil: The Origins of Genocide and Other Group Violence*, Cambridge: Cambridge University Press.

Steger, Manfred (2009), *Globalisms: The Great Ideological Struggle of the Twenty-First Century*, Lanham, MD: Rowan & Littlefield.

Steinert, Marlis G. (1977), *Hitler's War and the Germans: Public Mood and Attitude during the Second World War*, Athens, OH: Ohio University Press.

Stewart, Frances and Valpy Fitzgerald (2001), *War and Underdevelopment: Volume 1, The Economic and Social Consequences of Conflict*, Oxford: Oxford University Press.

Stromberg, Roland N. (1982). *Redemption by War: The Intellectuals and 1914*, Lawrence: Regents Press of Kansas.

Struett, Michael J. 2008. *The Politics of Constructing the International Criminal Court: NGOs, Discourse, and Agency*, New York: Palgrave Macmillan.

Sullivan, Dennis and Larry Tifft (2007), *Handbook of Restorative Justice. A Global Perspective*, London/New York: Routledge.

Sunder, M. (2012), "Keeping Faith: Reconciling Women's Human Rights and Religion," in John Witte, Jr. and M. Christian Green (eds.), *Religion & Human Rights: An Introduction*, 281–98, New York: Seven Stories.

Susan Willett (2010), "Introduction: Security Council Resolution 1325: Assessing The Impact on Women, Peace and Security," *International Peacekeeping* 17(2): 142–58.

Sussman, Robert W. (2013), "Why the Legend of the Killer Ape Never Dies: The Enduring Power of Cultural Beliefs to Distort Our View of Human Nature," in Douglas P. Fry (ed.), *War, Peace, and Human Nature: Convergence of Evolutionary and Cultural Views*, 97–111, New York: Oxford University Press.

Suttner, Bertha von (1905), "The Evolution of the Peace Movement." Available online: https://www.nobelprize.org/prizes/peace/1905/suttner/lecture/.

Swerdlow, Amy (1982), "Ladies' Day at the Capitol: Women Strike for Peace Versus HUAC," *Feminist Studies*, 8(3): 493–520.

Swidler, Leonard (2014), *Dialogue for Interreligious Understanding*, New York: Palgrave Macmillan.

Tahmasesebi, S. (2012), "A Civil-Society-Led Revolution: Promoting Civil Rights and Women's Rights in the Middle East," in Minky Worden, M. (ed.), *The Unfinished Revolution. Voices from the Global Right from Women's Rights*, 61–72, New York: Seven Stories.

Tam, Wai Lun (2007), "Subverting Hatred: Peace and Nonviolence in Confucianism and Daoism," in Daniel L. Smith-Christopher (ed.), *Subverting Hatred: The Challenge of Nonviolence in Religious Traditions*, 38–56, Maryknoll, NY: Orbis Books.

Tamale, Sylvia (1999), *When Hens Begin to Crow: Gender and Parliamentary Politics in Uganda*, Boulder, CO: Westview Press.

Tannenwald, Nina. (2008), *The Nuclear Taboo: The United States and the Non-Use of Nuclear Weapons Since 1945*, Cambridge: Cambridge University Press.

Taylor, Paul M. (2012), "Religion and Freedom of Choice," in John Witte Jr. and M. Christian Green (eds.), *Religion and Human Rights*, 170–87, Oxford: Oxford University Press.

Teitel, Rudi G. (2000), *Transitional Justice*, Oxford: Oxford University Press.

Teitel, Rudi G. (2015), *Globalizing Transitional Justice. Contemporary Essays*, Oxford: Oxford University Press.

Terrell, Mary Church. (1980), *A Colored Woman in a White World*, New York: Arno Press.

Tharoor, Ishaan. (2013), "Viewpoint: Why Was the Biggest Protest in World History Ignored?," *Time* February 13. Available online: http://world.time.com/2013/02/15/viewpoint-why-was-the-biggest-protest-in-world-history-ignored/.

The British Academy (2015), *The Role of Religion in Conflict and Peacebuilding*, London: British Academy.

The Conversation (2015), "From the Temple to the Street: How Sikh Kitchens Are Becoming the New Food Banks," *The Conversation*, July 22, 2015. Available online: http://theconversation.com/from-the-temple-to-the-street-how-sikh-kitchens-are-becoming-the-new-food-banks-44611.

Thich Nhat Hanh in Kotler, A. (1991), *Peace is Every Step, the Path of Mindfulness in Everyday Life*, New York: Bantam Books.

Tiercelin, Claudine (2015), "Les philosophes français face à la guerre," in Antoine Compagnon (ed.), *Actes du Colloque de rentrée du Collège de France. Autour de 1914–1918: Nouvelles figures de la pensée*, 1995-221, Paris: Odile Jacob.

Tilly, Charles (2004), *Social Movements, 1768–2004*, Boulder, CO: Paradigm Publishers.

Tilly, Charles and Lesley G. Wood (2012), *Social Movements. 1768–2012*, London: Routledge.

Tirosh-Samuelson, Hava, ed. (2003), *Judaism and Ecology: Created World and Revealed Word*, Cambridge, MA: Harvard University Press.

Toh, Swee-Hin (2004), "Uprooting Violence, Cultivating Peace: Education for an Engaged Spirituality," Lecture, 17 June, Griffith University, Australia. Available online: https://research-repository.griffith.edu.au/bitstream/handle/10072/368665/toh04.pdf?sequence=1&isAllowed=y.

Toh, Swee-Hin and Cawagas, Virginia (2010), "Peace Education, ESD and the Earth Charter: Interconnections and Synergies," *Journal of Education for Sustainable Development*, 4(2): 167–80.

Toh, Swee-Hin and Cawagas, Virginia (2010), "Transforming the Ecological Crisis. Challenges for Faith and Interfaith Education in Interesting Times," in F. Kagawa and D. Selby (eds.), *Education and Climate Change*, 175–96, New York: Routledge.

Toh, Swee-Hin and Cawagas, Virginia, eds. (2006), *Cultivating Wisdom, Harvesting Peace: Educating for a Culture of Peace Through Values, Virtues and Spirituality of Diverse Cultures, Faiths and Civilizations*, Brisbane: Multi-Faith Centre, Griffith University.

Tolstoy, Leo ([1869] 1966), *War and Peace*, New York: Norton.

Tomlinson, John (1999), *Globalization and Culture*, Chicago: University of Chicago Press.

Tonkinson, Robert (1974), *The Jigalong Mob: Aboriginal Victors of the Desert Crusade*, Menlo Park, CA: Cummings.

Tonkinson, Robert (1978), *The Mardudjara Aborigines: Living the Dream in Australia's Desert*, New York: Holt, Rinehart, and Winston.

Tonkinson, Robert (2004), "Resolving Conflict within the Law: The Mardu Aborigines of Australia," in Graham Kemp and Douglas P. Fry (eds.), *Keeping the Peace: Conflict Resolution and Peaceful Societies around the World*, 89–104, New York: Routledge.

Tooze, Adam (2015), *The Deluge: The Great War, America and the Remaking of the Global Order, 1916–1931*, London: Penguin.

Torres, Sergio and Fabella, Virginia, eds. (1978), *The Emergent Gospel: Theology from the Underside of History*, Maryknoll, NY: Orbis Books.

Toynbee, Arnold J. (1969), *Experiences*, New York: Oxford University Press.

Trachtenberg, Marc (1991), *History and Strategy*, Princeton, NJ: Princeton University Press.

Tripp, Aili Mari (2005), "Legislative Quotas for Women: Implications for Governance in Africa," *African Parliaments*: New York: 48–60.

Tripp, Aili Mari (2015), *Women and Power in Postconflict Africa*, Cambridge: Cambridge University Press.

Truman, Harry S (1956), *Years of Trial and Hope*, Garden City: Doubleday.

Tse Tung, Mao (1956), "Opening Address at the Eighth National Congress of the Communist Party of China," quoted in Tse Tung, Mao (1972), *Quotations from Chairman Mao Tsetung*. Beijing: Foreign Language Press, 65.

Tucker, Mary E. and William, Duncan R., eds. (1998), *Buddhism and Ecology*: The *Interconnections of Dharma and Deeds*, Cambridge, MA: Harvard University Press.
Tucker, Robert W. (2015), *Woodrow Wilson and the Great War: Reconsidering America's Neutrality 1914–1917*, Charlottesville: University of Virginia Press.
Tucker, Spencer C., and Priscilla Roberts, eds. (2005) *Encyclopedia of World War I*, 246, Santa Barbara, CA: ABC-CLIO.
Turse, Nick (2008), *The Complex: How The Military Invades Our Everyday Life*, New York: Henry Holt.
Turshen, Meredeth and Twagiramariya, Clotilde, eds. (1998), *What Women Do in Wartime*, London: Zed Press.
Tutu, Desmond (1984), "Nobel Lecture". Available online: www.nobelprize.org/nobel_prizes/peace/laureates/1984/tutu-lecture.html.
Tutu, Desmond (1999), *No Future Without Forgiveness*, New York: Doubleday.
Tyler, Aaron A. (2010), "Religion, Politics and Peacebuilding. The Method of Sant Egidio," *Journal of Culture and Politics* (Summer): 78–94.
UNESCO (1994), "UNESCO's Declaration on the Role of Religion in the Promotion of a Culture of Peace," Paris: UNESCO. Available online: http://fund-culturadepaz.org/eng/DECLARACIONES/religion%201994.pdf.
Union of Concerned Scientists (n.d.), "Global Warming Impacts: The Consequences of Climate Change Are Already Here," *Cambridge, MSA: Union of Concerned Scientists*. Available online: www.ucsusa.org/our-work/global-warming/science-and-impacts/global-warming-impacts#.WuNWmciFM2x.
United Nations (1994), *Human Development Report 1994. New Dimensions of Human Security*, New York: United Nations Development Program.
United Nations (2003), *Human Security Now. Protecting and Empowering People*, New York: United Nations Commission on Human Security.
United Nations (2013), *The Arms Trade Treaty*. Available online: https://unoda-web.s3-accelerate.amazonaws.com/wp-content/uploads/2013/06/English7.pdf.
United Nations Office for Disarmament Affairs, "Nuclear Weapon-Free Zones." Available online: www.un.org/disarmament/wmd/nuclear/nwfz/.
United States Institute of Peace (2002), "The Alexandria Declaration 2002." Available online: www.usip.org/programs/alexandria-declaration.
Universal House of Justice (1985), *The Promise of World Peace*, Haifa: Universal House of Justice.
Vagts, Alfred (1959), *A History of Militarism*, New York: Norton.
Van Der Veer, Peter, Ngo, Tam and Yu, Dan Smyer (2015), "Religion and Peace in Asia," in R. Scott Appleby, Atalia Omer, and David Little (eds.), *The Oxford Handbook of Religion, Conflict, and Peacebuilding*, 407–29, New York: Oxford University Press.
Van Dijck, José (2013), *The Culture of Connectivity: A Critical History of Social Media*, Oxford: Oxford University Press.
Van Leeuwen, M. (2009), *Partners in Peace: Discourses and Practices of Civil-Society Peacebuilding*, Abingdon: Routledge.
van Tongeren, P., Brenk, M., Hellema, M. and Verhoeven, J., eds. (2005), *People Building Peace II. Successful Stories of Civil Society*, London: Lynne Rienner Publishers.
Verbeek, Peter (2013), "An Ethological Perspective on War and Peace," in Douglas P. Fry (ed.), *War, Peace, and Human Nature: Convergence of Evolutionary and Cultural Views*, 54–78, New York: Oxford University Press.
Vickers, J. (1993) *Women and War*, London: Zed Books.

Victoria, Brian Daizen (2012), "Teaching Buddhism and Violence," in B.K. Pennington (ed.), *Teaching Religion and Violence*, 74–93, Oxford: Oxford University Press.

Vinthagen, Stellan (2015), *A Theory of Nonviolent Action: How Civil Resistance Works*, London: Zed Books.

Volkan, Vamik (2006), *Killing in the Name of Identity. A Study of Bloody Conflicts*, Durham, NC: Pitchstone Publishing.

Walgrave, Stefan and Rucht, Dieter (2010), *The World Says No to War: Demonstrations Against the War on Iraq*, Minneapolis: University of Minnesota Press.

Wallensteen, Peter (2011), *Peace Research: Theory and Practice*, New York and London: Routledge.

Walsh, Martha (2012), "Gendering International Justice: Progress and Pitfalls at International Criminal Tribunals," in Donna Pankhurst (ed.), *Gendered Peace: Women's Struggles for Post-War Justice and Reconciliation*, Abingdon: Routledge.

Waltz, Kenneth (2001), *Man, the State, and War: A Theoretical Analysis*. Revised Edition, New York: Columbia University Press.

Walzer, Michael ((1977) 2015), *Just and Unjust Wars. A Moral Argument with Historical Illustrations*, New York: Basic Books.

Walzer, Michael (2004), *Arguing about War*, New Haven, CT: Yale University Press.

Wank, Solomon (1988), "The Austrian Peace Movement and the Habsburg Ruling Elite, 1906–1914," in Charles Chatfield and Peter van den Dungen (eds.), *Peace Movements and Political Cultures*, 40–63, Knoxville, TN: University of Tennessee Press.

Ward, Paul (2004), "Gender and National Identity," in Ward, Paul, *Britishness Since 1870*, 37–53, London: Routledge.

Watson, Adam (2009), *The Evolution of International Society. A Comparative Historical Analysis*, 2nd ed., London: Routledge.

Watt, Donald Cameron (1989), *How War Came: The Immediate Origins of the Second World War*, New York: Pantheon.

Webel, Charles and Galtung, Johan, eds. (2009), *The Handbook of Peace and Conflict Studies*, London: Routledge.

Webel, Charles and Johansen, Jorgen, eds. (2012), *Peace and Conflict Studies: A Reader*, London: Routledge.

Wedgwood, C.V. (1938), *The Thirty Years War*, London: Jonathan Cape.

Weibel, Peter (2015), *Global Activism: Art and Conflict in the 21st Century*, Cambridge, MA: MIT Press.

Weinberg, Gerhard L. (1980), *The Foreign Policy of Hitler's Germany: Starting World War II, 1937–1939*, Chicago: University of Chicago Press.

Weiss, Thomas G. (2016), *Humanitarian Intervention*. 3rd ed., Cambridge: Polity.

Weiss, Thomas G., et al., eds. (2013), *The United Nations and Changing World Politics*, Boulder, CO: Westview Press.

Weissman, Deborah (2017), "Elements of Violence and Nonviolence in Judaism: A Contemporary Israeli Perspective," *Journal of Ecumenical Studies*, 52(1): 80–95.

Wendt, Alexander (1999), *Social Theory of International Politics*, Cambridge: Cambridge University Press.

Wheeler, Nicholas J. (2003), *Saving Strangers. Humanitarian Intervention in International Society*, Oxford: Oxford University Press.

Whelsh, J.M. (2006), *Humanitarian Intervention and International Relations*, Oxford: Oxford University Press.

Williams, Emma (2012), "The Velvet Fist," *The Economist 1843*, May/June.

Wilson, Edward O. (1978), *On Human Nature*, Cambridge, MA: Harvard University Press.

Wilson, Edward O. (2012), *The Social Conquest of the Earth*, New York: Norton.

Winfield, Nicole (2017), "Pope: Humanity Risks 'Suicide' with Nuclear Confrontation," *Religion News Service*, October 30. Available online: https://religionnews.com/2017/10/30/vatican-aims-to-head-off-us-north-korea-nuclear-standoff/#.

Witte, John Jr. and Christian Green, M. eds. (2012), *Religion and Human Rights*, Oxford: Oxford University Press.

Wittner, Lawrence S. (2009), *Confronting the Bomb: A Short History of the World Nuclear Disarmament Movement*, Palo Alto: Stanford University Press.

Wodiczko, Krzysztof (2012), *The Abolition of War*, London: Black Dog.

Wood, Elisabeth Jean (2006), "Variation in Sexual Violence During War," *Politics & Society*, 34(3): 307–42.

Wood, Elisabeth Jean (2009), "Armed Groups and Sexual Violence: When is Wartime Rape Rare?," *Politics & Society*, 37(1): 131–61.

World Council of Churches (1999), "A Basic Framework for the Decade to Overcome Violence," *Geneva: World Council of Churches*. Available online: www.oikoumene.org/en/resources/documents/commissions/international-affairs/peace-and-disarmament/peace-concerns/a-basic-framework-for-the-decade-to-overcome-violence.

World Council of Churches (2015), "Faith Communities Concerned about the Humanitarian Consequences of Nuclear Weapons." Available online: www.reachingcriticalwill.org/images/documents/Disarmament-fora/npt/revcon2015/statements/1May_Faith.Communities%20.pdf.

World's Parliament of Religions (1893), The World's Congress of Religions, Chicago, IL: World's Parliament of Religions. Available online: https://archive.org/details/worldscongressr00savagoog.

Worldwatch Institute (2017), *Earth Ed: Rethinking Education on a Changing Planet*, New York: Island Press.

Wrangham, Richard and Glowacki, Luke (2012), "Intergroup Aggression in Chimpanzees and War in Nomadic Hunter-Gatherers: Evaluating the Chimpanzee Model," *Human Nature*, 23: 5–29.

Wrangham, Richard, and Peterson, Dale (1996), *Demonic Males: Apes and the Origin of Human Violence*, Boston: Houghton Mifflin.

Wright, Quincy (1942), *A Study of War*, Chicago: University of Chicago Press.

Yaffe, Martin D., ed. (2001), *Judaism and Environmental Ethics: A Reader*, New York: Lexington Books.

Yanklowitz, Rabbi Dr. Shmuly (2014), *The Soul of Jewish Social Justice*, Jerusalem: Urim Publications.

Young, Nigel, J. (ed.) (2010), *The Oxford International Encyclopedia of Peace*, Oxford and New York: Oxford University Press.

Youngblood, Steven (2016), *Peace Journalism Principles and Practices. Responsibly Reporting Conflicts, Reconciliation, and Solutions*, London: Routledge.

Zacher, Mark (2001), "The Territorial Integrity Norm: International Boundaries and the Use of Force," *International Organization*, 55(2): 215–50.

Zwick, Mark and Louise (n.d.), "Pope John Paul II Calls War a Defeat for Humanity: Neoconservative Iraq Just War Theories Rejected," *Catholic Online*. Available online: www.catholic.org/featured/headline.php?ID=361.

CONTRIBUTORS

Ronald Edsforth has retired from teaching, but is still a Research Associate in History at Dartmouth College where he was a Distinguished Senior Lecturer in the History Department (1992–2014) and Professor and Chair of Globalization Studies in the Master of Liberal Studies Program (2006–16). He was also the first Coordinator of Dartmouth's interdisciplinary War and Peace Studies Program (1998–2004). Professor Edsforth is currently writing with his wife, Joanne Devine, a history of Save the Children dedicated to their son Nick, who died in 2009.

Douglas P. Fry is Professor and Chair of the Department of Peace and Conflict Studies at the University of North Carolina at Greensboro. Professor Fry earned his doctorate from Indiana University in 1986. He has written extensively on aggression, conflict resolution, and war and peace. He is author of *Beyond War* (2007), *The Human Potential for Peace* (2006) and co-editor of *Keeping the Peace: Conflict Resolution and Peaceful Societies Around the World* (2004) and *Cultural Variation in Conflict Resolution: Alternatives to Violence* (1997). Douglas Fry received the Peace and Justice Studies Association's Peace Scholar-Educator Award in 2015.

Marcel Kaba is currently a doctoral student in the Department of Government and International Relations at the University of Sydney. He previously studied in New York and Prague, and has spent the last seven years working on development issues in Afghanistan, South Sudan, and Kenya.

Cecelia Lynch is Professor of Political Science at the University of California, Irvine. She has authored, co-authored, or co-edited six books on international law, ethics, and international relations theory including the prize winning *Beyond Appeasement: Interpreting Interwar Peace Movements* (1999). Professor Lynch has received fellowships from the Social Science Research Council, MacArthur Foundation, American Association of University Women, Andrew W. Mellon Foundation, and the Henry Luce Foundation. She has published numerous articles on peace movements, IR theory, law, diplomacy, religion, ethics, and humanitarianism. Her newest book, *Wrestling with God*, will be published by Cambridge University Press in 2019.

John Mueller is Senior Research Scientist and Woody Hayes Chair of National Security Studies Emeritus, Mershon Center for International Security Studies, Ohio State University; and a Senior Fellow at the Cato Institute, Washington, DC. His numerous books include *Are We Safe Enough? Measuring and Assessing Aviation Security* (with Mark G. Stewart, 2018); *Chasing Ghosts: The Policing of Terrorism* (with Mark G. Stewart, 2016); *Atomic Obsession: Nuclear Alarmism from Hiroshima to Al-Qaeda* (2010); *Overblown: How Politicians and the Terrorism Industry Inflate National Security Threats, and Why We Believe Them* (2006); and *The Remnants of War* (2004).

Rune Ottosen is Professor Emeritus in journalism at Oslo Metropolitan University. He has written extensively on press history and media coverage of war and conflicts. He is co-author with Stig Arne Nohrstedt of several books, the latest *New War, New Medias and New War Journalism (2014)*. In 2010, he was one of the editors and co-author of the four-volume Norwegian Press History, *Norsk Presses historie (1767–2010)*. Rune Ottosen was for many years President of the Norwegian Association of Press History (2009–2015) and was President of the Norwegian Non-fiction Writers and Translators Association 2001–2005.

Donna Pankhurst is Professor of Peacebuilding and Development in "Peace Studies and International Development" at the University of Bradford, UK, where she teaches undergraduate, postgraduate and research students. Her research background is in post-conflict settlements and peacebuilding, with a focus on gender issues. Currently Professor Pankhurst researches other gendered aspects of "the afterwar," with a focus on what happens to military veterans.

Geneviève Souillac is an Associate Professor in the Department of Peace and Conflict Studies at the University of North Carolina at Greenboro. She has held academic positions in peace and conflict studies in Finland, Australia, Japan, and most recently in the Department of Anthropology at the University of Alabama, Birmingham. She combines philosophy and anthropology in studies of peace, human rights, ethics, religion, and global civics. Her numerous publications include *Human Rights in Crisis: The Sacred and the Secular in Contemporary French Thought* (2005), *The Burden of Democracy: The Claims of Cultures, Public Culture, and Democratic Memory* (2011), and *A Study in Transborder Ethics: Justice, Citizenship, Civility* (2012).

Toh Swee-Hin is Professor Emeritus, University of Alberta. He has been Distinguished Professor at the University of Peace in Costa Rica, and a founding director of the Multi-Faith Centre, Griffith University (Australia). His many publications and contributions to UNESCO, the World Council for Curriculum & Instruction, Parliament of the World's Religions, Religions for Peace, and the Asia-Pacific Centre for International Understanding reflect his belief that global peace culture is emerging in the intersection of conflict transformation, human rights, social justice, interfaith dialogue, sustainable development, and global citizenship. In 2000, Toh Swee Hin was awarded UNESCO Prize for Peace Education.

Charles Webel has been a peace and social justice activist since his high school days in New York. He is Professor of International Relations at the University of New York in Prague. He has been Delp-Wilkinson Chair in Peace Studies at Chapman University, and taught at Harvard and the University of California, Berkeley. A five-time Fulbright Scholar, Professor Webel's many publications include the fourth edition of the now classic *Peace and Conflict Studies* (with David Barash, 2017), the *Handbook of Peace and Conflict Studies* (with Johan Galtung, 2002), and *Terror, Terrorism, and the Human Condition* (2007).

INDEX

Page numbers: Figures are given in italics; notes as [page number]n.

9/11 attacks 67, 79, 83–5, 118

Abdi, Dekha Ibrahim 92
absence
 of peace 22
 of war 21, 27
Abu-Nimer, Mohammed 92
Acquino, Corazon *107*
activism, women's association with 73–4, 129, 134
Adams, John 43
Addams, Jane 113
Adenauer, Chancellor of Germany 169–70
Afghanistan 67–8, 141, 155–6, 157
Africa
 definitions of peace 27–9
 interfaith dialogue 100–1
 nuclear weapons 135
 peace movements 129
African Commission on Human and People's Rights 176
African National Congress (ANC) 138
agency, institutional integration 173
aggression 55–6, 116, 150, 154
Agnivesh, Swami 96
agonism concept 54, 55
ahimsa (nonkilling) 86, 90
aid-recipient countries 62
al-Qaeda group 159
All Quiet on the Western Front (Remarque) 130
Allen, Mark 45–6
Alliance of Religions and Conservation (ARC) 103–4
Allied nations, World War II 3, 11
American Civil War 148
American Convention on Human Rights 176
Anan, Kofi 112
anarchic interstate structure 173
Anasazi nomads 47
ANC (African National Congress) 103–4

ancient civilizations 43, *43*, 56
animal behavior studies 51, 54
annihilation, wars of 149
anticolonial struggles 71
antinuclear movements/protests 6–7, 135, 138
antiwar movements/protests 71–3, 106, 108, 136–8, 149–50
apartheid system 138–9, 177
Arab–Israeli conflict 87
Arab Spring 110–11, 141–3
arbitration 128, 131, 143
ARC (Alliance of Religions and Conservation) 103–4
archaeological data 45–7, 57
"archaic" societies 174
archetypal war stories 11–13
Ardrey, Robert 44–5
Arendt, Hannah 26
arms control strategies 135, 150
arms markets, trading in 143
Armstrong, Neil 17
Aron, Raymond 22
arts, peace movements 129–30, 139
Ascherman, Arik 92
Ashafa, Muhammed *103*
Asia
 definitions of peace 29–31
 peace movements 129
 see also China; Japan
Asia-Pacific Interfaith Symposium 98, 101
atheism 84
atmospheric testing, nuclear weapons 6–7
atomic bombings 3, 4, 168
 see also nuclear weapons
attrition strategies 10
Australia, Western Desert nomads 57
Axis nations, World War II 11

Babst, Dean V. 25
backlash discourse, gendered peace 77–8
Baha'i faith 93, 97

balance of power theories 172
Balkan wars 1912–13 165
Ball, George 170
Ban Ki-moon 76
band social life 48–9, 54
Barash, David 24
behavioral data, zoology 53–4
Bergson, Henri 165–7, 174
black recipients, Nobel Peace Prize 113
Blackhawk down, Somalia 157
Blackwell, Joyce 129
Bloomsbury Group 130
Blum, William 116
bodies of soldiers 13–14
Bondfield, Margaret *130*
bonobos *55*
Bonta, Bruce D. 50
border disputes 158
"bottom-up" peace initiatives 140–1
Bouazizi, Mohamed 141
Boulding, Elise 174
Brazil, Upper Xingu River tribes 42
Bread and Puppet Theater 139
Briand, Aristide 165–6
British Co-operative Women's Guild 71
British colonialism 132
Brodie, Bernard 147
Brown, Donald 42–3
Brussels, peace system *58*
Buddhism 85–6, 90–1, 93–8
Bush, George W. 118, 141

Caeymaex, Florence 167
Cambodia 90–1
Campaign for Nuclear Disarmament (CND) 106
Camus, Albert 4, 19
Capa, Robert 109
capitalist oppression 154
caring behavior 51–2
Carr, E.H. 133
Carrier, Alain *169*
Catholic Church 85, 89–90, 99
Central American peace movements 138
Chamberlain, Neville *117*, 153
CHCs (cosmopolitan harm conventions) 175
child dependency 51–2
children
    interfaith dialogue about 103
    sexual abuse 99
    in war 65, *149*
China 21, 23, 30, 154
Christian Peacemaker Teams 89, *90*

Christianity 87–9, 93–7, 102
    see also Catholic Church
Churchill, Winston 3, 11–12, 153
citizenship, normative approach 59
Civil Rights movement, United States 16, 34–5
civil society
    integrative approaches 167
    state scrutiny 174–5
    women 74
civil wars/conflicts
    American Civil War 148
    Arab Spring 142
    honor and 113
    international impact 184n.
    policing 156
    post-World War II 8
    terrorism and 158–9
    women's experiences 66–7, 73
civilian deaths
    gender and 65–7
    World War I 148, 181n.
civilization
    progress and 174
    war aversion 7–8
    World War I propaganda 167
Civilization and Its Discontents (Freud) 43–4
classical view, human nature 43–4
Clausewitz, Carl von 11, 116
climate change 17, 103–4
CND (Campaign for Nuclear Disarmament) 106
Cohen, Stanley 15
Cold War 153–6, 158
    balance of power theories 172
    integrating institutions 174
    just war theories 173
    news representations 116–17
    nuclear fear 5, 66
    peace movements 134–9
    peace-war continuum 22
    war aversion 8
Colombia 74, 76
colonial wars 156, 184n.
colonialism 132
commemorative sites 14, 78
Communism 116, 154, 155
conflicts
    peace movements 128–33
    transformations in 178
    see also civil conflicts; war. . .
Congress of Racial Equality (CORE) 134
conscientious objection 36

containment strategy 154–6
Convention of the Elimination of all Forms of Discrimination Against Women 75
cooperation 51–2, 169, 173
"cooperation circles" 101
CORE (Congress of Racial Equality) 134
Cortright, David 129, 137
cosmopolitan harm conventions (CHCs) 175
Costa Rica 31
Court of Human Rights 175–6
Crimean War 118, 181n.
crimes against humanity 140
criminal law 177
Cuban Missile Crisis 6, 32
cultural violence 25–7
culture of peace 142–3, 159–61, 182n.
Czechoslovakia 155

Dalai Lama 30, 31, 91
Daoism 86, 96–7
Dart, Raymond 44
de Gaulle, Charles 170
de Waal, Frans 53
Dear, John 89
deaths in war
    Balkan wars 165
    gender and 65–7
    Great Power warfare 8, 11
    historical perspective 3
    memorialization of 13–14
    numbers in 1990s 2
    peace movements' prevention of 36
    World War I 147–8, 181n.
democracy 16, 25, 31, 79, 161
democratic peace theory 25
democratization, UN facilitation 175
destructive power of war 164–8
deterrence 145–61
    nuclear weapons as 117, 135, 154
development and peace 25, 62–4, 80, 175
dialogue of action, peacebuilding 100
diplomacy 178
direct violence-cultural violence distinction 26
discriminatory practices, religion 99
"divine" peace 23
"domestic violence" 77
Dr. Strangelove (Kubrick) 117, 139
drone warfare 181n.
DuBois, W.E.B. 129, 135

Earth Day poster *18*
East Asia
    expansionism 150
    peace movements 129
eastern expansion, German policy 152
ecological crisis 96–7
economic devastation, European wars 148
economic development/growth 79–80, 148
economic systems, social justice 94–5
EEC (European Economic Community) 168
Egypt 27
Eichmann, Adolf 26
Einstein, Albert 5–6, 33–4
empathy 51–2
empire, demise of 156
END (European Nuclear Disarmament) movement 138
engaged Buddhism 91, 95
"enlightened patriotism" 132
Enlightenment morality 164–5
Entman, Robert 116
environmental programs 96–7, 103–4
Eritrea-Ethiopia conflict 157
Eritrean People's Liberation Front 67
essentialist narratives, human nature 173–4
Ethiopia-Eritrea conflict 157
ethnic cleansing 8
ethno-nationalism 164
EU *see* European Union
Europe
    backlash discourse 77
    changing attitudes to war 145–9
    Communist threat 155
    definitions of peace 33–6
    national liberation movements 135–6
    peace movements 128, 137
    World War II 151, 152–3
European Economic Community (EEC) 168
European Nuclear Disarmament (END) movement 138
European Union (EU) 58, *58*, 168–9, 171, 177, 178
evolutionary history 42
expansionism 158, 167, 172
    East Asia 150
    German policy 152
    see also territorial expansion

faith communities 97–8
    see also religion
Falk, Richard 24, 121, 180
Fanon, Frantz 137
fatwas 92

Felipe VI of Spain *131*
Fellowship of Reconciliation (FOR) 132
feminine role, women in peacetime 69
feminism 62, 70–2, 76
Ferguson, Niall 7–8
Figueres, José 31
Fontaine, François 169
FOR (Fellowship of Reconciliation) 132
forager societies 46–9, *48*, 52, 57
forgiveness 141
Forsberg, Randall 138
framing war news 116–18
France *166*, 168–71
Francis, Pope 36, 89, 94, 96
Franco-German reconciliation 169–71
freedom 99, 175
Freud, Sigmund 33, 43–5
Fry, Douglas 18, 49, 52, 55, 174
functionalist institutionalism 170

"gacaca courts" 141
Gaddafi, Muammar 119
Galtung, Johan 10, *120*
   definitions of peace 22–3, 26, 36–7
   gender and war 62, 71
   "journalism of attachment" 124
   peace movements 139
   peace research 119, 120
   war-peace journalism dichotomy 121–3
Gandhi, Mahatma 86–7, 88
Gandhi, Mohandas K. 27, 29–30, *29*, 41, *88*, 110–11, 132, 183n.
Gbowee, Leymah 141
GBV *see* gender-based violence
Gellner, Ernest 160
gender
   discrimination 99
   equality goals 63
   inequality discourse 62–3, 80
   interfaith dialogue 104
   war and peace 61–81
   "women" inter-changeability 64
gender analysis 62–4, 69, 80–1
gender-based violence (GBV) 68–9, 75, 77
Georgia 181n.
Germany
   dismemberment of 154
   EU formation 168
   Franco-German reconciliation 169–71
   freedom from international war 158
   war aversion 181n.
   World War I memorial *160*

World War II 151–3
Ghosananda, Maha 90–1
"global commons" 105–11, 182n.
global norms dynamics 176
Global North
   economic operations 80
   health problems of forces 78–9
global peace culture 1, 15–19, 108
Global South
   social justice 95
   UN interventions 77
globalization
   acceleration of 16–17
   peace talks 27
Glover, Jonathan 8
Goertz, Gary 172
Goldstein, Joshua 38
Gómez, José 54–6
Gopin, Marc 87
Gorbachev, Mikhail 32, 155–6
Gore, Al 181n.
grassroots initiatives *see* "bottom-up" peace initiatives
Great Power nations 4, 7–8, 9, 10–12
Great War *see* World War I
Greek civilization 43, *43*
Green, Christian 99
Green Revolution 110
Greenham Common protests 72–3, *73*
Griffin, Michael 109
Guernica (Picasso) 130, *131*
guerrilla soldiers 67
Gurus, Sikhism 93
Gusmao, Kay Rala Xanana 25

Hague Conferences, 1899/1907 131
Hanh, Thich Nhat 90–1, *91*
Hanitzch, Thomas 123–4
happiness-peace distinction 37
Hardt, Michael 108
Harlem Renaissance 129–30
Hart, Donna 45
Haudenosaunee system, Iroquois Confederacy *51*
HDI (Human Development Index) 63
health problems of forces 78–9
Heffermehl, Frederick 111–12
hegemonic masculinity 69
"Heroes' Day" commemorations 78
heroism narratives 11–13
Herrenvolk theory 26
hibakusha (survivors of nuclear war) 135

hierarchical social organization 46–7
Hinduism 86, 96, 97
Hinsley, F.H. 151
Hiroshima 53, 135, *136*, 168
Hitler, Adolf 151–2, *151*, 152–4, 158, 181n.
Hobbes, Thomas 43–5
Hobbesian view, human nature 44–5, 49, 59
Hobsbawn, Eric 147
Holocaust 65–6
Holsti, K.J. 147–8
Holtom, Gerald 106
homicide 46, 49
honor in warfare 3–4, 113
hostility 56–7
Howard, Michael 158
human community, global peace culture 15
Human Development Index (HDI) 63
human nature
  beliefs since 1920s 41–60
  classical view 43–4
  concept of 42–3
  definition 42
  essentialist narratives 173–4
  evidence evaluation 45–58
  narrative paradigm shift 59–60
  scientific understanding of 45
human rights
  democracy and 16
  freedoms 175
  institutional integration 168
  legal bodies 177
  peace movements 134
  public debate 176
  religion and 97–9
human security 175
  see also security
Human Universals (Brown) 42
humanitarian interventions 124, 139–42
humanity, shared/common 18–19
Huntington, Samuel 83
Hussein, Saddam 118–19
Huxley, Aldous 130
Hynes, Samuel 12

ICAN (International Campaign to Abolish Nuclear Weapons) 101
ICC (International Criminal Court) 143, 177
idealism 27, 164
ideational-institutional integration 168–74
ideational power 164–8

imperial wars 156
India
  environmental stewardship 97
  nonviolence 86–8, 132
  Pakistan war 157
  peace movements 129
  peacebuilding in 90
inequality, forms of 62–3, 80
inner peace 22–3, 27, 31
institutional development 161
institutional integration 168–79
institutionalized violence 39, 59
insurgency *see* terrorism
integrative approach
  institutions 168–74
  peace 163–80
interdependence principle, religion 96
interfaith dialogue 99–104
intergovernmental institutions 172
intergroup violence 50
internally peaceful societies 49–50
international boundaries, territorial expansion 158
International Campaign to Abolish Nuclear Weapons (ICAN) 101
International Criminal Court (ICC) 143, 177
international law 9, 85
International Panel on Climate Change (IPCC) 17–18
international political culture 142–3
international wars 150–8, 161
Internet 107, 115
"interpersonal/intersubjective" peace 23
IPCC (International Panel on Climate Change) 17–18
Iran-Iraq War 8, 157
Iraq War
  death toll estimates 2
  journalism 118–19
  as just war 85–6
  peace movements 141
  policing 157
  protests 1
  visual images 110
Iraq-Kuwait invasion 157–8
Iroquois Confederacy, Haudenosaunee system *51*
IS *see* Islamic State
Islam
  framed as terrorist religion 83
  nonviolence 87

peacebuilding 91–2
social justice 94
see also Muslims
Islamic State (IS) 118, 159
Islamist terrorists/militants 119, 159
Israeli-Palestine contests 157

Jahn, Gunnar 114–15
Jainism 86, 96, 97
James, William 119
Japan
 antinuclear movement 135
 bombings in World War II 3, 4–5, 135, 168
 peacebuilding in 90
 war ambitions 150–1, 153
 women's groups 79, 129
Jaurès, Jean 165, 167, 174
Jenkins, Brian 159
Jervis, Robert 154
Jewish organizations 92
 see also Judaism
jihad, multiple meanings 87
Johnson, Lyndon 23
Johnson, Robert 154
Jones, Terry 45–6
journalism
 in peace 109, 119–24
 in war 110, 115–19
"journalism of attachment" 123–4
Judaism 87, 94, 96, 97
 see also Jewish organizations
just war 85–7, 173
justice
 institutional integration 178
 peace and 25, 27–8, 31, 93–4, 133–4
 peace movements 127
 religious beliefs 93–6
"justpeace" concept 143

Kaba, Marcel 10
Kadayifci-Orellana, S. Ayse 92
Kant, Immanuel 27, 37
Kanzo, Uchimura 129
Keegan, John 152
Keeley, Lawrence 45
Kellogg-Briand Pact 131–2, 167
Kelly, Raymond C. 57
Kennedy, John F. 32
Kenya 28
Kershaw, Ian 152
Khan, Abdul Ghaffar 91–2
Khrushchev, Nikita 32

killer ape view 44–5, 56
killing
 aversion to 52–3
 justification 86
 within-species 54
King, Martin Luther Jr. *34*
 definitions of peace 24, 27, 34–5, 41
 nonviolence 113–15
 religion and pacifism 89
 Vietnam War speech 137
Kluckhom, Clyde 42
Knightley, Phillip 117–18
Kohl, Helmut 171
Korean War 154
Kosovo 123
Kubrick, Stanley 117, 139
Kung, Hans 99
Kuwait-Iraq invasion 157–8
Kyoto agreement 17

Lamas, Carlos Saavedra 113
lasting peacebuilding 174–9
Latin America 31, 78, 138, 140
law, women's recognition in 70
law of nations 173
League of Nations 128, 131–2, 134, 150, 166
Leakey, Louis B. 45
Lebow, Richard Ned 124
Lederach, John Paul 89, 143
Lee, Richard B. 59–60
legal bodies
 international wars 150
 war crimes 177
legal rights, women 73
legitimacy of global norms 176
Lenin, Vladimir Ilyich Ulyanov 32
lesbians, gay, bisexual, and transgendered
 people (LGBT) 97–9
lethal violence 54–6
Levy, Jack 160
LGBT (lesbians, gay, bisexual, and
 transgendered people) 97–9
liberal view of peace 27, 134–5, 143
liberation
 national movements 135–7
 theology of 85
 women's 66–8
Liberian peace movement *140*, 141
Libya 118–19, 142
Lifton, Robert Jay 179
Linklater, Andrew 175
Loyn, David 122–3

Luard, Evan 146, 156, 158
Lukacs, John 151–2
Lutuli, Albert 113–15, *114*
Lynch, Jake 122–3

Maathai, Wangari 28–9, *28*
McNamara, Robert 155
Macy, Joanna 91
MAD (Mutual Assured Deterrence) 117
Magnum Photos 109
Malaysia 50
male rape 68
Malinowki, Bronislaw 45
mammalian behavior patterns 51–2, 53–6
Manchester, William 151–2
mandate system, League of Nations 132
Mao Tse Tung 30–1
Mardu society, Australia 57
Marshall, S.L.A. 52
Maschner, Herbert 47
masculine experience of war 12, 14
masculinity ideologies 64, 68–9
mass killings/massacre strategy 3, 7, 11
Mastny, Vojtech 154
materialism 150
media coverage of war 8–9, 14–15, 108, 110
    see also news coverage
media framing, war news 116–18
memorialization 13–14
    France *166*
    Germany *160*
    United Kingdom *78*
men
    benefits of being a man 64
    gendered experiences 61–81
Mennonites 89
Middle East
    Arab Spring 143
    civil wars 159
    Nobel Peace Prize awards 112–13
    peace requirements 87
    policing wars 157
    religious-inspired violence 83
    war journalism 119
militarism 128–33, 150, 167
military defense organizations 171–2
military-industrial complexes 4
military science/technology 10–11, 52–3
Moll, Frank 110
Monnet, Jean 168–70, *171*
Montagu, Ashley 45
Montgomery Bus Boycott 34, *34*

moral force, peace as 163, 164–8, 174
"mother" concept 74
Mozambique 89
Mueller, John 2–3, 9
Multi-Faith Centre 102
Munich Agreement 116–17
music, World War I *146*
Muslims 92, 97, 102
    see also Islam
Mutual Assured Deterrence (MAD) 117
Myers, Fred 57

Nagasaki nuclear bombing 135, 168
Nagler, Michael 59
Nakao, Hisashi 46
"napalm girl" image 108–10, *108*
nation-building 157
nation-states, social complexification 56
National Committee for a Sane Nuclear Policy (SANE) 135
National Council for the Prevention of War (NCPW) 128
national liberation 135–7
National Peace Council (NPC) 128
nationalism
    critiques of 167
    emergence of 168
    ideological impact 164
    rationalism links 165
NATO *see* North Atlantic Treaty Organization
natural selection 42, 56
"natural" war 153
naval armaments 132
Nazism 152–3, 168, 173
NCPW (National Council for the Prevention of War) 128
Near East, war emergence 46, 57
negative peace concept 9, 22–3, 27, 127, 183n.
Negri, Antonio 108
Netherlands, Women's Peace Congress *147*
Neumayer, Eric 67
"New Wars" 66–7
news coverage 26, 105–25
NGOs (nongovernmental organizations) 134
Niebuhr, Reinhold 133
Nixon, Richard 35
Nobel, Alfred 111–12
Nobel Peace Prize 18, 111–15, 182n., 183n.
nomadic foragers 46–9, *48*, 52, 57
non-attachment principle 94
nongovernmental organizations (NGOs) 134

nonviolence
    Asia 29–30
    civil rights 34–5
    global peace culture 16
    inner peace 31
    justice-peace relationship 28
    peace movements 132
    in reform 173
    religion motivating 84, 86–8
    representations of peace 110–11, 113–15
nonwarring societies 50–1
normative approach
    citizenship 59
    institutional integration 172–3, 176
normative ideal, peace as 37
normative solidarity 178
North Africa, war journalism 119
North America, peace definitions 33–6
    see also United States
North Atlantic Treaty Organization (NATO) 118–19, 138
North Korea 154
North Vietnam 155
Northern Ireland 123
Norway, Nobel Peace Prize 111–12
NPC (National Peace Council) 128
NPT (Nuclear Non-Proliferation Treaty) 135
nuclear asymmetry 24
nuclear deterrence 23–4, 135, 154
nuclear fear 5–7, 16, 19, 66
"nuclear metaphysics" 154
Nuclear Non-Proliferation Treaty (NPT) 135
nuclear peace 23–4
nuclear symmetry 24
nuclear weapons
    atmospheric testing 6–7
    ban on 24, 72
    campaign to abolish 101
    CND disarmament campaign 106
    definitions of peace 32
    humanitarian interventions 139
    media framing 117
    peace movements and 37, 143
    testing 6–7, 135
    total war strategy 5
    see also atomic bombings
Nuremburg trials 25
nurturing behavior 51

Obama, Barack H. 35, 115, *131*
objectivity, journalism 123
occidental peace theories 21–2, 33

Ogata, Sadako 175
On War (Clausewitz) 116
Operation Gomorah, World War II 3
oppression, Soviet Union 154
Order Primates 54
Orwell, George 153
Oslo Accords 113
Otpor! group 110–11
Ottosen, Rune 12
outer peace 22–3, 27

pacifism
    passivism distinction 39
    religion and 83–104
    war-aversion 153
Pakistan-India war 157
Palestine *90*, 139, 157
Pankhurst, Donna 12
papal declarations 89, 94, 96
Paris Agreement 17
Parliament of the World's Religions (PWR) 100
passivism-pacifism distinction 39
patriarchy 98
patriotism 118
Pauling, Linus 5
peace
    absence of 22
    definitions 9–10, 19, 21–40, 183n.
    dialectical definition 39
    "evolution" of 38–9
    as integration 163–80
    representations of 105–25
    tensions with justice 133–4
    war as instrument for 35
"Peace Churches" 87, 89
peace journalism 109, 119–24
peace movements 36–7, 127–43
    Cold War 134–9
    growth of 167
    women and 69–75
    World War I 149–50
"peace race" 24
peace research 10, 84, 119, 120, 139
Peace Research Institute Oslo (PRIO) 119
peace studies, emergence of 10
"peace symbol" 106, *106*
peace systems 50–1, 57, *58*
peace talk 27, 36–7
peace-war continuum 22, 39
"peaceable diversity" 182n.
peacebuilding 120

institutional integration 178–9
interfaith dialogue 100–2
normative integration 176
peace movements 141
religious beliefs 84–5, 88–93
women and 69–77
peaceful societies 49–50
peacekeeping 78, 119–20, 176
peacemaking 36–7, 119
peaces, definitions 27
Pearson, Lester 183n.
People Power movements 16, 107, 110, *142*
Philippines 90, 107
photography 109
Phuc, Phan Thi Kim 108–9, *108*
Physicians for Social Responsibility (PSR) 135
Picasso, Pablo, *Guernica* 130, *131*
Pierson, Roach R. 77–8
Pinker, Steven 23, 38–9, 54, 160
Plümper, Thomas 67
policing wars 156–7
policy discourses, gender incorporation 63–4
political actors, integrative approaches 167
political communication, war as 9–10
political culture 142–3, 159–61, 182n.
political neutrality 183n.
political power, moral force 164–5
political violence 40, 84
poppy symbolism 182n.
positive peace concept 10, 19, 22–3, 27, 174
post-Cold War era, humanitarian interventions 139–42
"post-conflict" measures 141
postwar peace, gender and 77–80
poverty 94–5, 102
power
    balance of 172
    of gender 62–3
    of ideas 164–8
PRIO (Peace Research Institute Oslo) 119
progress and civilization 174
Prussia, Seven Years War 148
PSR (Physicians for Social Responsibility) 135
psychological need, peace as 37
public opinion, Nazi era 152
Putin, Vladimir 32–3
PWR (Parliament of the World's Religions) 100

R2P ("Responsibility to Protect") 140, 142
Rabbis for Human Rights 92
racial equality 134–5, 138–9

racism 129–30
"radical" factions, peace movements 143
Randolph, A. Philip 129
rape during warfare 68
rationalism-nationalism links 165
Rauchhaus, Robert 24
Reagan, Ronald 138
realism/realist view
    balance of power 172
    institutional integration 173
    morality and 164
    of peace 22, 27
Realpolitik perspective 22, 33
reason, nationalism and 165
reconciliation and peace 24–5, 169–71
regime change wars 118, 156, 157
religion
    human rights and 97–9
    institutional integration 178–9
    just war traditions 85–7
    pacifism and 83–104
    peace imperative 36
    peace movements 142
    social justice and 93–6
    sustainable development 96–7
Religions for Peace organization 100–1
Remarque, Erich Maria 130
"Remembrance Day" 78
Renan, Ernest 164
"Responsibility to Protect" (R2P) 140, 142
restorative justice 25, 178
restraint, primacy of 53–6
retributive justice 25
revenge, war as 3–4
Rich, Norman 152
Richmond, Oliver 176
rights discourse 175
    see also human rights
Romero, Oscar 138
Roosevelt, Franklin D. 11, 175
Roper, Marilyn 46
"Rosie the Riveter" icon 66
Rothblat, Joseph 5–6
Rousseau, Jean-Jacques 44–5
Russell, Bertrand 5–6, *6*, 130
Russell, Edith 6
Russell, William 118
Russell-Einstein Manifesto 5–6
Russia
    nuclear testing ban 7
    peace definitions 21, 32–3
    threat to United States 19

war with Georgia 181n.
  see also Soviet Union
Rustin, Bayard 132, *133*, 135
Ruta Pacifica de las Mujeres group 74

al-Sādāt, Muḥammad Anwar 25, 27–9
Sahlins, Marshall 41–3
SALT (Strategic Arms Limitation) 137–8
Sánchez, Oscar Arias 31
SANE (National Committee for a Sane Nuclear Policy) 135
Sant'Egidio Catholic Community 89
Sarvodaya Shramadama programs 96
Satha-Anand, Chaiwat 87
satyagraha (non-violence) 29–30
Saving Private Ryan (Spielberg) 12–13
Schell, Jonathan 7
Schuman, Robert 169
scientific views, human nature 45, 52–3
SDS (Students for a Democratic Society) 136–7
security 145–61, 172, 175
Security Council, UN 75–7
self-defense justification, war 85, 87
selfishness 43
Sen, Amartya 16, 64, 175
Seven Years War 148
sexism 62
sexual abuse 99
sexual violence 68–9, 77
SGI (Soka Gakkai International) 93
sharing behavior 49, 51–2
Shastri, Sunanda Y. 86
Shastri, Yajneshwar S. 86
Shibahara, Taeko 129
Shifferd, Kent D. 41
Shiva, Vandana 95, 96–7
Sikhism 93, 97
Silsilah Dialogue Movement 102
Simon, Yves 165
Smuts, Jan 132
social complexification 46–7, 56
social constructivism 164
social identity 56–7, 58
social justice 93–6
social organization 46, 48, 54
social responsibilities, gendered war 66
social structure, violence of 26
Soka Gakkai International (SGI) 93
soldiers
  definitions 78
  as survivors 12–13
  as victims 12

Solidarity movement 138
Somalia 74, 157
Sontag, Susan 109
Souillac, Geneviève 19, 49, 52, 59
Soulez, Philippe 166
South Africa
  apartheid system 138–9, 177
  Gandhi's campaigns 183n.
  nonviolent resistance 28
  peace movements 132
South Asia, peace movements 129
South Korea 154
"sovereign" states 158
sovereignty 171
Soviet Union
  Cold War 153–6
  disintegration of 32, 174
  nuclear arms race 137
  see also Russia
space travel 17
species consciousness 6, 17
species-typical behavior 42–3, 46, 48
Spielberg, Steven, *Saving Private Ryan* 12–13
state bureaucracies 80
states
  civil society scrutiny 174–5
  structural violence 59
  see also nation-states
stereotypes, gendered 61, 76, 80–1
Strategic Arms Limitation (SALT) 137–8
Strodbeck, Fred L. 42
structural violence 25–7
  citizenship 59
  economic systems 94
  gender inequality 62
  global peace culture 15–16
  interfaith dialogue 102
  peace research 10, 120
  positive peace and 23
Students for a Democratic Society (SDS) 136–7
Sudan peace agreement 76
superpowers, Cold War 154
survival of soldiers, as victory 12–13
Sussman, Robert W. 45, 52
sustainable development 28–9, 96–7
Sustainable Development Goals 63
sustainable futures 96–7
Suttner, Bertha von 38
Symons, Donald 42
Syria 119, 142
Szala, Anna 55

INDEX

TCs (Truth Commissions) 79
technological capabilities 17
Tennyson, Lord Alfred 59
territorial expansion 158, 172
terrorism 21–2, 67, 83, 158–9
Thirty Years War 148
Thompson, William 160
Tibet 31
Tiercelin, Claudine 167
Tilly, Charles 106
Tolstoy, Leo 145
Tonkinson, Robert 57
total war strategy 3, 5, 11, 12
totalitarianism, Nazi Germany 153
Toynbee, Arnold 146
trade, effects of war 161
transparency principle 123
TRC (Truth and Reconciliation Commissions) 141
Trojan War 148
Truman, Harry 154
Trump, Donald 115
Truth Commissions (TCs) 79
Truth and Reconciliation Commissions (TRC) 141
truthfulness 122–3
Tsar Bomba testing 6
Tutu, Desmond 28, 141

UDHR *see* Universal Declaration of Human Rights
UK *see* United Kingdom
UN *see* United Nations
United Kingdom (UK)
    antiwar protests 72–3
    feminist campaigns 70, 71
    memorialization 78
    peace movements 128, 141
    see also British...
United Nations (UN)
    civil society scrutiny 174–5
    conflict transformations 178
    expansion of 172, 173, 176
    gender equality goals 63
    gender stereotyping 80
    interfaith dialogue 99–100
    peace movements 134
    Resolution 1325 75
    Resolution 1820 76
    territorial expansion 158
    warfare legitimacy 9, 85
    women's associations 75–7

United Religions Initiative (URI) 101
United States (US)
    9/11 attacks 67, 79, 83–5, 118
    antiwar protests 72
    backlash discourse 77
    Civil War 148
    Cold War 153–6
    feminist campaigns 70
    gendered war 66, 79
    human rights 176
    interfaith dialogue 102
    Islamist terrorism 159
    just war tradition 85–6
    League of Nations 166
    news media 116–19
    nuclear arms race 137
    nuclear testing ban 7
    nuclear waste costs 24
    peace definitions 21
    peace movements 128–9, 132, 136–7, 141
    Russian threat 19
    Veterans Day 78
    World War I 148–9, 168
Universal Declaration of Human Rights (UDHR) 134, 168, *169*
Upper Xingu River tribes, Brazil 42
URI (United Religions Initiative) 101
US *see* United States
"Us versus Them" concept 56–8
USSR *see* Soviet Union
Ut, Nick 108–9

Veil, Simone 171
Veterans Day, United States 78
victims of war
    media coverage 14–15
    soldiers as 12
Vietnam War 155
    antiwar protests 72, *72*, 106, 137, *137*
    commemorative sites 78
    death tolls 2
    peace movements' role 36
    visual images 108–9
violence
    against women 77
    human nature 43, 45, 49–50, 54–6
    peace contrast 25–7
    religious-inspired 83–4
    unacceptibility of 19
    war definitions 182n.
    see also structural violence

visual representations, news 108–10, 115, 119, 124–5
von Suttner, Baroness 38, 111, 113
voting, women's right to 70, 79

war
  absence of 21, 27
  of annihilation 149
  consequences of 10–15
  definitions 182n.
  destructive power 164–8
  gender and 61–81
  human nature and 41–60
  ideology of 159
  as instrument for peace 35
  legitimacy 85
  opposition to 149–50
  origins of 46–7, 57
  peace-war continuum 22, 39
  as political communication 9–10
  racism and 129–30
  as revenge 3–4
  shift in attitudes to 145–7
  "winning the war on" 38
  see also civil conflicts; conflicts; deaths in war
war aversion 7–10, 14, 16, 160, 181n.
war crimes, law on 177
War Crimes Tribunal 79
war journalism 110, 115–19, 121–3
war stories 11–13
"war on terrorism" 67, 83
warlike human nature 41–2, 44
Waterloo, Battle of 13–14
Watt, Donald Cameron 152
weapons
  classification 143
  technological development 10–11
  see also nuclear weapons
weapons of mass destruction (WMDs) 118
Webel, Charles 10, 24
Weinberg, Gerhard 151–3
Wells, H.G. 130
Wells, Ida B. 129
Western Desert nomads, Australia 57
Western views
  civilization/progress debate 174
  human nature 43–4
  peace definitions 33–6
  positive peace 27
WHO (World Health Organization) 62–3

WILPF *see* Women's International League for Peace and Freedom
Wilson, Edward O. 44
Wilson, Woodrow 27, 166–7
Witte, John Jnr. 99
WMDs (weapons of mass destruction) 118
Wodiczko, Kyzysztof 41, *179*
women
  antinuclear protests 6
  archetypal war stories 12
  "gender" inter-changeability 64
  gendered experiences 61–81
  human rights 97–8
  interfaith dialogue 101, 104
  Nobel Peace Prize awards 113
  peace movements 73, 129, 130, 134
  sustainable development and 28–9
Women in Black organization 74
Women, Peace and Security (WPS) resolutions 76–8, 80–1
Women's International League for Peace and Freedom (WILPF) 71, 113, 129, *130*, 132
women's movements 73, 129, 134
Women's Peace Congress, Netherlands *147*
Women's Strike for Peace (WSP) 72
World Fellowship of Faiths 133
World Health Organization (WHO), gender analysis 62–3
World War I
  archetypal narratives 11
  definitions of peace 32
  gender and 61, 65–6
  impact of 145–50, 153
  memorials *160*, *166*
  military technologies 10–11
  nationalism's emergence 165, 168
  Nobel Peace Prize awards 112
  peace movements 128
  propaganda 167
  total war strategy 12
  war aversion 181n.
World War II 150–3
  Communist threat 154
  cyclical explanation 4
  death tolls 3, 8
  gender and 65–6, 71
  killing, aversion to 52
  massacre strategy 11
  Nobel Peace Prize awards 112
  nuclear fear 5
  peace movements 133–4

Worms, Frédéric 166
"worthiness, unity, numbers, and commitment" (WUNC) displays 106–7, 110
WPS (Women, Peace and Security) resolutions 76–8, 80–1
Wright, Quincy 25
WSP (Women's Strike for Peace) 72

WUNC ("worthiness, unity, numbers, and commitment") displays 106–7, 110
Wuye, James *103*

Youngblood, Steve 122
Yugoslavian wars 156

zoological contexts, human nature 53–6